AF447901

# Notes / Ex

# PRAISE FOR WEALTH IN NUMBERS

"Raising capital can be overwhelming, feeling out of reach for many. Wealth in Numbers reshapes the financial landscape, making it easier for both beginners and experienced individuals to navigate."
—Eve Chase, Investment & Acquisitions Manager, Tyton Holdings

"Wealth in Numbers is a must-read for anyone in real estate development or private investments. It offers a clear roadmap for using SPVs to fuel growth and manage assets effectively—a resource I wish I had earlier in my career."

—Ross A. Hillesheim, Principal, 1850 Properties

Throughout my career in Real Estate, I've made use of Special Purpose Vehicles countless times. In Wealth in Numbers, Jake and Max make a complex topic approachable, turning it into a powerful catalyst for growth. This book is a practical guide to leveraging private investment vehicles and unlocking their wealth-creation potential. For serious investors looking to elevate their portfolio, this resource is a must-have addition to their library.

-Dave Pinson, Partner, Mosch Capital

"A must-read for anyone looking to build wealth in the 21st century. Avery and Claver provide an inside peek into the world of SPVs, offering to the masses what was once a tool for only the financial elites. Highly recommend reading for anyone interested in the world of private investing!"

—Melissa Barall, Investor

# PRAISE FOR WEALTH IN NUMBERS

"This book takes the mystery out of SPVs with clear, practical, and step-by-step guidance. Packed with real-world examples, Jake and Max empower readers to confidently set up and manage SPVs—from setup and tax planning to profit distribution—for profitable and savvy private investments."

—Taylor Pierce, Vice President, Great Oaks Capital Partners, LLC.

"Must read! Without proper structuring through SPVs, even the best investment opportunities wither on the vine. On the other hand, an efficient SPV structure addresses multiple issues like a well engineered machine becomes a thing of beauty."

—Eric Wong, Director, Celera

"Max and Jake give an understanding of SPVs in an easy way for students to seasoned investors, there are great takeaways to in this guide for navigating the world of private investment."

—Dr. Manoj D. Mahajan,
Associate Professor and Senior Research Scientist
Stony Brook University Center of Excellence in Wireless & IT

"SPVs are essential in private investing, yet often confuse first-time investors. In this concise and practical guide, Jake & Max simplify the process with a clear, step-by-step approach to navigating the process of SPVs and syndicates. Whether you're new to the field or looking to deepen your understanding, this book is a must-read for anyone involved in private investments."

—Christian Durfee, Founder, InvestLink Social

# PRAISE FOR WEALTH IN NUMBERS

"What Jake and Max have written isn't a stuffy book of theory, it's actionable and practical. Investors of all stripes will get a lot out of this book."

—Nick Dimondi, Film Producer

"As someone who has spent 6 years in the small business acquisition world, I've seen how powerful SPVs can be in structuring simple and complex deals. Wealth in Numbers does a great job breaking down using SPVs in a clear, actionable way that's easy to grasp. From managing risks to optimizing tax strategies, it gives you the tools to simplify even the toughest transactions. If you're working on mergers or acquisitions of any size, Wealth in Numbers will help you understand how using SPVs can make your deals smoother and more efficient."

—Ben Kelly, President, Acquisiton Ace

"Wealth in Numbers" is the definitive guide for anyone seeking to demystify SPVs and syndication. Avery and Claver masterfully bridge the gap between complex investment strategies and practical, actionable insights. This book doesn't just teach you about SPVs; it empowers you to leverage them as a catalyst for financial growth and opportunity. Whether you're a seasoned investor or a newcomer, this is a must-read blueprint for navigating the private investment landscape with confidence and clarity."

—Gannon Coffman, Managing Partner, Vessel Capital Group

# The Ultimate Dealmaker's Guide to SPVs, Syndication, and Private Investment

## MAX AVERY & JAKE CLAVER

### FOREWORD BY JORDAN HUTCHINSON

PUBLISHED BY:
Trade Days Publishing; Dallas, Texas
ISBN: 9798218532659
Library of Congress Control Number: 2024923116
PRINTED IN THE U.S.A.
Written by Max Avery & Jake Claver
Cover: Max Avery
Edited by: Max Avery

Library of Congress Subject Headings (LCSH)
Investments
Limited Partnership
Venture Capital
Real Estate Investment
Real Estate Investment - Syndication
Private Equity Funds
Personal Finance

BISAC Subject Headings

BUS025000 — BUSINESS & ECONOMICS / Entrepreneurship
BUS036000 — BUSINESS & ECONOMICS / Investments & Securities / General
BUS050020 — BUSINESS & ECONOMICS / Personal Finance / Investing
BUS054000 — BUSINESS & ECONOMICS / Real Estate / General

## About
# Max Avery

Known for his relentless pursuit of excellence and his enthusiastic approach to expanding businesses in diverse industries, Avery's expertise spans the evolution of modern finance, from traditional capital markets to cutting-edge decentralized finance (DeFi).

His comprehensive understanding of both traditional and emerging financial markets is evidenced by his credentials, including certification as a Capital Markets & Securities Analyst (CMSA)® and FinTech Industry Professional (FTIP)™ as well as Advanced Blockchain Architectures, DeFi Infrastructure, and FinTech Law and Policy. His strategic acumen has been recognized at the highest levels, including his District Export Council appointment Secretary of Commerce Wilbur Ross in 2018. As a member of the National Small Business Association's Economic Development Committee, he has helped shape policies that impact capital formation and business growth.

Avery's philosophy, "If something is worth doing, it should be done with excellence," has guided his approach to capital raising and deal structuring in private investments. His track record of converting complex challenges into practical solutions has made him a sought-after business strategist and consultant.

Since 2016, Max has focused his talents on raising capital and funding deals in private investments for private equity and real estate. As he continues to push the boundaries, Max remains committed to making a lasting, positive impact on the world around him. His journey is a testament to the power of vision, hard work, and a commitment to excellence. Visit MaxAvery.org for more info.

Jake Claver is a distinguished leader in the Family Office arena. As Managing Director of Digital Ascension Group, a sophisticated multi-family office, he provides tailored investment solutions for High Net Worth (HNW) and Ultra High Net Worth (UHNW) individuals. His role in leading Syndicately, a specialized SPV investment management platform, demonstrates his deep expertise in structured investment vehicles.

Aside from his education in Finance at North Texas University, his credentials include certification as a Qualified Family Office Professional as well as various certifications in DeFi and blockchain technology, bridging traditional finance with innovative digital asset solutions.

Claver's experience in creating and managing SPVs positions him as an authority on modern investment vehicles. His work spans traditional family office investments to cutting-edge digital asset strategies, making him particularly adept at navigating both conventional and emerging financial markets.

His expertise in structuring investment vehicles and working with family office portfolios has earned him recognition as a thought leader in the space. He has demonstrated consistent success in capital formation, investment structuring, and wealth preservation for ultra-high-net-worth families, with a particular focus on creating anti-fragile investment strategies that incorporate both traditional and digital assets. Visit JakeClaver.com for more info.

# TABLE OF CONTENTS

# WEALTH IN NUMBERS

# FOREWORD

I first met Jake Claver while hosting Jets & Capital, one of our premiere family office and investor networking  events in Utah. With the fall colors of the sweeping rocky mountains as a backdrop, we brought together hundreds of family offices, high net worth investors, and entrepreneurs in a massive hangar; surrounded by private jets, helicopters, and supercars to network and make deals happen. Attendees at events have included billionaires and Presidents, with entrepreneurs from every industry collaborating to build a space for groundbreaking ideas. Many are looking to create and bring life to their ideas, but lack the funding to do so. Some have startups driven by passion for innovative tech. Others are real estate professionals with a new deal to develop or improve. Dreamers with a vision.

Jake was a well spoken guy in a nice suit, who constantly had a group of people around him anxiously listening in to his conversations. Our initial discussions centered around his work with family offices, digital assets and blockchain and unique deal structuring was just the start. This guy had a tremendous resume and was working on some stellar projects. The most significant was his work with unique deal syndications. As a capital raiser for funds and startups myself, having access to investors wasn't an issue, but the right structuring for deals was always a struggle. Traditionally to raise money for a project in my world, it had to be done either through a new startup company with operating agreements, or through a complex investment fund structured as a  506(b) with SEC regulations galore and a 100+ page private placement memorandum (the "fund bible") that put most lawyers to sleep. Creating a good deal and finding investors and raising money was already difficult, the structuring on top of that made it oftentimes impossible. I saw many visionary entrepreneurs work tirelessly to start funds or companies, only to give up after years of uphill battles on the most simple of structuring issues.

In that crowded private jet hangar, we were surrounded by people with deals and people with capital, what they needed was a system and structure to put those together - and Jake had an inside scoop on the solution. Something that democratized private investments. Jake's systems proved that access to deals and capital is not limited to the elite and well connected, but through a structure called Special Purpose Vehicles (SPV's), capital and success was accessible to anyone with a good deal. That initial conversation led to a deep friendship and collaboration on many deals and events.

I started hosting these unique events with a vision to bring together some of the highest caliber people in the world - family offices and investors, fund managers and founders, the movers and shakers that have built something significant. As the relationship with Jake and his partner Max Avery deepened, it became very apparent that they fit this criteria and I was anxious to collaborate more. I learned more about thier work in SPV's, and how their platform, Syndicately, wasn't just another investment tool; it was a paradigm shift in how we approach private equity.

Jake and Max soon partnered with me for an event at Caesars Palace, where private investors alongside Robert F. Kennedy Jr. met and networked while watching the inaugural Formula 1 race in Las Vegas. We had a private suite right by the track, hearing and feeling the roar of the F1 cars as they hurdled 200+ mph past the casinos and down the strip. After Jake presented to our audience, we sat down and discussed in depth about Max and his pursuits in SPV's, and soon I understood the magnitude of what was being built here. They were putting together a means of navigating the complex world of private investment, and this actively reshaping the investment landscape. Their business "Syndicately" was opening doors for entrepreneurs and investors, making once-exclusive opportunities accessible to a wider audience.

I've been pitched deals and capital raises hundreds of times. Plenty of vanilla average deals, and plenty of innovative ideas, but something about Jake and Max's approach to SPVs caught my attention in a not just a unique deal, but a change in dynamic of how the industry is being ran. Their deep understanding and forward-thinking vision for democratizing private investments aligned perfectly with what I've always strived for in my career - creating pathways for collective success and fostering an ecosystem where great ideas can find the capital they need to thrive.

I realized how transformative SPVs could be. I'd seen firsthand the frustration of brilliant entrepreneurs struggling to find funding, and equally, the disappointment of eager investors unable to access high-potential deals. Max and Jake were building bridges where only chasms had existed before.

When they approached me to write the foreword for their comprehensive guide on SPVs, I didn't hesitate. This book represents more than just a manual on investment vehicles; it's a manifesto for a new era of inclusive, dynamic, and impactful investing. Max and Jake's leadership in the SPV space has been nothing short of revolutionary. Their insights in this book are invaluable for anyone looking to navigate the future of private investments. This book could empower a new generation of investors and entrepreneurs. It could fuel world-changing innovations and create new paths to wealth for many. As we enter a new era of private investments, SPVs have become a powerful tool, offering a unique mix of flexibility, security, and scalability, thus making exclusive opportunities available to everyone and changing the way we think about building wealth.

Investment vehicles like funds, JV's and hold co's are complex and unnecessary for most deals. SPV's are the perfect fit for most, they are deal specific and focused, immensely simpler than other options, and offer fast set up and execution. This comprehensive guide does more than merely introduce readers to the world of SPVs; it serves as a roadmap through the intricacies of forming, managing, and scaling these powerful investment vehicles. This guidance is clear and practical. It makes SPVs accessible to all, from experienced GPs to first-time entrepreneurs seeking to raise capital for a great idea. SPV's can pool resources effectively, offer flexibility while mitigating risks, and make it so all parties are sharing in the success. Whether it's funding clean energy initiatives, supporting underrepresented entrepreneurs, or investing in community development projects, SPVs provide a mechanism for investors to generate wealth while making a positive impact on the world. Investors too get diversification, potentially higher returns, and the chance to be part of groundbreaking ventures at their inception. Jake and Max have dissected these strategies and created this phenomenal guidebook to help any dealmaker bring them to life.

For anyone serious about securing their financial future and making a meaningful impact through their investments, this book is an indispensable guide. It will equip you with the knowledge and tools needed to navigate the sophisticated world of SPVs and tap into the vast opportunities they provide. Whether you're an investor looking to expand your portfolio, an entrepreneur seeking to fund your next big idea, or a professional aiming to broaden your financial expertise, the insights contained within these pages will prove invaluable. This will help you, and you already have this book, now get started putting it to work.

Jordan Hutchinson,
President, And Capital Events
www.jetsandcapital.com
Expert Fundraiser & Investment Fund Advisor
Principal, Hutchinson Family Office

WEALTH IN NUMBERS

# INTRODUCTION

Lots of people want to take charge of their financial destiny and find ways to make their money grow. If this book has captured your attention, you're probably among those people. Guess what? You've just struck gold. So, to offer you a glimpse into what this book is all about, let's start with a story.

A group of friends gathers around a table at their favorite café, enjoying the rich aroma of fresh coffee. With warm mugs in hand, they're buzzing with excitement, tossing investment ideas back and forth. One of them leans forward, eyes sparkling as she talks about a promising tech startup that she believes will disrupt the industry. "I seriously think that this could be huge," she says, "but it's gonna need some serious support to take off."

There's another member in the group who wants to make it big in real estate and own properties all over the city. Looking across the table he says "It's possible, but I still think we should look into investing in multi-family units," he says, knowing there's a growing need for housing in the area. "The rental market's blowing up here and if we do it now, we could earn some solid returns."

A third friend chimes in and enthusiastically explains her idea for buying out a business. "This business already has a strong customer base and a solid brand. We could buy it and make it even better by adding new products, opening more locations, and giving it a fresh online presence."

The energy at the table is electric as they talk about their future investments. Yet, their smiles wane a bit when faced with the daunting question - "How can we make any of these a reality?"

So, where exactly do they begin? In the past, this enthusiasm could dwindle due to all the paperwork, confusing regulations, and other obstacles that ruin even the best business plans.

Sound familiar?

They're not discouraged. They sit back, sip their coffee, and begin to brainstorm. They discuss how they could team up, find some partners, and get guidance from some seasoned investors.

But what can they do to make their dreams into a reality?

Well, that's where this book comes in. Let us fill you in on an amazing tool for private and alternative investments. The funny thing is, most people still don't know about it. What we're talking about is called a Special Purpose Vehicle, or "SPV" for short, and it provides a versatile investment strategy that anyone can make use of to open up new opportunities.

The group of friends we mentioned can join together, create a Special Purpose Vehicle, and rally like-minded investors around their vision. This structure will let them focus on a single project so they tap into expertise and capital they couldn't access individually. With an SPV, their collective ambition can take flight, and those ideas that they tossed around over steaming mugs can become reality.

As you read through this book, you'll soon understand how SPVs have the power to reshape your investment strategy. You might be thinking, "Do I really need zero qualifications?" Well that's one of the great things about running a SPV. There aren't any requirements for special licenses, certifications, tests, or gatekeepers. SPVs provide a level playing field, accessible to everybody, whether you're a seasoned finance professional or just starting out. SPVs provide a practical approach that lets you reach for investment opportunities that you never thought possible. Another empowering aspect of SPVs is that they do not require the deal organizers to be Accredited Investors themselves. Whatever your background, you can form and manage an SPV today. All it takes is the willingness to learn and a solid plan for the investment opportunity you believe in. The field is open, and the barriers to entry are low—it's up to you to seize this opportunity.

The material in this book will provide you with what you need to run a SPV from start to finish. We'll guide you through every step of SPV creation and management. You'll learn to raise capital, structure deals, and maintain compliance through the process. We're glad you're here, so take a moment to pick up a notepad, grab your favorite beverage and let's get started.

WEALTH IN NUMBERS

*"The best way to predict the future is to create it."*
— *Peter Drucker, Management Consultant & Educator*

# WHAT IS AN SPV?

The most powerful tool in private investing isn't what you think. Enter the Special Purpose Vehicle - the unsung champion that's quietly rewriting the rules of financial strategy. It's time you got acquainted. SPVs are legal entities for a particular investment. They let multiple investors combine funds for a single project.

Despite being used at the highest levels for private investments, these tools are surprisingly easy to approach and helpful for newcomers who are starting out with finding opportunities, raising capital, and building a strong reputation. Imagine an SPV as a collaborative investment that allows participants to combine their resources for a bigger opportunity. Despite their versatility, SPVs often remain under-utilized by both novice and experienced investors, making them a hidden gem in the world of finance. This book examines SPV possibilities and reveals how they can entirely revolutionize your investment strategy.

In the US, it's common to form SPVs as LLCs. Later on, we'll go into more detail and explore the various options for setting up a SPV, such as partnerships, trusts, corporations, and LLCs. Becoming a Limited Partner (LP) through investing in a SPV opens doors to potential opportunities that may not be accessible otherwise. The investment managers, also referred to as General Partners or "GPs," act as the architects of these entities. Their aim is to secure, negotiate, finance, and complete deals to generate profits for themselves and their Limited Partners.

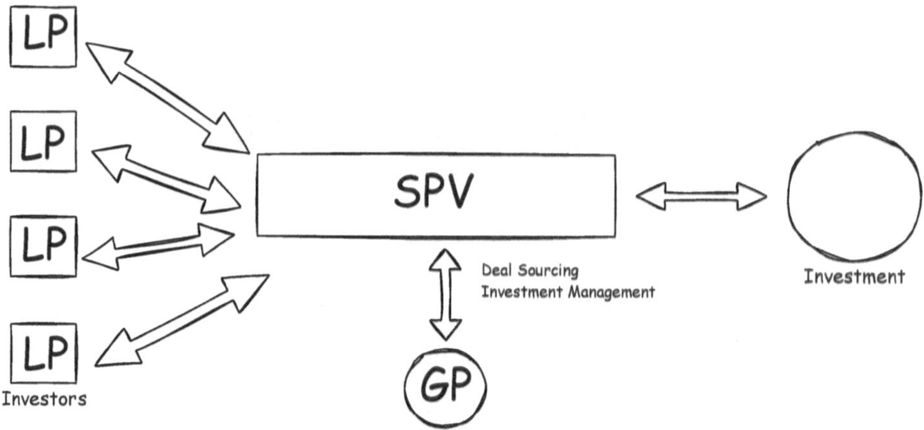


Despite being relatively unknown, SPVs have existed for a long time. Their origin dates back to the early 20th century when there was a demand to finance large-scale infrastructure developments like railways and bridges. The goal was to set up a separate entity to handle the project's finances on its own, without depending on the government agency or parent company.

As markets became more intricate and interconnected worldwide, more people and companies recognized the advantages of SPVs. They were a really attractive option because they could protect assets, reduce taxes, and help with getting access to capital.

During the 70s and 80s, large financial institutions and corporations employed SPVs more extensively for others, carrying out specific, often large-scale, transactions. This included mortgage-backed securities, asset-backed securities, and the securitization of different asset classes.

The dot-com boom of the 1990s and early 2000s, followed by the global financial crisis of 2007-2008, marked significant milestones in the evolution of SPVs. These events highlighted the importance of having investment structures that are transparent, regulated, and strategically planned. SPVs started being used for more than just their traditional purposes, including venture capital investments, private equity, real estate, and other areas.

SPVs are now more prevalent in a wide range of projects. SPVs are intricately woven into the fabric of global finance, providing a refined approach to private investments. It ensures a balance between risk, compliance, and strategic financial planning. SPVs can be used for various investment strategies, such as supporting startups and facilitating real estate deals, as well as enabling cross-border investments and mergers and acquisitions.

Furthermore, SPVs usually have fewer regulatory restrictions imposed on them. For that reason, they are a lot more appealing to folks raising capital and holding assets. They have allowed large corporations to be a lot more agile and have brought about a path for democratization for private investments to allow more opportunities to "the little guy". The transformation of SPVs, from highly specialized financial tools to becoming a major part of contemporary investment strategies really shows how versatile they are. The use of SPVs is expected to keep growing and hold even more importance in private markets.

Alright, so in the coming pages, we'll get into the details and discuss everything that is required for you to get started in setting up an SPV for your next investment deal. The info we have put together for you here will cover what you need to know for putting together the legal documents, onboarding your investors and maintaining compliance in the process.

# UNDERSTANDING SECURITIES

With our understanding of what Special Purpose Vehicles are, it's time to discuss the rules that govern them. Setting up a Special Purpose Vehicle for an investment means you're entering a highly regulated area. You should definitely understand securities and the regulations that come with them. Securities are financial instruments that represent ownership in a company or a debt. Knowing what qualifies as a security and the rules that govern them is essential for SPV managers. This knowledge helps ensure the SPV operates within legal boundaries and builds trust with stakeholders. Once you've got these concepts down, as the General Partner, you can build a solid foundation for running an effective and compliant investment deal.

To put it simply, a security is a financial item that can be bought and sold, and holds value. When you raise capital from investors, you give them securities in return. These securities can represent ownership in the SPV. They can show that the investor is a creditor of the SPV. Or, they can represent claims of future ownership. One important feature of securities is that they're fungible. This means that each security of the same type is basically identical and can be easily swapped for another. As a result, investors find securities more appealing. It streamlines trading and valuing them.

Investment agreements carry both profit potential and a level of risk. To figure out if something counts as a security under U.S. law, we use something called the Howey Test. This test was created by the U.S. Supreme Court back in 1946 and has four "prongs" of criteria that we can examine to be able to determine the status of an investment. If something meets the criteria to be a security, there are certain regulations that have to be followed. The Howey Test has become an important concept for those involved in investments to know what rules they need to follow.

**There are four key criteria that make up the Howey Test:**

- Investment of money (or something of value)

- In a common enterprise

- With the expectation of profits

- Solely through the efforts of the promoter or a third party

An investment is considered a security if it meets all four criteria of the Howey Test. Regulators set certain registration rules that must be followed when something is classified as a security. However, there are many exceptions to these rules. They are in a set of regulations called Regulation D. We'll discuss the details of Regulation D later in this book.

Depending on this classification, there are significant impacts on the legal and regulatory rules you need to follow. This can be complex and errors can result in grave repercussions. So, if you're unsure about your situation, it's best to consult an attorney who specializes in this area. They can help you figure out if your venture counts as a security and what rules you need to follow.

The Securities Act of 1933 and the Securities Exchange Act of 1934 are the two important laws that shape how the U.S. securities market operates. The 1933 Act came about during the Great Depression and focuses on how new securities are created and sold to the public. Its main goal is to protect investors by making sure companies tell the truth about what they're offering. The Securities Act of 1934, on the other hand, deals more with the buying and selling of existing securities. It requires public companies to keep sharing important business info over time. Both laws attempt to simultaneously accomplish two objectives. They aim to protect investors and to help businesses raise money to grow. It's all about finding a balance between these two goals.

Equity, debt, and hybrid are the three primary types of securities you'll find used in Special Purpose Vehicles.

Investors can have ownership rights in a Special Purpose Vehicle by holding equity securities. This includes a share of what the SPV owns (its assets) and a portion of the money it makes (its profits). Let's look at a couple of examples to make this clearer. In a real estate SPV, if you hold equity securities, you would own a part of the properties the SPV buys. So if the SPV owns apartment buildings, you'd own a slice of those buildings. In a tech startup SPV, equity securities might give you a stake in the company's ideas and inventions (called intellectual property). They may also give you a share of its future profits. This type of investment allows people to directly benefit from the success of the SPV's projects or business.

Debt securities are a way for financial backers to lend capital to a Special Purpose Vehicle. In this arrangement, the SPV borrows money from investors and promises to pay it back over time, plus interest. This can be useful in different situations. As an illustration, a real estate SPV might use debt securities to fund a property renovation. The investors would lend money to the SPV, and the SPV would pay them back using the rent money it collects after the renovation is complete. Similarly, a software development SPV could use debt securities to fund the creation of a new app. In this case, the SPV would repay the investors using money from future app sales. This approach allows SPVs to get the money they need for projects, while giving investors a way to earn interest on their money.

Hybrid securities are a mix of debt and equity, offering more options but also being more complicated. A good example is a convertible bond. This type of investment starts off like a loan, giving investors regular interest payments. However, it can change into ownership (equity) if certain things happen. Let's look at how this might work in a couple of different situations. For one example, a real estate SPV could offer convertible bonds that pay interest like a normal loan. With this strategy, if the value of the properties starts to rise, investors could choose to swap their bonds for a share of ownership in the properties. Along the same lines, a tech company SPV might want to provide bonds that can be converted into shares once they reach a specific number of users.

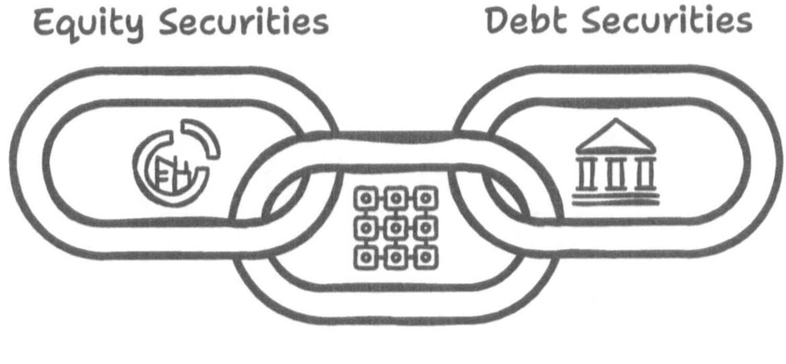


Regardless of the industry, anyone managing private investments must understand various securities. SPVs are used in this context to deal with different securities, raise capital, and organize investment deals. In later chapters, we'll dig into the specific steps you need to follow to stay on the right side about compliance. The bottom line is, the more you learn about securities, the better you can move forward with structuring private investment deals. This benefits you, as the General Partner, and your Limited Partner investors.

# WEALTH IN NUMBERS

*"You have to be burning with an idea, or a problem, or a wrong that you want to right. If you're not passionate enough from the start, you'll never stick it out."*

— *Steve Jobs, Co-Founder of Apple*

# STARTING WITH WHY

Now that we've explored securities and some SPV regulations, let's zoom out and see the bigger picture. Knowing the technical stuff is important. But, we must also consider why investors and entrepreneurs are drawn to these financial instruments. So what motivates individuals to get involved in the complex world of private markets and SPVs? To answer this we need to shift our focus from the "what" of SPVs to the essential "why." Although private markets can be intricate, they are highly appealing, and with good reason.

Throughout history, society has always been drawn to the idea of discovering new things. This drive has pushed them to explore unknown lands and come up with revolutionary ideas. In the world of finance, private markets are like these uncharted territories. They're full of potential opportunities for investors, but they're difficult to access. Many people don't even know where to begin with private investments. The mix of possibility and exclusivity in private markets is intriguing. Just as explorers sought new worlds, today's investors seek private markets for new ways to grow wealth and build businesses.

In contrast to the well-lit corridors of public markets, private markets demand a unique navigation strategy. The complexity and lack of transparency in private markets present challenges. As a result, people working in private markets must practice caution and pay close attention to detail. Due diligence in private market investments is a must. It requires dealmakers to be patient, analytical, and resourceful.

For these reasons, private investments appeal to our desire to reach into the unknown. Going with the traditional investment route can be a drag - slow and dull. SPVs open doors to an exciting frontier, granting more investors access to previously exclusive deals. Using an SPV to raise capital requires a clear vision and a solid plan for utilizing the funds effectively. It's crucial to understand not just what you're investing in, but why you're doing it.

An SPV is more than just a financial tool; it's a commitment to your investors, your vision, and yourself as you become a leader in unfamiliar territory. As you explore SPVs further, keep this sense of purpose in mind. It will guide you through challenges. The most successful SPVs aren't just about chasing returns, but about bringing visions to life and creating value in the world. You need to identify your goal and understand why you might want to use an SPV to raise capital. With that in mind, let's look at some examples of ways that SPVs can be used to bring your vision to life.

## Mergers & Acquisitions

Many Mergers and Acquisitions (M&A) professionals rely on Special Purpose Vehicles to streamline and safeguard the deal process and offer solutions to various challenges. One huge advantage of using a Special Purpose Vehicle in M&A is the protection it offers. When someone buys a company, they typically want to keep their personal assets separate from the business they're purchasing. An SPV acts as a protective barrier in this scenario if issues arise with the newly acquired business.

For instance, if the purchased company faces legal challenges or financial difficulties, the SPV limits the buyer's risk. Their potential losses are confined to what they've invested in that specific business through the SPV, rather than putting their entire personal wealth at stake. This setup provides peace of mind and financial security for buyers in business acquisitions.

Special Purpose Vehicles are particularly valuable in a strategy known as a "roll-up" in the mergers and acquisitions (M&A) world. This approach involves buying multiple businesses as part of a larger plan. In a roll-up, each acquired business can be purchased through its own separate SPV. This structure keeps the companies separate, so legal issues don't affect the other businesses. As a result, using SPVs in roll-ups allows investors to manage risk more effectively across their portfolio of acquired companies. This protects the overall investment strategy from any individual business setbacks.

Sometimes, when buying a business, a purchaser might only want certain parts of it rather than the whole company. In these situations, buyers can use a SPV to handle just the assets they're interested in. For example, if a buyer only wants to acquire a company's equipment, intellectual property, or customer lists, they can set up an SPV to manage these specific items.

This SPV acts as a separate entity, dedicated solely to overseeing the acquired assets. The separation has multiple benefits, including better asset management and improved financial tracking. Also, by keeping these assets in a separate entity, the buyer gains some legal and financial protection. This reduces their personal risk if something goes wrong with the assets. In general, SPVs increase the efficiency and make it easier to complete acquisitions that might otherwise be challenging or impractical.

## Real Estate

Chances are, your initial introduction to SPVs came in the form of a real estate investment. Special Purpose Vehicles have revolutionized real estate investing. They are now the top choice of industry professionals. They're extremely useful for private market property investments. These include opportunities in commercial buildings, residential properties, land, and development projects.

Since the 1980s, banks, developers, and investors have been using SPVs to streamline real estate transactions. SPVs facilitate the syndication of real estate deals, which have grown tremendously in popularity. Their appeal lies in the ability of an SPV to simplify forming partnerships and streamline financial management and asset transfers. For example, when a building or group of buildings is held under an SPV, it operates as its own business entity. SPV shareholders receive income from the property revenue and manage expenses through the SPV. This model enhances property investment access via fractional ownership. It gives investors the option to spread their investments across multiple properties. This approach allows more investors to participate in income-generating assets, taking a share of the deal. As a result, individuals with less available capital can now take part in real estate opportunities that were previously out of reach.

Another advantage of using an SPV in real estate is the potential for significant tax savings. For example, when property sales taxes exceed capital gains taxes, an SPV can be helpful. An organization can set up an SPV to hold a property, and when it's time to sell, the organization can sell the SPV entity, not the property itself. This approach could result in reduced liability for capital gains tax on the SPV sale, rather than facing higher property sales tax. Further benefit can be achieved by carefully structuring revenue against mortgage expenses to optimize financial gains and enhance a company's overall fiscal position. As a result, it could lead to easier access to capital and better terms.

## Secondaries

Secondary transactions involve buying and selling existing investments in private companies. Secondary investments let investors trade private equity interests. They offer liquidity, risk management, and diversification in private equity. As a result, secondary markets offer access to rare opportunities.

This allows early investors, founders, or employees to sell their shares before the company goes public or gets bought out. These shares can be common (usually owned by founders and employees) or preferred (typically held by investors). It's important to understand the difference between secondary transactions and primary investments. Secondary transactions involve buying existing shares. They don't raise new money for the company or change other shareholders' ownership. Primary investments bring new money into the company. But, they reduce existing shareholders' ownership percentages.

They allow sellers to receive cash earlier, while new investors can invest in promising private companies before they go public. These transactions also help establish valuations for companies not yet traded on public markets. While investing in private companies through Special Purpose Vehicles (SPVs) might lead to higher returns, it also carries increased risk. However, secondary markets help smaller investors. They allow pooling resources via SPVs. This grants access to opportunities that usually need substantial capital. These investments may provide quicker returns compared to early-stage investments. Smart investors can also find undervalued companies in secondary markets. The scarcity of information and limited access can lead to the discovery of excellent investment opportunities.

Secondary markets for private company shares become more active when companies choose to stay private for longer periods and delay going public. This trend is often seen when there are fewer company buyouts and mergers happening. In these situations, investors in private companies seek ways to sell their shares and recover their investments. As venture capital and private equity funds reach maturity, their Limited Partners (LPs) want to see returns on their investments. Secondary markets provide an opportunity for these LPs to sell their stakes and demonstrate the performance of the funds. Unlike public markets where trading is quick and easy, private investments are more challenging to buy and sell.

If you're interested in purchasing secondary shares for a SPV deal, you typically need to negotiate your allocation before raising capital. Once that's done, you'll need additional time to set up the SPV and raise capital from investors. So, where do you get an allocation? Many company employees get stock options or restricted stock units (RSUs) and might want to sell these before the company goes public. You can also work with brokers that deal in secondaries to negotiate a traunch for your deal.

The secondary market for private company shares can be challenging. This is especially true when negotiating with sellers. However, expertise in this area can set you apart as an investment manager.

## Infrastructure Projects

Large infrastructure projects rely heavily on SPVs, particularly in transportation, energy, and telecommunications. These projects often require complex financial arrangements and robust structures to manage risks and attract investment. This makes SPVs an ideal solution. SPVs create a separate entity for each project. This ensures that risks and rewards are fairly shared among project sponsors, investors, and lenders. This separation limits each party to only their agreed-upon risks. It makes these projects more attractive to investors.

SPVs are useful in public-private partnerships (PPPs). They facilitate a means for collaboration between governments and private companies. The SPV structure helps manage the financial, operational, and legal aspects of large infrastructure projects. It ensures they are handled well and benefit all parties. This framework works great for complex projects that need input from both public and private sectors.

SPVs allow project managers to create deals that cater to various investor needs. They may include investment options like senior debt, mezzanine debt, or preferred equity. Since they cater to different risk and reward preferences, these projects are more attractive to a wider range of investors.

## Startups

For startup founders looking for funding, a Special Purpose Vehicle can be a lifeline. Starting a new company is already tough, with lots of challenges to overcome. SPVs make it easier for startups to get funding, which could make a big difference in their success.

The complexities of managing multiple investors is simplified by consolidating them into a single entity. Rather than dealing with many individual investors, an SPV makes a single investment on their behalf. This approach simplifies the company's cap table, showing only one entry instead of a long list of separate investors. With fewer stakeholders, the startup has clearer governance. This makes management easier as it grows. This can speed up the funding process, cutting it from months to weeks. For example, a tech startup on the verge of a breakthrough could use an SPV to quickly secure funds. This would avoid the lengthy negotiations of traditional venture capital investments. This makes SPVs an efficient tool for addressing urgent funding needs.

For investors, SPVs offer a simple way to invest in promising startups. The rules are clear from the start, which is great for people who want to invest without having to manage things or negotiate all the time.

You might not realize this, but here's something to consider: SPVs can actually make a startup more attractive to future investors. How? By showing that the startup can get big chunks of investment all at once, SPVs tell other investors that the business is serious and has support. This can make it easier to raise more capital in later rounds.

Early capital raising and streamlined business operations are possible for startups through SPVs. This helps them build a strong base for growing their business over time. It's not just about getting the first round of funding, but about setting up for long-term success in the market.

## Natural Resources

The strategic use of SPVs has made them an important instrument in natural resource investment. Natural resource projects include those centered on things like minerals, oil and natural gas. Their flexibility and efficiency make them well-suited for this industry. They manage complex projects and balance investors' needs with the demands of large-scale resource extraction and processing.

Natural resource projects face several significant challenges. One major issue is the volatile nature of commodity prices, which can fluctuate widely and impact project profitability. Another obstacle is the complex regulatory landscape. These projects often require working with multiple government agencies. Also, many natural resource projects are in remote or harsh areas. This can make operations logistically difficult and expensive. These challenges may include extreme weather, poor infrastructure, or political instability. SPVs help handle these issues by letting you set up the investment in a way that fits the project. This also helps protect investors by keeping the project's risks separate from other investments.

Natural resource projects often require significant amounts of capital to get off the ground. Special Purpose Vehicles are a simple way to pool capital for these projects. These sources might include pension funds seeking stable, long-term returns. Or, they might be industry partners who bring valuable expertise with their investment. By using SPVs, project managers can more easily attract and coordinate the large sums of money needed for natural resource ventures. This approach simplifies the process of securing and managing the significant capital required for these complex and often expensive projects.

Managing a SPV for natural resource projects requires strong negotiation skills and sharp risk management ability. By effectively using an SPV, you can maximize the potential of these valuable, long-term ventures. This approach allows you to generate attractive returns for your investors while also contributing to the global supply of essential resources.

## Renewable Energy

The renewable energy sector benefits from SPVs as valuable tools for financing projects like solar farms. These projects can experience a range of obstacles, such as long permitting processes, volatile energy prices, and substantial upfront costs. The framework of SPVs enables an easier capital raising process to appeal to investors driven by environmental impact or financial gains.

Through the use of an SPV, solar companies can raise capital by offering bonds or shares as an investment opportunity. Renewable energy companies can enhance capital management and attract a variety of investors through the use of SPVs, which separate project risks and rewards. Since SPVs offer creative funding options beyond traditional bank loans, it is possible to customize deals to suit different investors' needs.

Renewable energy investments are risky. But, government subsidies and long-term power purchase agreements can provide more stable revenue. This stability makes renewable energy projects more appealing to investors. It offers financial security and reduces risk.

The strategic use of SPVs is now vital in renewable energy. It enables the successful development and operation of large-scale energy projects. They're a valuable asset for advancing clean energy projects since they can overcome funding challenges and draw in a wide range of investors.

## Intellectual Property

Raising capital for acquiring, developing, or licensing intellectual property can be simplified with a Special Purpose Vehicle. With this capital access, groundbreaking ideas can be turned into successful businesses.

Assessing the value of intellectual property can be a challenging process. An example is when a patent for a technology seems very profitable, but its market success is uncertain. As an example, sometimes a patent for a technology seems very lucrative, but it's tough to predict if it will actually do well in the market.

It's well known that licensing intellectual property (IP) can be a lucrative opportunity. When you hold valuable IP, your management team can develop strategies to commercialize it and negotiate terms for its acquisition and use. By granting other companies the right to use the IP, the SPV can earn steady royalty income while maintaining ownership. This approach is versatile and can work across different industries. One option is to license a pharmaceutical patent to multiple drug makers, allowing them to produce and sell the medication. Similarly, you could also consider licensing an algorithm to various tech firms, enabling them to utilize it in their products or services. The great thing about licensing is that it's scalable and can provide long-term, recurring revenue. Ultimately, this creates a unique way to support and benefit from innovative ideas. This not only generates attractive returns for investors but also encourages further innovation.

## Aircraft and Vessels

When it comes to overseeing investments in high-value assets such as aircraft and yachts, SPVs stand out. They streamline the ownership and operational processes extremely well. Through segregating financial and legal risks within the SPV, they safeguard investors' assets and enhance asset management. Unlike certain collectibles that may appreciate over time, aircraft and yachts typically depreciate. Having a private jet or yacht comes with significant ongoing expenses, such as maintenance, crew salaries, and insurance. To address these challenges, an SPV should plan its exit strategy from the start. This plan should also take into account depreciation and asset sale considerations. SPVs can implement depreciation recapture strategies to lower tax burdens resulting from asset depreciation. Managing a private jet or yacht means navigating through a maze of regulations, from licensing to international standards.

SPVs make this easier by letting multiple people own and manage these assets together. This spreads out the financial risks and allows experts to handle day-to-day operations. Think of an SPV as a central hub that keeps everything running smoothly and legally.

In the past, only very wealthy people could afford planes and yachts. But now, SPVs have made it possible for more people to own a piece of these luxury items with fractional ownership. By dividing ownership into smaller parts, SPVs allow more people to enjoy the perks of luxury travel without bearing all the costs and responsibilities alone. This has made owning a yacht or plane a more achievable dream for many. As the GP for these assets, you must negotiate good purchase agreements, manage maintenance and crew performance, and ensure efficient operations. You also need to think strategically about how to use these assets and plan when and how to sell them for the highest return. With skill and dedication, it becomes possible to capitalize on investments and generate value for everyone involved in the SPV.

## Derivatives and Financial Products

Managing investments in derivatives and complex financial products can be simplified through the use of Special Purpose Vehicles. They provide a flexible and efficient framework. Isolating specific financial activities within separate entities helps manage risks. It allows for customized approaches and may provide regulatory and tax benefits.

Situations where SPVs are particularly effective include:

## Futures Contracts:

Companies can effectively handle price volatility through the use of SPVs. To safeguard against price changes in commodities or financial instruments, it can create an SPV. The SPV enters into futures contracts on behalf of the company, providing a buffer against unfavorable price movements. If prices move against the company's interests, the futures contracts gain value, offsetting potential losses. On the other hand, if prices move in a positive direction, the company gains directly but the futures contracts may lose value. This method helps businesses control costs or revenues. It makes financial planning easier and may yield better futures market deals.

## Forward Contracts:

Companies can use SPVs to manage their future financial commitments. If a business knows it will have a future transaction in a foreign currency or commodity, it can use an SPV to enter into a forward contract. The SPV agrees to buy or sell the asset at a fixed price and date, basically sealing the deal for the future transaction. This strategy helps companies avoid the uncertainties of market fluctuations, providing a clear picture of future cash flows. Companies can keep their main operations separate from these hedging activities by isolating them in an SPV, which could simplify accounting and compliance.

## Options:

Using an SPV to manage options-based investments enables complex investment products. These SPVs can trade options on different assets to make personalized risk and return profiles for investors. An SPV could merge options with other financial instruments. This would create principal-protected notes with gains tied to market performance. By using this strategy, investors can create advanced investment products that separate risks and potentially offer tax advantages.

## Swaps:

Swap transactions using SPVs allow companies to effectively mitigate interest rates and currency risks. When businesses want to exchange cash flows, such as switching from fixed to floating interest rates, they can utilize an SPV for this purpose. The SPV enters into the swap agreement with a counterparty, effectively transforming the nature of the company's financial obligations. Businesses can use this strategy to match their liabilities with their desired risk profile, without making changes to their current debt structure. Companies can use an SPV to keep swap arrangements off their balance sheets, which can offer regulatory or accounting advantages while managing financial risk.

## Distressed Debt:

Troubled businesses can regain stability and find relief by leveraging a SPV. When a company is struggling financially, its debts often become available at lower prices. Investors can use SPVs to buy this discounted debt. By doing so, they might be able to help the company recover, or they could profit from the process of restructuring the company's finances. This approach gives investors a chance to potentially turn around a failing business while also aiming to make a return on their investment.

## Direct Lending:

Loans can be extended directly to companies, avoiding the need for traditional banks when through a Special Purpose Vehicle. This approach gives more flexibility in how loans are structured. Unlike regular banks, SPVs can tailor the loan terms to better fit what each company needs. This means companies can get loans that work well for their specific situation, even if those terms wouldn't be possible with a standard bank loan. It's a way for businesses to access financing that's more customized to their requirements.

## Asset Transfer:

SPVs simplify the process of packaging and selling specific assets. Imagine you have a box full of various items you want to sell. Instead of listing and selling each item separately, which could be time-consuming and complicated, you could put all these items in one big container and sell the entire container. This is essentially what an SPV does for companies

When a company has multiple assets it wants to sell, such as real estate, or equipment, it can transfer all of these assets into an SPV making it a distinct legal entity. This separation allows the company to sell the entire SPV as one unit, rather than dealing with the complexities of selling each asset individually.

This approach offers several advantages. First, it saves time and reduces paperwork, as the company only needs to manage one transaction instead of many. Second, it can make the sale more attractive to buyers, who might prefer to purchase a package of assets rather than individual pieces. Third, it can be especially useful for complex or hard-to-sell assets that might be challenging to value or transfer on their own.

### Structured Finance:

This complex area of finance creates specialized financial tools and entities. They meet specific investment needs and manage risk. It includes many products and techniques. They aim to turn financial assets into more marketable securities. Structured finance primarily revolves around the use of SPVs to create and manage various financial instruments. These instruments include Collateralized Loan Obligations (CLOs) and Collateralized Bond Obligations (CBOs). CLOs are securities that repackage pools of loans into different risk levels. CBOs are similar but use bonds as the underlying assets. Other common products are Collateralized Debt Obligations (CDOs) and Credit Default Swaps (CDSs). CDOs can include a mix of loans, bonds, and other assets. CDSs are contracts that transfer credit risk between parties.

The field also includes several types of asset-backed securities. Residential Mortgage-Backed Securities (RMBS) and Commercial Mortgage-Backed Securities (CMBS) are created by pooling mortgage loans. Asset-Backed Securities (ABS) can be based on other debts, like credit card receivables or auto loans. Real Estate Mortgage Investment Conduits (REMICs) are a tax-advantaged structure for issuing mortgage-backed securities. Structured finance also includes specialized products like Insurance-Linked Securities (ILS). They transfer insurance risk to the capital markets. It also includes synthetic financial instruments. They use derivatives to replicate the cash flows of other assets. Guaranteed Investment Contracts and syndicated loans are other examples of structured finance products.

A key concept in structured finance is securitization, where financial assets are pooled and transformed into tradable securities. This process often uses securitization trusts, which are SPVs that issue securities backed by the pooled assets. This not only provides liquidity to the original asset holders but also allows investors to access a wider range of investment opportunities. For example, a company with a large portfolio of car loans might use an SPV to package these loans into a single, tradable security. This process, known as loan securitization, allows the company to quickly convert its illiquid loan assets into cash, freeing up resources for other projects. It also transfers the loans' credit risk to investors. This protects the company's main operations from potential financial setbacks.

In essence, structured finance redistributes risk and creates new investment products. This plays a major role in modern financial markets by increasing liquidity through unique investment opportunities. As you can see, SPVs are particularly well-suited for handling derivatives and financial products. When you run an SPV for credit assets, you're in charge of managing risk and being able to carefully choose and control investments can result in major profits.

This role offers an exciting opportunity to uncover hidden value in various assets, drive financial innovation, and develop attractive investment options. It's a chance to participate in financial engineering, where traditional assets are transformed into new products that benefit both the market and investors.

WEALTH IN NUMBERS

*"You don't have to be a genius or a visionary or even a college graduate to be successful. You just need a framework and a dream."*

*— Michael Dell, Founder of Dell Inc.*

# KEY BENEFITS OF SPVS

So by now, we're sure you're starting to see why SPVs are attractive so many investors. As the General Partner, you'll be working to craft an attractive deal for potential investors that lays the groundwork for success. Whether you're a seasoned veteran or just stepping into the investment management world, mastering the power of Special Purpose Vehicles equips you with an edge to structure winning deals. Understanding the key benefits of SPVs could be the key to unlocking new potential. By creating a distinct legal and financial entity, SPVs provide a logical structure that's easy to communicate to potential investors.

As a General Partner, your role is to create an appealing investment opportunity that sets the stage for success. SPVs offer advantages that can give you an edge in structuring successful deals, regardless of your experience level in investment management.

Thanks to the clear structure of SPVs, you can easily explain your deal to potential investors in a way that anyone can grasp. At their core, SPVs follow a simple narrative: "Here's our investment deal, how it works, and what we plan to invest in." Remember that the goal here is not just to manage investments but to manage them well. SPVs can revolutionize your approach to investing by providing both security and access to new possibilities. As we explore the specific components of SPVs in the following pages, you'll gain a clear understanding of how they work and how they can benefit you. This knowledge will enable you to make informed decisions about your investments with confidence.

So, let's take a closer look at some key advantages that Special Purpose Vehicles bring to the table:

## Legal Protections

Investing always comes with some level of risk, but there are ways to protect yourself and your investors. An SPV keeps the investment's finances and potential legal issues separate from your other business activities. This separation is called "risk isolation." By using an SPV, you can limit your exposure to financial and legal problems that might arise from a specific investment. Even in the unfortunate scenario of an SPV facing losses or bankruptcy, the parent company's assets typically remain largely unaffected. This extra protection makes investments more attractive. It allows investors to explore, risky opportunities and encourages investment in promising, but complex, ventures.

Let's consider a real estate firm that owns multiple rental properties. Traditionally, if all these properties were owned by one company, a lawsuit against any single property could put the entire portfolio at risk. This is where Special Purpose Vehicles become valuable. Instead of directly owning all properties, the organization creates a separate SPV for each property. Each SPV holds the title to its specific property. The company then establishes a main "control center" SPV that owns all these individual property SPVs. With this structure, if a legal issue arises with one property, it only affects that property's specific SPV. The other properties and the main control center SPV remain protected. This approach effectively limits any problems to a sole SPV, shielding the rest of the company's assets from potential legal or financial issues.

## Build a Track Record

If you're aiming to manage a full-fledged investment fund in the future, you'll need to prove your worth to potential investors. They want evidence that you can pick winning deals and provide good returns. By successfully managing multiple SPVs, you can build a track record that demonstrates your investment skills. Each successful SPV shows your ability to find excellent opportunities and execute them well. You're not just talking about future plans; you're actively making investment decisions and building a portfolio.

As you run successful SPVs, you'll grow your network of Limited Partners who are interested in working with you. This process also helps you develop your investment strategy and establish yourself as an expert in your chosen area. Building your reputation takes time. With persistence and a history of successful SPVs, you'll be well-placed to advance your career. You might launch your own fund and make a big impact in the investment world.

## Streamlined and Swift Formation

So you've found a deal that has the potential to be huge, but there's a catch – the window of opportunity is narrow. Every day counts. You're thinking: "How can I move fast enough to secure this deal without getting bogged down in paperwork?"

The efficient formation process of an SPV is one of its most appealing features, making it possible to establish the legal framework in just days. This provides a huge advantage - you can stay agile and move quickly when time is of the essence.

## Clearly Established Guidelines

Clear regulations in a defined legal framework are major advantages of Special Purpose Vehicles. These structures make it easier for investors to comply with various rules, including those that apply across different countries. Compared to other investment methods, SPVs can significantly cut down on paperwork and administrative tasks. This simplicity is a major reason why many investors find SPVs appealing.

### Freedom to Choose Jurisdiction

When forming a Special Purpose Vehicle, you have the flexibility to choose where to set it up, even if it's not where you live. This is called "jurisdictional freedom." It lets you pick a location with the best laws and rules for your needs. This choice might lead to paying less in taxes compared to your home area. By setting up SPVs in a place with favorable regulations, it is possible to optimize finances and operations while complying with all necessary regulations.

### Ease of Asset Transfer

A solution for managing assets that are difficult to transfer can be found with SPVs. Instead of dealing with complex lists of individual assets, an SPV can hold ownership of a single asset on behalf of a group. This structure allows the entire SPV to be sold as a complete package, eliminating the need to divide up assets. SPVs are appealing because they simplify the process of converting assets into cash or establish a valuation. This makes it much easier for asset owners to sell their holdings.

### Enhanced Privacy Options

Using Special Purpose Vehicles enables companies to achieve improved confidentiality in business operations. An SPV allows a company to conceal projects or deals from competitors or to maintain secrecy about specific deals or resource utilization. Forming your LLC in states such as Delaware and Wyoming offer enhanced privacy for individual investors.

In essence, SPVs create a privacy shield. They let businesses and individuals work on projects without drawing unwanted attention. This privacy protection makes SPVs appealing to those wanting to keep their financial and business activities confidential.

## Financing

With the help of a SPV, companies can finance new projects without adding to their debt or diluting the ownership of current shareholders. Typically, the parent company contributes some funds, while external investors provide the rest. This structure allows investors to support a specific project without directly investing in the parent company.

SPVs also provide advantages when seeking loans. Since the SPV owns the assets directly, its creditworthiness is separate from the parent company's credit management. Essentially, SPVs create a financial buffer that can lead to more favorable financing terms and greater flexibility in project funding.

## Run Deals Outside of Investment Thesis

For fund managers, Special Purpose Vehicles offer a practical solution when they encounter lucrative deals that don't fit their fund's investment thesis. Remember that SPVs are separate legal entities for specific investments. They allowe fund managers to raise capital exclusively for these ventures. This approach allows funds to stick to their thesis while still pursuing promising off-strategy opportunities.

## Increased Leverage & Deal Term Control

By pooling their capital in a Special Purpose Vehicle, investors can gain enhanced control over deal terms. This collective approach gives them more negotiating power than individual investors typically have. The General Partner managing the SPV works hard to find and negotiate the best possible pricing for the deal, which benefits the participating Limited Partners. Because of the SPV's larger investment size, the GP has more influence in shaping the investment deal's structure. This increased leverage often makes it easier for the GP to negotiate and secure high-quality investment opportunities. Essentially, by joining forces in an SPV, investors gain more say in deal terms and potentially access better investments than they might on their own.

## Deal by Deal Profits

The structure of Special Purpose Vehicles benefits both the organizers (General Partners) and the investors. Unlike traditional funds, SPVs allow organizers to earn profits on each individual deal, rather than on the overall performance of a larger fund. This approach is particularly advantageous for newcomers to fund management, as it can offer quicker returns. Traditional fund-raising can be time-consuming, and since most funds are long-term investments, it can take years to see significant returns. In contrast, SPVs generate returns faster because profits and carried interest are paid out on a deal-by-deal basis. The success of an SPV investment depends on a single factor: a liquidity event, such as when the company being invested in is acquired or goes public through an IPO. This focused approach can lead to quicker and more tangible results for both organizers and investors.

## High Quality Dealflow:

Consistently backing successful projects is key to establishing a reputation as skilled investors. By identifying promising opportunities and generating strong returns for stakeholders, a General Partner can build a track record that fuels a virtuous cycle of achievement.

This proven ability to pick winners attracts higher-quality deal flow, as entrepreneurs seek out reputable investors. Simultaneously, it enhances the GP's credibility, making it easier to raise capital for future funds and potentially on more favorable terms. Success also expands the GP's network. It opens doors to co-investment opportunities and industry insights. Ultimately, a strong track record lays a solid foundation for achieving favorable outcomes in the competitive landscape of private investments. This helps position the GP as a trusted and sought-after partner for both entrepreneurs and investors alike.

## Specific Investment:

Investors enjoy feeling in control of their investments, and Special Purpose Vehicles cater to this desire by offering clarity and specificity. Unlike traditional funds, which spread investments across a portfolio, SPVs focus on a single opportunity. This lets investors choose whether to participate based on the specific venture. This targeted approach gives investors a clear view of where their money is going, which can boost their confidence and potentially lead to larger investments.

As we've discussed, SPVs can isolate risk. They protect investors' portfolios while they pursue high-return ventures. Each SPV can have unique terms for its investment. This makes them attractive to investors who value transparency and tailored opportunities. SPVs empower investors by offering control, clarity, and customization. This helps them make informed investment decisions. As a result, they are often more willing to commit funds.

## Cost Efficiency

It is typically far more affordable to make use of a SPV when compared to a traditional investment fund. Thanks to modern service providers like Syndicately, setting up and managing SPVs has become even more simplified and cost-effective. With this increased accessibility, more organizers and investors can join in, getting deals done quickly and without expensive overhead. SPVs are a great option for new managers who don't have a lot of resources.

These managers can now cut costs and go after big returns that could be out of reach for them with a traditional fund structure. SPVs are leveling the playing field by giving people the chance to invest in lucrative deals without expensive overhead.

## Access to Capital

The investment landscape is being revolutionized by SPVs, making it more accessible and inclusive. They allow for smaller investment amounts, which opens the door to a broader range of investors, including those who might not have had access to such opportunities before. This flexibility benefits both dealmakers and investors.

By pooling capital, General Partners can access lucrative investments that were previously out of reach due to high minimum thresholds. We work with a lot of investors that like SPVs because the hard work of sourcing, building relationships and closing the deal is done for them — they get to pick something they want to invest in. SPVs have lower barriers to entry and help in democratizing investment. SPVs enable emerging General Partners to structure deals while broadening investment accessibility. This dual benefit expands the investor base and democratizes access to promising opportunities. Ultimately, SPVs open up lucrative opportunities to a broader range of investors and provide emerging General Partners with more potential sources of capital.

## Opportunity for Follow-On Investments

Venture capital (VC) funds often use Special Purpose Vehicles to maintain their investment position in successful portfolio companies as they grow. If a promising startup in a VC's portfolio needs more funding, the VC may want to invest more, but their fund's allocation limits could be a constraint. This is the perfect situation for SPVs. They allow the VC to create a separate investment vehicle specifically for this follow-on round. Plus, the LPs who put money into the VC fund have the chance to exercise their pro-rata rights.

This means they can join the SPV and invest directly in the startup alongside the VC, maintaining or increasing their stake in the company. This way, VCs can support their best investments and give their LPs a chance to be more directly involved in a startup's growth.

# NOTABLE REAL-WORLD EXAMPLES OF SPVS

While Special Purpose Vehicles might not always grab the headlines, they are often the framework behind the scenes of many big business deals. Consistently, they have shown their significance in navigating complicated transactions to achieve success. If you're like us, you may find that real-life examples bring these concepts to life.

While the most notable transactions involve significant figures, it's important to understand that SPVs can be incredibly useful for (much) smaller deals. Whether you're looking at billion-dollar mergers or small investments, understanding SPVs can help. They play a key role in both cases. Here are a few fascinating examples of notable, high-profile deals shaped by SPVs so you can see how they operate in the real world.

- **Bain Capital's Acquisition of Burger King in 2002:**[i] Bain Capital, a private equity firm, used an SPV to acquire the fast-food giant Burger King in a deal valued at $1.5 billion. The SPV structure likely facilitated the financing and offered specific advantages such as risk isolation and potential tax benefits.

- **KKR's Acquisition of Toys "R" Us:**[ii] Private equity giant KKR, along with other investors, used an SPV to acquire Toys "R" Us in a leveraged buyout deal valued at $6.6 billion. The SPV structure allowed for risk isolation from KKR's other investments, potential tax optimization, and tailored financing and management strategies for the acquisition.

- **SL Green Realty Corp.'s Acquisition of Equity One :**[iii] SL Green, a real estate investment trust, utilized an SPV to acquire Equity

---


i      *https://www.bizjournals.com/boston/stories/2002/07/22/daily53.html*

ii    *https://www.wsj.com/articles/SB111103595420582128*

iii   *https://slgreen.gcs-web.com/static-files/0a3e4d2c-d147-477b-b88a-b7afe22c48bc*

One, another REIT, in a deal worth $11 billion. The SPV likely played a crucial role in the financing and integration of the two companies' assets.

- **Hilton Worldwide's Acquisition of Waldorf Astoria Hotels & Resorts:**[iv] Hilton used an SPV to acquire the iconic Waldorf Astoria hotel chain for $1.95 billion. The SPV provided flexibility in financing and asset management for this specific hotel acquisition.

- **Starwood Capital's Acquisition of Extended Stay Hotels:**[v] Starwood Capital, specializing in real estate investments, utilized an SPV to acquire Extended Stay Hotels for $8 billion. The SPV likely offered flexibility in financing and asset management.

These stories are more than just about money; they show how flexible and useful Special Purpose Vehicles can be. Each SPV is designed to meet the specific needs of a deal, proving that in the world of big finance, there's no one-size-fits-all solution. Looking forward, the importance of SPVs in global finance is expected to grow, so by reading this book - you're definitely positioning yourself in the right place. SPV are great at adapting to the complicated challenges that modern business deals bring.

---

iv      *https://www.sec.gov/Archives/edgar/data/1585689/000158568915000009/wanypressrelease.htm*

v      *https://www.globenewswire.com/news-release/2021/06/16/2248347/0/en/Blackstone-and-Starwood-Capital-Group-Complete-Acquisition-of-Extended-Stay-America.html*

# WEALTH IN NUMBERS

*"The most successful investors are those who put the time and effort into knowing their investments inside and out."*

*— Peter Lynch, Investor and Mutual Fund Manager*

# YOUR ROLE AS GP

So, you've finally made up your mind to jump into an investment deal. You're stoked about the possibilities and ready to take action. But then, you hit a roadblock and realize that simply having some knowledge and a positive mindset isn't gonna get things moving. To really grow and reach your investment goals, you need a steady flow of excellent opportunities to invest in. Without this constant supply of promising deals, it's tough to move forward.

The real winners in investing are the ones who excel at finding great investment opportunities. This is known as "deal flow," and is a key element for any successful investment manager. Mastering deal flow can significantly impact your investment career. However, it's important to note that deal flow isn't just about the quantity of investment opportunities you encounter. The quality of these opportunities is equally, if not more, important. Being able to consistently find high-quality investment options is what sets apart the most successful investors from the rest.

To find really amazing opportunities, you need to take two key steps. First, you should be purposeful and strategic in how you search for opportunities. This means actively looking for investments that fit your goals and criteria, rather than just waiting for them to come to you. Second, you need to look at a lot of different possibilities. The more potential investments you examine, the better your chances of finding truly excellent ones. It's a bit like panning for gold - the more river bed you sift through, the more likely you are to find valuable nuggets. Successful investors work hard to see many opportunities, but they also develop the skills to quickly identify which ones are worth pursuing further.

In a nutshell, deal flow is all about building relationships. It's all about making connections with people who bring you unique opportunities that others might miss. In the investment world, the saying "It's not what you know, but who you know" is particularly true. A Harvard Business Review survey found that 60% of venture capital deals come from an investor's networks and referrals, highlighting how important it is to nurture and expand your professional connections.

However, building a network isn't just about collecting business cards or adding LinkedIn connections. It's about creating genuine relationships based on trust, mutual respect, and shared interests. This is especially important in investments. They often involve long-term partnerships with high stakes for all parties.

Referrals don't just stem from other investors. Some of the best leads can emerge from unexpected sources like attorneys, accountants, consultants, and other service providers. These professionals are often well-positioned to spot promising ventures before they become widely known. Cultivating relationships with them can provide a steady stream of pre-vetted opportunities.

There are also ways to find deals on your own by actively seeking out potential opportunities. For example, many successful real estate investors scout for properties they see potential in. They then contact the owners to see if they'd like to sell.

Nailing deal flow requires you to balance networking, relationship building, and a genuine drive to make an impact on your professional network. Whether you're an experienced investor or just starting out, the key principles remain the same.

### Effective Strategies for Finding Deal Flow

Cultivate Personal Networks & Collaborate with Other Dealmakers Successful general partners (GPs) in the investment world know the importance of building and maintaining strong personal networks. Think of these networks as gardens that need constant care and attention to thrive. By nurturing these connections, you can create a valuable source of deal flow. It's crucial to foster relationships with other dealmakers and make it a habit to regularly exchange potential investment opportunities with your peers. This collaboration can significantly boost your access to promising deals. Don't forget to tap into your connections with co-investors, leads, and Limited Partners. Additionally, encourage founders you work with to refer their peers and colleagues, as this can lead to new opportunities. By building a network of trusted sources, you can ensure a consistent flow of potential deals. In essence, cultivating personal networks and collaborating with other dealmakers is a key strategy for success in the investment world.

- **Leverage Online Platforms and Communities:** Explore niche-specific online directories relevant to your investment focus (e.g., startups, real estate, M&A) for curated lists of potential opportunities. Actively engage on social media platforms like X, YouTube, and LinkedIn to discover trends, identify promising ventures, and connect with industry players. Participate in digital communities such as Discord or private forums where insiders share insights and opportunities. Follow thought leaders and join relevant conversations to gain early access to valuable information and potential deals. By strategically using these diverse online resources, you can significantly expand your reach and enhance your deal flow pipeline.

- **Attend and Host Events:** Attending and hosting events is a crucial strategy for dealmakers to expand their network and discover new opportunities. Make it a priority to regularly participate in industry events, conferences, and networking gatherings. They are great chances to meet potential partners, learn about trends, and stay connected with the business community. Don't limit yourself to just attending, though. Hosting your own functions, such as intimate dinners for target companies, can be highly effective in building stronger relationships and sourcing deals. Pitch competitions and startup events are also worth attending, as they offer exposure to new ventures and fresh ideas. However, keep in mind that the most promising deals often require earlier engagement, before startups reach the stage of presenting at such events. By joining and creating these networking events, you'll find and profit from valuable investment opportunities.

- **Offer Valuable Services:** Building a robust deal flow in the investment world relies heavily on offering valuable services. The most successful investors understand that networking is a two-way street, and they focus on giving as much as they take. This approach creates a virtuous cycle of reciprocity. By providing value to your network, you increase the likelihood that people will think of you when opportunities arise. There are many ways to offer value: you can mentor young entrepreneurs, facilitate introductions between complementary businesses, or share insights through thought leadership content. The key is to position yourself as a helpful, knowledgeable resource in your industry. This isn't just about being nice – it's smart business. When you consistently offer valuable services and expertise, you become an important node in your network. As a result, high-quality deals are more likely to find their way to you. Keep in mind, in business, one of your most powerful asset is your reputation for adding value.

- **Conduct Strategic Cold Outreach:** Dealmakers can utilize strategic cold outreach to uncover promising investment opportunities effectively. This approach involves proactively identifying potential startups using various research tools and databases. Once you've identified promising companies, the next step is to reach out directly to their founders. The key to success in cold outreach is personalization – tailor your messages to show that you've done your homework and understand what makes each startup unique. Don't be discouraged if you don't get immediate responses. Persistence is crucial in this process, as it often takes multiple attempts to establish contact. However, when done correctly, this method can yield high response rates and potentially lead to valuable deals. Remember, the goal is to initiate meaningful conversations that could evolve into mutually beneficial partnerships. By combining thorough research, personalized communication, and persistent follow-up, you can turn cold outreach into a powerful tool for expanding your deal flow.

Also, when sharing deal flow, practice good ethics with your opportunities. Always prioritize privacy and obtain consent when sharing information on a potential deal. Keep in mind that creating a strong deal pipeline is not only about discovering immediate opportunities—it's also about establishing the groundwork for a prosperous, long-term investment career.

As you progress in your career, find ways to back the investment community. It'll help you build your network and reputation. If you focus on these principles, you'll not only increase your chances of finding great investments, but also establish yourself as a respected player in the field.

# UNDERSTANDING LIMITED PARTNERSHIP

Mastering these deal flow strategies is key for investors nowadays, but it's important to acknowledge the historical roots of connecting capital with promising ventures. Let's take a step back and explore how this tradition of investment has shaped the landscape we operate in today.

The idea of investors supporting entrepreneurs in risky business ventures isn't new. It goes back hundreds of years, even to the days when Marco Polo sailed the seas looking for treasures. Over time, investors have always tried to make money from successful business ideas. They've put money into all sorts of things, from companies that built canals and railways to businesses that traded goods with faraway colonies. This kind of investing has continued into modern times. In the early 1900s, a group of rich people and families became well-known for their investments. We still recognize names like the Vanderbilts, Whitneys, Rockefellers, and Warburgs today. These wealthy families played a big role in shaping the world of investing as we know it.

Fast forward to today and you have names like Ray Dalio, Warren Buffet & Charlie Munger, Peter Thiel, Bill Ackman, Alfred Lin, Carl Icahn that come to mind. Deals with global impact are consistently being orchestrated by high-profile investors.

Limited Partnerships offer a unique combination of flexibility and protection. They can be structured in complex and sophisticated ways to suit various business needs. At the same time, they provide a crucial safeguard for Limited Partners: these investors can't lose more money than they initially invested, similar to how shareholders in a company are protected. Because of these advantages, Limited Partnerships have become the preferred structure for many private investments. They offer benefits that other legal structures simply can't match. As you may already know, a Limited Partnership involves two types of partners:

General Partners (GPs) and Limited Partners (LPs). Each type has its own role and level of involvement in the partnership.

The relationships between the General Partner and Limited Partners in investment partnerships follow a structured format. We'll discuss the documents that outline this relationship in more detail when we cover how to set up your Special Purpose Vehicle entity. Over the last three decades, these agreements have become more standardized in many areas, which has helped make the investment process more efficient. However, they still maintain flexibility in important business terms. The standardization, plus the ability to customize when needed, supports complex, adaptable investment deals. They can be tailored to each specific deal. The framework of limited partnerships provides the legal structure for these flexible investment setups.

As a General Partner, you embody the spirit of entrepreneurship by taking on significant responsibility and risk. You manage the daily operations and investment details, putting your time, money, effort, and reputation on the line to make deals happen. LPs must have a solid understanding of their rights and your decision-making authority as the GP in any investment, considering your important role. Typically, instead of acting as an individual, you'll set up the GP as a separate Limited Liability Company. This structure helps protect you from personal liability for the Special Purpose Vehicle's debts or losses and may offer tax benefits.

While some may underestimate the GP's role, viewing them as just a middleman, that couldn't be further from the truth. GPs are playing a huge role in making the deal happen thanks to their expertise, network, and hustle. The misconception that GPs have an easy job or contribute little value is a gross underestimation. Managing investments and creating value for all parties is complex. It requires significant effort.

Being a GP is demanding and comes with a lot of responsibility. Odds are, unless your LPs read this book, they probably have no idea how much effort you're putting in. Consider passing them a copy of this book once you're done with it.

You'll need a blend of business acumen, dedicated effort, and long hours to achieve success. After all, you're the one finding a deal, running the due diligence and evaluating it. By connecting investors with amazing opportunities, you enable them to prioritize their day-to-day activities. When you take on this role, you become a key player in driving progress and innovation in the business world.

Leading investment deals is a journey with its ups and downs. You'll constantly be raising capital for multiple investments, closing deals, and searching for new opportunities. Perhaps most importantly, you're responsible for the SPV's decisions, can make legally binding commitments. We'll get into it a bit more in the coming pages, but to mitigate personal risk, GPs often structure a corporation or LLC entity to fill the GP role.

While you're working to manage the compexities, it's a great idea to  develop a clear timeline for each deal. Establish some milestones for fundraising, securing commitments, receiving funds, and deploying capital. If you can stick to this schedule, it'll help you maintain a smooth operation and also maintain your sanity in the process.

Now that you have a general idea of what's involved, being a General Partner comes with several key responsibilities, including:

### Due Diligence

You're responsible for thoroughly vetting potential investments. This involves critically evaluating the deal's value to investors and assessing both risks and potential returns. Your industry knowledge is crucial here - you must stay informed about the sector you're operating in. If you lack specific expertise, don't hesitate to seek outside opinions. The ability to take a hard, objective look at what's being offered and judge its actual value to investors is essential. Your judgment in evaluating deals properly is paramount.

## Capital Raising

Your role is instrumental in securing funds from investors. It involves building relationships with potential Limited Partners. You must communicate investment opportunities and potential returns effectively. Remember, in capital raising, there are often no second chances. You need to be persuasive and clear in your presentations, as you may only get one shot at convincing investors to commit their funds.

## Investor Relations

You're responsible for keeping your Limited Partners informed throughout the investment lifecycle. This means giving regular updates on the SPV's performance and sharing detailed financial reports and investment updates. Also, communicate any changes in the investment strategy. Transparency and clear communication are key to maintaining trust with your investors.

## Team Building

You'll need to assemble a team of professionals to support the SPV's operations. This team may include investment professionals, finance and accounting specialists, legal advisors, and other experts crucial to the SPV's success. Your ability to recruit and manage a diverse group of talented individuals will significantly impact the overall performance of the SPV.

## SPV Management

You oversee the day-to-day operations of the SPV. This involves managing administrative tasks, ensuring compliance with relevant regulations, and maintaining operational efficiency. Your attention to detail and ability to multitask are integral Smooth operations are key to the SPV's investment strategy.

Now that we've covered your role as the General Partner, let's talk about what's expected from limited partners and how they fit into the structure.

Limited partners are investors. They provide capital to the partnership. But, they don't run the business day-to-day. Their role is to follow through and fund their commitments. They must provide capital as outlined in the investment documents. It is essential for LPs to meet capital calls promptly so you can operate smoothly to fulfill your responsibilities. Trust, communication, and mutual benefit form the foundation of the GP-LP relationship. While GPs handle daily operations of the SPV, LPs expect to stay informed and receive investment returns.

As we've mentioned, LPs have a unique advantage. Their risk is capped at their initial investment. If the partnership goes into debt, creditors can't touch their personal assets. This setup allows limited partners to invest in potentially profitable ventures while keeping their risk in check. There's also a tax benefit to this arrangement. The partnership's profits are "passed through" to all partners, who then report this income on their personal tax returns. This makes the whole structure tax-efficient for everyone involved.

Some LPs may contribute in other ways, such as helping the GP source investment opportunities or serving on advisory boards. When LPs serve on advisory boards they can offer valuable insights and expertise without interfering with daily operations. This role enhances oversight, aligns interests, and contributes to strategic decision-making. However, an LP's participation as an advisory board member depends on the specific terms of the SPV agreement. There may be a need for safeguards and disclosure to deal with potential conflicts of interest. Thoroughly evaluating the legal and ethical consequences is important.

One thing to consider...your Limited Partners aren't just names on a spreadsheet - These are real people, with real dreams and real money that they're putting in your hands. They've bought into your vision and have handed you the keys to their financial future, at least a part of it. Your LPs are relying on you to make decisions with their best interests in mind. So, what's the takeaway here? With great power comes great responsibility. Yeah, I know, it's cliché, but it's true and can make you sit up a little straighter once you let that sink in.

The key to successful partnerships lies in effective communication and understanding the needs of all parties involved. By nurturing these relationships, you can improve the experience of your Limited Partners and achieve greater success together.

# GENERAL PARTNER TIPS & BEST PRACTICES

Understanding the relationship between General Partners and Limited Partners is key, but it's not the only thing you need to make it in private investment. To really excel at making deals, you need practical strategies and insights to help you through all the complexities. So, let's check out some valuable tips to make your life easier and more productive as you start managing private investments:

> *Know your limits - When you come across something that is outside your area of expertise or capacity, bring in a specialist who can handle it effectively rather than struggling alone.*

Recognizing your own strengths and weaknesses is crucial for successful business management. While it's important to develop a broad skill set, it's equally vital to acknowledge areas where you may lack expertise. Instead of struggling with tasks outside your core competencies, consider outsourcing these functions or hiring specialized talent. This approach allows you to focus on your strengths and the areas where you add the most value to your business.

Outsourcing or hiring experts can improve efficiency and work quality. It can boost overall performance, too. Remember, effective leadership often involves knowing when to delegate and leveraging the skills of others to complement your own abilities. By addressing your limitations proactively, you can build a more robust and well-rounded operation.

## Never Stop Learning

Learn all you can about private investment, regulations and running deals. The book provides a strong foundation, but there are countless opportunities for you to continue learning and expanding your knowledge. The greater your understanding of private investments and your involvement in deals, the smoother your operations will be to manage. Prioritize ongoing education in finance, taxation, and regulations. When you are proficient in these areas, it will boost the confidence of potential investors for your role as a General Partner.

## Get your first money in

When raising capital, you need momentum and securing your initial investment is crucial for building momentum in your efforts. This initial investment, no matter how modest, creates a vital sense of forward movement for your deal. This initial commitment can provide the validation and confidence needed to approach larger investors and potentially secure more substantial funding.

## Determine Your Deal Frequency

We have ran and closed a lot of SPVs over the years. But in doing so, we have to consider how often we present deals to potential investors, especially during tough economic times. Too many deals too often can cause analysis paralysis. There is also a possibility of overwhelming investors with too many offers, causing them to ignore or lose interest in your deals. This may leave deals underfunded and slow the process. Work to to prioritize your top deals and maintain a manageable pace when presenting new opportunities.

## Find a Mentor

Having a good mentor can change the course of your entire journey. Truth be told, they can make all the difference between a successful program and one that fails. The input of someone with lots of experiecne will help you to find your way around the whole process. Remember, your mentor has passed through whatever stage you're currently in. They understand the nature of the business and can guide you to avoid the pitfalls others have faced. There are lots of people that have used SPVs, so seek them out and soak up their knowledge.

## Document Your Processes

Raising capital is all about following the right steps. Investors want to work with professionals who are serious about their work, have a long-term mindset, and don't cut corners. Investors may view sloppy or irregular practices as a warning sign. For these reasons, documenting clear systems and processes are essential and it's surprising how few people will take the time to do this. It costs nothing and provides leverage, quality, and repeatability. Figure out the most important steps in your capital-raising operation and write them down. Make sure to focus on actions that keep giving value, and write down anything you do more than once. When processes are well documented, it's easier to delegate and ensure that team members are following the guidelines.

# WEALTH IN NUMBERS

*"Vision without action is a daydream. Action without vision is a nightmare."*
— *Japanese Proverb*

# PLANNING AND GOAL SETTING FOR SPVS

Now that we've got the essentials down, let's dig into the strategic side of handling Special Purpose Vehicles. The previous advice helps with daily deal-making challenges. But, for long-term success, you need to consider different investment strategies.

When you design Special Purpose Vehicles with specific investment goals in mind, it helps you make them more effective. To manage them successfully, you need to plan ahead. Start by clearly defining what you want to achieve with your investments. Set ambitious yet realistic goals for yourself and create a plan to reach them. The plan should encompass both short-term objectives (what you aim to achieve in the next year) and long-term goals (where you aspire to be in five years or as your ultimate lifetime achievement). You'll see this ultimate goal often referred to as your BAHG. A Big Hairy Audacious Goal, or BHAG for short is a bold and ambitious goal that you set for yourself. The term was first mentioned in the 1994 book Built to Last: Successful Habits of Visionary Companies by Jim Collins and Jerry Porras. Key to this approach is to break the long-term goal into steps. Be flexible in your process so you can review and adjust your strategy as you progress.

Let's break down the goal-setting strategy using this more ambitious financial objective:

- **Someday Goal:** "Achieve a net worth of $10 million+ and attain complete financial freedom." This is a big financial goal. It aims for a comfortable retirement and possibly generational wealth.

- **5-Year Goal:** "Grow investment portfolio to $3 million and establish multiple income streams." This goal is a big step toward the $10 million target. It recognizes that wealth often grows faster over time.

- **1-Year Goal:** "Increase net worth by $500,000 through savings and investments." This ambitious yearly target reflects the high-growth strategy needed to reach the long-term goal.

- **Monthly Goal:** "Add $42,000 to investment portfolio and identify one new potential income stream." This could mean saving aggressively, investing for high returns, and exploring business opportunities.

- **Weekly Goal:** "Invest $10,500 and spend 5 hours on financial education or business development." This goal keeps us on track for the monthly target. It also stresses the need for ongoing learning and skill growth.

- **Daily Goal:** "Save/earn an extra $1,500 for investments and dedicate 1 hour to financial strategy or networking." This daily goal reflects the high level of commitment required for ambitious wealth accumulation.

- **Right Now:** "Check your investments and research high-growth strategies." This immediate action step initiates the journey towards the ambitious long-term goal.

This framework, when applied to a $10 million net worth goal, illustrates several key points:

- **Aggressive Growth Strategy:** Each level's goals require rapid growth. They likely involve high-paying jobs, successful businesses, and smart, high-return investments.

- **Multiple Income Streams:** To achieve high net worth, one needs more than just one source of income. So, we must develop new revenue generating opportunities.

- **Continuous Learning:** The focus on financial education and networking at the weekly and daily levels reflects the need for advanced financial skills to manage and grow significant wealth.

- **Compounding Effects:** The framework considers that, as wealth grows, so does the potential for further growth. This is reflected in the accelerating targets at each level.

- **Risk Management:** The high targets imply a need for careful risk management, diversification, and possibly using complex financial instruments.

- **Lifestyle Considerations:** To meet those financial goals, you may need to make tough lifestyle choices. This includes saving a lot, even as your income rises.

- **Long-Term Perspective:** This goal structure highlights that building great wealth takes time. It shows how consistent, focused efforts compound over years.

Going through these steps will help you be a more effective General Partner. When setting personal goals, consider your SPV activities and how running investment deals will fit into your broader strategy. This approach will help you align your deal-making with your long-term goals and investment philosophy. Doing so will also help you build investment opportunities that align with your vision. Reference your goals to make important decisions about your SPV structure and legal framework. You'll want to consider factors like your risk tolerance, investment timeline, and expected returns. By aligning your personal objectives with your SPV's structure you'll improve your chances of success.

## Strategic Goal Setting for Success

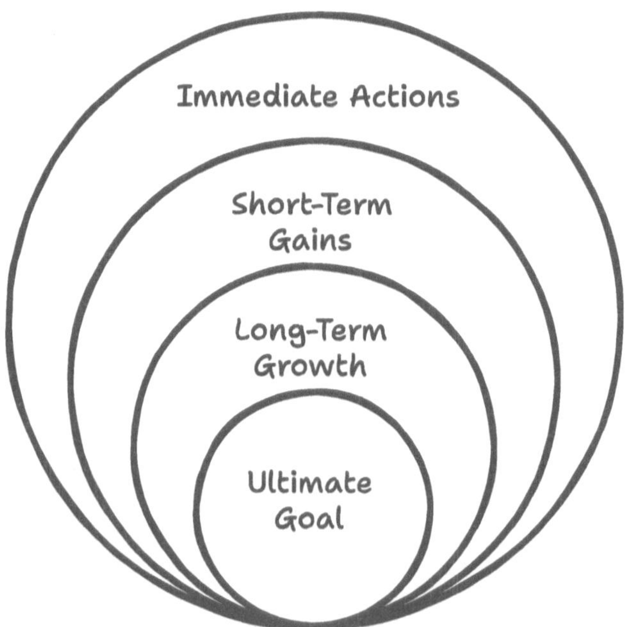


Now, let's take a moment to discuss long-term and short-term investment strategies. To succeed as a dealmaker, it's essential to understand each of these approaches. The key difference isn't just about the time frame, but also the underlying philosophy. By knowing both perspectives, you can adjust your approach to fit the specific opportunity and your overall portfolio goals.

Long-term Investment SPVs aim to grow, increase value, or generate income over many years. They typically invest in assets like real estate, large infrastructure projects, or long-term equity investments. The main objective with long-term investment is to create stability and growth by choosing opportunities that could pay off significantly over time. These SPVs rely heavily on careful market research and thorough due diligence processes.

Solid governance and control is necessary to thrive in the long term. These SPVs need a strong leader to manage investments. Such management provides clear direction and helps investors feel confident and committed to the deal. However, it's also important to be flexible enough to make changes when needed. While stability is key, being able to adapt to market changes or unexpected events is just as important. Having this flexibility is key for the SPV to succeed and minimize risks over the full investment lifecycle.

In contrast, short-term SPVs are designed for quick, specific investment goals. Unlike their long-term counterparts, these SPVs aim for quick profits. They seek to exploit temporary market inefficiencies and arbitrage opportunities. They also buy and sell assets quickly. They're built to be fast and flexible, often trying to use money quickly and then get it back out again in a short time. These SPVs need to be set up in a way that allows for agility and quick decisions. This is important because they often work in high-pressure situations where time is of the essence.

Managing risk for short-term SPV) is quite different from long-term ones. Long-term investments can usually handle short-term market changes without much worry. They have the time to wait for things to improve. However, short-term SPVs don't have this luxury. They must have robust risk assessment and management frameworks in order to navigate market volatility and protect their investment.

Operational efficiency is equally important for short-term SPVs. It involves agile investment management. It often uses tech to analyze data, make decisions, and communicate with investors quickly. Their efficiency lets these SPVs quickly react to market changes. They aim to maximize profits in a short investment window.

| | Long-term Investment SPVs | Short-term Investment SPVs |
|---|---|---|
| Time Horizon | Years or decades | Months to a few years |
| Primary Goal | Achieve sustained growth, capital appreciation, or income generation | Capitalize on temporary market inefficiencies or execute rapid-fire investment strategies |
| Risk Profile | Lower risk, able to weather short-term fluctuations | Higher risk, potential for higher short-term returns |
| Asset Focus | Tangible, stable assets (e.g., real estate, infrastructure) or established companies | Liquid assets, opportunities for quick profit |
| Investment Approach | Careful market research and thorough due diligence | Swift capital deployment and efficient exit strategies |
| Governance Structure | Complex, for sustained oversight and active management | Streamlined for rapid decision-making and flexibility |
| Investor Involvement | More active participation in strategic decisions | Less direct involvement due to need for quick actions |
| Adaptability | Emphasis on long-term stability with flexibility for future adjustments | High emphasis on agility and quick response to market dynamics |
| Risk Management | Can often ride out short-term market fluctuations | Requires robust, swift risk assessment and management frameworks |
| Operational Focus | Thorough market analysis and strategic oversight | Operational efficiency and agile investment management |

It's important to understand both long-term and short-term investment strategies. These strategies are like tools that smart investors use to make money. Each strategy has its own benefits, and the key is knowing when to use which one. The top investors don't stick to only one approach. Instead, they combine strategies to create a balanced plan that matches their goals. It's about blending stable, long-term investments with exciting quick-return opportunities.

This mix is more than just spreading out the risk. It also helps investors roll with the punches while staying focused on what they want to achieve. Investors who maintain a strategic outlook while remaining committed to their goals have the power to shape the market and achieve their financial aspirations.

# WEALTH IN NUMBERS

*"Choosing the right location can reduce operating costs and boost morale—two things that are critical for growth."*

*— Carlos Slim, Business Magnate and Investor*

# SELECT THE RIGHT JURISDICTION

While understanding the strategic aspects investment approaches is crucial for successful SPV management, it's equally important to consider where you establish your Special Purpose Vehicle. When setting up a SPV, you have the flexibility to choose the most advantageous location. This choice involves balancing legal benefits, tax advantages, and operational ease.

First, check the tax implications in potential jurisdictions. Lower taxes can greatly improve your SPV's financial efficiency. Next, consider the legal aspects, including bankruptcy laws, contract enforcement, and securities regulations. These factors affect your operations' stability and security. Also, evaluate the overall business environment and ease of conducting business in each location.

While it may seem logical to simply go for the place with the lowest taxes, this isn't always the best strategy. Some areas with slightly higher tax rates might provide improved legal protections or more streamlined regulatory processes. Your SPV could actually benefit more from these factors in the long term. They could help you steer clear of costly legal issues in the future, possibly saving you more money overall than what you'd save on taxes. That's why it's important to do your homework and pick a jurisdiction that suits your SPV's needs and objectives.

Now, let's discuss what it looks like when you take the domestic route we do. When it comes to attractive options in the United States, Wyoming and Delaware are hard to beat. They're worlds apart in terms of geography and culture, both states have an established reputation of being a great place to do business, especially for private investments.

## DELAWARE

Delaware has always been known as a top spot for business formation, especially for SPVs. Investors and entrepreneurs favor Delaware for its corporate laws. They are backed by a specialized Court of Chancery and legal precedents. In addition, most experienced investors and financial institutions are familiar with them. These factors can be particularly important for complex SPVs or those that may encounter litigation. Here are some key benefits of forming a Delaware LLC for your SPV:

- **Robust Legal Framework:** Delaware boasts a sophisticated and well-established body of business law. The state's Court of Chancery, a specialized court dealing exclusively with business matters, provides predictable and consistent rulings. This legal certainty is invaluable for SPVs, which often involve complex financial transactions.

- **Flexibility in Structure:** Delaware LLCs offer significant flexibility in management and ownership structures. The Operating Agreement can be tailored to meet specific needs, allowing for creative solutions in SPV design. This adaptability is particularly useful for complex investment structures or multi-party arrangements.

- **Strong Asset Protection:** Delaware law provides strong asset protection for LLC members. The "charging order" is typically the sole remedy for creditors of an LLC member, which helps protect the LLC's assets from claims against individual members.

- **Privacy:** Delaware does not require public disclosure of LLC member or manager names in formation documents. This level of privacy can be crucial for certain types of SPVs, especially those involving high-profile investors or sensitive transactions.

- **Series LLCs:** Delaware allows for the formation of Series LLCs, which can be particularly useful for SPVs. This structure enables the creation of separate "series" within a single LLC, each with its own assets, liabilities, and members. This can be an efficient way to manage multiple investments or projects under one umbrella entity.

- **No State Corporate Income Tax:** For LLCs not operating within Delaware, there's no state corporate income tax. However, there is an annual franchise tax.

- **Ease of Formation and Maintenance:** Delaware offers a streamlined formation process and does not require annual meetings or reports (though annual taxes must be paid).

- **Familiarity:** Delaware's reputation as a business-friendly state can lend credibility to your SPV, potentially making it more attractive to investors, partners, and financial institutions.

## WYOMING

Wyoming has positioned itself as an attractive choice for business formation, emerging as a strong competitor to conventional business hubs. The state's legislature has been proactive in creating an ecosystem that supports the establishment and operation of SPVs. Businesses are increasingly choosing Wyoming because of its attractive incentives, protections, and flexibility. Here are the key benefits of forming a Wyoming LLC for your SPV:

- **Strong Asset Protection:** Wyoming offers some of the strongest asset protection laws in the United States. The state provides charging order protection for both single-member and multi-member LLCs, making it difficult for creditors to reach the LLC's assets.

- **Enhanced Privacy:** Wyoming takes privacy a step further than many states. It does not require public disclosure of LLC members or managers and does not share information with other states or federal agencies unless compelled by law.

- **Low Costs:** Wyoming offers some of the lowest formation and maintenance costs in the country. The initial filing fee and annual report fees are significantly lower than many other states, including Delaware.

- **No State Income Tax:** Wyoming does not impose a state income tax on individuals or businesses, which can result in significant tax savings for SPV members.

- **Lifetime Proxy:** Wyoming allows for lifetime proxies, which can be useful in maintaining control in certain SPV structures.

- **No Citizenship Requirements:** There are no citizenship or residency requirements for forming an LLC in Wyoming, making it attractive for international investors.

- **Flexible Management Structure:** Like Delaware, Wyoming allows for flexible management structures, which can be outlined in the Operating Agreement.

- **Close LLC:** Wyoming offers the option of forming a "Close LLC," which combines some of the characteristics of an LLC and a corporation, potentially useful for certain SPV structures.

- **Simplified Maintenance:** Wyoming has relatively simple ongoing compliance requirements, with just an annual report and fee to maintain good standing.

**Those were some long winded explanations, so to make all this information a bit easier for you to digest, here's a comparison of both jurisdictions in a table:**

| | Delaware LLC | Wyoming LLC |
| --- | --- | --- |
| Specialized Business Court | ✓ | |
| Series LLC Structure | ✓ | ✓ |
| Strong Asset Protection | ✓ | ✓ |
| Enhanced Privacy | ✓ | ✓ |
| No State Income Tax for Non-Residents | ✓ | ✓ |
| Low Formation and Maintenance Costs | | ✓ |
| Lifetime Proxy | | ✓ |
| Flexible Management Structure | ✓ | ✓ |
| Charging Order Protection for Single-Member LLCs | | ✓ |
| Familiarity in Business | ✓ | |
| No Citizenship Requirements | ✓ | ✓ |

Based on our experience conducting deals in both jurisdictions, we can confidently say that both Wyoming and Delaware can be great choices for operating an SPV. The choice between them often depends on specific business needs, long-term goals, and the nature of the SPV's intended activities.

# INTERNATIONAL JURISDICTIONS

This book primarily explores how to set up SPVs in the United States, outlining the specific steps involved in the U.S. process. However, it's worth noting that SPV regulations and requirements differ around the world. While our main audience is people working with SPVs in the U.S., we recognize that readers from other countries can also benefit from much of this information. That's why we've included some details about international SPVs as well. We believe this broader perspective will be valuable, even though the book's main focus is on U.S.-based SPVs.

Whether it's the bustling financial hubs of Singapore or the sun-soaked beaches of the Cayman Islands, each jurisdiction has its own flavor of SPV regulations and requirements. Understanding the specificities related to the location is essential when setting up offshore. These rules can also change depending on what industry you're in. It's important to know which government agencies oversee SPVs in your area, like the SEC in the United States or the FCA in the United Kingdom. When choosing where to set up an SPV, look for a place with a well-developed financial sector, clear laws, and a convenient time zone for doing business globally. Keep in mind that regulations are always evolving.

When looking into international jurisdictions, you'll need to take into account a bunch of factors, like the investment type and the tax treaty network in the place you pick. These agreements between countries are the key to your SPV's tax efficiency. They stop double taxation and tackle tax evasion. While these treaties can be complicated, understanding them can really help your SPV save on taxes. But tax agreements aren't the only thing to consider. You also need to consider local taxes and rules about having an actual presence in the country.

Okay, before you start imagining yourself in a tropical paradise for your next SPV, let's face reality for a moment. Regardless of the location, setting up an SPV is not without challenges. Despite the attraction of international jurisdictions, it's important to carefully consider the downsides. When you compare these options to the US, you'll see why it's often better to keep your SPV domestic.

Let's start with the most obvious challenge: jurisdictional complexity. Imagine trying to set up your SPV in Luxembourg. Sounds glamorous, right? Well, prepare yourself for a crash course in Luxembourgish law, because you're going to need it. Each of these jurisdictions has different guidelines you must know. They all have their own rules. What works in one place might land you in hot water in another. Compliance with regulations across jurisdictions can be a never-ending game of whack-a-mole. Each rule you satisfy is replaced by three more that pop up in its place.

Now, let's talk about money. After all, isn't that why we're here? The promise of tax benefits in places like the Cayman Islands can be as seductive as a siren's call. But here's the kicker - those potential savings can quickly be swallowed up by the costs of setting up and maintaining your offshore SPV. And let's not forget about the day-to-day operations. Running an SPV abroad via Zoom calls, with half your team in different time zones can be a recipe for chaos.

Yet, the most harmful risk present in these offshore waters is the potential to make your investors apprehensive. Today, perception is reality, and public opinion can be more brutal than any legal process. Operating an SPV in certain offshore jurisdictions will have some folks raising an eyebrow where you might as well be wearing a t-shirt that says, "Please scrutinize my finances!" It's the reality we have to accept, even if it's not fair. Trust holds as much value as any physical asset in the world of investments.

So, what's an ambitious investor to do? Well, here's a thought that might seem counterintuitive at first: sometimes, the best way to think outside the box is to stay inside it. The United States, with all its complexities and challenges, offers a stable, well-regulated environment for SPVs that's hard to beat.

Think about it. When you set up an SPV in the U.S., you're operating in a system that's as familiar as your favorite pair of jeans. The legal terrain, though complex, is familiar and well-explored. You've got access to top-notch legal and financial professionals who speak your language (both literally and figuratively). And when it comes to investor confidence, there's something to be said for the stability and transparency that comes with operating under U.S. regulations.

Let us paint you a picture. Imagine you're at a cocktail party, chatting with potential investors. Which is more appealing? "Our SPV is based in a well-regulated U.S. jurisdiction, providing transparency and stability for our investors," or "Our SPV is in an offshore tax haven, but it's totally legit"? We think you know which one is more likely to have investors reaching for their checkbooks rather than the nearest exit.

But don't just take our word for it. Let's consider a practical example. Picture two identical SPVs, both investing in real estate. One is set up in the Cayman Islands, the other in Delaware. On paper, the Cayman Islands SPV might show a slight edge in terms of tax benefits. But, the higher setup and maintenance costs, and the complexities of international banking reduce that advantage. The potential reputational risks and the challenges of managing properties from afar add to the problem.

The Delaware SPV, on the other hand, operates in a familiar legal environment. It can easily open bank accounts, work with local property managers, and provide clear, transparent reports to its investors. When issues arise (and they always do), there's a well-established legal system to fall back on. It might not have the exotic allure of an offshore entity, but it has something far more valuable: reliability.

Now, we're not saying that international SPVs don't have their place. In certain specific circumstances, they can be the right tool for the job. However, many investors, especially those new to SPV investing, find that staying local is the wisest choice.

Remember, in the world of investments, slow and steady often wins the race. It's not about finding the flashiest solution or the cleverest tax loophole. It's about creating a stable, sustainable structure that can weather the storms of market fluctuations and regulatory changes. And when it comes to stability and sustainability, it's hard to beat the good old U.S. of A.

So the next time you find yourself dreaming of offshore SPVs and tax haven beaches, take a moment to consider the hidden currents beneath those tempting waters. Sometimes, the best adventures are the ones closest to home. Especially when home offers you a solid foundation, a clear regulatory framework, and the confidence of your investors. And isn't that what we're all really after in the end?

*"The most important thing about investment is structure."*
*— Charlie Munger, Vice Chairman, Berkshire Hathaway*

# HOW TO STRUCTURE YOUR SPV

Now that we've covered the importance of choosing the right jurisdiction for your SPV, let's switch gears and talk about the SPV structure itself. When we put together our first SPV, it was a bit overwhelming. But don't stress, you'll catch on quickly. As you get more experience, everything will feel more organized and purposeful, so no need to feel intimidated.

It's important to plan ahead for how you structure your SPV, but why exactly should you care about how your SPV is structured? It is important because it sets your investment's framework. Your structure outlines the relationship between investors and managers, and it manages legal and tax obligations. At the end of the day, this ensures everything runs as smoothly as possible. Keep in mind, each deal and SPV negotiation is distinct, allowing for flexible structuring that benefits everyone involved. When we talk about "structure," we mean the interconnected economic and legal structure of your investment deal.

Key decisions include choosing the jurisdiction, legal form (e.g., LLC, Trust, Corporation), capital structure, and governance mechanisms. Optimizing these elements helps meet investment goals and ensures compliance. It requires considering regulatory, tax, investor, and risk factors. A clear governance structure, such as an independent board, safeguards investor interests and resolves potential conflicts.

Before you decide on the structure of your SPV, make sure to consider these important questions. Understanding the considerations and implications of your answers is essential when creating an SPV. This is because these questions address multiple elements of the structure.

- **How much capital do I need to raise and over what time period?:** This question is vital as it determines the scale of your SPV and influences your fundraising strategy. It helps you set realistic goals and timelines for capital acquisition.

- **What is the minimum investment amount?:** The minimum investment amount sets a barrier for investors. It ensures the deal attracts those with enough financial capacity. This amount can vary based on the nature of the investment opportunity and the targeted investor base.

- **What sort of fees are appropriate?:** Determining a fair fee structure is crucial for attracting investors while ensuring the SPV's operational costs are covered. It impacts the SPV's profitability and investor returns.

- **What sort of returns do I expect to produce for investors? How do I know?:** This question helps you set realistic expectations for investors and guides your investment strategy. It's essential for transparency and building trust with potential investors.

- **How much can I expect to make?:** Understanding your potential earnings helps you align your interests with those of the investors and ensures fair compensation for your efforts in managing the SPV.

- **How much of my own capital (if any) should I invest alongside other investors?:** This question addresses the concept of "skin in the game." Your personal investment can demonstrate confidence in the SPV and align your interests with those of other investors.

- **What should my management team look like, and what roles/ responsibilities will be necessary?:** Defining the management structure is crucial for efficient operation of the SPV. It helps clarify roles, responsibilities, and decision-making processes.

- **When is the investment timeline and how does this impact potential investors?:** The investment timeline provides clarity on the expected holding period and exit strategy. Building with a planned liquidity timeline is important as it can attract certain types of investors based on its length. It also helps in planning the SPV's overall strategy and exit options.

By carefully considering these factors, you can design an SPV structure that both aligns with your objectives and meets investor expectations. This thoughtful approach not only enhances the appeal of your offering but also lays the groundwork for a more robust investment vehicle.

# INTRODUCTION TO SECURITIES EXEMPTIONS

Now that we've covered the key points to think about when setting up your SPV, let's circle back to an important legal aspect: securities exemptions.

When you're in this line of work, you need to take the time to understand what these exemptions are and how they work. They allow your SPV to remain compliant while you raise capital and run your deal. Think of it this way: if the structure of your SPV is like the blueprint of a house, then choosing the right securities exemption is like getting the proper building permits.

It gives you the legal pathway to offer investment opportunities without having to go through the long and expensive process of registering with the SEC. Understanding these exemptions is key to making sure your SPV stays on the right side of the law. Let's take a look at some of the most common exemptions that SPVs use and how they can affect the way you raise capital.

When companies in the United States want to sell securities to investors, they usually have to register them with the government first. This was designed to protect investors by making sure companies provide accurate information about what they're selling. However, this registration process can take a long time and cost a lot of money. For smaller companies or those that need capital quickly, this can be a big problem. It might even stop some businesses from getting started at all.

To help solve this issue, the government created some exceptions to these rules. These exceptions are called "exemptions." They allow certain companies to sell securities without going through the full registration process. The main law that governs this is called the Securities Act. It says that all securities must be registered with the Securities and Exchange Commission (SEC) unless they qualify for one of these exemptions. These exemptions can make it easier and faster for companies to raise money, while still providing some protection for investors.

Regulation S, introduced by the SEC in 1990, provides an exemption from registration requirements for securities offers and sales made outside the United States. It's relevant for SPVs in certain international investment scenarios. For example, a United States-based company could use an SPV to issue securities only to foreign investors, taking advantage of Regulation S to avoid SEC registration. This is useful for accessing international capital markets without the complexities and costs of full SEC registration.

Regulation S requires that the offer and sale occur in an "offshore transaction" and prohibits "directed selling efforts" in the United States.

To comply, the entire transaction must happen outside the United States and not direct any marketing efforts towards American investors.

Regulation S has its upsides like compliance and cost savings, but it also has some strict requirements and risks. SPVs have to deal with resale restrictions on securities and make sure they follow United States and local securities laws.

For SPVs solely looking to raise capital from investors outside the United States, considering Regulation S can still be a good option. When deciding which rules to follow, you need to think about what you want to achieve, who you want to invest in your deal, and how your SPV is set up. There's no one-size-fits-all answer – the best choice depends on your specific situation.

If you're trying to raise capital inside the United States, you'll want to become familiar with the rules under Regulation D. The government first introduced these rules in 1982 to make it easier for companies to get funding without going through the full, complicated process of registering their securities. Regulation D includes several different rules, but the ones you really need to pay attention to are Rules 504, 505, and 506. These rules are especially important because they outline different ways companies can raise money. Each rule has its own set of requirements and benefits, so companies can choose the one that best fits their needs. By using these rules, many businesses have been able to get the money they need to grow, without getting stuck in red tape.

Rule 506 is especially popular for companies set up to handle investments, often called Special Purpose Vehicles (SPVs). It comes in two versions: 506(b) and 506(c). Both allow companies to raise money, but they have different rules about advertising and who can invest.

These exemptions can save companies time and money. They still protect investors by requiring key information to be provided. This balance helps support new businesses while also looking out for people's investments. That's why Rule 506 is often a good choice for SPVs in the

United States that want to raise capital. Allow us to elaborate on the specific regulations mentioned in Regulation D:

- **Rule 504:** Allows companies to raise up to $5 million from both accredited and non-Accredited Investors without extensive SEC disclosure requirements. While the SEC doesn't mandate specific disclosures under Rule 504, companies should still prepare an offering document, like a PPM, to protect against potential fraud or liability claims. Historically, Rule 504 was popular for capital raising and syndication because of its relaxed offering limits. Its peak usage was before the 2012 JOBS Act, which introduced changes to Regulation D. After the JOBS Act, Rule 504's popularity for syndication declined as other exemptions, particularly Rule 506(b) and (c), became more attractive with their larger offering limits and broader investor base. While Rule 504 still exists, it's no longer the preferred choice for most syndications in the current regulatory environment.

- **Rule 505:** Allows companies to raise up to $5 million from up to 35 non-Accredited Investors and an unlimited number of Accredited Investors. While the offering can target both accredited and non-Accredited Investors, the non-Accredited Investors must have a pre-existing relationship with the company or its officers, directors, or general partners. Companies utilizing Rule 505 are required to provide specific disclosures to all investors and file Form D with the SEC.

- **Rule 506(b):** Allows companies to raise an unlimited amount of capital from non-Accredited Investors (up to 35) and/or Accredited Investors without general solicitation. No specific information is required to be furnised if only Accredited Investors are involved, which can result in a lot of saved time and cost. However, if any non-Accredited Investors are involved, the private placement rules require the delivery of written information of the same type that would be contained in a registration statement filed with the SEC. The GP must have a reasonable basis to conclude that any non-Accredited Investor has the investment sophistication to evaluate the merits and risks.

- **Rule 506(c):** Allows general solicitation and advertising of a Rule 506 Regulation D fund, subject to certain key conditions. Sales are restricted to Accredited Investors only. This rule opens doors to a wider pool of potential investors, enabling issuers to tap into a diverse network of individuals who share their investment vision.

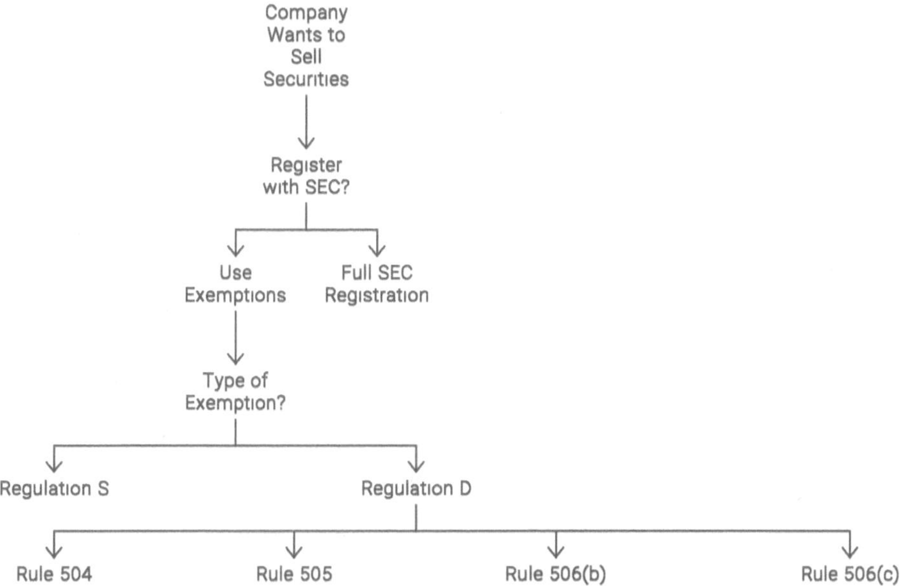

WEALTH IN NUMBERS

*"Every choice you make has an end result. Choose wisely, even between two good things."*

— *Zig Ziglar, Author and Motivational Speaker*

# RULE 506(B) & 506(C)

We get asked all the time if Rule 506(b) or 506(c) is the way to go, and the truth is, there are things to think about for each option that depend on specific circumstances. Private investment deals benefit from these exemptions by providing flexibility and reducing regulatory burden. It's important to carefully consider the specific guidelines for each of them.

Each exemption has nuances. For private securities offerings, it is necessary for issuers, investors, and financial professionals to have a foundational level of knowledge. Both Rule 506(b) and Rule 506(c) share several important characteristics:

## Unlimited Capital Raising Potential

Rule 506 offerings are highly attractive to businesses because they allow for unlimited capital raising. This means companies can raise as much money as they need without any caps or restrictions. Both Rule 506(b) and 506(c) offer this benefit, setting them apart from other investment options that may limit fundraising amounts. The ability to scale fundraising efforts without regulatory limitations is a significant advantage for deals that require substantial amounts of capital.

### No Cap on the Number of Accredited Investors

Rule 506 offerings have a big advantage: there's no limit on how many Accredited Investors can take part. This means a SPV can accept investments from as many Accredited Investors as they want, which can help them reach their fundraising goals more easily. By allowing unlimited Accredited Investors, companies can build a diverse group of investors. This isn't just good for raising capital - it can also help create valuable business connections for the future. Overall, this feature gives businesses a lot of flexibility in how they raise funds and grow their investor base.

### Regulatory Compliance

Both Rule 506(b) and 506(c) offerings have common regulatory requirements. Issuers must file Form D with the SEC within 15 days of the first securities sale, providing basic offering information. All securities sold under Rule 506 are "restricted," meaning they have resale limitations to prevent immediate public resale. While these offerings are exempt from state registration due to federal preemption, some states may still require notice filings or fees. It's crucial for issuers to research and comply with any remaining state-level requirements to ensure full regulatory compliance in all jurisdictions where they offer securities.

### Flexibility in Investment Structure

Rule 506(b) and 506(c) offer great flexibility for structuring Special Purpose Vehicles (SPVs) across various investment types, including real estate, venture capital, and private equity. This versatility allows SPV managers to create vehicles that precisely match their investment goals and investor preferences. The adaptability of these rules enables SPVs to adjust their focus as market conditions change without major regulatory overhauls. This flexibility not only makes the offerings more attractive to investors but also allows SPVs to remain responsive to evolving investment opportunities.

## Federal Preemption of State Registration

Rule 506(c) and 506(b) offerings have a big advantage: they don't need to be registered separately in each state. This is called federal preemption. It means that companies, including Special Purpose Vehicles (SPVs), can offer their investments across multiple states without dealing with different state regulators. By eliminating the need to navigate complex state-specific rules, this makes things more affordable and less complicated. This is especially helpful for Rule 506(c) offerings, which can advertise widely without triggering extra state rules. While some states might still ask for a notice or a fee, the process is much simpler overall.

## Faster Time to Market

Rule 506(b) and 506(c) offerings help companies raise money faster and more easily than traditional public offerings. These special rules, part of something called Regulation D, cut down on a lot of red tape. Unlike public offerings, companies don't need to register with the SEC, which saves a lot of time and effort. They also use simpler paperwork that's quicker to prepare. Companies can start these offerings whenever they think the time is right, without waiting for the SEC to review everything. Once they're ready, they can immediately start collecting money from investors. With Rule 506(c), they can even advertise to find more investors quickly. These offerings are flexible too - companies can get money as soon as each investor commits, instead of waiting for everyone to invest at once. After the offering, there's less ongoing paperwork compared to public companies, so business leaders can focus more on growing their company. While Rule 506(c) does require checking that investors are wealthy enough to participate, which takes a bit of time, both types of offerings are still much faster than going public. This speed is really important for businesses that need to move quickly to take advantage of opportunities or deal with tough market conditions.

## Disclosure Requirements

Both Rule 506(b) and 506(c) offerings require issuers to provide essential information to potential investors, typically through a document called a private placement memorandum (PPM). While these offerings don't need the extensive disclosures required for public companies, the PPM is still crucial. It outlines investment terms, risks, and other important details, helping investors make informed decisions. The specific content may differ slightly between 506(b) and 506(c) offerings because of their unique regulatory requirements, but the core purpose remains the same: to provide clear, accurate, and important information to investors. This ensures transparency and helps investors understand the opportunity, even though the disclosure isn't as extensive as for public offerings.

## Bad Actor Rules

Rule 506(b) and 506(c) offer a "safe harbor" that allows issuers to sell securities without SEC registration. However, this protection is lost if any key team member, known as a "covered person," is a "Bad Actor." Covered persons include the issuer, affiliates, directors, certain stockholders, officers, and paid solicitors. It's the issuer's responsibility to verify that no covered person is a Bad Actor. Failing to do so can lead to accusations of misleading investors and potential legal consequences. This requirement, called "Bad Actor disqualification," is crucial for maintaining the offering's exempt status and avoiding regulatory issues.

## Triggers for Registration

When a company raises money through Rule 506(b) or 506(c) offerings, they might still need to register with the Securities and Exchange Commission (SEC) under certain circumstances. This usually happens when the company grows significantly or attracts many investors.

Specifically, if a company has more than 2,000 investors overall, or more than 500 non-Accredited Investors, and its total assets exceed $10 million, it must register under the Securities Exchange Act of 1934.

Rule 506(b) offerings are typically aimed at a smaller group of investors, including up to 35 non-accredited individuals who already have a relationship with the General Partner. Rule 506(c) offerings allow for broader advertising but require all investors to be accredited. However, even with these private offerings, companies need to be careful about how many investors they bring in, as exceeding certain limits can trigger registration requirements.

This becomes more complex when companies use multiple Special Purpose Vehicles (SPVs) for their offerings. The SEC considers all these SPVs together when counting investors, so companies need to be mindful of the total investor count across all their investment pools, or they might accidentally trigger rules they were trying to avoid.

If a company does need to register with the SEC, it faces significant changes in its operations. This includes regular reporting requirements, such as filing annual (Form 10-K), quarterly (Form 10-Q), and current reports (Form 8-K). The company must also comply with SEC regulations on corporate governance and financial disclosures.

For example, imagine a startup that initially raises $15 million through a Rule 506(b) offering with 150 investors, including 30 non-accredited ones. At this point, they don't need to register. However, as they grow and do more fundraising, their investor count might exceed 2,000, and their assets might grow beyond $10 million. At this stage, they would have to register with the SEC and comply with all the associated reporting and disclosure requirements.

# UNDERSTANDING RULE 506(B)

Rule 506(b) of Regulation D can make it easier and more appealing for people to organize investment deals with SPVs. The advantage of Rule 506(b) is its ability to offer a flexible path for capital raising and allows for unlimited Accredited Investor participation. In addition, you can include up to 35 other savvy investors who might not meet the "accredited" criteria. If you're unsure about the meaning of that status, don't worry, we'll explain later in this book. This rule is extremely beneficial for dealmakers with existing investor connections.

One important thing to note is that in order to comply with the rule, you must refrain from general solicitation and public marketing. Instead, rely on your existing network and substantive pre-existing relationships. We'll also fill you in on qualifying relationships in the pages ahead. Some people might think it's limiting, but it's great for GPs with strong investor connections.

When including non-Accredited Investors, 506(b) offerings trigger additional disclosure obligations. Issuers must provide these investors with extensive information, similar to disclosures in Regulation A offerings. This requirement makes things more transparent, but also makes the offering process more complicated.

While 506(b) offerings require careful navigation of these rules and restrictions, they offer a balance of capital-raising flexibility and investor protection. This makes them a popular choice for many private offerings, especially those seeking to leverage existing investor relationships while maintaining the option to include a limited number of sophisticated non-Accredited Investors.

When discussing investment deals, it's important to avoid language that could violate the regulations. If you want to stay within the guidelines, you could consider saying something like "We're always eager to connect with potential new partners. If you're interested in exploring opportunities, please complete our questionnaire or contact us directly." or "We'd love to learn about your interests and explore potential collaborations."

Instead of providing information about specific investment deals, these methods concentrate on fostering relationships and gathering information. The most effective strategy is to prompt interested individuals to fill out an information form or reach out to you directly, setting the foundation for a potential business relationship in the future.

Avoid mentioning specific investment amounts or deals in your communications. For instance, don't say you're raising a certain amount of money for a particular company or organizing an investment vehicle for a specific property. This kind of direct language about investment opportunities could lead to regulatory scrutiny.

When talking about investments in public, it's important to keep things general and avoid getting into specifics. You can discuss investing as a broad topic and even mention the idea of investing together someday. However, it's best not to directly ask people to join any particular investment opportunity. By following these guidelines, you can stay on the right side of the rules while still having meaningful conversations about investing. This approach lets you explore potential partnerships without crossing any legal lines. Remember, the goal is to have open discussions about investing without making specific offers or promises. Now, let's go over the specific and unique requirements for 506(b) offerings.

### Investor Base Composition

In the world of Special Purpose Vehicles (SPVs), Rule 506(b) offers a unique advantage when it comes to investor base composition. This exemption provides a balanced approach to capital raising, allowing SPVs to tap into a diverse pool of investors while maintaining control and discretion.

Under Rule 506(b), SPVs can accept investments from an unlimited number of Accredited Investors. These are typically high-net-worth individuals or entities with the financial sophistication to understand and bear the risks associated with private investments. This opens the door to a potentially large reservoir of capital from experienced investors.

What sets Rule 506(b) apart is its provision for including up to 35 non-Accredited Investors in the mix. These individuals must be financially sophisticated, possessing sufficient knowledge and experience to evaluate the merits and risks of the investment. This flexibility allows SPVs to broaden their investor base beyond the typical Accredited Investor pool, potentially tapping into valuable networks and expertise. However, including non-Accredited Investors comes with additional responsibilities. This ensures transparency and helps protect less experienced investors.

## No Public Marketing or Solicitation

Under Rule 506(b), there are strict limitations on how you can market your investment opportunity. This rule prohibits any form of public marketing or general solicitation, which means you can't advertise your offering through TV, radio, social media, or other public channels.

The key to complying with Rule 506(b) is the concept of a "substantive pre-existing relationship" with potential investors. This means that before you can discuss specific terms or details of your offering, you must have an established relationship with the investor. This relationship should be deep enough that you understand their financial position, professional background, and risk tolerance. We'll explore this topic a bit further in the coming pages.

While you can discuss your business in general terms, any specific details about the investment offering should be reserved for these pre-existing relationships. This restriction promotes a more personalized and targeted approach to fundraising, focusing on quality connections rather than quantity.

It's crucial to understand that even seemingly innocent actions can violate these rules. For example, posting about your fund on the internet or mentioning investment terms at a public seminar could be considered general solicitation, which is strictly forbidden under Rule 506(b). This approach may limit your reach, but it often results in a more engaged and suitable investor base for your offering.

## Disclosure Requirements

Rule 506(b) offerings for Special Purpose Vehicles (SPVs) have different disclosure requirements based on investor type. For Accredited Investors, only material information is needed, significantly reducing paperwork and costs. This allows SPVs to focus on their investment strategy and deal execution, making the process more efficient and economical. However, if non-Accredited Investors are involved, the issuer must provide extensive disclosures similar to those in registered offerings. To manage risks with non-Accredited Investors, it's recommended to conduct investor suitability assessments and maintain accurate records. This approach balances providing necessary information to investors while maintaining confidentiality for private investment vehicles, creating a more agile capital raising environment for SPVs.

## Operational and Administrative Benefits

Rule 506(b) offerings provide significant operational and administrative benefits for Special Purpose Vehicles (SPVs). After initial filing, ongoing compliance becomes simpler, reducing long-term administrative work. This allows SPV managers to focus more on core investment activities, potentially improving performance and returns. The streamlined process saves time and reduces the risk of compliance errors. Additionally, under certain conditions, securities issued through 506(b) offerings may have potential for secondary market development, which could attract more investors due to the possibility of future liquidity.

Overall, these benefits create a more efficient investment vehicle, enabling managers to concentrate on value creation rather than regulatory tasks.

## Enhanced Privacy and Network-Based Fundraising

Rule 506(b) offerings provide SPVs with enhanced privacy and network-based fundraising advantages. This structure allows for greater confidentiality during capital-raising, encouraging a relationship-driven approach where managers use their professional networks to attract investors. This method often results in a more engaged and committed investor base, potentially offering valuable insights beyond capital. The combination of privacy and targeted fundraising can lead to a more supportive ecosystem around the SPV, improving its chances of long-term success. Additionally, the lower public profile afforded by 506(b) offerings gives SPVs more control over their investor base and direction, which is vital for managing long-term success.

## Financial Statement Requirements

Financial statement requirements for Rule 506(b) offerings vary based on the amount raised and the inclusion of non-Accredited Investors. For offerings up to $2 million, an audited balance sheet dated within 120 days of the offering start is required if non-Accredited Investors are involved. For offerings between $2 million and $7.5 million, financial statements must meet smaller reporting company standards, with at least an audited balance sheet if full audits are impractical. Offerings over $7.5 million require comprehensive audited financial statements typically found in registration statements, though an audited balance sheet may suffice if full audits are unfeasible. Generally, audit requirements become more stringent as the offering size increases, especially when non-Accredited Investors participate. The focus shifts from basic balance sheet audits for smaller offerings to more comprehensive financial audits for larger ones, ensuring appropriate disclosure and investor protection.

## Cost Efficiency

Rule 506(b) offerings provide a cost-efficient option for Special Purpose Vehicles (SPVs) to raise capital. The prohibition on general solicitation in these offerings naturally limits marketing expenses, allowing SPVs to allocate more resources to their investment strategies. Additionally, the well-established nature of 506(b) offerings often leads to savings in legal costs due to attorneys' familiarity with the process. This cost efficiency improves the overall economics of the capital raise and can potentially allow for better terms or returns for investors. As a result, 506(b) offerings are particularly appealing for SPVs operating with limited initial capital or those aiming to maximize the efficiency of their fundraising efforts.

## Flexibility in Deal Terms

Rule 506(b) offerings give Special Purpose Vehicles (SPVs) significant flexibility in structuring deal terms, especially when working with sophisticated investors. This allows SPV managers to create investment structures that align with their goals and investor preferences. Unlike more rigid offerings, 506(b) deals can be customized to suit specific risk profiles, return expectations, and investment timeframes. Managers can negotiate unique provisions for liquidity, voting rights, or profit-sharing, making their offerings more attractive and fostering stronger partnerships with investors. This flexibility enables SPVs to optimize their capital structure and operational framework, potentially improving their chances of achieving investment goals while meeting investor expectations.

## International and Future Scalability

Rule 506(b) offerings provide advantages in international reach and future growth. These offerings easily accommodate international investors, broadening the capital base and diversifying the investor pool. This is particularly useful for SPVs targeting international investments or seeking foreign expertise. This flexibility enables dealmakers to scale and adapt to changing market conditions and investment opportunities, providing a pathway for long-term growth in private investments.

### Reduced Liability Risk

Rule 506(b) offerings help Special Purpose Vehicles (SPVs) reduce liability risks by focusing on accredited and sophisticated investors. These investors are assumed to have more financial knowledge and risk tolerance, leading to better-informed decisions. They're more likely to understand complex investments and market changes, which can lower the chances of legal disputes. This focus on experienced investors can also offer some protection for SPV managers if investments don't perform well, as these investors are expected to do their own research and understand the risks. While this approach doesn't eliminate all legal risks, it creates a more stable environment for SPVs to operate in, allowing managers to concentrate more on investment strategies.

# ESTABLISHING A SUBSTANTIVE PRE-EXISTING RELATIONSHIP

In 1940, the Investment Company Act introduced restrictions on how private securities could be offered to investors. Because of this Act and the rules that came after, companies and fund managers had a tough time raising capital because they couldn't openly discuss their investment opportunities. Instead, they were limited to talk about deals with people they already knew and had a "substantive pre-existing relationship" with. This created challenges for raising capital. As part of the JOBS Act in 2012, rule 506(b) was implemented to loosen restrictions, simplifying the process for dealmakers to find investors and raise capital.

In securities law, the idea of a "substantive pre-existing business relationship" is important but not clearly defined by the Securities and

Exchange Commission (SEC). This lack of clarity has led legal professionals to interpret it differently, with some taking a cautious approach and others being more bold in their interpretations.

While the SEC hasn't given a strict definition, they did provide some insight in 2015. Citizen.VC, a Venture Capital firm based in Palo Alto, California asked the SEC for guidance on how to establish these relationships with potential investors before raising capital. In response to a question from Citizen.VC about general solicitation and what counts as a "substantive pre-existing relationship," the SEC issued a "No Action" letter saying they wouldn't take action against the company's practices. This letter suggested that a "substantive" relationship means having enough information to judge a potential investor's financial situation and an understanding of investments. This guidance helps, but still leaves room for interpretation in the financial world.

Citizen.VC set up a private website where all investments were made. To use this site, Prospective investors had to register, confirm their Accredited Investor status, and gain approval before accessing investment opportunities. This approval process involved a thorough check of each investor's financial knowledge and experience. The SEC pointed out that each situation is different, and while the SEC didn't completely endorse Citizen.VC's methods, their approach can be helpful for others to learn from about how to properly build relationships with investors while following securities laws.

The assessment consisted of a few key elements. Citizen.VC communicated with potential investors over the phone to learn about what their financial goals were, investment preferences, and risk tolerance. In addition, they emailed investors to provide basic information, answer questions, and assess their investment knowledge. Citizen.VC also examined the credit history of every potential investor and provided access to relevant sections of their website outlining the company's investment strategy, principles, and management objectives.

# WEALTH IN NUMBERS

**Securities Act of 1933**
**Regulation D — Rule 502**

August 6, 2015

**Response of the Office of Chief Counsel**
**Division of Corporation Finance**

Re: Citizen VC, Inc.
   Incoming letter dated August 3, 2015

Based on the facts presented, the Division's views are as follows. Capitalized terms used in this response have the same meaning as defined in your letter.

You have requested the staff concur in your conclusion that the policies and procedures described in your letter will create a substantive, pre-existing relationship between CitizenVC and prospective investors such that the offering and sale on the Site of Interests in SPVs that will invest in a particular Portfolio Company will not constitute general solicitation or general advertising within the meaning of Rule 502(c) of Regulation D.

We agree that the quality of the relationship between an issuer (or its agent) and an investor is the most important factor in determining whether a "substantive" relationship exists. As the Division has stated before, a "substantive" relationship is one in which the issuer (or a person acting on its behalf) has sufficient information to evaluate, and does, in fact, evaluate, a prospective offeree's financial circumstances and sophistication, in determining his or her status as an accredited or sophisticated investor. See, e.g., *Bateman Eichler, Hill Richards, Inc.* (Dec. 3, 1985). We note your representation that CVC's policies and procedures are designed to evaluate the prospective investor's sophistication, financial circumstances and ability to understand the nature and risks of the securities to be offered. We also agree that there is no specific duration of time or particular short form accreditation questionnaire that can be relied upon solely to create such a relationship. Whether an issuer has sufficient information to evaluate, and does in fact evaluate, a prospective offeree's financial circumstances and sophistication will depend on the facts and circumstances.

In expressing these views, we note your representation that the relationship with new Members will pre-exist any offering, consistent with the Division's previous guidance. In this regard, we note that a prospective Member is not presented with any investment opportunity when being qualified to join the platform. Any investment opportunity would only be presented after the prospective investor becomes a Member. Further, we understand that CVC creates SPVs for investment in particular Portfolio Companies and not as blind pools for a later investment opportunity.

Because this position is based on the representations in your letter, any different facts or conditions might require the Division to reach a different conclusion.

        Sincerely,

        David R. Fredrickson
        Chief Counsel

---

**Incoming Letter:**

The Incoming Letter is in Acrobat format.

*http://www.sec.gov/divisions/corpfin/cf-noaction/2015/citizen-vc-inc-080615-502.htm*

On top of that, Citizen.VC made sure their team and potential investors could meet online or in person. Citizen.VC granted access to investment opportunities only after confirming that an investor met the criteria for knowledge and suitability. The key point to remember is that Citizen.VC made sure to build a real connection with each investor before showing them any chances to invest. This shows how important it was for Citizen.VC to have a relationship with investors before trying to present an investment deal. They didn't just rush into asking for investments. Instead, they took the time to get to know the investors first, which was a central part of their strategy for finding new funding.

To build a strong relationship with potential investors before offering them investment opportunities, you need to have real, personalized interactions with them. This process begins by asking investors to fill out a detailed form about their financial situation and experience with investing. It's important to have the investor sign and date this form for record-keeping.

Afterwards, continue the conversation through phone or in-person to gather further information about the investor's financial objectives and circumstances. It's important to keep notes about all these conversations to demonstrate how the relationship has grown over time.

Take these steps to establish a solid, legal relationship with the investor. This approach is about more than just casual conversation and demonstrates your effort to understand their financial background and investment experience.

Timing plays a crucial role in establishing investor relationships that comply with SEC requirements. While the SEC mandates a "passage of time" before making an offer, it doesn't specify an exact duration. As a best practice, allow for a "cooling-off period" after initial contact before presenting investment opportunities. Aim to maintain a relationship with a prospective investor, ideally for at least two to three months before presenting your investment deal. This helps make sure you're only talking to investors who are truly qualified and interested.

During this period, it's important to keep in regular contact with the investor. This shows that you're building a genuine relationship. Just meeting someone once, adding their name to a list, and then suddenly offering them an investment isn't enough to satisfy the SEC's rules. Instead, focus on having meaningful conversations with the investor regularly. This builds a strong foundation for possibly talking about investments in the future.

Recently, a new trend called "raising in public" has become popular, especially among social media influencers who want to use their followers to raise capital. This new way of doing things has led to questions about how to follow the rules that limit public advertising for investments.

To stay within the law, influencers and people managing funds should use general language when they talk about investments in public. They shouldn't directly invite people to invest. Instead, they should ask potential investors to share more information about themselves. This helps create the "substantial pre-existing relationship" that the law requires, while also getting more people involved. This approach lets them reach more potential investors while still following the rules. However, they need to be very careful about what they say in public. They must make sure their messages can't be seen as directly asking people to invest. It's a delicate balance between wanting to get attention and following the regulations.

The main idea is to build genuine relationships with people and share broad information about what you're doing without asking them to invest. This way, interested people can reach out to you first, giving you a chance to build the relationship the law requires before talking about specific investments. To attract new potential investors within the rules, use marketing and PR to show off your general success as an investor and give people ways to contact you.

To attract investors while following the rules, focus on promoting yourself and your overall success as an investor, rather than talking about specific investment deals or funds. This helps you stay within the guidelines of Rule 506(b). Use a step-by-step approach to build relationships: start by sharing general content on platforms like LinkedIn, X (Twitter) and YouTube, then encourage people to sign up for a newsletter or ask them to join private chat groups, and finally, have one-on-one conversations.

This gradual process helps you build the relationships required by law before discussing specific investment opportunities. While this method might take more time than directly asking for investments, it allows you to turn your audience into a group of investors that follows the rules. The key is to develop a smooth, organized way of building relationships and sharing information. This ensures that connections made through social media or newsletter sign-ups can grow into proper investment partnerships.

# UNDERSTANDING RULE 506(C)

Rule 506(c) is a powerful capital-raising tool that allows public advertising of investment opportunities, breaking traditional private placement restrictions. This can be particularly beneficial for dealmakers with a strong personal brand on social media platforms like X (Twitter), YouTube, and LinkedIn, as they can attract LP capital by discussing investment opportunities with their audience.

However, 506(c) comes with specific requirements. Only Accredited Investors, meeting SEC-defined criteria can participate. The GP must take "reasonable steps" to verify each investor's accredited status, which can be complex and time-consuming. All marketing materials must be truthful and accurate, adhering to strict anti-fraud provisions. This includes brochures, website content, social media posts, and public presentations.

GPs must comply with state-specific regulations in addition to federal requirements when marketing these deals.

While 506(c) allows unlimited capital raising and investor numbers, it imposes restrictions on security resales, potentially limiting liquidity. In addition, the increased public exposure that comes with a 506(c) offering can be a double-edged sword. While it may attract more potential investors, it also draws more attention from regulators and existing investors. This heightened scrutiny means that you'll need to be prepared for more detailed due diligence processes. As a result, the fundraising timeline might be longer than with other types of offerings. To address this increased attention, you should have comprehensive and transparent documentation ready.

Rule 506(c) remains a powerful choice for General Partners who are willing to work exclusively with Accredited Investors and can handle the associated regulatory challenges. While this option does come with its own set of hurdles, it definitely offers several advantages. The suitability of a 506(c) offering depends on the unique objectives and circumstances of that deal. To help you decide if this route is right for your situation, let's explore some of the key benefits that come with choosing a 506(c) offering.

### Expanded Investor Reach

Rule 506(c) offers significant advantages for issuers seeking to raise capital. It allows for general solicitation and advertising, enabling companies to reach a much wider pool of potential investors through various marketing channels like websites, social media, and press releases. This expanded reach and marketing flexibility not only helps in raising capital more efficiently but also provides opportunities for brand building and establishing credibility in the market. Unlike the more restrictive Rule 506(b), which limits outreach to personal business relationships, 506(c) allows for a comprehensive marketing strategy.

### Increased Investor Credibility

The strict verification process for Accredited Investors in 506(c) offerings boosts the credibility of these investments. It attracts sophisticated Accredited Investors who value transparency and compliance. The process implies participants are financially stable and understand risks, which reassures other potential investors. This vetting not only meets regulatory requirements but also improves the perceived quality of the investment opportunity. As a result, it can make raising capital easier and more successful.

## Unlimited Fundraising Potential

Rule 506(c) offers a flexible approach to fundraising with no limits on the number of investors or the amount of capital that can be raised. This allows companies to customize their fundraising strategies, whether they want to target a few wealthy investors or a larger group of smaller investors. The rule's flexibility can potentially lead to significant capital raises, comparable to or even exceeding traditional funding methods. This approach not only makes investing more accessible but also allows companies to build a more diverse investor base. Ultimately, Rule 506(c) gives companies the freedom to market ambitious projects without restrictions on investor numbers or fundraising amounts.

## Disclosure Requirements

While 506(c) offerings don't require the extensive disclosures mandated for public offerings, they typically have stricter disclosure requirements than 506(b) due to their broader reach through general solicitation.

# DECIDING BETWEEN 506(B) AND 506(C)

When choosing between Rule 506(b) and Rule 506(c) offerings, you'll need to carefully consider your options. As you've just learned, these two exemptions, while both falling under Rule 506, have distinct characteristics. Which path you choose can affect your ability to attract investors, manage regulatory obligations, and achieve your financial goals. This can come in ways that may not be immediately apparent but can have far-reaching consequences. On the next page, you'll find a comparsion table for your review.

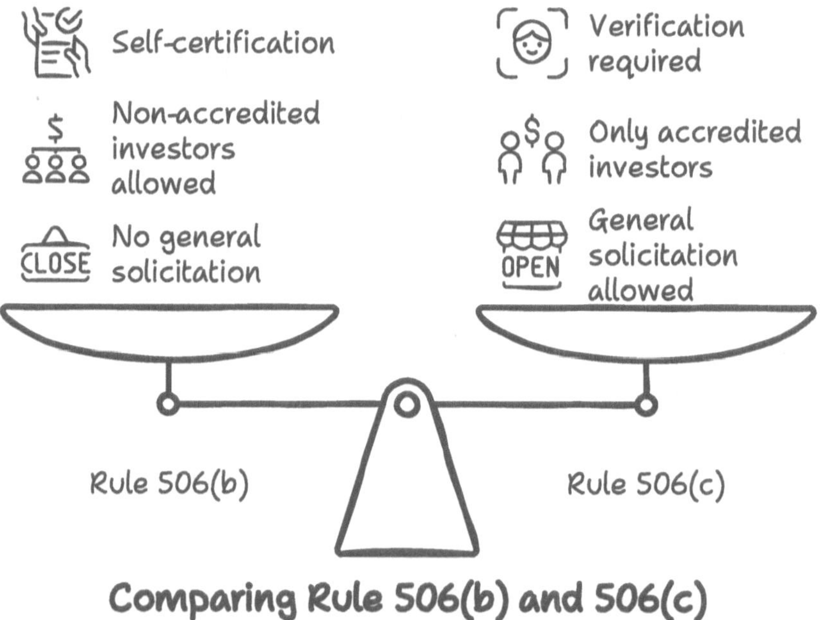


Comparing Rule 506(b) and 506(c)

| | Reg D – 506(b) | Reg D – 506(c) |
|---|---|---|
| Capital Limits | None on amount raised; None on each investor amount | None on amount raised; None on each investor amount |
| Investor Eligibility | Accredited Investors & up to 35 Non-Accredited Investors | Accredited Investors only |
| Investor Suitability Verification | Self-certification ok | Verification required; (Can be by CPA, attorney, financial planner) |
| Limit on Investment Amount | No limit | No limit |
| Financial Statements | Required only if non-accredited investors and 20M+ AUM | Not required |
| Advertising / General Solicitation: | Limited marketing directly to known investors without "general solicitation" (substantial pre-existing relationship required); Intermediaries may be used. | No limitations on solicitation, can be marketed over the internet; TV, advertisements and solicitation on social media permitted |
| Investor Status Verification: | Accredited investors typically self-certify accredited status through an investor questionnaire | Issuers must take reasonable steps to "verify" accredited status; may use various methods; non-exclusive list of methods that may be relied on as meeting requirements |
| Use of Offering Materials Outside of Mandated Disclosure: | Mandated disclosure only if non-accredited investors involved (same disclosure should be given to all investors) | Not required |
| Liability: | Liability under general Section 17/Rule 10b-5 anti-fraud provisions for any person making untrue statements; state law liability; potential "willful participant" liability for intermediary | Liability under general Section 17/Rule 10b-5 anti-fraud provisions for any person making untrue statements; state law liability; potential "willful participant" liability for intermediary |
| Intermediaries: | Intermediaries not required; any intermediaries used must be registered broker dealers or entities exempt from B/D registration | Intermediaries not required; any intermediaries used must be registered broker dealers or entities exempt from B/D registration |
| "Bad Actor" Rules: | Offering cannot be made if "Bad Actor" involved; issuer must take "reasonable care" to exclude Bad Actors, may use questionnaires | Offering cannot be made if "Bad Actor" involved; issuer must take "reasonable care" to exclude Bad Actors, may use questionnaires |

*"Profit is not a dirty word. It's a necessary part of doing business."*
*— Paul Clitheroe, Financial Analyist and Advisor*

# SPV FEES AND COMPENSATION

When you're considering doing an investment deal with an SPV, the biggest question is usually about how you'll get compensated. Unlike traditional fund structures that rely heavily on annual management fees, SPVs offer unique ways to get paid. It's natural to wonder how you'll be rewarded for your hard work, especially when faced with enticing promises of quick wealth and luxury lifestyles from so-called "gurus" in the industry.

However, it's important to understand the reality behind these glossy promises. While SPVs do provide more flexible compensation options compared to traditional funds, they're not a shortcut to instant riches. Building a successful business running investment deals requires significant effort, personal growth, and resilience. What many self-proclaimed experts fail to mention are the challenges involved - the long hours, setbacks, and difficult lessons that come with navigating this complex field.

The truth is, succeeding in this business is a journey that demands dedication and perseverance. It's not about making millions overnight and retiring to a tropical island. Instead, it's about putting in the work, learning from experiences, and gradually building a sustainable and profitable venture. Understanding this realistic perspective is crucial for anyone considering a career as a General Partner in the world of SPVs.

It's great to have big goals in this business - in fact, it's encouraged. However, it's crucial to understand that achieving these goals is a long-term process, not something that happens overnight. Success in this field is about commitment to your vision and building a business that can stand the test of time. This approach means putting integrity first, even if it means slower profits initially. It also involves creating positive relationships and maintaining an excellent reputation in the industry.

In this business, news travels fast - both good and bad. Those who compromise their integrity for quick gains often struggle later on, finding it hard to rebuild damaged relationships and repair their reputation. On the other hand, General Partners who focus on long-term success become known for their reliability and ability to create partnerships that benefit everyone involved. In an industry where trust and relationships are everything, having a good reputation can be your most valuable asset.

It's important to understand the realistic timelines for investment deals. Depending on the type of investment, it can often take several years before you're ready to exit and see any profits. This can be challenging, especially for newcomers who are eager to see quick returns on their efforts. The gap between expectations and reality in this regard often leads to misunderstandings about how financially successful new General Partners actually are. Many people assume GPs are making substantial money right away, but the truth is that it often takes time and patience before significant profits are realized. You need to understand and accept that success in private investment is a long-term game.

To set yourself up for long-term success in this field, prioritize establishing good relationships with your investors. Open and honest communication is crucial. Don't avoid important conversations about investment amounts, expected returns, and how you'll measure success. Discuss exit strategies and be clear about how the SPV will handle selling investments. These talks might seem challenging, but they're essential for building trust and making sure everyone's goals are aligned.

One advantage of SPVs is that they naturally align the interests of General Partners and investors. As a GP, your rewards are directly tied to the SPV's success, which motivates you to maximize returns for both yourself and your investors. This creates a situation where everyone benefits when the SPV does well. Besides the ownership stake you get from running the deal, there are other creative ways to earn income.

However, be careful not to charge too many fees. Smart investors will be put off by a deal structure that takes too much profit through excessive charges. They want to see a fair arrangement where your compensation is reasonable and linked to their success. Also, make sure your deal structure complies with local regulations to avoid legal issues that could harm your business and reputation.

Ultimately, success in the SPV business isn't about quick profits or a luxurious lifestyle. It's about building a lasting, respected business that creates value for both you and your investors. It involves thinking long-term, dealing with ups and downs, and continuously learning and improving. While the journey might not be as glamorous as some people claim, the rewards – both financial and personal – can be truly life-changing for those willing to put in the effort and stay committed.

Let's explore a handful of strategies that can help you generate profits from your deal:

### Management Fees

Managing investment deals can be a financial struggle when you're starting out and waiting for them to mature. To address this, one option is to introduce management fees for every deal. These fees can be tailored to the size and complexity of the SPV, serving two purposes: compensating you for structuring the deal and covering operational costs. Many SPVs opt for a one-time upfront fee, typically 2-5% of the total committed capital, instead of annual fees. This method offers investors a cost structure that is transparent and easy to understand.

However, some General Partners decide against charging management fees. If you're not planning on taking management fees, just make sure you've got some other income to cover your expenses and manage the SPV effectively while waiting for potential profits from exits and Carried Interest. A balanced approach often works best: charging lower upfront management fees for the SPV while using income from other ventures to cover personal expenses. This strategy helps keep investors satisfied and your finances stable.

## Carried Interest

Compensation for General Partners' work and expertise primarily comes in the form of Carried Interest, commonly referred to as "Carry." With this system, they can get a share of the profits from successful investments, as a reward for their skill in selecting and managing successful investments. So, when an investment turns out to be profitable, the GP gets to share in that success through their Carried Interest, even if they didn't contribute capital to the deal.

Carried Interest helps align the goals of General Partners and Limited Partners. This system ties the General Partner's pay to the investment performance. If the investments don't do well, the General Partner earns little or no Carried Interest. This structure creates a powerful incentive for the General Partner to work hard and make wise decisions for the success of the investment and shows a shared commitment to success between both parties.

Many SPVs follow a compensation structure known as "Two and Twenty." This formula typically works as follows: the General Partners receive 2% of the total capital raised upfront as a management fee, and then 20% of the profits generated by the investment.

However, it's important to note that Carried Interest, can vary and may be anywhere between 10% and 20% depending on the specific deal. In some cases, the deal structure might include a condition called a hurdle rate.

The hurdle rate in investments acts as a performance threshold that must be exceeded before a General Partner can claim Carried Interest. Typically, hurdle rates are set around 7-8%, slightly higher than returns from less risky investments like public stocks. This higher rate works to build confidence with investors considering tying up their money in less liquid investments.

Interestingly, hurdle rates are more common in venture capital funds than in SPV investments. This difference arises because SPVs don't typically have ongoing management fees. Whether or not you use a hurdle rate, understanding these concepts will help you make informed decisions that balance investor needs with potential rewards.

It's a good idea to consult your CPA about the tax implications of Carried Interest. The tax treatment of Carried Interest could vary depending on your circumstances. In some cases, it might be classified as a return on investment and taxed as a capital gain, which might result in a lower tax rate compared to ordinary income.

The way Carried Interest is distributed could cause a tax deferral benefit, similar to how unrealized capital gains are treated in the stock market. Just as you don't pay taxes on stock appreciation until you sell, you might delay paying taxes on Carried Interest until you actually receive the cash distribution. There are several ways in which this deferral can be beneficial. You get more time to prepare for the tax bill, can invest the money instead of paying it immediately, and might end up with a better tax situation later on, depending on your circumstances.

This tax deferral aspect of Carried Interest can provide significant flexibility in your overall tax planning. For instance, you might be able to time the receipt of Carried Interest to coincide with years when your income from other sources is lower, potentially reducing your total tax burden. However, it's important to note that tax laws surrounding Carried Interest are complex and subject to change. The specific tax treatment can vary based on factors such as the structure of the investment, how long it's held, and current tax regulations.

Given this complexity and the potential for significant tax savings, it's crucial to work with a qualified tax professional who specializes in this area. They can provide personalized advice based on your specific situation, explain how current tax laws apply to your Carried Interest, help develop strategies to optimize your tax position, and ensure you're complying with all relevant tax rules. Seek expert advice to navigate Carried Interest taxation to potentially save money and make the most of your investment success.

## Ongoing Distributions

When it comes to profits from assets like rental properties held in an investment vehicle, ongoing distributions must be taken into account. The distributions from investments represent the profits shared with investors once management fees and operational costs have been deducted.

But who gets to enjoy these fruits of labor, and in what order?

Investment distributions can vary widely in their frequency and structure, depending on the type of investment and deal arrangement. These payouts might occur in different ways. They might be quarterly (common in real estate), monthly (typical for high-yield debt), or annually (often in private equity or venture capital). They might even trigger on specific events like reaching milestones or selling assets. The method of profit distribution also differs. Some use a simple method. They pay a fixed percentage of each investor's contribution regularly. Others use a more complex "waterfall" method. In a waterfall structure, profits are distributed in stages with different rates applying as performance thresholds are met. This can potentially reward superior performance but is more complicated to manage.

The deal's structure can greatly affect your profits from these distributions. A common arrangement is for you to receive your portion only after your Limited Partners have recouped their initial investment. This patient approach aligns interests and creates a shared sense of purpose between you and your partners, fostering a strong, cooperative relationship. Managing investor returns and expectations effectively requires a deep understanding of distribution methods. This is particularly true with the intricacies of waterfall distributions. Take some time to think about how often, how, and when you distribute, so you can make your investment strategy perfect for you and your partners.

In the context of Reg D offerings, waterfall distributions typically follow this general structure:

- **Return of Capital:** Investors are prioritized in receiving their initial investment back first before any profits or additional distributions are made to other stakeholders.

- **Preferred Return:** A predetermined rate of return (often 6-8%) is paid to investors before any profit-sharing occurs.

- **Catch-Up:** The deal sponsor may receive a larger share of profits until they "catch up" to a certain percentage of the total returns.

- **Carried Interest:** Remaining profits are split between investors and the sponsor according to a predetermined ratio (e.g., 80/20).

This structure aligns the interests of investors and sponsors by ensuring that investors are prioritized in the return of capital and achievement of a baseline return. It also incentivizes the sponsor to maximize performance, as their profit share increases significantly once investor thresholds are met.

It's worth emphasizing that waterfall structures can be highly customized to fit the specific needs of a deal. They can be tailored to accommodate different investor classes, risk profiles, and investment objectives. For 506(b) offerings, which prohibit general solicitation, the waterfall structure can be a key selling point when presenting to Accredited Investors.

Implementing a clear, fair waterfall distribution model can prove beneficial. It not only helps in attracting investors but also in managing the complexities of profit distribution throughout the life of the investment. It outlines how returns will be allocated. This reduces conflicts and clarifies everyone's financial position in the deal.

To understand waterfall distributions, let's examine their use in SPV investments. We want you to see how this mechanism can adapt to various investment scenarios. When it comes to startup investments, waterfall structures are key for balancing risk and reward. Early-stage investors, who often take on the highest risk, are typically positioned at the top of the waterfall. This means they receive their initial investment plus a preferred return before other participants see any profits. For instance, an SPV investing in a promising tech startup might structure its waterfall so that investors recoup their principal plus a 20% preferred return before any additional profits are distributed.

Real estate development SPVs frequently employ waterfall distributions to manage complex, multi-phase projects. In this context, the waterfall might be tied to specific milestones or performance metrics. For example, when the property hits a target occupancy or cash flow, the distribution waterfall kicks in. It rewards investors and developers based on the project's success.

When it comes to film financing SPVs, waterfall distributions can be particularly complex. They might include provisions to recoup production costs, pay investors, and then share profits. This would be based on box office or streaming revenues among producers, talent, and other stakeholders. This structure incentivizes all parties to work towards the film's success while providing a clear framework for how profits will be shared.

In all these cases, the waterfall distribution is a strong tool. It aligns interests, manages risk, and sets clear profit-sharing rules. When you're able to clearly show investors how and when they'll get returns, it helps attract a range of investors.

## Waterfall Distribution Process

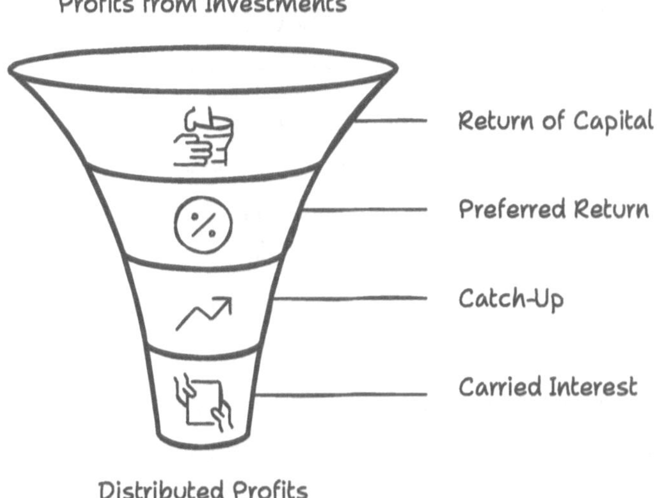


### Exits & Liquidity Events

The exit phase of your SPV is essentially the final stage of the investment. It involves selling the assets, paying off any debts, and then distributing the profits to investors based on their ownership stake. This process turns investments that were previously hard to cash out into real, tangible returns. While we'll explore exits and liquidity events in more detail later, it's important to understand that these are the moments that truly matter in investing. They're when all the planning and waiting pay off and transform illiquid investments into tangible returns for investors.

But there's more to it than just making money, although that's certainly a major part. When a General Partner successfully manages an exit, it proves their investment skills, strengthens their track record, and enhances their reputation. This success can open doors for more investments and partnerships, paving the way for more growth and success.

# OFFERING SIZE AND MINIMUM INVESTMENT

When creating your SPV, one very important piece is figuring out how much money you need to raise in total and how much each investor will need to contribute at a minimum. It's not just about the numbers, it's about the art of making this decision that can really make your venture succeed. You want to ensure that investors are seriously committed to the project, while keeping the opportunity accessible.

When you're crunching the numbers for your offering, it's not only about the investment cost. Keep in mind all the other expenses when figuring out how much money you'll need. To establish cost baselines, start by researching comparable projects. Remember to factor in buffers for unexpected events, regulatory requirements, fees, and ongoing operational expenses tied to the SPV.

Once you know how much capital you need, you can start thinking about the investment minimum. The trick is to find a sweet spot that gets the right investors, sufficient capital, and drives project success. That's why good General Partners think long and hard about these factors before launching their SPV. On one hand, you want to ensure that your investors are genuinely committed to your project. A higher minimum investment can serve as a filter, attracting those who truly believe in the opportunity and are willing to back it with substantial capital. These committed investors are more likely to be patient, understanding, and supportive throughout the project's lifecycle, especially during challenging times. Keep in mind that the pendulum can easily swing too far in this direction. You run the risk of alienating potential investors if you set the bar too high.

Setting your investment requirements too low can lead to problems. You might attract investors who aren't as sophisticated or committed to your project. These less experienced investors often require more hand-holding and can consume a lot of your time and energy. Additionally, with lower investment minimums, you risk not meeting your fundraising goals. This could leave you without enough money to finish your project. It's important to find a balance that attracts serious, capable investors while still meeting your financial needs. The key to nailing your fundraising goals is finding this middle ground.

To set the right investment terms, it's important to research similar opportunities in the market. This helps ensure your offer is competitive. Look at what other projects are doing: How much are they asking investors to put in? How well are they attracting investors? This research gives you a good starting point. But don't just copy others. Think about what makes your project special. Is it in a hot, fast-growing industry? This might justify asking for more money. Or are you trying something new that could benefit from including more people? Also, consider how the current market feels about your type of investment. Think about how any fees you charge might affect investors' decisions. By understanding the market and your project's unique features, you can set investment terms that are attractive to investors and right for your goals.

The expected length of your investment project is another important factor to consider when setting the minimum investment amount. Generally, investors might be willing to put more money into long-term projects that have the potential for big returns. For shorter projects, it might be better to ask for less money from each investor which could help you attract a larger pool of potential investors. TThink back to your goal-setting strategies and decide if this project will be a quick venture or a long-term commitment. When you consider the time horizon along with the other factors we've discussed, you can create an investment opportunity that meets your needs, attracts the right kind of committed investors and works in both your and your investors' favor.

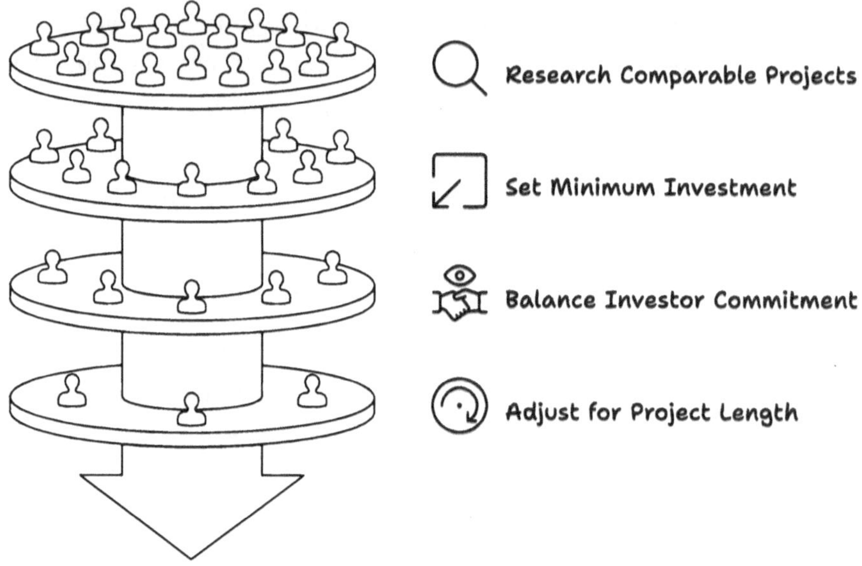


Ultimately, you're looking for the right balance where your offer seems valuable but also accessible. The minimum investment amount you choose says a lot about your project. It tells investors what you expect, how serious you want them to be, and even what kind of investor group you're trying to build. You want to structure deals that not not only bring in money but also keep you on track of building a strong, varied group of committed investors. This kind of investor base is really important for any successful project and for the future projects you'll have come across your desk. Remember, it's not just about the capital – it's about creating the right community.

# WEALTH IN NUMBERS

*"Begin with the end in mind."*
— *Stephen R. Covey, Author of The 7 Habits of Highly Effective People*

# PLANNING YOUR EXIT STRATEGY

Unwinding your deal can seem far off when you're just getting started, but it's important to plan for how you'll eventually exit from the investment. Thinking through this process before forming your SPV will help you structure it in a way that makes your later stages a lot less hectic. As a result, it'll be easier to wrap things up when it's time to exit the investment.

Your exit strategy has two main purposes. It tells investors when and how they might get returns on their investment. It also emphasizes the importance of the General Partner's decision-making authority and what rights (if any) the investors have in the decision making process. It helps individual investors have a clear picture of how long they can expect to have their money invested in the deal and their options for selling their position. At the same time, this will guide your decision-making process, motivate your investors, and increase the likelihood of achieving a profitable exit. When you define and communicate these decision points to investors, you'll be able to  rest easy knowing all your stakeholders are informed and aligned with the plan.

Careful consideration should be given to the exit provisions to avoid potential constraints. If you don't clearly outline these, it may be hard to sell your position or hinder a buyer's ability to make an acquisition. A flexible structure with clearly defined terms around transferability and liquidity is essential. It provides investors with clear pathways to exit their investment when desired or necessary. Depending on the deal structure, these could include the following possibilities:

- **Rights of First Refusal:** These rights give existing investors priority to purchase additional shares or interests before outside parties are invited. Let's say an investor wants to sell - the other SPV members have the chance to buy their allocation first to keep control and safeguard the asset's stability.

- **Drag-Along Rights:** These rights allow majority stakeholders to compel minority investors to participate in a sale. This could occur if a majority of investors decide to sell the SPV assets and want to avoid minority holdouts. Drag-along rights ensure that all investors sell their interests under the same terms, facilitating a smooth transaction.

- **Tag-Along Rights:** These rights serve to protect minority investors by allowing them to join in the sale when a majority investor decides to sell their stake. This ensures minority investors are not left behind if a majority interest sale occurs, giving them an option to sell on similar terms.

- **Predetermined Timelines or Conditions for Selling Interests:** A SPV may include predetermined exit strategies or conditions under which assets are sold or stakes are transferred, such as a specific investment horizon, achieving a certain valuation, or reaching a particular stage. This clarity helps align all investors on when or how an exit might occur, minimizing disputes.

Your valuation methods and dispute resolution procedures should back these up. By negotiating these terms upfront, investors can avoid their capital being tied up indefinitely or having trouble transferring ownership due to unclear or restrictive rules. The documentation should address practical issues, like cost allocation for transactions, required approvals, and compliance with regulations. Take time to establish clear criteria for each exit option so everyone involved has a full understanding.

Make sure to include a projection of potential returns for investors. One way to form your projected returns is by creating a comparison to similar deals in the industry and making use of using historical data. You should think about how timing can impact your exit and how market conditions can affect it. To meet investor objectives and maintain their confidence, this level of transparency is essential.

It's important to recognize that different industries need unique approaches for the best financial outcome. Some strategies suit certain deals better than others and your approach should be designed to fit the specific circumstances of each market. The secret is to know what matters in your industry and create an exit strategy that lines up to create the best exit. For example, in the startup world, founders might have a set amount they're looking for before considering an acquisition offer. They might also choose to go public through an IPO or direct listing once they meet certain financial goals. When it comes to real estate investments, the strategy could be to sell a property once it hits a specific revenue goal or market value. Consider these examples of different investment types and their potential scenarios:

### Real Estate Investments

In real estate, options include individual asset sales, portfolio sales to attract larger investors, conversion to a Real Estate Investment Trust (REIT), or sale-leaseback arrangements. Each of these strategies offers different benefits, such as unlocking capital while maintaining operational control or attracting significant investor interest through portfolio sales.

## Mergers & Acquisitions (M&A) Deals

For M&A-focused SPVs, strategic mergers with complementary companies can create synergies and enhance market position. Acquisitions by larger entities can provide substantial returns, while reverse mergers offer a path to public markets without the complexities of a traditional IPO. Management buyouts are another option, allowing leadership teams to align ownership with operational expertise.

## Startup Investments

Startup-focused SPVs often aim for high-growth exits. An IPO is a coveted option that offers liquidity and potential for significant returns. Acquisitions by established companies provide rapid exits, while secondary sales allow for partial liquidity without full public exposure. Licensing strategies can also monetize intellectual property without relinquishing ownership.

## Natural Resources Investments

In the natural resources sector, SPVs may pursue asset sales of individual properties or resource rights. Joint ventures with larger companies can mitigate risk and accelerate development. Royalty agreements offer upfront capital in exchange for future production rights, while resource-specific IPOs create focused public entities attractive to specialized investors.

## Intellectual Property Investments

Intellectual property SPVs have unique exit strategies. Outright sales of patents or IP portfolios can be highly lucrative, especially for groundbreaking or industry-essential IP. Companies seeking to bolster their competitive position or enter new markets may be willing to pay premium prices for strategic IP assets.

## Secondary Equity Deals

Secondary equity SPVs focus on providing liquidity in private markets. SPV managers exercise significant control in scenarios such as secondary sales and company buybacks. They are responsible for finding buyers, negotiating prices, and managing the distribution of proceeds to Limited Partners (LPs). In the event of a portfolio company's IPO, SPV managers have control over the timing and distribution of capital post-lock-up period, a decision that can significantly impact investor returns.

## Tangible Assets

For SPVs holding tangible assets like aircraft, fleet sales may attract operators or investors seeking scale, while sale-leaseback arrangements allow for capital recovery without operational disruption. Asset-backed securitization can transform these hard assets into tradable securities, tapping into broader capital markets.

Just a reminder, every deal is unique, so there are lots of other scenarios that could be considered for your specific deal. Bottom line, make sure you've got a solid exit plan for your SPV investment. Make sure you're working to maximize returns and fulfill your fiduciary duties. A well-thought-out exit plan guides the entire investment process, making sure everyone's interests are aligned. When done properly, you'll impress potential investors and build your reputation as a skilled dealmaker.

WEALTH IN NUMBERS

*"I knew that if I failed I wouldn't regret that, but I knew the one thing I might regret is not trying."*

*— Jeff Bezos, Founder of Amazon*

# CREATING YOUR SPV

With a clear understanding of your deal, you're now ready to put pen to paper—or more accurately, fingers to keyboard. Let's discuss the practical process of creating the essential documents for your SPV. We'll move from theory to action, translating your carefully planned structure into the legal and financial documents that will form the backbone of your investment vehicle. This step is key in turning your SPV into something tangible, ready for investments and to fulfill its purpose.

## MISTAKES TO AVOID

Don't let a preventable mistake to ruin your Special Purpose Vehicle and cause a financial disaster. You really need to make sure everything is set up properly from the start. If you don't, you might face major issues down the road. By getting things right initially, you protect yourself and your assets. This becomes especially important if your Special Purpose Vehicle runs into legal or financial troubles later on. When you've done everything properly, you can relax knowing that you've taken steps to shield yourself from potential problems. This foresight gives you peace of mind as you move forward with your business ventures. Let's look into the key areas that, if ignored, could pierce the protective veil transforming it from a safety net into a potential liability.

### Using Generic Templates from a Search Engine:

Beware the copy-and-paste trap. Finding a free online legal template might seem like a quick fix for creating your SPV documents, but they can be a ticking time bomb. Generic templates are often outdated and lack the specificity needed for your unique situation. They're a lot like ill-fitting clothes – they might look okay from a distance, but they won't provide the tailored protection your SPV deserves.

### Using Your Home Address:

While it may seem like the more convenient option, using your home address on your LLC documents will broadcast your personal information. Consider renting a virtual mailbox or using a registered agent service to maintain professionalism and privacy.

### Ignoring Annual Filings and Fees:

The state jurisdiction you form your LLC in will have you file annual reports and pay fees to stay compliant. Missing these deadlines can result in penalty fees and even the dreaded "revoked" status of your LLC – not exactly a recipe for success.

### Skipping Details in Your Operating Agreement:

Things might go great until disputes over ownership, profits, and management style cause a mess. That's the potential pitfall of skipping important details in your Operating Agreement. This document acts as your rulebook, outlining ownership percentages, profits and how you'll run the show. Don't leave things to chance and hope for the best – always take time to get it in writing!

### Commingling Personal and Business Finances:

Think of your business bank account as a sacred space, separate from your personal funds. Dipping into it for everyday expenses blurs the lines of liability. If your SPV faces a lawsuit, this commingling can make it harder to prove your business is a distinct entity, potentially putting your personal assets at risk.

### Failing to Maintain Proper Records:

Never underestimate the importance of keeping detailed records. Keeping detailed records of your business finances is essential for navigating tax season and legal situations. If your SPV experiences difficulties, detailed documentation could come to the rescue.

### Not Understanding Tax Implications:

Be cautious of the misconception that LLCs automatically decrease your tax burden. Depending on how an LLC is structured and how its profits are distributed, it could actually result in unexpected tax liabilities. Avoid tax issues and maintain compliance by partnering with a tax professional.

# THE VALUE OF LEGAL ADVICE

Once you start making things official, keep in mind that setting up a SPV comes with a lot of paperwork and it's important that you have the legal side of things handled properly. Having a skilled attorney on your side is a smart move, even if you're experienced in investment deals.

Look for an attorney who specializes in investment deals and financial transactions. They need to be capable of producing and evaluating Special Purpose Vehicle documents that adhere to regulations and best practices. These documents should clearly establish the rights, responsibilities, and restrictions regarding redemption and transferability, protecting both you and your Limited Partners.

Make sure you do your homework when choosing an attorney for your SPV. Check out their experience - how many deals they've done, who they usually work with, and if they specialize in any specific market. See how well they know tax law and get to know their support team. Asking these questions will help you choose an attorney who can support your SPV ambitions effectively. It's also a good idea to see if they're in good professional standing and if they've had any problems with the state bar.

Getting legal advice when setting up an SPV is important, but don't just let your attorney make all the decisions. One of the potential drawbacks of attorneys' strong emphasis on risk identification is that it can lead to excessive caution and higher expenses. As the GP, your job is to balance risk management with moving the deal forward. Don't get bogged down in endless contract revisions. Instead, use your judgment to make smart decisions that consider both risks and rewards. Stay directly involved in contract negotiations and maintain contact with potential investors. Your attorney's advice is valuable, but the final decisions are yours to make.

Attorneys are like consultants, they give advice but don't make the final call. Your ability to navigate these complexities effectively, considering both legal advice and business relationships, is what will ultimately determine the success of your SPV. Focus on what's best for you and your investors to create a successful deal.

# FORMING THE SPV

The first step in running a Special Purpose Vehicle is getting it legally established, usually with a Limited Liability Company (LLC) as the entity for your deal. When you do this the first time, you'll typically need to create two separate entities. The first is called the Investment Entity, which is the SPV itself. This serves as a secure vault for capital contributed by Limited Partners and holds the investment assets. The second is the Sponsor Entity, which represents you and your team as the General Partner, in charge of handling everything for SPV operations.

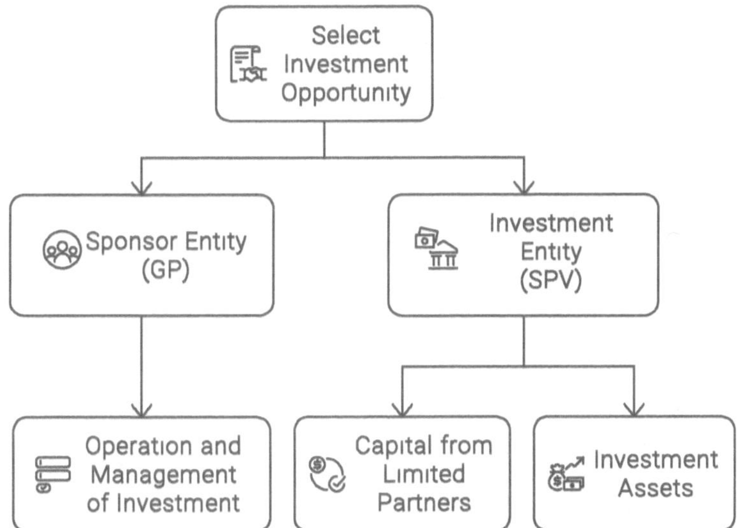


This dual-entity approach has a few benefits. First, it helps LPs by protecting their personal assets from potential SPV losses and only holding the GP responsible for the Sponsor Entity's assets. Roles are clearly defined, with Limited Partners providing capital and potentially receiving returns, while the General Partner takes an active role in managing investments. This setup gives LPs the chance to invest with limited risk and empowers GPs to make decisions without putting their personal assets at stake. Ultimately, this framework creates the foundation for successful investments in the SPV structure. By using LLCs for your SPV, you have more freedom to arrange ownership and management compared to other business structures. The great thing about this flexibility is that the SPV can be tailored to everyone's needs.

While you're going through this process, you might come across the term "formation document." and wonder what exactly that means. To add to the confusion, it can have different names depending on where you're forming the entity and what type of company it is. Other names that get used for this document are Certificate of Formation, Articles of

Organization, Corporate Charter, or Articles of Incorporation. If you hear these terms used interchangeably, don't stress - what they're referring to is the document that establishes your LLC as a legal entity. What you call it varies based on where and what type of entity you're forming. So, what is it? The thing to understand is that this document, whatever it's called, is the official paperwork that brings your company into existence in the eyes of the law. It marks the official start of your SPV as a legal entity, like a birth certificate for your SPV.

So you know, creating an LLC involves following state-specific rules, but the process is similar across the US. You'll need to provide some basic information like your SPV's name, business address, and details about its members and managers. You'll also need to choose a registered agent, which we'll talk more about in a bit. You may also need to provide a brief description of your business purpose.

The main part of the process is actually filing with your chosen state's business registration office handled by the Secretary of State. They'll review your application and, once approved, send you the official formation document. Each state has a website where you can submit this paperwork. Filing fees vary by jurisdiction, but they're not too expensive no matter where you file.

This whole process can seem intimidating due to legal terms and state-specific requirements, but don't worry, you have a couple of options. One option is to enlist the help of a professional service. They are great for making the process simple, and are especially valuable if you don't feel comfortable filling everything out yourself. It takes the work off your hands but does add a bit of cost. You can always choose to file the LLC documents yourself. This can be cheaper and give you more control. But, you must know the legal requirements for forming the LLC in your chosen jurisdiction. Between the two, we definitely suggest making use of a professional service to avoid any issues down the line. If you need to change any information later, you can file an amendment or restatement.

This keeps your LLC's records up-to-date with any changes in membership, address, or other details.

When going through this for the first time, it can be time-consuming as you learn the process and review the information for accuracy. Don't forget, countless businesses make it through this process each year, and you can too. With a little patience and expert help, you can set up a solid legal foundation for your SPV. It might seem overwhelming at first, but finishing this process is a big step toward reaching your investment goals.

# CHOOSING A REGISTERED AGENT

As we just mentioned, when you're forming your SPV, you'll have to decide if you want to hire a registered agent or do it yourself. A registered agent, sometimes called a statutory agent, receives official documents and legal notices on behalf of your SPV. Proper communication and legal compliance rely heavily on this role.

Every state requires businesses to designate a registered agent with a physical address within the state where the entity is established and who is available during regular business hours. This ensures the receipt of crucial legal documents, which is necessary for due process. Don't underestimate the importance of picking the right registered agent for your SPV.

Without a reliable registered agent, you might not know about legal proceedings and risk complications like a default judgment in a lawsuit. Some of the most common things handled by a registered agent include:

- **Corporate Governance Documents:** Includes receiving, forwarding, or filing documents like shareholder minutes, resolutions, articles of incorporation, and other state-required filings. The registered agent may also retain these documents for the business.

- **Service of Process:** Involves formally receiving legal documents such as subpoenas, lawsuits, and other legal notices, and promptly forwarding them to the appropriate parties.

- **Annual Reports:** Encompasses tax return documents and updated information about the company's structure, officers, and directors.

- **Regulatory Compliance Documents:** Includes handling permit applications and various renewal forms

- **State Tax Forms:** These include franchise tax returns, sales tax returns, and other tax-related documents.

You might wonder why a registered agent is so important. You can certainly choose to be your own registered agent, but this has drawbacks. You have to be available during business hours at an address in your SPV's state of registration. This address becomes part of public record and you might have to deal with privacy issues and unwanted mail.

When you hire a professional registered agent, you get a bunch of advantages. It helps protect your privacy, makes sure you don't miss any important documents or deadlines when you're not available, and makes it simpler to comply with regulations if your SPV operates in multiple states. Basically, a registered agent is like a middleman who takes care of state-specific requirements so you can focus on running your SPV, no matter where you are or how busy you are.

When deciding on a registered agent for your SPV, there are a few factors to consider. First, compare the services and prices of different providers. Look for customer reviews to see if the agent is reliable and easy to get in touch with. Pay attention to the specific services each agent offers, such as mail forwarding or document scanning. These can vary between providers, so pick one that best suits your needs. As for cost, you can expect to pay between $50 and $300 per year for registered agent services. Keep in mind that some providers may also charge a one-time setup fee. If you pick the right registered agent, you won't have to stress about legal notices or deadlines. This opportunity allows you to focus on your operations and enjoy some peace of mind.

## NAICS Code

When setting up your first LLC, you may come across a term you're not familiar with: the NAICS code[i]. Among all the paperwork and legal jargon, this six-digit code can seem like just another hurdle. Initially, many new business owners see it as an unnecessary complication in an already complex process. But as you go further into the LLC filing requirements, you'll discover that the NAICS code is more than just a random series of numbers.

The North American Industry Classification System or NAICS for short, is a classification system for industries in North America. Agencies from the United States, Canada and Mexico worked together to develop it and in 1997, the NAICS (pronounced "nakes") system was introduced to replace the older Standard Industrial Classification (SIC) system. This updated system offers a more comprehensive approach to categorizing businesses and industries.

NAICS codes play an important role in business. The government uses these six-digit codes to analyze data from different industries. They hold great importance for entrepreneurs due to their impact on tax liabilities and eligibility for tax incentives. You have the responsibility of selecting your own NAICS code based on the category that best describes your operations. No government agency will assign this code for you. The IRS uses these codes to verify the accuracy of your tax return and determine if your business qualifies for specific tax benefits, so it's important to make an informed decision.

---

*i        The United States Census Bureau maintains a website with NAICS data at https:// www.census.gov/naics/*

While most states don't require a NAICS code when forming an LLC, some states may have specific requirements for including a NAICS code in the formation process. Additionally, NAICS codes may be necessary for both federal and state-level filings. For instance, the federal government often requires NAICS codes when filing taxes using Form 1040. The IRS leverages these codes to collect statistical information and distribute relevant data to specific industries.

The most common entities in the financial sector are typically formed under the NAICS Code "525990 - Other Financial Vehicles". This industry classification has a mix of legal entities, like funds, but not insurance and employee benefit funds, open-end investment funds, trusts, estates, and agency accounts. Notable examples within this industry encompass mortgage real estate investment trusts (REITs), closed-end investment funds, special purpose financial vehicles, collateralized mortgage obligations (CMOs), unit investment trust funds, face-amount certificate funds, and real estate mortgage investment conduits (REMICs).

NAICS may seem confusing at first, but the more you learn about it, the more you realize its importance for your business identity. Every time you look at it in the future, know that this minor detail helped you set the stage for your SPV's success.

## Operating Agreement

The Operating Agreement serves as the key document for SPVs, defining their operations, member roles, and financial and managerial principles. Defining the relationship between the General Partner and Limited Partners requires this essential "rulebook".

Now, you might be thinking, "Isn't this just like the bylaws of a corporation?" Well, while there are similarities, the Operating Agreement offers greater flexibility, particularly for LLCs. The Operating Agreement can steer your decision making process and serves as a way to avoid unexpected events. The flexibility here means you can customize your Operating Agreement to match the deal's specific needs and your preferences as an investor or partner.

Like we said, you'll find lots of LLC Operating Agreement templates online, but it's a good idea to work with a law firm that specializes in investment deals to make sure the documents are exactly what you need. So, what does this "rulebook" actually cover?  Well, a lot goes into it, so pay close attention to these key elements:

- **Entity Information:** First things first, the basics. You'll need to include the entity name, business address, and state of formation. Give the legal name of the LLC, a description of its purpose and activities, its principal place of business, and its registered agent.

- **Members Details:** List the names and addresses of all members of the LLC. Note that you'll need to update these details anytime a new member is added to your LLC.

- **Ownership Structure:** List the ownership percentages and types of membership interest units held by each member of the LLC.

- **Contributions:** Specify the initial member contributions to the LLC. These contributions could include a financial investment, property, or professional expertise and services.

- **Allocation of Profits and Losses:** Describe how any profits, losses, or other distributions will be shared among the members of the LLC.

- **Transfer of LLC ownership:** Establish the ground rules under which a full or partial transfer of LLC ownership might occur in the event of a sale, the dissolution of the LLC, or any other events that might impact ownership.

- **Accounting Information:** Address how the LLC will maintain its financial records for tax purposes and bookkeeping for the IRS.

- **Member Roles and Responsibilities:** This section needs to clearly define the roles and responsibilities of its members. This includes specifying who the General Partner (GP) and Limited Partners (LPs) are, and what their respective roles entail. The GP typically acts as the decision-maker, and LPs, on the other hand, are those who have invested money but aren't involved in day-to-day operations. The agreement must include a clear outline of the GP's authority. This includes specifying whether the GP can make all decisions independently or if some decisions require input from LPs. The agreement should also establish voting procedures if LPs have voting rights, detailing the percentage of ownership required for approving various matters. For managing members, the agreement should cover who they are, their roles, compensation, removal procedures if necessary, and the limits of their responsibilities. However, it's worth noting that in many cases, the individual investors' information is not included in the Operating Agreement. Instead, a separate document called a subscription agreement may be used to give investors ownership, disclose their qualifications to invest, and tie them to the Operating Agreement.

- **Management and Operations:** This section of your Operating Agreement is all about the details of running your SPV. How will you raise more capital if needed? What happens if an investor wants to jump ship and sell their stake? Can they sell to anyone, or do existing members get first dibs? Here's where you can really flex your creative muscle.

- **Fiduciary Duties:** Now, let's talk ethics. As the GP, you have a big responsibility on your shoulders. The fiduciary duties section of an SPV Operating Agreement outlines the General Partner's ethical responsibilities. It should explicitly state the GP's obligation to act in the best interests of the SPV and its members. This goes beyond avoiding conflicts of interest, emphasizing ethical leadership and transparency. By including this, the agreement establishes trust, reassures Limited Partners, and sets clear standards for the GP's conduct. This section is crucial for ensuring responsible management and protecting all members' interests throughout the SPV's lifecycle.

- **Dispute Resolution:** While most deals will go along smoothly, it's definitely possible that even in a well managed SPV, you might still run into a dispute. For that reason, your agreement should detail the procedures for resolving conflicts between managers or members when informal negotiations fail. Take the time to outline an in-depth dispute resolution process. This could include steps such as mediation and arbitration.. By establishing a clear roadmap for conflict resolution, you're more likely to avoid costly and time-consuming litigation. Always work towards maintaining productive relationships and have measures in place so the SPV can continue operations even in a challenging situation.

- **Dissolution:** All good things must come to an end, and your SPV is no exception. An important but often overlooked aspect of an SPV Operating Agreement is the dissolution process. Addressing how the venture will be wound down is a crucial mark of a well-prepared SPV. The agreement should outline the steps for dissolving the company when the time comes, which can be much more complex than simply selling all assets and dividing the cash. It should detail how assets will be liquidated and how the proceeds will be distributed among members. Even though dissolution may not be on your mind right now, it's important to talk about it from the start. It provides clarity and helps prevent potential conflicts or complications when the SPV reaches the end of its lifecycle. Make sure to include these details in your Operating Agreement so everyone's on the same page when winding down.

More often than not, people will pay attention to their Operating Agreement when they're in the process of forming a SPV and hardly ever touch it again. As a result, some investors don't give it much thought. If everything goes according to plan, that shouldn't be a problem. But if something unexpected happens, you'll have to depend on the Operating Agreement for guidance. Moreover, it will undoubtedly be necessary for reference during the dissolution process.

# ESTABLISH A DEDICATED BANK ACCOUNT FOR YOUR SPV

After creating your LLC entity, the next important thing that you need to do is to open a dedicated bank account for your SPV. In addition to this, you need to open a separate bank account for your General Partner LLC entity that you'll use for things like outside expenses and profit distributions.

When we decided to launch our first Special Purpose Vehicle, we thought the toughest part would be finding investors to join us. Man, we were way off! Setting up a bank account for your Special Purpose Vehicle isn't as simple as opening a regular business account. Not all banks will handle SPV accounts, so unfortunately, you can't just pick any bank or credit union at random. SPVs have some unique needs due to their structure. Some banks have policies that won't allow you to collect money or invest on behalf of others.

We started off by calling a bunch of local banks, and each time they either didn't know what to say or flat out said no. "SPV? What's that," they'd say, or "Sorry, we don't handle those kinds of accounts." We felt like we were speaking a foreign language. Just when we were about to give up, we stumbled upon a banker that actually lit up at the mention of "SPV." He knew exactly what we were working on and how they could support us.

What we needed was an omnibus account. This type of account serves as a dedicated bank account for your Special Purpose Vehicle and plays a vital role in maintaining a clear separation between your SPV's finances and your personal or business accounts. Keeping this separation is necessary for legal purposes, aids in record-keeping, and safeguards the interests of all parties. It's important to have this account set up before you start collecting funds from LPs or purchasing assets for the SPV. The invested capital from your Limited Partners is deposited into the omnibus account, which acts as the main hub for receiving funds from Limited Partners after the onboarding process and issuing a capital call.

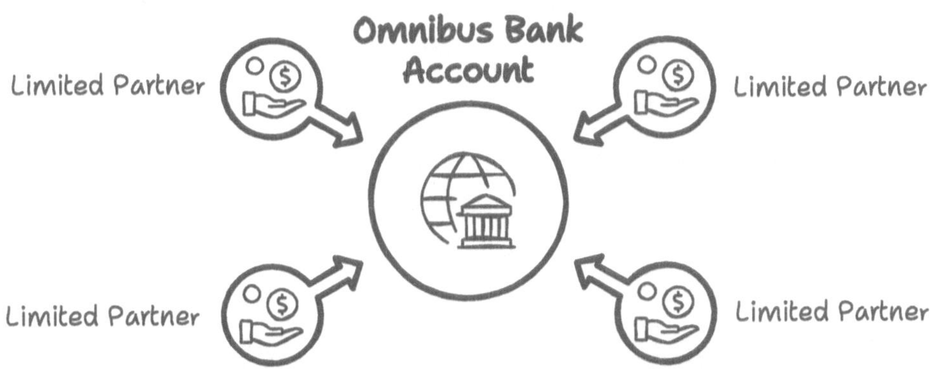


All this being said, you need to find a specialized financial partner that understands SPVs and fund administration. Consider working with third-party administrators, as they often have connections to banks that are familiar with SPVs.

Syndicately and similar platforms have pre-established banking arrangements in place to simplify the process. If you're not sure where to start, you can always reach out to us and we can provide you with some banks that may be a good fit. When choosing a bank, here are a few things to consider:

- **Account Features:** Evaluate the account features that match your SPV's needs, such as digital banking platforms, international transfer options, and specialized transaction support.

- **Fees & Minimum Balance:** Analyze the fee schedule and minimum balance requirements to ensure they align with your budget and operational plans.

- **Welcome Incentives:** Research any promotional offers available for new account holders that could benefit your SPV.

- **Yield Potential:** Compare the interest rates offered on various account types, including both operational and savings accounts, as well as any credit facilities.

- **Transaction Fees:** Review the fee structure for different transaction types to minimize unexpected costs during regular activities.

- **Termination Fee:** Investigate any potential charges associated with account closure, especially if your SPV has a predetermined lifespan, to avoid unforeseen expenses during the wind-down process.

Once you've selected a bank that supports SPVs, opening a business bank account is a simple process. Some banks let you open an account online, while others might need you to go to a branch. When we work with a client at Syndicately, we help them with setting up the bank accounts to make things easier. When setting up a bank account for your SPV, be prepared to present the following:

**Proof of SPV's Legal Existence**

- Formation Documents

- Operating Agreement

- Employer Identification Number (EIN)

**Ownership Documentation**
- Official list of members of your GP entity
- List of individuals authorized to manage the account and conduct transactions
- Share certificates or commercial registry documents with beneficial ownership information
- IDs for all Ultimate Beneficial Owners

**Address Verification**
- Recent bank statement or utility bill (dated within last six months) for the responsible party

**Defined Purpose and Account Details**
- Purpose of the SPV
- Account purpose
- Expected monthly transaction volumes
- Currencies involved
- Countries involved

## Applying for an EIN

An Employer Identification Number (EIN) is like a Social Security number for your business. Having its own Employer Identification Number (EIN), which is a type of Taxpayer Identification Number (TIN), allows the SPV to separate its business activities and simplify tax compliance.

You will want to obtain an EIN for your SPV as soon as it's formed since it will be necessary for doing important things such as opening a business bank account and filing taxes with the IRS. Getting an EIN for your SPV is easy.

We'd be willing to wager that you'll most likely be filing for your EIN online. Most folks go that route and it's much faster than other methods. Just head over to the IRS website and find the "EIN Online Assistant" page. You'll need to fill in some info about your SPV, like its legal name and address, along with your own email and phone number. Don't forget to include the Tax Identification Number (TIN) of the person responsible for the SPV.

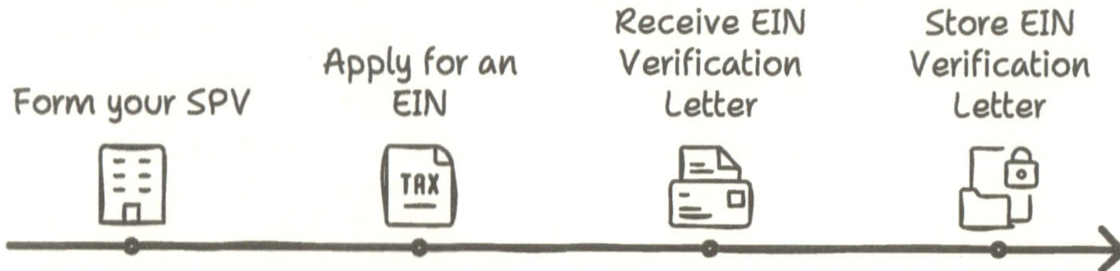


Not a Fan of Online Stuff? You can also apply by phone, by mail, or by fax. No matter which method you choose, make sure you have all your SPV documents handy. It'll make the process smoother and save you time!

When you get an Employer Identification Number (EIN) for your business, the IRS sends you a confirmation letter known as the EIN Verification Letter - CP-575. This letter is important because it proves your EIN is valid and you might be asked to present a copy of it rather than just providing the number for certain things like opening your business bank account. It's kindof what you could consider the birth certificate for your EIN.

So what happens if you lose this document? They won't mail you a new copy of the CP-575 but you can request a replacement letter that is called a "147c Letter" from the IRS. This serves the same purpose and you can request the replacement by calling their Business & Specialty Tax Line at 1-800-829-4933. They'll ask you some questions to verify your identity and then send you a new copy.

## International Requirements

If you're a General Partner that's not a United States citizen, there are additional considerations. While a TIN is not required by the SEC, you'll need it to establish and operate your SPV. Non-U.S. citizen partners who are ineligible for a Social Security Number may need to obtain an Individual Taxpayer Identification Number (ITIN) from the IRS.

It's important to note that state requirements for LLCs can vary significantly. Some states may have additional filing or tax requirements beyond federal obligations, and many require annual reports to maintain good standing. Always consult with a tax professional familiar with both federal and state requirements in your specific location. Your SPV requires a TIN for several critical reasons:

- **Tax filing requirements:** If your SPV is a single-member LLC, it will likely have to file its own federal and state income tax returns

- **Banking requirements:** Your SPV will usually be required to have a TIN in order to open a business bank account at most financial institutions.

- **Regulatory compliance:** A TIN is required to fulfill the Compliance process under Regulation D Rule 506.

- **Relevant TIN type:** In this context, the Individual Taxpayer Identification Number (ITIN) is the most relevant type of TIN. An ITIN is issued by the Internal Revenue Service (IRS) to individuals who need to comply with U.S. tax laws but are not eligible for a Social Security Number (SSN).

### Steps to Obtain an ITIN:

- **Complete Form W-7:** This is the Application for IRS Individual Taxpayer Identification Number.

- **Gather Required Documentation:** You'll need to provide documents proving your foreign status and identity.

- **File a Tax Return:** Attach your completed U.S. tax return to the Form W-7.

- **Submit to IRS:** Mail your application, documentation, and tax return to the IRS.

As an international GP, understanding and obtaining the appropriate TIN is important for regulatory compliance, financial operations, and investment activities in the United States. Although it may appear complicated, it is actually quite simple with proper guidance. Don't forget, it's smart to consult with a tax professional who's experienced with international taxes and securities to make sure you're following all the U.S. regulations.

### How to Get Your Central Index Key (CIK)

To raise capital in your SPV, you'll need to get a special code from the government. This code is called a Central Index Key (CIK), and it's given out by the Securities and Exchange Commission (SEC).

The process of obtaining a CIK requires filling out forms, having them notarized, and sending them to the SEC. Once the CIK lands in your inbox, you've got access to the SEC's Electronic Data Gathering, Analysis, and Retrieval system (commonly known as EDGAR). This system serves as the SEC's electronic archive. By using this key, you will be able to easily file the necessary forms that are required to provide the SEC with information about your SPVs. Here's a guide to walk you through the process.

### Step 1: Apply for EDGAR Access

Depending on your situation, follow these steps to apply for EDGAR access:

- **No Existing CIK:** Use the online Form ID application through the SEC's EDGAR Filer Management website. This involves providing company information, ownership details, and designating a contact person.

- **Existing CIK (No EDGAR Access):** If you have a CIK but haven't filed electronically before, submit a Form ID application, choosing the option "Apply for EDGAR Access: Applicants With a CIK but Without EDGAR Access Codes."

## Step 2: Completing the Form ID Application

Filling out the Form ID is straightforward but requires attention to detail. Here's what you'll need:

- **Company Information:** Legal name, registered address, and IRS Employer Identification Number (EIN).

- **Business Type:** Indicate whether your company is a corporation, LLC, etc.

- **Public Accounting Firm:** If subject to audit, provide the name and contact info of your independent public accounting firm.

- **Company Officers:** List names, titles, SSNs, and addresses of LLC managing members

- **Filing Representative:** Designate who will be responsible for EDGAR filings and maintaining your CIK and access codes.

Example: Imagine you're managing an SPV called "Tech Ventures LLC." You'd enter "Tech Ventures LLC" as the legal name, provide your business address, and include your EIN. You'd list your members details and designate the filing representative.

## Step 3: Notarize and Submit the Form ID

After completing the Form ID online, print it out and get it notarized. This step is crucial for verifying the authenticity of your submission. You can then fax the notarized form to the SEC's Filer Support Department or attach a PDF scan to your online application.

> *Tip: Keep the notarized copy safe, as you might need it for future reference or additional filings.*

## Step 4: Receive Your CIK and Access Codes

Once the SEC processes your application, you'll receive your CIK and a set of access codes via email. These include:

- Central Index Key (CIK)

- CIK Confirmation Code (CCC)

- Password

- Password Modification Authorization Code (PMAC)

- Passphrase

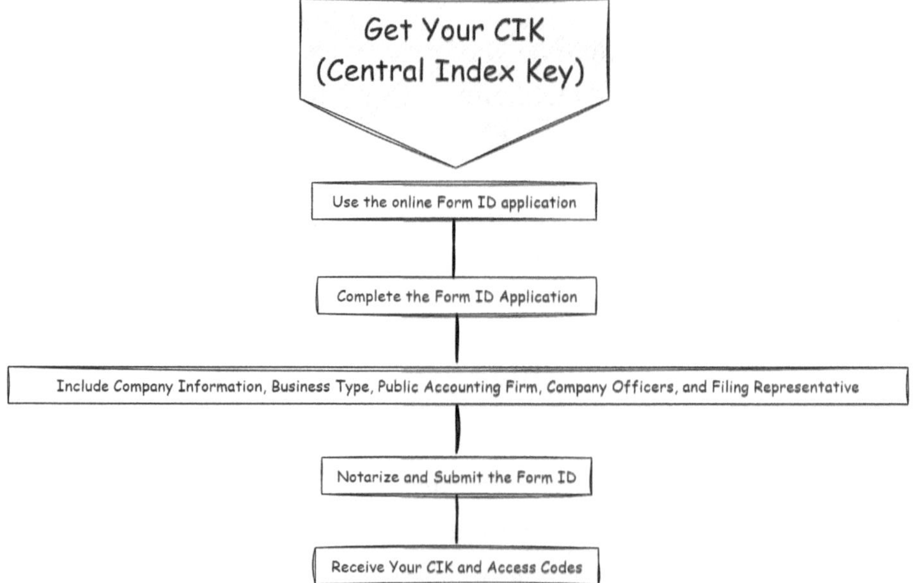

## Step 5: Logging Into EDGAR

With your new access codes, log into the EDGAR system. Here's what you'll do:

- Visit the EDGAR Filer Management website.

- Enter your CIK, CCC, and temporary password.

- Follow the prompts to create permanent access codes and a passphrase.

## Step 6: Maintain Your CIK and EDGAR Access

Keeping your company's paperwork up to date is really important. You need to make sure all the information you give to the government is accurate and sent in on time. Every year, you might need to fill out a form called Form IDW. This form lets you tell the government about any changes in your company, like if you have new officers or if the people who handle your paperwork have changed.

# WEALTH IN NUMBERS

*"The language of business is contained in its contracts. Every word matters, every clause counts, and assumptions are your enemy."*
*— Larry Sonsini, Founding Partner, Wilson Sonsini Goodrich & Rosati*

# CREATING THE SPV DOCUMENTS

Once an investor agrees to join your SPV, they'll need to sign a series of documents as part of their onboarding process. These documents formalize the partnership, ensure regulatory compliance, and clearly outline the terms and expectations of the investment. This process helps safeguard the interests of investors and the General Partner.

The documents you're looking at include several key components: a private placement memorandum, a subscription agreement, an investor questionnaire, and an anti-money laundering agreement. These work together to explain how your Special Purpose Vehicle will function. Thoroughly understanding these documents is imperative, regardless of how much fundraising experience you have.

Given the level of complexity involved in preparing your SPV documents, it's strongly advised to engage the services of an attorney who specializes in this field. With their expertise, your offering will meet all the regulations, give investors all the info they need, and protect everyone involved.

If you want to see how the SPV process usually works, let's look at a story from rockstar entrepreneur named Sarah. She's the brains behind an awesome health tech app. Sarah crushed her pitch, and now she's got several investors ready to commit capital to her Special Purpose Vehicle. Sarah gives the investors a heads up that they need to do some important paperwork to make their investment official. Sarah's got these documents ready to present to the investors:

- **Investor Questionnaire:** Investors fill out a questionnaire that gathers information about their financial status and investment experience. This helps confirm if they are Accredited Investors and comply with regulatory requirements.

- **Private Placement Memorandum (PPM):** Sarah provides each investor with a PPM, which details the investment opportunity, the business plan, potential risks, financial projections, and the terms of the investment. This document ensures that all investors are fully informed about where their money is going.

- **Subscription Agreement:** Each investor signs a subscription agreement, committing to the amount they are investing in the SPV. This contract outlines the terms of the investment, including any conditions or restrictions.

- **Know-Your-Customer (KYC) and Anti-Money Laundering (AML) Agreement:** To comply with legal regulations, investors also sign an AML agreement. This document requires them to verify their identities and affirm that their investment funds are from legitimate sources.

- **ACH Authorization Form:** Investors complete an ACH authorization form, allowing the SPV to electronically transfer funds from their bank accounts via the Automated Clearing House (ACH) network. This facilitates the efficient and secure transfer of their investment funds.

- **W-9/W-8 Tax Forms:** Investors provide the appropriate tax forms—W-9 for U.S. citizens or residents, and W-8 series forms for non-U.S. investors. These forms supply necessary tax identification information to ensure compliance with IRS reporting requirements.

Sarah and her investors need to understand these documents to make the investment process smooth and legally compliant. Next, we'll take a closer look at each of these components. By exploring these documents in detail, you'll gain valuable insights into how they function individually so you can navigate the complexities of fundraising and investment within an SPV structure.

# INVESTOR QUESTIONNAIRE

First things first, when we first start working with a potential investor, we have them fill out an investor questionnaire, which is a must for Regulation D Investments. We use this questionnaire to learn more about the investor and check if they are eligible to work with us. The form gathers info on how they found us, investment objectives, preferred investment timeframe, accreditation status, and available investment capital.

By using the questionnaire, you can not only assess if the investor is suitable, but also make sure the investment is only offered to those who meet the criteria.

**The key components you'll want included in the questionnaire are:**

- **Personal Information:** Basic identifying details of the investor.

- **Accreditation Status:** Questions to determine if the investor meets the SEC's definition of an Accredited Investor.

- **Financial Status:** Net worth, annual income, and liquid assets available for investment.

- **Investment Experience:** Past involvement in private placements, real estate investments, or other relevant sectors.

- **Risk Tolerance:** Assessment of the investor's ability and willingness to bear investment risks.

- **Investment Objectives:** Short-term and long-term financial goals.

- **Source of Funds:** Origin of the capital to be invested, crucial for anti-money laundering (AML) compliance.

- **Sophistication Assessment:** For non-Accredited Investors in 506(b) offerings, questions to evaluate their financial knowledge and capability to assess investment risks.

- **Relationship with Issuer:** In 506(b) offerings, documentation of how the investor became aware of the opportunity.

Although investor questionnaires for 506(b) and 506(c) offerings share some basic elements, they have important differences. Questionnaires for 506(c) offerings put a strong emphasis on verifying an investor's accredited status. This often involves asking for supporting documents or getting verification from a third party. On the other hand, questionnaires for 506(b) offerings tend to focus more on the investor's existing relationship and their level of financial sophistication. Regardless of the offering type, these questionnaires help assess whether the investment aligns with the investor's goals, gauge their risk tolerance, and ensure they understand the nature of the investment.

When you're creating your own questionnaire, it's crucial to make sure your questions are easy to understand and cover all the important aspects of determining if an investor is qualified.

Here is an example investor questionnaire so you can get a better idea of what how they will typically be formatted:

**INVESTOR QUESTIONNAIRE**

[Company/SPV Name] - [Offering Name]

CONFIDENTIAL

This questionnaire must be completed by each prospective investor in [Company/SPV Name]'s [Offering Name]. The information provided will be used to determine eligibility for participation in this investment opportunity and ensure compliance with applicable securities laws.

### 1. PERSONAL INFORMATION

- Full Name: ____________________
- Date of Birth: ____________________
- Social Security Number or Tax ID: ____________________
- Primary Residence Address: ____________________
- Mailing Address (if different): ____________________
- Phone Number: ____________________
- Email Address: ____________________

### 2. ACCREDITATION STATUS

- [ ] I have a net worth, or joint net worth with my spouse or spousal equivalent, exceeding $1,000,000 (excluding the value of my primary residence).
- [ ] I had an individual income exceeding $200,000 in each of the last two years, or joint income with my spouse or spousal equivalent exceeding $300,000, with a reasonable expectation of reaching the same income level in the current year.
- [ ] I hold in good standing one or more professional certifications, designations, or credentials from an accredited educational institution, as designated by the SEC.
- [ ] I am a director, executive officer, or general partner of the issuer of the securities or of a general partner of that issuer.
- [ ] None of the above apply to me.

### 3. FINANCIAL STATUS

- Approximate Net Worth (excluding primary residence): $____________
- Annual Income:
- [ ] Less than $100,000
- [ ] $100,000 - $200,000
- [ ] $200,000 - $500,000
- [ ] $500,000 - $1,000,000
- [ ] Over $1,000,000
- Liquid Assets Available for This Investment: $____________

### 4. INVESTMENT EXPERIENCE

- Private Placements:    [ ] None [ ] Limited [ ] Moderate [ ] Extensive
- Real Estate Investments: [ ] None [ ] Limited [ ] Moderate [ ] Extensive
- Stocks/Bonds:        [ ] None [ ] Limited [ ] Moderate [ ] Extensive
- Venture Capital:      [ ] None [ ] Limited [ ] Moderate [ ] Extensive
- Hedge Funds:        [ ] None [ ] Limited [ ] Moderate [ ] Extensive
- Number of private placements invested in over the past 5 years: ______

### 5. RISK TOLERANCE

- Risk Tolerance (1-5, with 1 being the lowest): ______
- Are you comfortable with the possibility of losing your entire investment? [ ] Yes [ ] No

## 6. INVESTMENT OBJECTIVES

Primary Investment Objective (select one):

- [ ] Capital Preservation
- [ ] Income
- [ ] Growth
- [ ] Speculation

Investment Time Horizon:

- [ ] Short-term (0-3 years)
- [ ] Medium-term (3-7 years)
- [ ] Long-term (7+ years)

## 7. SOURCE OF FUNDS

The funds for this investment will come from:

- [ ] Personal Savings
- [ ] Business Income
- [ ] Inheritance
- [ ] Sale of Assets
- [ ] Other (please specify): ______________________

## 8. SOPHISTICATION ASSESSMENT

(For non-accredited investors in 506(b) offerings)
- Education Level: ______________________
- Occupation: ______________________
- Please describe your understanding of the risks associated with private placements:

______________________________________________________________
______________________________________________________________

- Have you ever lost money in an investment? [ ] Yes [ ] No
- If yes, how did this experience affect your investment approach?

______________________________________________________________

## 9. RELATIONSHIP WITH ISSUER

How did you become aware of this investment opportunity?

- [ ] Pre-existing relationship with the issuer
- [ ] Referral from a friend/family member
- [ ] Through a broker or financial advisor
- [ ] Other (please specify): ______________________
- Length of relationship with the issuer or its principals (if applicable): ______________

## 10. ADDITIONAL INFORMATION

1. Are you investing on behalf of any other person or entity? [ ] Yes [ ] No
   If yes, please explain: ______________________
2. Are you subject to backup withholding? [ ] Yes [ ] No
3. Are you a U.S. person (including a U.S. resident alien)? [ ] Yes [ ] No

## 11. CERTIFICATION

By signing below, I certify that:

- The information provided is true, accurate, and complete to the best of my knowledge.
- I understand this information will be relied upon by the issuer to determine my eligibility.
- I agree to promptly notify the issuer of any changes to the information provided.
- I acknowledge that investing in private placements involves significant risks, including the possible loss of my entire investment.
- I have sufficient knowledge and experience to evaluate the merits and risks of this investment.

Print Name: ______________________ Signature: ______________________ Date: ______________________

# PRIVATE PLACEMENT MEMORANDUM

When raising private capital, Special Purpose Vehicles under Rule 506(b) and 506(c) use Private Placement Memorandums (PPMs) instead of the SEC-registered prospectuses used in public offerings. PPMs are required documents that serve multiple important purposes. They provide detailed information about the investment, including the business model, market opportunity, financial projections, and investment terms. A solid PPM isn't just about checking off a box—You can use it to make a compelling narrative for your SPV. By offering in-depth information to potential investors, PPMs allow you to meet regulatory requirements while effectively communicating the investment opportunity. Now, let's look at the sections your PPM should include.

- **Executive Summary:** This brief overview captures the essence of your offering. It should outline the security type, the fundraising target, and provide an interesting snapshot of your opportunity. This is your chance to craft a message that resonates with investors. Highlight key milestones, and articulate your long-term vision.

  - **Purpose of the SPV:** Explains the specific goals and objectives of the Special Purpose Vehicle (SPV). This section should articulate the strategic vision and mission of the SPV.

  - **Target Market:** Identifies the market segment the SPV aims to serve. This includes any relevant demographic details, market size, and growth potential.

  - **Business Strategy:** Outlines the approach the SPV will take to achieve its goals. This should include marketing strategies, sales tactics, and any partnerships or collaborations.

- **Offering Details:** This section further specifies whether the security is equity, debt, or another financial instrument. For instance, it could be common stock, preferred stock, bonds, notes, or convertible securities.

- **Equity PPMs:** Equity Private Placement Memorandums (PPMs) are used when a company is offering ownership stakes, such as shares in a corporation or units in a limited liability company (LLC). These documents typically highlight the company's growth potential, market positioning, and how the additional capital will drive expansion.

- **Debt PPMs:** Debt Private Placement Memorandums are utilized when offering bonds, notes, or other debt instruments. These memorandums usually focus on the company's ability to service the debt, providing detailed information on cash flows, interest rates, maturity dates, and any collateral securing the debt.

> *Some offerings may combine elements of both, such as convertible notes that can transform from debt to equity under certain conditions. Regardless of the security type, the PPM must provide a clear and comprehensive picture of the investment opportunity.*

- **Offering Price:** The price at which the security is being offered. This includes details on any discounts or premiums applied to the offering.

- **Minimum Investment:** The minimum amount an investor must commit. This threshold helps filter out investors who may not have sufficient resources to support the investment.

- **Use of Proceeds:** Detailed explanation of how the funds raised will be utilized by the issuer. This section should outline specific projects, operational costs, or debt repayment plans that the capital will fund.

- **Management Team:** Investors often say they invest in people as much as ideas. Showcase your team's expertise, track record of success, and unique qualifications that make them suited to execute the business plan. Includes biographical information about the SPV's management team. This should cover their professional background, qualifications, and relevant experience. Highlights the expertise and track record of key individuals. This can include past successes, notable projects, and industry recognition.

- **Market Analysis:** Use authoritative data sources to quantify your market size and growth potential. Segment your target audience, outline key trends shaping the industry, and clearly articulate your competitive advantages. A SWOT analysis can be effective here.

- **Business Strategy:** Detail your go-to-market approach, revenue streams, and key partnerships. Outline your product roadmap and explain how additional capital will accelerate growth. Include key performance indicators (KPIs) you use to measure success.

- **Risk Factors:** This section requires brutal honesty. Address industry-specific risks, competitive threats, regulatory challenges, and operational vulnerabilities. Discuss potential obstacles to scaling and how you plan to mitigate these risks.

- **Use of Proceeds:** Provide a detailed allocation of funds, linking expenditures to specific growth initiatives. Consider using a table or chart to break down major categories (e.g., R&D, marketing, hiring) and their respective allocations.

- **Financial Information:** Present historical data (if applicable) and forward-looking projections. Include income statements, balance sheets, and cash flow statements. Clearly state your assumptions and provide sensitivity analyses for key variables.

- **Capitalization Table:** Show current ownership structure and model how it will evolve post-investment. Include any outstanding options or warrants. Consider showing multiple scenarios if there are variable funding targets.

- **Description of Securities:** Explain in clear language the specific rights attached to the offered securities. This may include voting rights, liquidation preferences, anti-dilution protections, or conversion features for convertible instruments.

- **Investor Suitability:** Clearly define accreditation requirements and any other criteria (e.g., minimum investment amounts). Explain the rationale behind these requirements and how they align with regulatory compliance.

- **Subscription Process:** Provide a step-by-step guide for investment participation. Include details on wire transfers, required documentation, and any digital platforms used for the process. Specify key dates and deadlines.

- **Tax Considerations:** While emphasizing the need for individual tax advice, highlight potential tax implications such as capital gains treatment, potential for tax credits (e.g., for qualified small business stock), or implications for international investors.

- **Legal Disclaimers:** Include standard legal language to limit liability, but also use this section to reinforce the importance of investor due diligence and the speculative nature of the investment.

A Private Placement Memorandum (PPM) must be transparent, clear, and tailored to investors, disclosing all key information accurately. Keep it consistent with other documents, regularly updated, and aligned with all communications. Proper disclosure is crucial to avoid misrepresentation claims and maintain exemption status. Verify investor qualifications, adhere to state requirements, and include legal, tax, and risk disclosures. Given the complexity of regulations, consult legal counsel throughout the process.

## Legal and Tax Disclosures:

Covering every aspect of legal proceedings in the legal disclosures is extremely important. This covers all legal matters involving the issuer, like ongoing lawsuits, regulatory probes, or intellectual property disputes. Additionally, disclosures regarding any licenses or permits required by the issuer's business operations, such as regulatory approvals or professional certifications, should be provided.

Tax disclosures should outline the potential tax implications for investors. These disclosures should cover the tax treatment of income, capital gains, or losses derived from the investment, taking into account any applicable tax laws, regulations, or exemptions. Be detailed and review everything carefully to make sure it's accurate and complete.

## Risk Factors Disclosure:

The risk factors disclosure serves as a fundamental element in offering documents. The disclosure thoroughly outlines investment risks, including industry-specific and issuer-specific risks. It is important to provide a clear explanation of each risk, along with an assessment of its potential impact and the mitigation strategies. This supports investors in making informed choices and safeguards issuers with complete transparency. Here are some key considerations for preparing your Risk Factors Disclosure.

- **Introduction:** Begin with a statement that investing in securities involves risks and should only be undertaken by those who can bear the potential loss.

- **Categorization of Risks:** Organize risks into categories such as operational, financial, market, and regulatory risks for easier comprehension. This helps investors quickly understand the nature of the risks.

- **Specificity and Relevance:** Describe each risk factor specific to the issuer and the investment opportunity. Avoid generic risks and focus on those unique to your business model, industry, and operational geography.

- **Order of Presentation:** Present risk factors in order of importance, starting with the most significant. Use judgment to prioritize based on potential impact.

- **Nature of the Risk:** Explain the risk and its relevance.

- **Potential Impact:** Describe how the risk could affect the issuer's business, financial condition, or investment performance.

- **Mitigation Strategies:** Outline measures in place to manage the risk.

- **Market and Economic Risks:** Discuss how market conditions or economic factors, such as interest rate changes, inflation, or recession, could affect the issuer's business or investment value.

- **Regulatory Risks:** Highlight any regulatory changes or uncertainties that could impact the issuer's operations or the legal landscape of the investment, including new laws, tax changes, or compliance costs

- **Competition and Industry Risks:** Detail the competitive landscape and how emerging competitors or industry shifts could pose risks to the issuer's market position and profitability.

- **Operational Risks:** Address risks related to operational capabilities, such as reliance on key personnel, supply chain vulnerabilities, or technological infrastructure.

- **Legal and Litigation Risks:** Inform investors about ongoing or potential legal challenges that could adversely affect the issuer's business.

- **Conflict of Interest:** Disclose any potential conflicts of interest that management might have, which could influence their decision-making to favor their interests over those of investors. End the section with a reminder that the listed risks are not exhaustive and that investing in securities inherently carries potential for loss. Encourage investors to consult with financial advisors or legal counsel to fully understand the risks before making an investment decision.

As you can see, a well-crafted Private Placement Memorandum serves multiple purposes beyond legal compliance. It provides potential investors with a clear understanding of both the opportunities and risks associated with an investment. By presenting a comprehensive assessment of the deal, including detailed risk factors, the document enables investors to make an informed decision.

This transparency builds trust between the company and its investors, turning an otherwise opaque transaction into a clearer proposition. The PPM also showcases the company's vision, preparedness, and commitment to open communication. As it's often an investor's first detailed look at the company, a thorough PPM can be a powerful tool for attracting investment and establishing strong, trust-based relationships with Limited Partners.

# SUBSCRIPTION AGREEMENT

A Subscription Agreement is a formal document that an investor signs to officially join your Special Purpose Vehicle as a Limited Partner. This agreement spells out all the important details of the investment, such as how much capital the investor will commit in and what they expect in return.

This document protects both the investor and the investment group by clearly stating how the money will be used and what the goals are for making a profit. By signing this agreement, everyone involved knows exactly what they're getting into and what to expect from the investment. While templates can be a useful starting point, remember that each offering is unique. Work with your attorney to tailor a subscription agreement to reflect the specific terms of your offering, the nature of your business, and the characteristics of your target investors. For example, a real estate fund might include specific provisions about property valuations and distributions, while a tech startup might focus on intellectual property protections and future funding rounds. To give you more details, here are the main parts of a Subscription Agreement.

## Capital Commitment

The capital commitment is a key part of a subscription agreement. It specifies the exact amount an investor is committing to the SPV. The agreement outlines how and when the investor will pay this amount, as one lump sum or in stages or as needed. It also covers how to handle committed but unused funds, and what happens if an investor fails to pay when required. Some agreements may allow the fund to ask for more than the originally committed amount in certain situations. This commitment is crucial as it helps the fund plan its investments and operations.

## Subscription Process

The Subscription Process section of an SPV Subscription Agreement outlines how an investor becomes an official stakeholder. It typically involves completing an Investor Questionnaire and providing proof of Accredited Investor status, such as tax returns or bank statements. The agreement specifies how to transfer funds, usually by wire or ACH, and provides account details. It may include minimum investment amounts and deadlines. Investors might also need to review and sign the SPV's Operating Agreement and other legal documents. This section creates a standardized procedure to ensure regulatory compliance and smooth the transition from prospective to official investor, minimizing confusion in the process.

## Rights and Responsibilities

The Rights and Responsibilities section of an SPV Subscription Agreement outlines what investors and the General Partner can expect from each other. Investors typically have voting rights on major decisions, receive regular financial reports, and can attend annual meetings. Their profit-sharing structure and exit conditions are also defined. The General Partner must follow the agreed investment strategy, provide timely financial reports, and maintain accurate records. They must act in the investors' best interests and may have restrictions on certain activities. This section details performance update frequency, audit requirements, and other obligations. By clearly defining these mutual expectations, the agreement promotes transparency and establishes a strong foundation for the relationship between the SPV's management and its investors.

## Redemption Provisions & Transferability Restrictions

The Redemption Provisions section of a Subscription Agreement for an SPV outlines how investors can exit their investment early. It typically includes a lock-up period after the initial investment. Here you'll set rules for how investors can sell or transfer their shares. It may also give existing investors first rights to buy shares that others want to sell. These restrictions help the SPV maintain control over its investor base, comply with regulations, and protect all investors' interests. The agreement usually specifies the process for requesting transfers, any related fees, and how transferred shares are valued.The agreement specifies how often redemptions are allowed (e.g., quarterly or annually) and how redemption values are calculated. It may include early redemption fees. Lastly, it outlines any situations where redemptions or transfers might need to be suspended.

## Distributions:

The Operating Agreement should outline clearly the manager's responsibility to distribute company profits to members. This is one of those things I tend to keep at the manager's discretion because pushing out too much profit can hurt the company if there are expected upcoming expenses. This is part of the manager's role in acting in the investors' best interest. Paying them as much as you can may not be in their long-term interest if it means hindering the company's long-term solvency.

## Confidentiality and Non-Disclosure

The Confidentiality clause in an SPV Subscription Agreement protects sensitive investment information. It defines what is confidential, typically including the fund's strategy, holdings, and performance metrics. The clause outlines how both investors and the General Partner should safeguard this information and prohibits disclosure to third parties without written consent. It may include exceptions, such as legally required disclosures. The agreement often specifies how long these confidentiality obligations last, sometimes extending beyond an investor's participation. This clause helps prevent information leaks, protects the SPV's competitive edge, and maintains trust among all parties involved in the investment.

## Investor Representations and Warranties

The Investor Representations and Warranties section of an SPV Subscription Agreement is crucial for compliance and risk management. Here, investors certify their qualifications, typically confirming their status as Accredited Investors under SEC rules. They acknowledge the investment risks and affirm they've read and understood all provided materials, including the Private Placement Memorandum. Investors may also represent their financial sophistication, ability to bear potential losses, and investment intentions. This section ensures investors are suitable for the offering, protecting both the SPV and the investors from legal and financial risks. It serves as a safeguard, confirming that investors fully understand their commitment and the potential outcomes of their investment.

## Handling of Investor Funds

Investor funds are typically held in a secure escrow account managed by a trusted third party until a minimum funding threshold is reached within a specified timeframe. Once met, funds are released to the SPV for use according to the investment strategy. If the minimum isn't reached, funds are returned to investors with interest. The SPV may accept oversubscriptions up to a maximum amount and might use a small percentage for pre-launch operations, with full disclosure to investors. Throughout the process, the SPV commits to transparency, providing regular updates on funding progress, expenses, and capital deployment. This approach ensures investors are informed about how their money is managed and used, fostering trust between the SPV and its partners.

## Time Period of Making the Investment

The "Time Period of Making the Investment" section in an SPV Subscription Agreement sets the timeline for investors to contribute their committed funds. It typically defines an investment period during which the SPV manager can request capital. This section explains when and how investors must pay, whether in set installments or as needed for specific opportunities. It may offer some flexibility in payment timing but also outline penalties for late or missed payments. The agreement might allow for extending the investment period or returning unused funds. Essentially, this section ensures everyone understands the schedule for fulfilling investment commitments. A sample clause might state: "Investors agree to provide their full commitment over 24 months, in up to four installments, each due within 10 business days of the manager's request."

## Reporting and Communication

The Reporting and Communication section of an SPV Subscription Agreement sets out how the fund will keep investors informed. It specifies what financial reports investors will receive and when, such as quarterly updates and yearly audited statements. This section also describes how often investor meetings will happen, whether in person or online, to discuss the fund's performance and plans. It might explain how investors can ask for extra information or talks with the management team. Some agreements may mention online tools for accessing fund data. This section lets knows how they'll get updates about their investment.

## Fees and Expenses

The Fees and Expenses section of an SPV Subscription Agreement explains all the costs investors will face. It typically covers three main areas: management fees, performance fees, and operational expenses. Management fees, usually a percentage of invested money, pay for the fund's day-to-day running. Performance fees such as carried interest reward managers for good results. Operational expenses cover things like legal and accounting costs. This section helps investors understand exactly what they're paying for and how it might affect their returns. For example, a fund might charge 2% on the initial raise and take 20% of profits above an 8% return, and in some cases depending on the type of SPV, bill Limited Partners for certain operational costs.

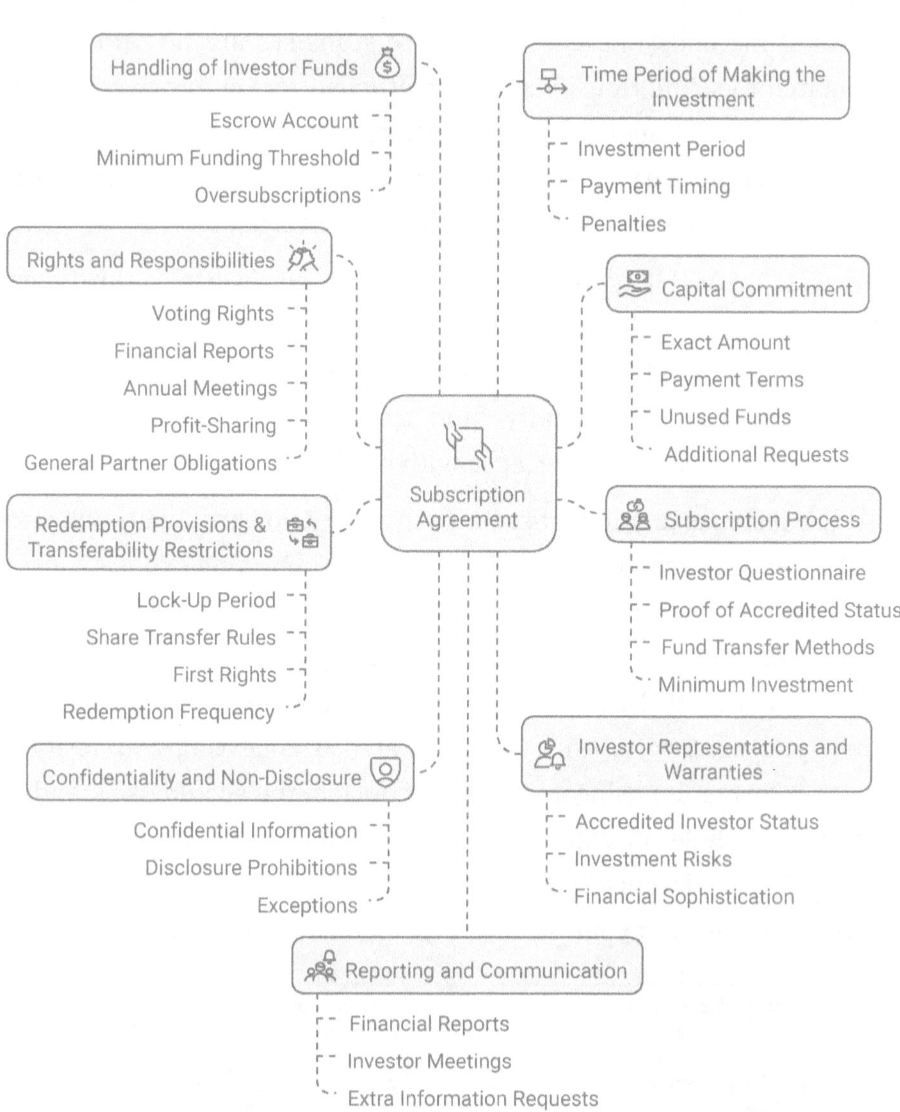
Handling of Investor Funds
Escrow Account
Minimum Funding Threshold
Oversubscriptions

Time Period of Making the Investment
Investment Period
Payment Timing
Penalties

Rights and Responsibilities
Voting Rights
Financial Reports
Annual Meetings
Profit-Sharing
General Partner Obligations

Capital Commitment
Exact Amount
Payment Terms
Unused Funds
Additional Requests

Subscription Agreement

Subscription Process
Investor Questionnaire
Proof of Accredited Status
Fund Transfer Methods
Minimum Investment

Redemption Provisions & Transferability Restrictions
Lock-Up Period
Share Transfer Rules
First Rights
Redemption Frequency

Investor Representations and Warranties
Accredited Investor Status
Investment Risks
Financial Sophistication

Confidentiality and Non-Disclosure
Confidential Information
Disclosure Prohibitions
Exceptions

Reporting and Communication
Financial Reports
Investor Meetings
Extra Information Requests

# ACH AUTHORIZATION FORM

You'll need a way to collect funds from your Limited Partners. While traditional methods like checks or wire transfers are an option, ACH (Automated Clearing House) is a more efficient for investors within the United States. ACH allows for direct electronic transfers between bank accounts, making it easier to handle both capital calls and distributions. This method is secure, efficient, and cost-effective.

To set up ACH payments, you'll likely need to use a third-party software platform and comply with relevant regulations. You'll also need to get authorization forms from your investors and verify their banking information. ACH will simplify fund transfers, cut admin work, and improve your investors' experience with timely, accurate transactions.

When it comes to ACH transactions in an SPV, you are legally obligated to fulfill certain responsibilities. This involves obtaining explicit consent from investors and maintaining detailed records. If you want to set up ACH transactions, you can use software that supports it. You might have to register with NACHA or find a bank that offers ACH services, depending on how you want to do this. The next step is collecting and verifying banking information using authorization forms. You should use standard forms that include an explanation of how ACH transactions work. To comply with regulations such as the Gramm-Leach-Bliley Act, you need to ensure the security of your investors' personal information.

> **COMPLIANCE NOTICE:** All participants in ACH transactions must adhere to the NACHA Operating Rules, which establish the standards for electronic payments. These comprehensive rules govern various aspects of ACH transactions, including processing times, authorization requirements, and dispute resolution procedures. Additionally, Federal Reserve regulations play a crucial role in ACH compliance. Notably, Regulation E provides essential protections for consumers engaged in electronic fund transfers. This regulation mandates the implementation of robust authentication methods to prevent unauthorized ACH transactions and outlines procedures for error resolution and handling unauthorized transactions. SPV managers must be well-versed in these regulations to ensure their ACH processes are fully compliant, protecting both their operations and their investors' interests.

Depending on your ACH process setup, you may need specific forms required by software or a bank. For reference, the next page includes an example ACH Authorization document.

---

### ACH Authorization Form for [SPV Name]

I, [Investor Name], hereby authorize [General Partner/SPV Manager Name] to initiate electronic debit and credit entries to my bank account listed below for the purpose of capital calls and distributions related to my investment in [SPV Name].

**Investor Information:**

Full Name: ______________________________

Address: ______________________________

City, State, ZIP: ______________________________

Phone Number: ______________________________

Email: ______________________________

**Bank Account Information:**

Bank Name: ______________________________

Account Holder Name: ______________________________

Routing Number (ABA): ______________________________

Account Number: ______________________________

Account Type: ☐ Checking ☐ Savings

---

### Terms and Conditions:

1. I understand that this authorization will remain in effect until I cancel it in writing, and I agree to notify [General Partner/SPV Manager Name] of any changes in my account information or termination of this authorization at least 15 days prior to the next billing date.

2. I acknowledge that the origination of ACH transactions to my account must comply with the provisions of U.S. law and the rules of the National Automated Clearing House Association (NACHA).

3. In the case of an ACH transaction being rejected for Non-Sufficient Funds (NSF), I understand that [General Partner/SPV Manager Name] may, at its discretion, attempt to process the charge again within 30 days.

4. I certify that I am an authorized user of this bank account and will not dispute these scheduled transactions with my bank, so long as the transactions correspond to the terms indicated in this authorization form.

5. I understand that my personal and financial information will be treated confidentially and in accordance with applicable privacy laws, including the Gramm-Leach-Bliley Act.

### Authorization:

By signing below, I authorize [General Partner/SPV Manager Name] to process ACH debits and credits to the bank account provided above for the purposes stated in this document.

Signature: ______________________________

Date: ______________________________

Please return this completed form along with a voided check or bank letter verifying your account details to:

[General Partner/SPV Manager Name]

[Address]

[City, State, ZIP]

[Email]

**For any questions or concerns, please contact us at [Phone Number] or [Email Address].**

# W-8 & W-9 DOCUMENTS

Collecting and managing tax documents correctly is an important part of SPV management to ensure compliance with IRS regulations. To manage these important documents effectively, start by including blank W-9 or W-8 forms along with your investment paperwork. Provide clear instructions on how to fill out these forms and explain how they should be returned to you.

Once you receive the completed forms, store them securely under IRS guidelines. If you notice any forms are incomplete or missing, follow up with the investors promptly. While this outline covers the general process, it's always best to consult with legal and tax professionals for specific advice.

> **NOTE: Investors must provide updated forms if their circumstances change.**

## For US Investors (W-9)

The W-9 tax form, formally known as the "Request for Taxpayer Identification Number and Certification," is used by the IRS to gather essential taxpayer information. Limited Partners based in the US must complete this form to ensure accurate transaction reporting to the IRS. The W-9 forms are used by US citizens, resident aliens, and domestic entities to gather information such as the investor's name, address, and TIN or SSN. There is no expiration date on W-9 forms.

# Completing Form W-9

- Provide full legal name as shown on tax returns.

- Enter business name/disregarded entity name if applicable.

- Check the appropriate box for federal tax classification.

- Enter address and TIN (SSN for individuals, EIN for entities).

- Sign and date the form.

---

**Form W-9**
(Rev. March 2024)
Department of the Treasury
Internal Revenue Service

**Request for Taxpayer Identification Number and Certification**

Go to *www.irs.gov/FormW9* for instructions and the latest information.

Give form to the requester. Do not send to the IRS.

**Before you begin.** For guidance related to the purpose of Form W-9, see *Purpose of Form*, below.

**1** Name of entity/individual. An entry is required. (For a sole proprietor or disregarded entity, enter the owner's name on line 1, and enter the business/disregarded entity's name on line 2.)

**2** Business name/disregarded entity name, if different from above.

**3a** Check the appropriate box for federal tax classification of the entity/individual whose name is entered on line 1. Check only **one** of the following seven boxes.

☐ Individual/sole proprietor  ☐ C corporation  ☐ S corporation  ☐ Partnership  ☐ Trust/estate

☐ LLC. Enter the tax classification (C = C corporation, S = S corporation, P = Partnership) . . . . ______

**Note:** Check the "LLC" box above and, in the entry space, enter the appropriate code (C, S, or P) for the tax classification of the LLC, unless it is a disregarded entity. A disregarded entity should instead check the appropriate box for the tax classification of its owner.

☐ Other (see instructions)

**4** Exemptions (codes apply only to certain entities, not individuals; see instructions on page 3):

Exempt payee code (if any) ______

Exemption from Foreign Account Tax Compliance Act (FATCA) reporting code (if any) ______

*(Applies to accounts maintained outside the United States.)*

**3b** If on line 3a you checked "Partnership" or "Trust/estate," or checked "LLC" and entered "P" as its tax classification, and you are providing this form to a partnership, trust, or estate in which you have an ownership interest, check this box if you have any foreign partners, owners, or beneficiaries. See instructions . . . . . . . . . . ☐

**5** Address (number, street, and apt. or suite no.). See instructions.

Requester's name and address (optional)

**6** City, state, and ZIP code

**7** List account number(s) here (optional)

*Print or type. See Specific Instructions on page 3.*

**Part I**   **Taxpayer Identification Number (TIN)**

Enter your TIN in the appropriate box. The TIN provided must match the name given on line 1 to avoid backup withholding. For individuals, this is generally your social security number (SSN). However, for a resident alien, sole proprietor, or disregarded entity, see the instructions for Part I, later. For other entities, it is your employer identification number (EIN). If you do not have a number, see *How to get a TIN*, later.

**Note:** If the account is in more than one name, see the instructions for line 1. See also *What Name and Number To Give the Requester* for guidelines on whose number to enter.

Social security number

or

Employer identification number

**Part II**   **Certification**

Under penalties of perjury, I certify that:

1. The number shown on this form is my correct taxpayer identification number (or I am waiting for a number to be issued to me); and
2. I am not subject to backup withholding because (a) I am exempt from backup withholding, or (b) I have not been notified by the Internal Revenue Service (IRS) that I am subject to backup withholding as a result of a failure to report all interest or dividends, or (c) the IRS has notified me that I am no longer subject to backup withholding; and
3. I am a U.S. citizen or other U.S. person (defined below); and
4. The FATCA code(s) entered on this form (if any) indicating that I am exempt from FATCA reporting is correct.

**Certification instructions.** You must cross out item 2 above if you have been notified by the IRS that you are currently subject to backup withholding because you have failed to report all interest and dividends on your tax return. For real estate transactions, item 2 does not apply. For mortgage interest paid, acquisition or abandonment of secured property, cancellation of debt, contributions to an individual retirement arrangement (IRA), and, generally, payments other than interest and dividends, you are not required to sign the certification, but you must provide your correct TIN. See the instructions for Part II, later.

**Sign Here**   Signature of U.S. person     Date

## General Instructions

Section references are to the Internal Revenue Code unless otherwise noted.

**Future developments.** For the latest information about developments related to Form W-9 and its instructions, such as legislation enacted after they were published, go to *www.irs.gov/FormW9*.

## What's New

Line 3a has been modified to clarify how a disregarded entity completes this line. An LLC that is a disregarded entity should check the appropriate box for the tax classification of its owner. Otherwise, it should check the "LLC" box and enter its appropriate tax classification.

New line 3b has been added to this form. A flow-through entity is required to complete this line to indicate that it has direct or indirect foreign partners, owners, or beneficiaries when it provides the Form W-9 to another flow-through entity in which it has an ownership interest. This change is intended to provide a flow-through entity with information regarding the status of its indirect foreign partners, owners, or beneficiaries, so that it can satisfy any applicable reporting requirements. For example, a partnership that has any indirect foreign partners may be required to complete Schedules K-2 and K-3. See the Partnership Instructions for Schedules K-2 and K-3 (Form 1065).

## Purpose of Form

An individual or entity (Form W-9 requester) who is required to file an information return with the IRS is giving you this form because they

Cat. No. 10231X     Form **W-9** (Rev. 3-2024)

### For Non-US Investors (W-8 Series)

International Limited Partners will need to complete a series W-8 form. Normally, foreign individuals or companies receiving US income face a standard 30% tax withholding. However, by filling out the correct W-8 form, they can establish their foreign status and claim any applicable tax treaty benefits they may be entitled to. This could potentially lower the taxes on their US investments. These forms remain valid for three years after the year they're signed.

### Form W-8BEN

The W-8BEN form, formally known as the "Certificate of Foreign Status of Beneficial Owner for United States Tax Withholding and Reporting," is used by non-US individual investors to certify their foreign status and claim treaty benefits if applicable.

### Completing Form W-8BEN (for individuals)

- Provide full name, country of citizenship, and permanent residence address.
- Enter US taxpayer identification number if applicable.
- Include foreign tax identifying number if required.
- Claim treaty benefits if applicable (specify article and rate).
- Sign and date the form.

Form **W-8BEN**
(Rev. October 2021)
Department of the Treasury
Internal Revenue Service

**Certificate of Foreign Status of Beneficial Owner for United States Tax Withholding and Reporting (Individuals)**
▶ For use by individuals. Entities must use Form W-8BEN-E.
▶ Go to *www.irs.gov/FormW8BEN* for instructions and the latest information.
▶ Give this form to the withholding agent or payer. Do not send to the IRS.

OMB No. 1545-1621

**Do NOT use this form if:** — **Instead, use Form:**

- You are NOT an individual . . . . . . . . . . . . . . . . . . . . . . . . . . . . . . . . . W-8BEN-E
- You are a U.S. citizen or other U.S. person, including a resident alien individual . . . . . . . . . . . . . . . . . . . W-9
- You are a beneficial owner claiming that income is effectively connected with the conduct of trade or business within the United States (other than personal services) . . . . . . . . . . . . . . . . . . . . . . . . . . . . . . . . . W-8ECI
- You are a beneficial owner who is receiving compensation for personal services performed in the United States . . . . . . . . . . 8233 or W-4
- You are a person acting as an intermediary . . . . . . . . . . . . . . . . . . . . . . . . . W-8IMY

**Note:** If you are resident in a FATCA partner jurisdiction (that is, a Model 1 IGA jurisdiction with reciprocity), certain tax account information may be provided to your jurisdiction of residence.

**Part I**    **Identification of Beneficial Owner** (see instructions)

**1**   Name of individual who is the beneficial owner     **2**   Country of citizenship

**3**   Permanent residence address (street, apt. or suite no., or rural route). **Do not use a P.O. box or in-care-of address.**

   City or town, state or province. Include postal code where appropriate.     Country

**4**   Mailing address (if different from above)

   City or town, state or province. Include postal code where appropriate.     Country

**5**   U.S. taxpayer identification number (SSN or ITIN), if required (see instructions)

**6a**   Foreign tax identifying number (see instructions)     **6b**   Check if FTIN not legally required . . . . . . . . . . . . . ☐

**7**   Reference number(s) (see instructions)     **8**   Date of birth (MM-DD-YYYY) (see instructions)

**Part II**    **Claim of Tax Treaty Benefits** (for chapter 3 purposes only) (see instructions)

**9**   I certify that the beneficial owner is a resident of _________________________ within the meaning of the income tax treaty between the United States and that country.

**10**   **Special rates and conditions** (if applicable—see instructions): The beneficial owner is claiming the provisions of Article and paragraph _________________ of the treaty identified on line 9 above to claim a _____ % rate of withholding on (specify type of income): _________________________ .

   Explain the additional conditions in the Article and paragraph the beneficial owner meets to be eligible for the rate of withholding: _________

**Part III**    **Certification**

Under penalties of perjury, I declare that I have examined the information on this form and to the best of my knowledge and belief it is true, correct, and complete. I further certify under penalties of perjury that:

- I am the individual that is the beneficial owner (or am authorized to sign for the individual that is the beneficial owner) of all the income or proceeds to which this form relates or am using this form to document myself for chapter 4 purposes;
- The person named on line 1 of this form is not a U.S. person;
- This form relates to:
  (a) income not effectively connected with the conduct of a trade or business in the United States;
  (b) income effectively connected with the conduct of a trade or business in the United States but is not subject to tax under an applicable income tax treaty;
  (c) the partner's share of a partnership's effectively connected taxable income; or
  (d) the partner's amount realized from the transfer of a partnership interest subject to withholding under section 1446(f);
- The person named on line 1 of this form is a resident of the treaty country listed on line 9 of the form (if any) within the meaning of the income tax treaty between the United States and that country; and
- For broker transactions or barter exchanges, the beneficial owner is an exempt foreign person as defined in the instructions.

Furthermore, I authorize this form to be provided to any withholding agent that has control, receipt, or custody of the income of which I am the beneficial owner or any withholding agent that can disburse or make payments of the income of which I am the beneficial owner. **I agree that I will submit a new form within 30 days if any certification made on this form becomes incorrect.**

**Sign Here** ▶   ☐ I certify that I have the capacity to sign for the person identified on line 1 of this form.

   Signature of beneficial owner (or individual authorized to sign for beneficial owner)     Date (MM-DD-YYYY)

   Print name of signer

**For Paperwork Reduction Act Notice, see separate instructions.**     Cat. No. 25047Z     Form **W-8BEN** (Rev. 10-2021)

## Form W-8BEN-E

The W-8BEN-E form, or the "Certificate of Foreign Status of Beneficial Owner for United States Tax Withholding and Reporting (Entities)," is similar to the W-8BEN but is used by foreign entities, such as businesses or organizations, investing in the SPV. This form serves to establish the foreign status of these entities and claim any applicable tax treaty benefits.

## Completing Form W-8BEN-E (for entities)

- Enter the organization's name and country of incorporation.

- Specify the entity type (corporation, partnership, etc.).

- Identify the applicable chapter 4 status (FATCA status).

- Provide permanent residence address and mailing address if different.

- Enter US TIN if applicable and foreign TIN if required.

- Claim treaty benefits if applicable.

- Sign and date the form.

| Form **W-8BEN-E** | **Certificate of Status of Beneficial Owner for United States Tax Withholding and Reporting (Entities)** | |
|---|---|---|
| (Rev. October 2021)<br>Department of the Treasury<br>Internal Revenue Service | ▶ For use by entities. Individuals must use Form W-8BEN. ▶ Section references are to the Internal Revenue Code.<br>▶ Go to *www.irs.gov/FormW8BENE* for instructions and the latest information.<br>▶ Give this form to the withholding agent or payer. Do not send to the IRS. | OMB No. 1545-1621 |

**Do NOT use this form for:** | **Instead use Form:**

- U.S. entity or U.S. citizen or resident . . . . . . . . . . . . . . . . . . . . . . . . . . . . . . . . W-9
- A foreign individual . . . . . . . . . . . . . . . . . . . . . . . W-8BEN (Individual) or Form 8233
- A foreign individual or entity claiming that income is effectively connected with the conduct of trade or business within the United States (unless claiming treaty benefits) . . . . . . . . . . . . . . . . . . . . . . . . . . . . . . . . W-8ECI
- A foreign partnership, a foreign simple trust, or a foreign grantor trust (unless claiming treaty benefits) (see instructions for exceptions) . . W-8IMY
- A foreign government, international organization, foreign central bank of issue, foreign tax-exempt organization, foreign private foundation, or government of a U.S. possession claiming that income is effectively connected U.S. income or that is claiming the applicability of section(s) 115(2), 501(c), 892, 895, or 1443(b) (unless claiming treaty benefits) (see instructions for other exceptions) . . . . . . . . . . W-8ECI or W-8EXP
- Any person acting as an intermediary (including a qualified intermediary acting as a qualified derivatives dealer) . . . . . . . . . W-8IMY

---

**Part I**    **Identification of Beneficial Owner**

**1** Name of organization that is the beneficial owner | **2** Country of incorporation or organization

**3** Name of disregarded entity receiving the payment (if applicable, see instructions)

**4** Chapter 3 Status (entity type) (Must check one box only):
☐ Corporation ☐ Partnership
☐ Simple trust ☐ Tax-exempt organization ☐ Complex trust ☐ Foreign Government - Controlled Entity
☐ Central Bank of Issue ☐ Private foundation ☐ Estate ☐ Foreign Government - Integral Part
☐ Grantor trust ☐ Disregarded entity ☐ International organization

If you entered disregarded entity, partnership, simple trust, or grantor trust above, is the entity a hybrid making a treaty claim? If "Yes," complete Part III. ☐ Yes ☐ No

**5** Chapter 4 Status (FATCA status) (See instructions for details and complete the certification below for the entity's applicable status.)

☐ Nonparticipating FFI (including an FFI related to a Reporting IGA FFI other than a deemed-compliant FFI, participating FFI, or exempt beneficial owner).

☐ Participating FFI.

☐ Reporting Model 1 FFI.

☐ Reporting Model 2 FFI.

☐ Registered deemed-compliant FFI (other than a reporting Model 1 FFI, sponsored FFI, or nonreporting IGA FFI covered in Part XII). See instructions.

☐ Sponsored FFI. Complete Part IV.

☐ Certified deemed-compliant nonregistering local bank. Complete Part V.

☐ Certified deemed-compliant FFI with only low-value accounts. Complete Part VI.

☐ Certified deemed-compliant sponsored, closely held investment vehicle. Complete Part VII.

☐ Certified deemed-compliant limited life debt investment entity. Complete Part VIII.

☐ Certain investment entities that do not maintain financial accounts. Complete Part IX.

☐ Owner-documented FFI. Complete Part X.

☐ Restricted distributor. Complete Part XI.

☐ Nonreporting IGA FFI. Complete Part XII.

☐ Foreign government, government of a U.S. possession, or foreign central bank of issue. Complete Part XIII.

☐ International organization. Complete Part XIV.

☐ Exempt retirement plans. Complete Part XV.

☐ Entity wholly owned by exempt beneficial owners. Complete Part XVI.

☐ Territory financial institution. Complete Part XVII.

☐ Excepted nonfinancial group entity. Complete Part XVIII.

☐ Excepted nonfinancial start-up company. Complete Part XIX.

☐ Excepted nonfinancial entity in liquidation or bankruptcy. Complete Part XX.

☐ 501(c) organization. Complete Part XXI.

☐ Nonprofit organization. Complete Part XXII.

☐ Publicly traded NFFE or NFFE affiliate of a publicly traded corporation. Complete Part XXIII.

☐ Excepted territory NFFE. Complete Part XXIV.

☐ Active NFFE. Complete Part XXV.

☐ Passive NFFE. Complete Part XXVI.

☐ Excepted inter-affiliate FFI. Complete Part XXVII.

☐ Direct reporting NFFE.

☐ Sponsored direct reporting NFFE. Complete Part XXVIII.

☐ Account that is not a financial account.

**6** Permanent residence address (street, apt. or suite no., or rural route). **Do not use a P.O. box or in-care-of address** (other than a registered address).

City or town, state or province. Include postal code where appropriate. | Country

**7** Mailing address (if different from above)

City or town, state or province. Include postal code where appropriate. | Country

---

**For Paperwork Reduction Act Notice, see separate instructions.**     Cat. No. 59689N     Form **W-8BEN-E** (Rev. 10-2021)

WEALTH IN NUMBERS

*"By a network I don't necessarily mean your customers or clients. I mean a network of people who know you, like you, and trust you. They might never buy a thing from you, but they've always got you in the backs of their minds. They're people who are personally invested in seeing you succeed... They're your army of personal walking ambassadors."*

— *Bob Burg Author of The Go-Giver*

# THE POWER OF CONNECTIONS

Alright, we've covered the basics of setting up the SPV and paperwork. Now, it's time to shift our attention to finding investors, the next piece of the puzzle. Even the best-planned SPV won't succeed without the right people investing in it. This part is key - it's what turns your SPV from just an idea on paper into a real, working investment.

Have you ever noticed how some individuals seem to move effortlessly from one exciting opportunity to the next in their careers, while others struggle to make progress? The key often lies in the power of connections. If you plan on having any success in this business, it's simply a fact of life that you're going to have to get out and introduce yourself to people. There's no way around it–you must constantly grow your network and there are no excuses for failing to do so. There's a well-known saying, often attributed to Jim Rohn, that states, "You are the average of the five people you spend the most time with." In my experience, this has proven to be true more often than not.

If you find that you're the most successful person in your current network, it might be time to get out there and meet new people who can inspire and challenge you to reach greater heights. When you're at events, be open about your work. Many people will find the management of private investments intriguing.

Having interesting topics to discuss can attract influential people who may be curious about your projects. The real benefit of knowing successful individuals is that they can introduce you to even more accomplished people in their networks. This means that when you have a great opportunity, these connections can help you reach high-level potential investors. Before you know it, your network can grow significantly, opening doors to many more possibilities.

Building relationships is like planting seeds - you never know exactly how they'll grow. It requires patience and it won't happen overnight. Sadly, everyone's chasing instant gratification these days (maybe give a dopamine detox a shot!). When networking, focus on building genuine connections with people rather than just collecting business cards. Some relationships may prove useful right away, while others might not show their value for years. You can't predict which connections will be most beneficial, as everyone has unique talents and perspectives that could help you in unexpected ways. The important thing is to keep making new connections and maintain your existing ones.

As these relationship seeds mature and your network grows, you'll find yourself in an increasingly powerful position. Having a robust network enables you to assist others by connecting them with the resources necessary to achieve their goals. Your ability to become a power connector who can leverage relationships will help you expand your reach exponentially. Connectors play a crucial role in smoothing social interactions, often by introducing people who might benefit from knowing each other. This could mean connecting brilliant minds, potential collaborators, or individuals with shared interests.

These introductions aren't just friendly gestures, they're calculated moves that subtly enhance the connector's status. By being the link between important parties, connectors can kickstart new ventures and alliances, cementing their position in social circles. This strategy is common among the elite. It shows their social skill and increases their influence without seeming too ambitious. It's a refined way of showing influence, expressed through subtle cues within sophisticated professional networks.

To become a successful connector, focus on building deep understanding of your contacts to add maximum value to your network. Diversify your connections across various disciplines, organizational levels, locations, and age groups. Engage authentically with new people by sharing your passions and listening to theirs. If you consistently make valuable introductions, your network will see you as an invaluable resource and turn to you when they need connections.

To reach your full potential as a dealmaker, concentrate on building relationships with other connectors. These individuals are typically competent, responsive, and well-connected themselves. By connecting with connectors in different industries or spheres of influence, you create a multiplier effect for your networking efforts. Always look for ways to add value to these relationships and be proactive in making thoughtful introductions within your network. As you cultivate your reputation as a connector, unexpected opportunities will come your way. Your ability to add value and make connections will precede you. It may lead to new investments, partnerships, or insights.

As someone leading private investments, your network will likely be your greatest asset and will directly affect your level of success. Be genuine and lend a hand when you can. Your next big break could be just one conversation away. In the end, the power of connections lies not in what they can do for you right now, but in the potential they hold for the future. Every person you meet, every conversation you have, every relationship you nurture is a thread in the tapestry of your career. You might not see the full picture yet, but trust that it's being woven, one connection at a time.

To excel at networking, prioritize giving without expecting reciprocation. Think about how you feel when someone asks you for a favor out of the blue - it's not great, right? They broke the golden rule of networking - you gotta give before you can get.

It's not all about the money you make, but about the value you bring to the table. If you prioritize giving value, the money tends to come on its own. Your income and influence depend on how many people you've helped and how much your help has impacted them. To network effectively, especially with those more successful than you, you need to offer some real value and go above and beyond for them. This doesn't mean you need to make grand gestures. Small, consistent acts of value go a long way. Even if you think you don't have anything to offer, remember that genuine connections are priceless. Just show up and help where you can.

Surround yourself with high-quality people who can help you reach your long-term goals. Take the time to understand their goals too.

How are you able to offer support to others? Is there a resource you found valuable that you could share? Is it possible for you to introduce them to a suitable mentor? Can you evaluate their proposal for a deal they're working on and give some insight?

Before asking for a favor, consider how you can add value to the other person's life. This shift in mindset can significantly improve your networking approach. By creating mutually beneficial connections, you may get better opportunities. This is due to reciprocity, and you won't even have to ask.

You already know that warm introductions are generally more effective than cold approaches. When you consistently provide positive experiences for people in your network, your reputation grows, leading to more referrals. Your network most likely knows people who are like them and might be interested in your next deal. Like they say, birds of a feather flock together. When wrapping up a conversation, a natural way to request a referral is to ask if there are any people in their network that you should meet. Make a mental note that professionals like attorneys, CPAs, and financial planners can be excellent sources for new introductions, especially once you earn their trust.

Don't forget to show your appreciation to those who refer you. Make sure to acknowledge every investor referral, even if they don't end up investing. Showing appreciation for your referral partners encourages ongoing support. Show your gratitude with a personal thank-you card or better yet, step into your role as a power connector and hook them up with valuable connections from your own network.

Being genuine matters and saying thank you regularly helps you get more referrals. To build strong relationships with your referral partners, keep in touch, share helpful insights and resources, and always provide value, not just when you need something. When you prioritize long-term relationships and mutual benefits, you create a referral network that boosts your success.

Here's a quick idea - If you'd like to help us and other entrepreneurs right away, here is one way you can do it. If this book has given you any value, can you do us a favor? It'll only take a minute to leave an honest review, and it would really make a difference. Also, when you show someone something valuable, they start associating that value with you. Got any entrepreneur friends who might enjoy this book? When you're done reading this, pass it their way or send them a copy! It's a great way to boost your rep and build some goodwill with others.

# THE IMPORTANCE OF AUTHORITY

As we've explored the importance of building and nurturing your network, it's clear that connections are the lifeblood of successful dealmaking. However, to truly maximize the potential of your network and stand out in the competitive world of private investments, you need to establish yourself as a trusted authority in your field. The level of authority you've build up over time can give you an edge that can help you make real difference in investment outcomes, attract top-notch investors, and close those big, high-level deals. When you're seen as an expert or leader in your industry, people are more likely to trust your judgment and be convinced by your ideas. When it comes down to it, having authority takes you from being a regular participant in private investing to being a leader in the space.

Check out this story that'll give you a whole new perspective on authority's influence. Yale University ran this experiment in 1972 that stirred up a lot of controversy about the power of authority to make people do what they're told. It may sound extreme, but they had to use a device to shock someone in another room for each wrong answer, and the voltage increased each time. This study, known as the Milgram experiment, demonstrated the powerful influence of perceived authority on human behavior, even when it conflicts with personal morals.

Psychologists thought less than 1% of people would go to the highest voltage level, but 67% actually did. The recorded high voltage levels became pretty concerning, but people didn't stop shocking even after they heard screams and then it got quiet in the other room, all because the guy in the lab coat told them to keep going.

The experiment was performed with different groups of people and in various situations, and the outcomes remained the same. It is common for individuals to follow authority figures, even if they have reservations.

It's not due to any specific script or technique, but rather a profound psychological response.

Authority might be considered the biggest factor in influencing human behavior. By displaying authority, effective communication, charisma, and empathy, you can significantly influence others. It's like a form of "social hacking." This could be rooted in humanity's history, where disobeying leaders often led to dire consequences. Tapping into this instinct can seriously impact decision-making.

There are four things - focus, authority, tribe, and emotion - that really impact how we act, especially when it comes to following along. These things work together to shape how we react. The first step to being a strong leader is getting people's attention and holding onto it. The biggest challenge for a leader is to make sure their team, colleagues, or audience are fully engaged, not just there. Without this fundamental level of attention, even the most insightful ideas or well-crafted strategies will fall flat. Another thing, you need to prove your authority to effectively guide the team. If you don't have this, your leadership role won't be effective. Third, one cannot underestimate the importance of fostering a feeling of belonging among the group. If people feel isolated or left out, they won't feel connected to the group, and that can mess with how well they perform. Lastly, make sure to keep things positive and enjoyable. People need emotional engagement in order to sustain the positive behaviors that drive success. So in short, leadership is all about grabbing attention, taking charge, making everyone feel like they're part of the team, and keeping them motivated with positive feedback.

We tend to pay more attention to new and interesting things. Our ancestors had to keep their eyes peeled to spot any risks or unique opportunities for their survival. In modern contexts, unexpected situations or information can create this same intense focus. The Milgram experiment exemplifies how novelty generates focus. The people who were participating had never experienced anything like it before - the place, the task, the equipment, and the whole situation. This novelty-induced focus then allows authority to take hold more easily. Interrupting established patterns or habits can also generate focus. This technique is a big deal when it comes to influencing behavior, whether it's in personal interactions or on social media. So, if you switch gears in the middle of a conversation, it can really shake things up and make people more open to fresh ideas.

It's not just about having tangible power, but how people perceive it that gives authority. To have authority, you need confidence, discipline, leadership skills, gratitude, and an element of enjoyment. When you've got all these things, people will start seeing you as an authority and listening to you more. Authority comes first, but "tribe" is a close second. Being social is just part of being human and we naturally want to fit in with a group. If someone seems like they're in charge, we're more likely to trust and follow them. The last element in this sequence is all about emotions and how when people enjoy what they're doing, they're more likely to keep doing it.

When trying to convince others, it's important to talk in a way that connects with their basic instincts. This approach, focusing on these four elements and communicating through non-verbal cues, can be more effective in eliciting desired responses than purely logical or verbal arguments.

# ESTABLISHING YOUR ONLINE PRESENCE

Let's build on what we talked about and see how authority and influence play out online. In today's world, being an online authority can make a big difference in how credible and influential you are in your field.

Building a strong online presence through social media and content creation shows that you know your stuff. Having a strong online presence can make a great first impression when people plug your name into a search engine. Here are a few ways you can build your online authority:

- Consistently sharing valuable, relevant content in your area of expertise

- Engaging with others in your field through thoughtful discussions and collaborations

- Showcasing your achievements, qualifications, and experiences

- Developing a distinctive personal brand that aligns with your professional goals

- Leveraging social proof through testimonials, endorsements, and case studies

When people find you online, they can have the same reactions we talked about earlier - they'll be interested in your unique ideas, see you as an expert, feel like they're part of your professional community, and have positive feelings about your work.

Just remember, it's all about being ethical and authentic when establishing your online authority. Don't try to deceive or manipulate, just focus on providing real value and building trust. When you do this, you can create a strong synergy between your online presence and real-life interactions, which boosts your ability to lead, influence, and make a positive impact in your field.

Now, let's shift our focus to the strategies that will help you build a strong personal brand and position yourself as an expert. By combining a robust network with a reputation for expertise, you'll create a powerful foundation for attracting high-quality investors and closing deals more effectively.

Taking time to build authority and a personal brand is an important piece of the puzzle in successful dealmaking that often gets forgotten. Authority is valuable social proof to investors and will help you stand out from the competition. It's essential to share your expertise consistently, engage with your audience, and gain recognition to build a solid reputation and earn trust. This can be achieved by leveraging multiple channels such as LinkedIn, X (Twitter), YouTube, and Substack, as well as through blogging, podcasting, and public speaking engagements. This approach helps you build a loyal community and compete effectively with bigger players in the investment world. You can really stand out in a saturated market when you highlight your unique qualities and become an influential figure in your industry.

Consistency and repetition are vital in establishing yourself as an authority. Successful dealmakers have become synonymous with their fields by maintaining consistent messaging and demonstrating expertise regularly. Think of how Chris Voss is associated with negotiation or Warren Buffett with investing. The more you create and share content about your work, the quicker you'll establish your authority.

It's really worth it to be seen as an expert in private investing. Because you're a trusted expert, you naturally attract more lucrative deals and collaborations, and your opinions will carry more weight. This elevated status significantly enhances your deal-making capabilities, extending your reach and impact in the industry. If you're new to this, creating content can be tough, but it's not impossible. Keep it real and share authentic updates about your day, celebrate when you close a deal, and don't be shy about discussing challenges and lessons. This transparency helps build trust and relatability with your audience.

Once you have a potential investor's interest, they'll likely look you up online. Not having a strong online presence can make it difficult to win over investors. On the other hand, a killer online presence makes it so much easier to close deals. As you start seeing profits, think about putting more into creating content at a larger scale. Eventually, this strategy will bring in a bunch of leads that convert really well, all because of the trust you built with your content.

If you're confused about where to start, I can point you in the right direction by introducing you to my friend Clifton Sellers and his team at Legacy Builder (https://www.legacybuilder.co/). They've done an awesome job helping some folks in my network make a real impact online. And don't forget, in the investment and dealmaking world, having a strong online presence is not just good, it's absolutely essential for establishing authority and attracting the right investors to your ventures.

# CREATE A NEWSLETTER

In addition to building social media content, creating your own newsletter is one of the best ways to grow your audience and establish authority for your brand. It's a straightforward way to stay connected and boost your brand. It doesn't have to be fancy, just a quick update on what's been going on in your life or business in the past month can work wonders. The main goal is to keep your audience informed and build a list of contacts who really want to know what you're up to.

We've been doing these personal newsletter updates for a while now. This is a chance for investors to see our progress firsthand and we've found that many get emotionally invested in our projects. Sharing our journey, challenges, and successes online on a regular basis helps us keep our readers connected and interested in our work. This approach works great for building relationships with investors and partners and establishing our credibility.

Platforms like Beehiiv, Substack, and LinkedIn have totally shaken up the content game, and I gotta give a shoutout to Tyler Denk and the folks at Beehiiv (www.beehiiv.com) - they're doing amazing things. These platforms allow you to publish articles, send updates to subscribers, and have a public page for readers. This approach helps more people see your content and keeps it around for a long time.

When it comes to creating content for your newsletter, try these strategies: go over your sent emails for common questions or topics you've covered with clients, keep a place to quickly write down ideas, and read a bunch to expand what you know. With these approaches, you'll never be short on content when you need to write.

Newsletters aren't just for immediate results, you never know when someone might reach out because of something you wrote ages ago. Lots of people hold back because they think they don't have anything important to say, but that's hardly ever the case. Even if you're new to the industry, your perspective and experiences matter.

Newsletter writing has benefits beyond audience building. The act of expressing your thoughts on paper consistently can deepen your understanding and expertise in your field. Engaging in the process of "writing to learn" hones your communication skills and cements your understanding of complex topics. Start small, stay consistent, and watch your influence grow over time.

# GET A QUALITY HEADSHOT

Another thing to consider is that your personal image can be just as important as your financial skills. The importance of a professional headshot cannot be overstated and this small detail can have a significant impact on your ability to attract investors and build trust.

First impressions are formed with remarkable speed. A study published in the Cognition And Emotion Journal in 2012[i] found that trust decisions are made within a mere 100 milliseconds of seeing a face. Your headshot is super important in shaping how potential investors see you before you even get a chance to pitch your SPV.

---

i     *https://www.ncbi.nlm.nih.gov/pmc/articles/PMC7424118/*

Having a good photo helps people connect with you, which is especially important in an industry that's often seen as impersonal and focused on numbers.

The style of your headshot should align with your brand and target audience. While traditional corporate shots work well in some contexts, a more relaxed yet professional image can be equally effective in some industries. The key is to balance approachability and professionalism. Skip the casual selfies or AI pictures - they won't make you look credible. Invest in a pro photographer to highlight your best features.

Make sure to use the same headshot on all your professional profiles, like LinkedIn, X (Twitter), and other social networks. Virtual personal branding is super important in today's digital world, just like a firm handshake. A professional headshot is far more than just a photograph – it's a powerful tool that can boost your first impression, earn client trust, and show your commitment to quality.

# LEVERAGE PUBLIC RELATIONS

Leveraging Public Relations (PR) is a powerful strategy to gain media exposure and establish yourself as an industry expert. Start by building relationships with journalists, bloggers, and influencers in your field through social media engagement and offering your expertise.

Create a comprehensive media kit with your headshots, bio, and key talking points to facilitate pitching to media outlets. Share press releases for important milestones and look for chances to be featured in top publications. Don't forget, PR is about getting your name out there and building up your reputation. Mentions in prestigious publications like Forbes or Business Insider can significantly boost your credibility.

When your media appearances align with your social media and content marketing, you've got a powerful PR engine. Treat PR as a marathon, start slow and keep growing your efforts. As you refine your purpose and message, your PR efforts will become more focused and effective.

When pitching journalists for PR, make sure your messages are interesting and to the point. Your pitch needs to be brief and impactful, with a subject line that grabs attention in 8-10 words. Keep your pitch organized and easy to follow. Give a brief intro that builds on the headline, followed by a more detailed paragraph about your work and the people you're targeting. Make the third section easy to read with bullet points. Make it brief, around 30-40 words, and end it with a clear call to action.

Ensure your email signature is professional and includes your name, contact information, and links to your active social media profiles. Success requires both patience and the flexibility to refine your approach based on feedback and results.

# PODCAST APPEARANCES

Podcasting has really emerged as a great way to connect with people and boost your personal brand. Its power lies in its ability to foster intimate, in-depth conversations that resonate deeply with listeners. Lots of industry leaders are into podcasts now because they can dive deep into complex topics in a more interesting way.

You don't have to start your own podcast, but going on other podcasts is a brilliant way to grow your audience. Being a guest on a popular show lets you demonstrate your expertise and attract new followers to your own platforms, kick-starting your own following. This head start can majorly ramp up your growth and influence in your niche.

When reaching out to podcast hosts, craft a personalized message that showcases what makes you unique. Podcast hosts aim to bring on guests who are both intriguing and can offer valuable insights, with the goal of boosting engagement and viewership/listenership.

These interviews can help you build a strong personal brand and establish authority. Consider creating a one-page summary to share with journalists and podcast hosts to strengthen your outreach efforts. We've put together an example to give you some inspiration.

[Your Name]: [Your Primary Expertise]

- [2-3 sentences summarizing your key experience, current role, and area of expertise]

**Extended Biography**

- [5-7 sentences detailing your entrepreneurial journey, major achievements, current projects, etc]

**Expertise & Topics**

- [Topic 1]
- [Topic 2]
- [Topic 3]

**Notable Achievements**

- [Achievement 1]
- [Achievement 2]
- [Any relevant awards or recognitions]

**Top Podcast Appearances**

- [Podcast Name] - Episode: "Title"
- [Podcast Name] - Episode: "Title"
- [Podcast Name] - Episode: "Title"

**Social Media & Online Presence**

- LinkedIn: [URL]
- Twitter: [URL]
- Instagram: [URL]
- Facebook: [URL]
- YouTube: [URL]
- Persona website: [URL]
- Business website: [URL]

**Value for Your Audience**

[Your Name] offers actionable insights on:

- [Key topic 1]
- [Key topic 2]
- [Key topic 3]
- [Key topic 4]

**Promotional Support**

- Will actively promote the episode across all social media platforms
- Can provide [any specific offers or resources] for your audience

**Booking Information**

Email: [Your email]
Phone: [Your phone number]
Calendar Link: [URL to your scheduling tool]

Another option for securing podcast appearances is to use a service like PodPitch (www.podpitch.com). Created by Parker Olson, PodPitch offers a monthly subscription that helps you identify relevant podcasts, draft and send outreach emails, and secure a lot of bookings—all within the platform. We've personally used it with great results. Once you've gotten an appearance scheduled, take time to prepare for the interview so you can make the most of the opportunity.

### Optimize Your Technical Setup

When prepping for a podcast, especially one with video, it's super important to get your technical setup right. First, get yourself a good mic and headphones for top-notch audio. A strong internet connection is a must. When you're on video, pick a quiet place with nice lighting to look professional. Don't forget to test your gear and software well in advance to avoid any last-minute glitches.

If you want to step up your on-camera skills, we seriously recommend checking out Sky Stack (www.skykstack.com). He's an absolute genius when it comes to making streams and video appearances look amazing. With the right tweaks, you can transform your home setup into a professional-looking studio, so you look and sound your best.

### Research and Prepare Content

Preparation is crucial for podcast success. Listen to some recent episodes to get a feel for the show's style. Plan some key points and stories, but be cool with going off script. Think about possible questions and practice your responses, keeping the audience's main points in mind. This balanced approach makes sure you're prepared but still yourself, so you can share useful insights while going with the flow. What's the end result? An episode of the podcast that really connects with listeners.

### Engage with the Host and Show

Building a good rapport with the host could make your interview more engaging. If it feels right, drop a thoughtful review on podcast platforms.

### Provide Comprehensive Materials

Don't forget to send the host what they need before your podcast spot so it goes smoothly. Just send a short bio with your top accomplishments, a good headshot, and any links to your work or social media. Include a brief list of specific topics or areas of expertise you're able to to discuss.

### Pre-Interview Preparation

Don't forget to check all your equipment one last time so everything goes smoothly. Hop on the call a few minutes early to handle any last-minute issues. Make sure you have water nearby and turn off all notifications on your devices so you don't get distracted. Before you dive into the interview, take a moment to get yourself in a good mindset. This preparation not only shows professionalism, but also helps you feel more relaxed and focused.

### Post-Interview Planning

Help the host spread the word about the episode after you're done recording. Share your strategies for getting the content out there. Don't forget to have some killer social media posts and email notifications ready to launch when the episode comes out. Get the word out there to reach more people, gain new listeners, and prove your dedication to making the show a success. When you're done with the podcast, make sure to drop the host a nice thank-you email. Don't forget to share any additional info they might need for the show notes. Being proactive and gracious after the interview can help you build a strong professional reputation and maybe even score future collaborations in your industry.

# WEALTH IN NUMBERS

*"The richest people in the world look for and build networks, everyone else looks for work."*

*— Robert Kiyosaki, Investor and Author of Rich Dad Poor Dad*

# GETTING IN THE RIGHT ROOMS

Now that we've explored the importance of building authority and buiilding a valuable network, let's address a common concern. For many dealmakers, the challenge isn't just finding good ideas or opportunities—it's getting in touch with the right people who can stroke a check to get your deal across the line. You know you need to connect with potential investors, but don't have a clue where to begin.

While your growing reputation and community-building efforts will naturally attract some prospects, that's not quite enough. Don't neglect the power of in-person connections to bring your expertise to life. It's important to actively search for other key players to fund your deals. To rub shoulders with wealthy potential investors, you must become part of their social circles. The saying "It's not what you know, but who you know" is totally true, especially for raising capital. But where exactly do you find these affluent individuals? Look for places in your area where you think wealthy people are likely to be and ask yourself, how can you break into these circles? Investors tend have their own networks, but they aren't hiding in some secret enclave.

Sometimes we'll hear someone say that there are "no investors in the area" and they couldn't possibly make a deal happen. Well, unless you're hiding out in the mountains, this is absolutely not true. Investors are all around us every day.

Just keep in mind, when you go to events, it's about forming genuine relationships that can benefit both parties. The reason people go to these events is to make connections. Don't shy away from introducing yourself to key players. Just remember, they want to network too. Nobody wants to miss out on making friends or connections, especially at public events.

They're interested in meeting people who are just as interesting as they are. So, when you go to these events, be ready to socialize and make connections. Start conversations, ask questions, and show genuine interest in others. If you play your cards right, a casual meet-up can become a valuable investment opportunity. The trick is figuring out where these circles overlap with yours and knowing how to navigate them. It's not only about being in the right places—it's about establishing yourself as someone worth knowing and investing in.

## The Networking Cycle for Career Success

Now that we've set the stage for effective networking, let's explore some specific venues and opportunities where you can put these principles into action. Here are a few ideas for where to go to meet potential investors and build your network. These suggestions range from traditional business settings to more unconventional social gatherings, each offering unique opportunities to connect with affluent individuals who might be interested in your deals. Whether you're a seasoned dealmaker or just starting out, these environments can provide fertile ground for expanding your circle of potential investors.

## Mastermind Groups

Joining mastermind groups and professional organizations can really help you grow, just like Napoleon Hill talked about in "Think and Grow Rich." These groups gather people with similar interests in self-improvement, goal-setting, and supporting each other. You have the option to join groups in person or online, or start your own using social media. Joining networks like EO, YPO, and Tiger 21 opens up valuable opportunities, and there are niche-specific mastermind groups you can more easily get involved in. We have our own mastermind group and are fortunate to have curated a really awesome community.

One mistake we often see in mastermind groups is not meeting with other members one-on-one outside of group events. Meeting up for lunch or coffee can help you connect with someone, understand their goals, and uncover potential synergies you may have overlooked. Coordinating these meetups is a bit of work, but it'll really boost your network's value in the long run. Take this extra step and turn casual acquaintances into potential allies, making your professional circle more valuable.

## Conferences

Attending a conferences is a great opportunity to make new connections and build your relationships. Be strategic when deciding which conferences to attend. Don't limit yourself to your industry, explore events where you can meet a diverse group of successful people. A tech conference could have not just software developers, but also venture capitalists, industry leaders, and innovative thinkers from all kinds of sectors. When different ideas and skills come together, some pretty awesome connections can happen.

Take the initiative at the event. A thoughtful question after the panel can pave the way for a more meaningful conversation later on. Think about attending the smaller breakout sessions or workshops. These more intimate settings often provide better opportunities for one-on-one interactions with speakers and other attendees. They're also fantastic spots to showcase your expertise and make a lasting impression on others.

Don't underestimate the power of social events surrounding the conference. Cocktail hours, networking dinners, and even informal gatherings at nearby venues can be where the real magic happens. In these relaxed settings, conversations flow more freely, and relationships can develop naturally. Lastly, don't limit yourself to traditional business conferences in your niche. The key is to stay curious and open to opportunities across various fields.

## Private Clubs, Upscale Bars & Cocktail Parties

Just imagine being in a place where success fills the air and power is all around. You can expect this kind of atmosphere at spots like Soho House, 5 Hertford Street, or The Club at The Ivy. These members-only clubs are more than just luxurious spaces – they're about being in the right place at the right time, mingling with influential individuals who can open doors you didn't even know existed.

But hey, getting into these exclusive places isn't always easy. A lot of times, you'll need a referral from an existing member to get in. Oh, and by the way, there's usually a price tag—annual fees can start at around $2,500 and increase from there. But for a lot of people, it's an investment in their future, a price to play with the big leagues.

If you can't afford fancy clubs, don't stress. The wealthy don't always sequester themselves behind closed doors. Sometimes, they're just looking to unwind like anyone else—albeit in more refined settings. This is where upscale bars and lounges come into play. Picture a discreet, elegantly appointed bar near the financial district, where deal-makers come to decompress after a long day of high-stakes negotiations. If you can blend in and start a conversation at the right time, these venues are a good way to get into the world of wealth.

For those with a taste for the finer things in life, wine tastings and gourmet events can be goldmines of opportunity. Here, you're not just meeting wealthy individuals; you're connecting with them over shared passions. It's amazing how a discussion about the merits of a particular vintage can develop into talks of business ventures or investment opportunities.

## Car Clubs

Car clubs are a hub for wealthy car enthusiasts who have a passion for luxury and high-performance vehicles. These clubs throw awesome parties, track days, and drives for car enthusiasts. When you join these clubs, you'll be able to chat about the newest car models, racing, and the latest car tech. If you want to enjoy it to the fullest, it's good to know about cars and be ready to share your own experiences and interests in the car world.

Maybe you've seen the classic Burt Reynolds movie Cannonball Run, well there's real groups that take their sports cars on a cruise across multiple states. Our first taste of this was in 2002 with the release of the movie "Mischief 3000," which documented the Teckademics crew crashing the Gumball 3000 rally. Besides the Gumball 3000, there are other cool car rally groups like Express Rally, Corsa America, GoldRush Rally, and LongTail Rally.

These exclusive rallies and events offer car enthusiasts the ultimate opportunity to indulge their passion on the open road. While not without controversy, they continue to attract wealthy gearheads seeking adventure and camaraderie. For those with the means and desire, joining one of these elite car clubs can provide access to unforgettable experiences and connections in the world of high-performance automobiles. Just remember to be responsible and stay safe when you're out on the road.

## Country Clubs, Golf and Racquet Clubs

Country clubs have a longstanding reputation as a venue for high-end networking opportunities that have stood the test of time. In the world of high-end clubs and golf courses, where wealth and opportunity meet like morning dew on perfectly manicured greens. And let's admit it, sinking a challenging putt can make even the most poker-faced investor warm up to you.

It's common knowledge that wealthy folks love to socialize, and these venues are perfect for mingling with potential investors and high-class individuals. They offer the best of both worlds: leisure and networking, allowing relationships to develop naturally.

If you've never been to one, a country club is a private place that offers a range of social events and sports. These clubs usually have a clubhouse and lots of space, with amenities like golf courses, tennis courts, swimming pools, pickleball courts, and platform tennis facilities. Additionally, country clubs often offer dining options, bars, and fitness centers for their members.

But don't worry if your golf game isn't up to par (pun intended). Lots of country clubs and golf courses offer lessons, so you can meet other beginners who might also be successful professionals looking to make new connections. Keep in mind, it's not about being the best golfer, it's about being an interesting person to chat with while playing.

The key to success in these environments is authenticity. Yes, you're there to network, but you're also there to enjoy the sport. Show genuine interest in improving your game, and you'll find that advice flows freely – both on and off the court. This shared passion creates an instant bond, making it easier to steer conversations towards business and investment opportunities when the time is right.

Don't be discouraged if you're not immediately rubbing elbows with millionaires. Many of these clubs have different membership tiers or guest policies. Start where you can, and work your way up. Attend club events, participate in tournaments, or become a volunteer for charity games. These activities not only improve your visibility but also demonstrate your commitment to the community – a trait highly valued in business circles.

## Antique Fairs

Enter the world of antique and vintage fairs and get ready to be amazed by the captivating mix of history, wealth, and passion. These events are way more than just places to find old knick-knacks. They're where rich collectors, savvy investors, and history fanatics come together to indulge in their love for rare and exquisite items.

If you're not familiar with these fairs, they can seem pretty overwhelming. But don't let that deter you. You can have deep conversations that go way beyond talking about prices and where things come from. Just remember, many people think their antique collections are a smart way to invest, not just a luxury.

The relaxed atmosphere at these fairs makes it easier to approach wealthy folks than in formal situations. Whether it's a charming local fair or a fancy international event, the important thing is to approach each interaction with curiosity and respect for the history on display. Ask thoughtful questions, share interesting tidbits you've learned, and don't be afraid to admit when you're encountering something new.

## Luxury Gyms

High-end gyms attract health-conscious, affluent individuals who value exclusivity and premium facilities. These gyms often double as informal networking hubs, where business deals can be casually discussed between sets or in the sauna. Stay open to friendly chats during your workout - you never know who you might meet! It's important to respect others' space, as many people use the gym as a sanctuary to unwind and decompress.

If you're near a major city, consider visiting well-known gym chains with multiple locations, such as Equinox and Life Time. These spots are popular with the more affluent gym crowd and offer a chance to network while getting fit.

## Art Galleries

Enter a world where culture, wealth, and opportunity combine like colors on a painter's palette. Art galleries have long been magnets for the affluent, drawing in those who see value not just in brushstrokes and sculptures, but in the cultural cachet and investment potential that fine art represents. These spaces are more than mere showrooms; they're sophisticated social arenas where people come to see and be seen, and to discuss artwork with the same passion others might reserve for sports or politics.

Opening nights are the best chance to go. These events often feel like a who's who of local society, with wealthy donors, art investors, and cultural tastemakers mingling over champagne. But don't let the glitz intimidate you. Approach these gatherings with a blend of respect for the art and openness to connection. As you make your way through this high-class environment, always remember that your genuine interest in art is your strongest advantage. If you're curious, ask about the artist's technique or the piece's background. A thoughtful comment about a bold sculpture or an intriguing painting can be the perfect conversation starter with that distinguished-looking individual admiring the same piece. Your curiosity might grab the attention of a collector or gallery visitor who's equally excited – or, hey, they might be on the lookout for unique art perspectives and investment chances.

If you don't immediately click with someone at your first gallery event, don't let it get you down. It takes time and dedication to build relationships in this world. Try to attend openings often, get to know the local art scene, and maybe even think about volunteering or donating to arts organizations. When you do these things, you show you're committed and become more a part of this cultured community.

## Airport Lounges

Take refuge in an oasis from the chaos of a busy airport with plush seating, ambient lighting, and the gentle clinking of ice in crystal tumblers for a far more welcoming atmosphere during your layover. These exclusive spaces are more than just a refuge from crowded terminals; they're impromptu boardrooms, casual meeting spots, and havens for the jet-setting elite. They give you a chance to mingle with successful people in a laid-back yet professional environment. Next time you have a layover, make the most of it. Look at it as a golden chance to make new connections.

Here, you'll find a concentrated pool of successful individuals—C-suite executives, entrepreneurs, and investors—all sharing one common denominator: the means and motivation to travel in style. We were first introduced to airport lounges through the the American Express Centurion Lounge some time ago. Over the years, we have made a ton of great connections there while sharing hors d'oeuvres and discussing our travel destinations.

Don't underestimate how accessible some lounges can be, they're not all ultra-exclusive. Many business travelers gain entry through company perks or premium credit cards. Keep in mind that these lounges are also sanctuaries. Travelers often use them as peaceful workspaces or a chance to take a breather. Respect for privacy is paramount. Your approach should be casual and unforced – perhaps a comment about a delayed flight or a recommendation for a good book can open the door to further conversation.

Lounge networking is awesome because it's super casual. Airport lounges are way more relaxed than formal networking events. We're all travelers here, so we automatically have something in common. Take advantage of this shared experience, but if the chance comes up, you can switch the conversation to business or investments.

Just a reminder, not every interaction has to be about business. The real value is in the connection. The person you talked to about the best Tokyo restaurants might hit you up in six months for a new investment. When you become a regular, you'll start recognizing familiar faces - other frequent flyers who could become valuable connections. If you run into each other, go ahead and say hello again. These repeated encounters can build the familiarity and trust necessary for deeper professional relationships.

## Auction Houses

Auction houses are where the wealthy go to find rare and valuable things, like art, antiques, and jewelry. These events are as much about socializing as they are about business. Even if you're not bidding, talking about the pieces can help you make valuable connections.

When you enter the world of auction houses and you'll be in a place where money, art, and excitement come together in a thrilling mix of paddles and price tags. You might be thinking, "I'm not here to drop a ton of cash on a painting!" Don't be afraid, there's more to attending an auction than just bidding. It's about immersing yourself in this world of wealth and culture. Dress up, but not too flashy. Your attire should hint at success, not shout it from the rooftops.

When there's a break in the bidding wars, start up a casual conversation. "What caught your eye in today's lineup?" can be a great icebreaker. Don't forget, people come to these events to socialize as much as to shop. Chatting about a vintage watch could seamlessly transition into talking about your cool business idea or investment opportunity.

But here's the golden rule: subtlety is key. This isn't the place to push your investment opportunity among the Monets and Renoirs. Instead, just make real connections with people who have similar interests. The wealthy individuals at these events are often drawn to passion and knowledge – demonstrate both, and you'll find doors opening. So, the next time you hear about a high-profile auction in your area, don't dismiss it. See it as your chance to step into a world where art, wealth, and opportunity intersect.

## Open Houses for Luxury Properties

Wealthy people check out luxury property open houses for new homes or investment chances. These events often feature high-end catering and exclusive previews, making them social occasions as well. If you've watched real estate shows like Million Dollar Listing or Selling Sunset, you know how much effort these realtors put into their open houses to attract wealthy buyers. No need to be a potential buyer or in real estate - all are welcome! And who knows, maybe you'll find someone you know who'd be interested in the property. Just reach out to the listing agent if you do. Keep up with the latest events by following posh realtors on social media.

The laid-back atmosphere helps foster open conversations and connections. When you attend luxury property open houses, you meet wealthy investors who appreciate the finer things and have the means to invest in exciting projects.

## Investment & Wealth Management Seminars

These events are for professionals who are looking to make wise investments. Wealthy folks attend these seminars to grow and safeguard their money. They offer valuable information and networking opportunities with both financial experts and other affluent attendees. They offer a chance to network with people who are serious about investing wisely. By attending investment and wealth management seminars, you position yourself in a fertile environment for networking with affluent individuals who are both capable and interested in exploring lucrative investment opportunities.

Dress sharp to make a positive first impression and carry yourself with confidence. Ask insightful questions during Q&A and be ready to talk about your own investment beliefs during breaks. This not only shows your engagement but also positions you as a knowledgeable participant. Mix confidence and humility when you talk to others. Share your insights and genuinely care about what others think. Being yourself can help you connect with investors who appreciate a blend of intelligence, ambition, and genuine curiosity. These interactions can pave the way for discussing possible investment opportunities.

## Hotel Bars

Affluent travelers who are often on the road need a place to stay and as a result, hotel bars in upscale establishments naturally become the place to be. They frequent these bars not only for their ambiance but also for the opportunity to unwind and socialize. These spots offer a sophisticated, yet laid-back atmosphere that is ideal for informal meetups and unexpected encounters. Imagine sitting at the bar, enjoying a well-crafted cocktail, and striking up conversations with people who are well-traveled and knowledgeable.

To increase your chances of meeting someone influential, frequent the bars of top-tier hotels in your area. Upscale hotels are known for their luxurious vibes and attract people who appreciate quality and sophistication. It's important to dress well so you look polished and put-together to make a strong first impression.

Since the atmosphere of an upscale hotel bar is conducive to organic, relaxed conversations, use this to your advantage to take time building rapport. As conversations progress, naturally steer the discussion towards your areas of expertise and what deals you have an interest in.

## Charity Events & Galas

Charity galas and fundraising events are not just about philanthropy; they're sophisticated gatherings where the who's who of the wealthy and influential come together to support causes close to their hearts. These events are really elegant and have top-notch attendees, so it's a great opportunity to network with potential investors that are there to support their favorite charity.

Do some digging and see what events are coming up nearby. To attend, you can usually get a ticket or sponsor the event somehow. In the beginning, just buy a seat, and as you get more successful, upgrade to buying a table and bring more people along with you. Just get in the same room, hang out, and make connections. If you're strapped for cash, reach out to the event organizers and find out if you can volunteer to get in.

These dinners are all about giving back, but they're also a great way to make a name for yourself in society. But make sure you look your best, first impressions count. Everyone at the event cares about making a difference, so it's a great way to start conversations.

When you're walking around, spot those key players who can not only afford it, but also have a history of supporting innovative ventures. Approach them with respect and enthusiasm, showing that you share their commitment to social impact. It's powerful when you discuss how your work can contribute to making a real impact.

## High End Vacations

Luxury resorts, exclusive beaches, and high-end ski destinations are the playgrounds of the wealthy, providing them with a serene escape from the demands of their busy lives. These luxurious retreats offer more than just relaxation—they become informal networking hubs where affluent individuals gather to unwind and enjoy premium experiences.

Choosing the right destination is key. Pick the swanky resorts and popular vacation spots that attract wealthy people. Engage in activities that are favored by the affluent, such as golfing at a renowned course, taking a culinary class at a five-star resort, or skiing at an exclusive mountain retreat. These activities are not only fun but also give you a chance to meet new people.

While it's important to be open to casual conversations, always respect others' privacy and their need for downtime. Wealthy people like to take these vacations to unwind after a busy work schedule. Take it easy and be polite when you're talking to others, let the conversation happen naturally without being pushy. While the number of potential connections may be limited, the quality of interactions is often higher, with individuals more inclined to have meaningful conversations.

## Yacht Clubs

Yacht clubs are a key gathering place for affluent individuals who have a passion for sailing, boating, and the luxurious lifestyle that accompanies these activities. These swanky clubs put on regattas and social events and have awesome facilities, building a vibrant community centered around maritime culture. Picture yourself at a stunning marina, the sun setting over a fleet of pristine yachts, as you engage in conversations with seasoned sailors and wealthy boating enthusiasts.

If you have an interest in sailing or boating, joining a prestigious yacht club can open doors to a network of wealthy individuals. Participation in club events is a fantastic way to immerse yourself in the community and demonstrate your genuine interest in maritime activities. The exclusivity of yacht clubs means that membership is often selective and may require sponsorship from an existing member. However, the investment in becoming a member can be well worth it, providing access to a network of affluent individuals who share common interests.

## Aviation Events

Rub shoulders with wealthy aviation fans at exclusive airport events, air races, and private aviation shows. Whether they are pilots, private jet owners, or enthusiasts of the luxurious aviation lifestyle, these events attract a sophisticated crowd where technical interest meets high-end living. Imagine strolling through an airfield lined with sleek, state-of-the-art aircraft, the hum of engines in the background, as you engage in conversations with affluent attendees.

To truly soar in this rarefied air, you need to speak the language. Brush up on your knowledge of avionics, fuel efficiency, and the latest in luxury cabin design. Remember, for many attendees, these aren't just modes of transport – they're symbols of success and freedom. Your goal is to position yourself as a peer, someone who "gets it."

And let's not forget the air races and flight demonstrations. These high-octane events attract a special breed of thrill-seekers – wealthy individuals who are used to calculated risks and high returns. As you watch pilots push the boundaries of physics, you might just find yourself standing next to a potential investor who's equally interested in pushing the boundaries of business and finance.

When you're mingling at these events, be excited and respectful when discussing technical topics with others. Engage in discussions about the latest aircraft technology, innovative aviation solutions, and the joys of flying. Share your own travel experiences or any insights you have gained about the industry. Be prepared to discuss the pros and cons of fractional ownership versus full jet ownership, after all, it's a great way to start talking about the use of Special Purpose Vehicles. These interactions can pave the way for deeper discussions about potential investment opportunities.

As the sun sets on the airfield and the last of the demonstration flights touch down, the real action often moves to exclusive after-parties in airport hangars or nearby luxury resorts. Here, in more relaxed settings, is where many of the most lucrative connections are made. Be prepared to continue the conversation over a drink, always keeping in mind that in this world, today's casual acquaintance could be tomorrow's key investor.

## Fashion Week

Imagine being seated among the fashion elite, the runway lights casting a sophisticated glow, as you immerse yourself in the world of haute couture and style. Fashion Week events are a major draw for wealthy people who are obsessed with luxury fashion, whether they're big spenders, designers, or industry insiders. These glamorous events show off the latest trends and designs and are important social gatherings for wealthy people.

To make the most of Fashion Week, stay in the loop with fashion trends and know your stuff when it comes to top designers and their collections. When you're prepared, you can have really interesting talks with people at the event. Demonstrating your enthusiasm and understanding of fashion can help you build rapport with influential attendees.

Make sure your outfit is stylish and appropriate for the event. Looking sharp not only helps you fit in but also makes a great first impression. These events are a great opportunity to meet wealthy people who love style and sophistication.

## Sporting Events

Don't underestimate the power of sporting events - they're perfect for networking and building connections. The best places to meet people at these events are tailgates and box seats. Think of tailgates as laid-back parking lot parties where fans meet up, eat, drink, and have a good time before going to the game. This casual atmosphere is perfect for connecting with people who have similar interests. The excitement of the game brings people together, making it easier to connect with strangers.

On the other hand, box seats give you a more exclusive place to network. You'll find business leaders, celebrities, and influential folks in these high-end areas. When you're in a box seat, you're bound to run into some well-connected people.

You can score these awesome box seats without breaking the bank. Here are a few strategies to think about.

Leverage your relationships to gain access to exclusive box seats at sporting events. As an example, many financial institutions have partnerships with sports teams or own box seats themselves. By building a strong relationship with your banker, you might receive invitations to these exclusive areas. Alternatively, if you know someone who has access to a box, you could offer to sponsor the food and beverages for the event. This approach can be a cost-effective way to gain access while also showcasing your generosity.

Whether you're cheering from a rowdy tailgate or sipping champagne in a luxurious box seat, sporting events provide unique opportunities to expand your network. With the right approach, you can turn your passion for sports into valuable professional connections.

### High-Stakes Poker

Welcome to the crazy world of high-stakes poker, where fortunes are made and lost with every card, and the real game goes way beyond the table. These events, often held in luxurious settings, provide a unique blend of excitement and exclusivity, attracting those who have millions to wager. This isn't your average casino floor. We're talking about exclusive events where the buy-in might be more than most people's annual salary.

Between hands, or in the lounges next to the gaming rooms, people strike deals, form partnerships, and discuss investment opportunities with the same casualness as ordering another round of single malt scotch.

Don't be surprised if you find yourself in a casual conversation about your investment deals while waiting for the next hand to be dealt. The beauty of these events is that business and pleasure blend seamlessly. Remember, discretion is key. What happens in these rooms stays in these rooms. If people trust you with secrets and opportunities, you'll be amazed at the doors that will open for you. Even if you don't play poker, it's still worth being part of this scene. Spectators are encouraged at many high-stakes games, especially if you're recommended by someone already in the circle.

## High-End Spas

High-end spas are the epitome of relaxation and luxury, attracting wealthy individuals who seek to rejuvenate and unwind in serene environments. Imagine yourself at a luxurious spa resort, surrounded by tranquil gardens and soothing treatments, as you engage in calm, meaningful conversations with affluent patrons.

The relaxed environment of a spa is conducive to composed, genuine interactions. Wealthy individuals at these retreats are there to de-stress and enjoy their time, making them more open to meeting new people. Approach conversations with an easygoing attitude, discussing the various treatments and experiences you've enjoyed at the spa.

While you won't find the rowdy atmosphere of a sports bar, the serene setting of a high-end spa fosters a different kind of connection—one that is more personal and thoughtful. Engage in light conversation about the benefits of different treatments, your favorite relaxation techniques, and perhaps even the luxurious amenities the spa offers. The calm ambiance of a spa allows for more meaningful interactions, where connections can be made on a personal level before transitioning to professional interests.

## Film Festivals

If you want to rub shoulders with wealthy folks in showbiz and beyond, film festivals like Cannes, Sundance, and Toronto are the place to be. You don't want to miss these events - they combine culture, parties, and networking like nothing else.

Be prepared to discuss films, directors, and industry trends. Your passion and understanding of the art will make you a more engaging conversation partner. Securing a ticket to a red carpet event and the accompanying party can be a golden opportunity, as these social gatherings are often filled with influential individuals. Preparation is key. Make sure you're familiar with the people, movies, and projects at the festival. This awareness will help you have good conversations and find genuine connections. Just so you know, SPVs are commonly used to finance film projects.

Dress to impress, reflecting the sophisticated and stylish ambiance of the festival. Remember, talk time may be limited prior to the film screenings, so make your interactions count. Express genuine curiosity about the attendees' experiences and contributions to the industry. This approach helps you form stronger connections and shows you're serious about the film community. These events offer a unique platform to connect with influential figures who appreciate both the art of cinema and the opportunities for investment in innovative ventures.

## Fine Dining Establishments

There are lots of affluent individuals that might fashion themselves as "foodies" and appreciate the art of fine dining. They work hard and enjoy indulging in exquisite meals, making fine dining establishments prime locations to make connections. These individuals frequent both high-end restaurants and charming local spots near their homes or workplaces, where they can enjoy a meal and unwind from a busy week.

If you want a casual and friendly vibe, grab a seat at the bar to mingle with new folks. Go ahead and strike up a conversation with the bartender at these spots. Bartenders often have the inside scoop on the regulars and can help you meet them.

Know your stuff when it comes to different cuisines, wine pairings, and dining etiquette. This knowledge will allow you to participate in sophisticated dinner discussions, making you an engaging companion at the table. These venues are perfect for mingling with wealthy folks who know how to live it up. It's a great chance to talk about investments and make some solid connections.

## Political Party Events

Political fundraisers and events are like magnets for wealthy people who want to influence policy and support their favorite candidates. These get-togethers are where the elite mingle, network, and have a say in shaping the future.

Make sure you dress appropriately to match the occasion. Your appearance should convey professionalism and respect for the political environment. Make sure you're up to speed on current political issues and ready to have respectful discussions to really make the most of these events. You can score some major brownie points with the VIPs by adding to the right conversations.

These events go beyond the here and now. They're all about playing the long game. That person you're talking to might not be an investor right now, but they could be your ticket to success later on.

## Alumni Gatherings

For prestigious colleges and universities, alumni gatherings are relatively common. These events attract successful and affluent individuals who value their alma mater and the connections it brings. Attending gives you the opportunity to network with accomplished professionals, increasing your chances of forming important relationships.

Alumni get-togethers are valuable, even if you didn't attend the school. You might have to answer some questions about your affiliation, but showing genuine interest in the institution can help bring you closer. Discussing the school's latest achievements, notable alumni, or recent developments can serve as excellent icebreakers. Be ready to chat about common interests and your professional background. Be confident and authentic in your interactions. People value genuine conversations that go beyond surface-level networking.

## Volunteering

Last but not least, volunteering with a nonprofit offers a unique opportunity to build a powerful network while making a positive impact in your community. A lot of people miss out on this strategy, but working with a nonprofit can provide you with a rewarding experience and connect you with amazing people.

During our time volunteering for nonprofit boards, we never tried to pitch our deals. Instead, we observed, served, and learned from the committee members. Our genuine efforts did not go unnoticed, and we gradually had opportunities to interact more closely with them, including a few lunches. At the time, we were seeking capital for one of our first deals, but we approached these interactions with the intention to learn, not to sell.

One gentleman, a successful real estate investor with hundreds of properties, became a significant mentor. Instead of asking him for money, we sought his advice on finding investors for an opportunity we were working on. Impressed with our volunteer work, he referred potential investors to us, significantly aiding our early efforts.

We didn't really ask for anything on this journey, we were more about learning and giving back. This approach helped us gain trust and respect.

Our mentors began actively supporting us, recommending us to others. Humbling ourselves and committing to service has paid off immensely, both personally and professionally.

## Hosting Your Own Events

When we first started out, we put together a small investment group. We set out to form a group with different professionals from all walks of life: lawyers, real estate professionals, accountants, business owners. We let them know how being part of the group would benefit everyone and help us all grow.

Despite being new to private investments, our vision and initiative brought them together. They didn't care that we didn't have much experience and liked that we worked hard to start the group. Taking the time to do this helped us bring together a team of successful pros with loads of experience and capital to invest. We soon realized the importance of surrounding yourself with skilled and motivated people. You can shape your network, even without a lot of resources.

Since we had a good start, we realized that hosting or speaking at live events is a fantastic way to attract potential investors, build authority and grow our network. These events give you the chance to establish your reputation and meet with potential investors. You should think about teaming up with people who have big networks to co-host the event or even ask them to sponsor refreshments. It can make the gathering even better by offering food, drinks, and giveaways to boost attendance. Make sure your events have a clear investor-focused theme and takeaway so they provide value. When you host events and build a community, you're not just growing your network - you're actually shaping it, creating opportunities for yourself and others along the way.

*"Information is power, but relationships are prosperity."*
— *Tom Peters, Management Expert and Author*

# BUILD YOUR CONTACT DATABASE

The power of connections and networking we've discussed is the foundation for building a successful investment venture. But to really make the most out of this power, you need a system to manage and take advantage of your expanding network. This is why having a comprehensive contact database will prove to be a valuable asset when it's time to start raising capital. As we shift our focus to the practical aspects of networking, let's explore how to start and nurture this list to transform your networking efforts into tangible opportunities.

When you meet someone new, it's a good idea to take notes—while mental notes are helpful, writing things down can be more effective as your list expands. Even having brief notes like "searching for real estate partnerships," "venture capital for tech startups," or "diverse portfolio seeking passive income investments" is a firm foundation.

Although it requires time and effort, creating and maintaining this list at first, it can end up saving you time in the long run. It will be much easier for you to contact the right folks and present your deal. The best time to start creating your investor database was yesterday, but the next best time is now. In practical terms, the person with the most extensive database of potential investors has a significant advantage.

Begin by mining your existing network. Look through your current contacts before seeking new connections. Your database should include a wide range of contacts, from long-term investors to recent acquaintances.

Start by creating a list with all potential investors. Include family members, old classmates, business acquaintances, and even interesting people you've met at social gatherings. Don't self-censor; add anyone who might remotely fit the investor profile, even if you're hesitant to approach them now. Your social media friends list can be a valuable resource to jog your memory.

For each contact, gather comprehensive information: full name, contact details, location, and how you met them. When possible, note their preferred investment areas. Make note of your contacts with any helpful information you may know like their investment activity or interests. You can also include notes about your past interactions or any relevant personal insights.

Now that you have your list of new connections as well as old friends and acquaintances, you'll be able to organize your efforts a bit better. As you make new connections, follow up with them to make sure those valuable leads don't go cold. Send a personalized message within a day or two of meeting someone new. You can reference specific points from your conversation, mention an interesting event that's coming up in the near future or suggest some ways collaborate.

In addition to the contacts you've already made, start a target list of "whales" - high-net-worth individuals you haven't met yet but want to connect with. These should be people who you think could make a substantial difference in your deals. Note any mutual connections or events you think you could attend and meet these people.

As your network expands, this list can become difficult to manage, so it's a good idea to think about making use of CRM software for tracking everything. Good CRM software will integrate with your calendar and email for seamless management. When you're just getting started, if you don't have the cash to invest in a CRM, there are lots of online database management tools that are free and easy-to-use. You can start to build a list there for free and transfer your data over to another platform once you have the ability to invest in something more sophisticated. Either way, the key is to organize your contacts and maintain consistent communication with them. If you're getting started with a free solution, you can start to build out a list that looks something like this:

| A Name | Email | Phone | Focus | Status | Location | Notes |
|---|---|---|---|---|---|---|
| John Doe | johndoe@doemail.com | (555) 555-5555 | AI Robotics | Reached Out | Bentonville | |
| John Doe | johndoe@doemail.com | (555) 555-5555 | Enterprise SaaS | Reached Out | Boston | |
| Jane Doe | janedoe@doemail.com | (555) 555-5555 | Blockchain | Meeting Scheduled | Miami | Introduced by Big Jim |
| John Doe | johndoe@doemail.com | (555) 555-5555 | Enterprise SaaS | First Meeting Complete | Miami | |
| Jane Doe | janedoe@doemail.com | (555) 555-5555 | FinTech | Second Meeting Complete | San Francisco | |
| Jane Doe | janedoe@doemail.com | (555) 555-5555 | Enterprise SaaS | Second Meeting Complete | Boston | |
| John Doe | johndoe@doemail.com | (555) 555-5555 | Consumer | Declined | San Francisco | |
| Jane Doe | janedoe@doemail.com | (555) 555-5555 | Real Estate | In Dilligence | Boston | |
| John Doe | johndoe@doemail.com | (555) 555-5555 | Enterprise SaaS | In Dilligence | Bentonville | |
| Jane Doe | janedoe@doemail.com | (555) 555-5555 | Enterprise SaaS | Declined | Boston | |
| Jane Doe | janedoe@doemail.com | (555) 555-5555 | Consumer | Meeting Scheduled | Bentonville | |
| John Doe | johndoe@doemail.com | (555) 555-5555 | Enterprise SaaS | First Meeting Complete | Dallas | Early NewCo investor |
| Jane Doe | janedoe@doemail.com | (555) 555-5555 | Consumer | Second Meeting Complete | Dallas | |
| John Doe | johndoe@doemail.com | (555) 555-5555 | FinTech | Declined | San Francisco | |
| Jane Doe | janedoe@doemail.com | (555) 555-5555 | Consumer | In Dilligence | Boston | |
| John Doe | johndoe@doemail.com | (555) 555-5555 | Enterprise SaaS | Reached Out | Dallas | |
| Jane Doe | janedoe@doemail.com | (555) 555-5555 | Consumer | Second Meeting Complete | Boston | |
| John Doe | johndoe@doemail.com | (555) 555-5555 | Enterprise SaaS | In Dilligence | New York | Loves the Nets |
| Jane Doe | janedoe@doemail.com | (555) 555-5555 | Enterprise SaaS | Declined | Boston | |

Your database should be constantly growing and changing along with your network, and it's what makes your fundraising efforts possible. By carefully managing this valuable resource you're building a path to potential partnerships and opportunities. Our database is like gold to us, the heart of everything we do. We absolutely need it, no exaggeration. That's why we keep pouring a ton of resources into maintaining, expanding, and improving it. Knowledge is power, and a well-kept database is an amazing knowledge hub. Start today, be thorough, and watch your network and potential for success skyrocket.

# WEALTH IN NUMBERS

*"The quality of your investors matters as much as the quality of your team."*
*— Ben Horowitz, Co-founder of Andreessen Horowitz*

# THE ART OF INVESTOR SELECTION

One of the biggest mistakes people make when trying to raise money is rushing the process. If you show up out of the blue, pitch a deal, and expect an immediate investment, you're likely setting yourself up for disappointment. Before people invest with you, you need to establish some level of trust and build a relationship. Raising capital can be challenging and time-consuming, so it's important to be proactive and have a reliable process established. Timing is key—you don't want to find yourself scrambling for funds at the last minute. Plan ahead and give yourself plenty of time to secure the investment you need.

Beginning conversations about potential deals in your pipeline well in advance of your raise's official launch is a strategic move that puts you ahead of the game. Engaging in early conversations allows you to gauge how much interest there is in your deal before officially launching the fundraising process. This approach also helps you strengthen relationships with potential investors, making them feel involved and valued from the outset. Plus, you'll have a list of investors who show interest, so you'll be ready to call them back when you're ready to get capital commitments in place.

Making this effort to be proactive can make all the difference in how your next deal goes. Instead of scrambling to secure funding at the eleventh hour, you'll be in a position to confidently fill your raise with a strong network of committed investors.

When you're on the hunt for people to approach for your SPV, your immediate network of friends and family is a good place to start. You might feel uneasy about pitching investment deals to friends and family, but remember that these people are not investing as a favor to you. This is a chance for them to grow their wealth. In today's investment landscape, they need your expertise. It's your responsibility to educate them about becoming passive partners in your venture. Even if they don't invest, sharing your excitement can turn them into your greatest supporters.

Friends and family can serve as a great funding option. They've seen for themselves how dedicated you are and are more likely to believe in your ambitious dreams. Their investment is not just financial support but also a vote of confidence that can be a powerful motivator. Discussing your vision over a casual dinner with your closest circle can make the fundraising process more approachable.

Some people hesitate to involve their friends and family due to fear of failure. However, if you're planning to fail, you shouldn't be pursuing the venture at all. While it's important to discuss your projects with them, you must also acknowledge the risks involved. Use these risks as motivation to push for your deal's success.

That being said, you've gotta communicate clearly when dealing with friends and family investors. Don't hide the risks and don't make the challenges seem easier than they are. They should understand the risk they're signing up for and know that there's a chance they won't see their money again. Provide a realistic timeline and outline potential returns or lack thereof. Honesty is key in managing their expectations. It's super important that you formalize agreements instead of relying on handshakes.

Don't underestimate this group of potential investors. Even if they're not Accredited Investors who can participate in a 506(c) offering, they can likely still invest in a 506(b) raise. Your personal connection allows you to communicate with them directly about investment opportunities without solicitation restrictions.

Leverage your existing relationships to find potential investors. Let them know what you're working on and give them the chance to get involved. Show appreciation to those who invest or refer you to other investors. Nurturing these relationships can provide ongoing benefits when seeking future investments. By managing expectations, fostering open communication, and establishing clear legal boundaries, you can turn friends and family investment into a launchpad for success rather than a source of conflict. Remember, protecting your relationships is just as important as protecting your business.

# INVESTOR CLASSIFICATION

It's important to consider other aspects of finding capital for your deal. While individual investors can be valuable, don't overlook networks of professional investors who might be interested in your project. The type of deal you're proposing will influence which investor groups are most suitable. Take the time to research various types of professional investors and determine where your capital is likely to come from. This research will help you identify which groups are most likely to be interested in funding your business idea and could become your best long-term partners. By understanding the landscape of potential investors, you can target your efforts more effectively and increase your chances of securing the right funding for your venture.

As an example, while Angel Investors tend to invest in a wide range of industries, an Angel Groups may have specific niches they prefer. For more formal organizations like a Venture Funds or Private Equity Firm or Family Office, research their investment preferences to narrow down your choices. By answering a few basic questions about these different investor categories, you can better understand which segments to focus on for your funding needs. This targeted approach will help you connect with investors who are more likely to be interested in your business idea and potentially become valuable long-term partners.

## Angel Investors

Angel Investors are typically wealthy individuals who invest their own capital into early-stage companies. Unlike venture capitalists, who invest other people's money through managed funds, Angel Investors use their own funds to support new and growing businesses and typically operate more flexibly and personally. They often come from various professional backgrounds, including attorneys, accountants, and successful entrepreneurs, sharing a common enthusiasm for fostering innovation. These are individuals you might encounter in your everyday business life, waiting to be approached for their potential to fuel your venture. Angel Investors bring more than just money to the table. They often have specialized knowledge and can provide valuable insights.

Finding people in your social and business networks who share your vision and have knowledge of your industry can be incredibly helpful. These individuals, known as Angel Investors, can provide valuable resources and support. Angel Investors are often willing to take on more risk than other types of investors, and they frequently invest in multiple startup companies. This willingness to take risks makes them great partners for new businesses that are just starting out. Unlike venture capital firms (VCs), which tend to be more cautious, Angel Investors are more likely to support ventures that are still developing and haven't fully established themselves yet. This makes Angel Investors particularly valuable for early-stage companies.

It's usually easy to approach an angel investor. You'd be surprised how often you can pique their interest with a quick chat and a solid pitch deck. Since the investments are usually small, you won't typically encounter long negotiations and might secure funding quickly.

While individual angels are important, angel groups have a different approach. These groups are like clubs where people come together and invest money in new businesses. They can be formal organizations with set rules or informal networks of people who are passionate about supporting new ideas. Getting funding from an angel group usually takes longer than from an individual investor because the group needs time to discuss and agree on the investment.

Finding angel groups, especially informal ones, can be tricky as they don't always have a strong online presence. To find them, try asking people in your business network, successful entrepreneurs, or professionals like lawyers, accountants, and bankers. These people often know about informal groups or have connections in the angel investing world.

Founders and investors often misunderstand the term "angel" as a stage of funding. "Angel investment" is often associated with the earliest stage of raising capital, but that's not the whole story. Angel Investors have diverse roles in funding. Angel Investors and syndicates aren't limited to the initial idea stage. Angels invest at different stages, from the start to early growth, and some invest at every stage. The range of possibilities suggests that "angel" isn't really tied to a distinct funding stage, but more like an investor who can jump in at different stages of a company's progress.

### Venture Capital Funds

Venture Capital (VC) is a form of investment where professional investors put money into promising young companies. VC firms manage funds that target specific types of businesses based on factors like industry, size, and location. When VCs invest, they set up complex agreements that give them certain rights and protections. They aim to make a profit within a few years by selling their stake or taking the company public. Most of this profit (70-80%) goes back to the investors who provided the money for the VC fund.

VC firms are willing to take risks, but they're more cautious than individual Angel Investors who might put smaller amounts into very early-stage companies. They look for businesses that have done their homework, have a strong team, and show some early signs of success. VCs usually want to see their investment pay off within 3-5 years.

It usually takes 2-3 months to complete the various steps involved in securing VC funding. It's a cutthroat industry, with VC firms battling it out to invest in the best companies. In the past, VC firms were managed by accomplished entrepreneurs. Throughout the years, they've grown to cover various professional roles, but VC partners with practical business experience are preferred.

For businesses that have progressed to having a product, customers, a solid team, potential partnerships, and a clear growth strategy, VC could be a good fit. They are especially suitable if you need a large investment and can wait a few months for the funding to come through.

## Private Equity Funds

Private Equity (PE) is an investment strategy that focuses on acquiring stakes in privately held companies or taking public companies private. Unlike publicly traded stocks, PE investments are typically funded by high-net-worth individuals and institutional investors. While similar to Venture Capital (VC), PE generally targets larger and more established companies.

PE firms are known for their hands-on approach to investment management. They actively identify opportunities and manage the companies they invest in, often specializing in specific industries to develop deep expertise. This specialization allows them to add value through operational improvements, strategic changes, and cost optimization, setting PE apart from other investment forms.

To maintain flexibility in their investment strategies, PE firms sometimes use Special Purpose Vehicles (SPVs). These allow firms to pursue attractive opportunities that may fall outside their core fund's parameters without disrupting its focus. SPVs also enable PE firms to isolate risk and potentially take larger stakes in high-potential, higher-risk investments.

The active management style of PE firms involves working closely with the leadership of their portfolio companies. They often acquire controlling stakes through buyouts, leveraging their expertise and resources to drive growth, increase efficiency, and ultimately enhance the company's value and profitability.

In essence, private equity is a sophisticated investment approach that utilizes capital from wealthy individuals and institutions to actively manage and improve companies, with the goal of generating substantial returns through operational enhancements and strategic decision-making.

## Family Offices

Family offices are discreet but powerful players in managing the fortunes of the world's wealthiest families.

But what does "family office" even mean? At its core, a family office is a private wealth management firm established to handle the financial and investment affairs of one or more extremely affluent families. Trust me, these organizations are a lot more intricate than you might think. Family offices aren't just investment tools; they're like protectors of generational wealth. They handle everything from day-to-day accounting to long-term estate planning, tax optimization, and even philanthropic strategy.

The world of family offices is as diverse as the families they serve. On one end of the spectrum, we have Single-Family Offices (SFOs), bespoke operations dedicated to managing the wealth of a single, ultra-high-net-worth family. These SFOs might oversee anywhere from $100 million to several billion dollars in assets, offering a level of personalized service and attention that is unmatched in the financial world. On the other end, we find Multi-Family Offices (MFOs), which pool resources to serve multiple wealthy families, managing portfolios that can stretch into the tens of billions.

Family offices are not only financially powerful, but also have a unique position in the investment world. Unlike traditional institutional investors or venture capital firms, family offices are unencumbered by external pressures or rigid mandates. They have the freedom to set their own rules, follow their own timelines, and pursue investments that align not just with financial goals, but with the values, passions, and legacy aspirations of the families they represent. Understanding the unique approach for family offices is crucial for securing their investment.

Forget solely focusing on high returns. Family offices prioritize aligning your venture with their core values. These values could be social impact, industry expertise, or entrepreneurial spirit. Research the family's background and philanthropic efforts to identify their core values. Demonstrate how your fund complements these values in your pitch.

Not all family offices invest in everything. Some focus on specific asset classes or risk profiles. Before reaching out, understand their investment mandate. Does their mandate align with your fund's strategy? Highlighting this alignment demonstrates you've done your homework and increases your chances of success.

Family offices often have unique established systems and processes that they use for evaluating investments. Some might have strict deadlines or specific investment committee structures. Respect these processes. Don't be discouraged if you miss a deadline; some families have quarterly investment cycles.

Many times, family offices often have ethical investment policies. Gambling ventures, for example, might not align with a family's moral compass. Research potential red flags before pitching to them. Understanding their ethical considerations demonstrates respect and increases your chances of a successful partnership.

Family offices may desire to act as direct investors (limited partners) or as a co-GP. The level of involvement they desire varies. Be upfront about your expectations and ask about theirs. Some families might invest passively, while others might seek active participation.

The key is good communication, so ask them about their investment style and how much they want to be involved. When you have an open dialogue, you can personalize your approach and establish a strong foundation for a successful partnership. Our advice is to start getting to know family offices well in advance of when you need funding. Get involved with them at industry events, through mutual contacts, and by consistently demonstrating progress and aligning strategically with their interests.

Remember, family offices prioritize fit over pure financial returns. Demonstrate alignment with their values, investment mandates, and ethical considerations – and watch your pitch go from silent to successful.

## Fund of Funds

A Fund-of-Funds (FOF) is like a big investment basket that collects money from many investors and then spreads it out into other investment funds, including Special Purpose Vehicles. This setup offers several benefits to investors. First, it helps reduce risk by spreading investments across multiple funds, which is especially helpful for investors with limited money. Second, experts who are skilled at selecting investments usually manage FOFs. This means investors can benefit from their knowledge without having to manage investments themselves.

For those running SPVs, FOFs can be a useful tool. Let's say you've found a great investment opportunity and gotten some investors on board, but you want to spread your skills across more deals. This is where FOFs can help. They typically invest in a wide range of fund types, each focusing on different areas or strategies. This approach gives the FOF, and its investors, access to a broader set of opportunities than a single fund could offer on its own.

## Investment Banks

Investment banks typically deal with large transactions and focus on managing risk for their clients, although they may make use of SPVs for their own purposes, their involvement in small Special Purpose Vehicles uncommon. These banks cater to various investors, including institutions like pension funds and everyday retail investors. They consider different transaction structures based on a company's size and needs. Investment bankers often rely on intermediaries or brokers to find deals and bring together buyers and sellers. They play a crucial role in the capital-raising process, pitching deals to both parties involved.

## Co-Syndication Opportunities

While various investor groups provide essential capital, one often-overlooked source is fellow dealmakers within your industry. These professionals can offer valuable pathways to raising funds and closing deals. Working with experienced GPs can really help you succeed. Partnering with an established GP can really speed things up and improve your chances of a successful outcome.

We call this collaborative approach co-syndication. Co-syndication is when a group of GPs join forces to invest in deals. This partnership model builds solid relationships and a trusted network among GPs. Co-syndication usually leads to ongoing collaborations that benefit everyone involved. This is a great opportunity for new dealmakers to learn from established GPs and get access to more investment opportunities. This can really amp up a solid deal by tapping into the networks of established GPs to attract more Limited Partners and money.

Some folks are iffy about sharing their best deals, wanting to keep all the economic benefits to themselves. They might not be keen on sharing their LP base with others. Not every deal has to be shared. It's cool to keep some deals "in-house", but if you only share "so-so" deals with other GPs, they might not be as interested in working with you later on. Going solo can totally work, but it usually means slower growth.

Each GP in a co-syndication has a specific role. The Co-Syndicate Lead's job is to find deals, run the SPV, and handle the money. The Co-Syndicate Partner lends a hand by using their experience and network to bring in LPs and promote the investment opportunity. When GPs work together, they can give LPs better investment opportunities without slowing down the process. Consider co-syndication to unlock amazing opportunities in private investments and achieve rapid growth while accessing great opportunities.

# PROFILING THE IDEAL INVESTOR

As we move from the art of networking to the science of investor profiling, recognize that these elements have a close connection in the world of private investments. Just as you are strategic in your networking, you must also be discerning in identifying potential investors, as not everyone will translate into capital for your deal. You've taken a big step in starting this process by building your database and keeping notes of your interactions so you'll have some place to start with defining your ideal investor.

The goal isn't just to find people who have money to throw around. It's about finding people who share your investment goals, share a similar risk tolerance, and can bring more than just money to the table.

Your knack for building genuine relationships will help you understand potential investors. You're looking for partners, not just funders.

While it may be obvious, it is essential to clearly outline the qualities you are looking for in a financial partner. This clarity can significantly impact your success in raising capital. To be effective, you need to understand the mindset of your ideal investor. Even if an investor has a lot of experience and invests often, it doesn't mean they're the perfect fit.

Look for individuals who value patience, portfolio diversification, and long-term wealth building. The ideal investor should be cautious but also open to calculated risks, especially when there's a possibility for high returns. If you're working with a new investor, be prepared to navigate the learning curve together.

When you connect your investment opportunities with people's psychological traits and financial goals, you'll find investors who will want to stick with you. Find investors who are on the ball, can evaluate your deals thoroughly, make timely decisions, and keep their word. They should have confidence in your abilities and recognize the value you bring. Ideal investors should be patient about timing and be open to future collaborations if they're satisfied with the results.

To get started, make a detailed avatar that reflects your research and experience, with stuff like age, interests, investing goals, and challenges. Take a look at your contact list and circle people who fit that profile. Make a system to score prospects based on how well they match your ideal investor traits. This way, you'll be able to target the right folks.

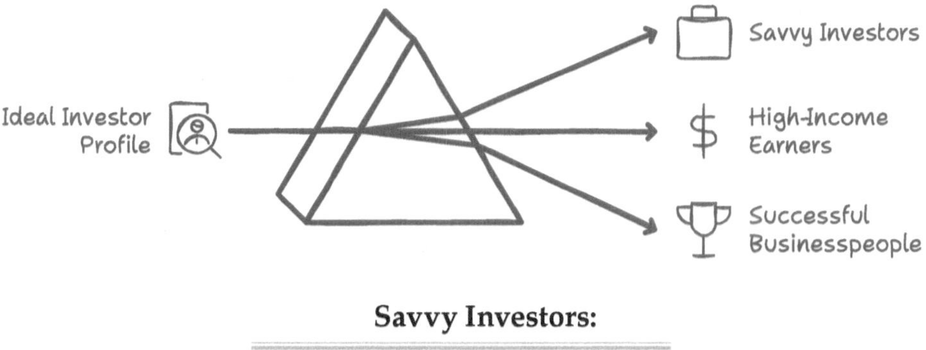


## Savvy Investors:

People with finance backgrounds or extensive investing experience make up the group of savvy investors. They ask detailed questions about financial metrics, market research, and risk management. It's super important to be well-prepared and transparent when dealing with these investors. They deal with stuff like low market returns and the need for a more diverse portfolio with the ability to mitigate taxes. You have the chance to pitch your investment as the solution to these issues. These investors usually have a clear idea of what they like to invest in. If they pass on the deal, ask for feedback to know more about their objectives. Just be upfront and ask them about the kind of deals they're into and what they're looking for in investments. Keep them in the loop as you gain experience and you could win them over for a future deal.

## High-Income Earners:

High-earning professionals can make excellent investors. These professionals are often seeking passive investment opportunities to grow their wealth. It's common for certain professionals to have a good amount of extra income available for investment, but they struggle to find the time to manage it. However, despite their income, people's financial situations can be very different. Keep in mind that having a big paycheck doesn't automatically mean that someone has lots of investable capital. Their lifestyle and expenses come into play.

## Successful Businesspeople:

Successful businesspeople, whether they built their own companies or inherited family wealth, are valuable potential investors and mentors. They often have lots of money, experience, and industry connections. Their success stories can inspire and guide you in your own business journey. Keep in mind that these people have their own perspectives on risk, growth, and market trends. Some people might just want to invest passively and diversify a bit, while others might want to get more involved in new ventures. Their business know-how can help improve your investment pitches. Building relationships with successful businesspeople can bring opportunities for funding, partnerships, and mentorship, not just financial help.

It can be a struggle to build and maintain wealth these days. The economy has changed, and so have the ways that people make money and the role of investment professionals.. Traditional methods are no longer enough. It's now vital to find and profile investors who share your vision. Instead of casting a wide net, focus on building relationships with those who match a carefully crafted investor profile. They should share your values, risk tolerance, and investment goals. Immerse yourself in their world and it will become easier to gain their trust and learn what drives their decisions.

Understanding how your investors generated their wealth provides invaluable perspective. Each success story holds clues to their motivations. Use them to tailor your approach and build lasting partnerships. Today, people want creative financial solutions. Lots of folks are starting to recognize the need for alternative financial strategies to achieve their long-term goals. They want to work with people like you that can offer both opportunity and expertise.

Just to give you an example of a great long-term partner, one of our investors is a business owner we got to know through mutual connections. She works long hours and wants to maximize her family time when possible. With limited capacity to explore new investment opportunities independently, she became interested in partnering with us as a Limited Partner. She checked a lot of the boxes for our ideal investor avatar and we were happy to get her involved. Since then, she consistently supports nearly all our deals, not with substantial amounts of money, but with consistent investment in the opportunities we offer. She's not just investing because we're friends, she invests because she trusts us to find great opportunities and do our job managing the deal.

Effective investor profiling is an ongoing process. With each interaction, adapt and refine your approach, building a network of aligned investors ready to fuel your ventures and lay the groundwork for lasting success.

## INVESTOR ACCREDIATION

When creating your ideal investor profile, you need to consider their accreditation status. This is important because it affects who can participate and under what conditions. For instance, in a 506(b) deal, you're limited in how many non-Accredited Investors can be involved.

At the same time, for a 506(c) deal, all investors must be accredited to participate. Don't forget about these restrictions while you're working on your investor avatar and fundraising plan.

Accredited Investor status[i] applies to individuals who earn over $200,000 annually (or $300,000 for couples) or have a net worth exceeding $1 million, excluding their primary residence. Additionally, people that have financial licenses like Series 7, 65, and 82 can meet this criteria. Investing entities can be banks, savings associations, registered investment advisors, insurance companies, brokers and dealers, small business investment firms, and rural business investment companies, among others. Private business development firms and organizations under Section 501(c)(3) are also included if they own assets over $5 million and weren't created solely to purchase securities under Regulation D.

You may be wondering what steps international investors take to get involved. While the SEC's definitions are for U.S. citizens, you can still find equivalent criteria. We'll get more into Accredited Investor verification a bit later in the book.

Sophisticated, non-Accredited Investors hold a special place in the investment landscape. These individuals don't meet the SEC's financial requirements to be considered Accredited Investors, but they make up for it with their knowledge and experience. This expertise allows them to manage investments more effectively. As a result, they can get involved in private investments through 506(b) deals.

Being a sophisticated investor isn't an official classification – there's no formal test or certification for it. Instead, the determination is based on information provided by the investor. To be considered sophisticated, an investor must prove their knowledge and experience to the issuing company, usually by providing documentation or answering questions about their investment history, financial knowledge, and business

---

*i        https://www.sec.gov/resources-small-businesses/capital-raising-building-blocks/accredited-investors*

experience. We give non-Accredited Investors some extra educational material to learn more about the opportunity and private investments. It's a way for us to be transparent and help them make informed decisions.

# UNDERSTANDING INVESTORS

While creating detailed investor profiles is crucial for identifying potential partners, it's only the first step in building meaningful relationships with them. Once you've identified promising investors who match your ideal profiles, the next critical skill is engaging them effectively. The beginning of this process is all about asking the right questions. By mastering the ability to ask insightful and strategic questions, you can move beyond surface-level interactions and truly understand an investor's motivations, preferences, and decision-making processes. This deeper level of engagement not only helps you refine your investor profiles but also allows you to tailor your approach and build stronger relationships.

Asking good questions is key to getting the most out of a conversation. Sometimes, people leave conversations feeling unsatisfied or like they didn't really connect because they either ask the wrong questions or ask the right questions in the wrong way.

If you're strategic with what you ask, you'll show off your expertise, understand people's motivations, and have a better shot at securing their investment. Productive conversations require you to practice active listening and understanding of their perspective. Ask relevant questions that fit your potential investor and the deal you're discussing. By doing this, you'll create a dialogue that goes beyond surface level and resonates with your potential investors on a deeper level.

These conversations serve two purposes: gauging investor interest and gaining insights into their preferences and decision-making processes. Start by discussing the investor's financial goals, which helps tailor your approach. Encourage them to elaborate on their goals and potential uses for the money. This naturally leads to specific questions about investment sizes, expected returns, and current holdings.

Pay close attention to how investors describe their investments, as this reveals their requirements. Active listening builds rapport and shows you value their input. Treat investor qualification like a sales process, aiming to determine if there's a good fit and understanding their decision-making timeline. Be strategic in meetings, assessing genuine interest and establishing clear expectations from the start.

By asking insightful questions and carefully noting their answers, you can detect subtle signals of an investor's interest and alignment with your objectives. Finding the right investor for your SPV is about ensuring a good fit for both parties. If you do this right, you're sure to build strong, productive relationships that support your long-term success.

We thought it would be a good idea to include some questions for you to consider asking your prospect. That being said, having a list of questions is great, but let them come out naturally during your conversations. You don't want to launch directly into a bunch of boilerplate questions without context. If nothing else, it can seem awkward or off-putting. Put in the effort to become a great conversationalist and with practice, you'll be able to effortlessly weave these questions in your discussions with potential investors, making each interaction more interesting and impactful.

- **Question:** What is your investment decision-making process? Understanding if decisions are made individually or by committee helps tailor your approach and align your fundraising process with their timeline.

- **Question:** Do you have experience in similar investments? Investors with relevant experience can provide valuable guidance and credibility beyond capital. Their past successes and challenges can inform your strategy.

- **Question:** What is your preferred investment time horizon?
  Aligning investment horizons is crucial for business strategy and exit plans. This ensures matching expectations between you and the investor.

- **Question:** What is the typical size of investments you make?
  Understanding their investment scale helps you tailor your ask to fit their typical range, increasing the likelihood of a successful pitch.

- **Question:** How important is liquidity to you?
  Clarifying liquidity preferences ensures your opportunity fits within their portfolio strategy and risk tolerance.

- **Question:** Who else needs to approve this investment?
  Knowing the decision-making chain helps you prepare comprehensive information packets and ensures you're talking to the right person.

- **Question:** What is your risk tolerance?
  Understanding their risk tolerance helps in presenting your opportunity appropriately and addressing potential concerns.

- **Question:** What does your due diligence process look like?
  Knowing their due diligence specifics helps you anticipate demands and prepare necessary documentation, streamlining the process.

- **Question:** What are you looking for in an investment?
  Understanding their priorities helps you highlight the most relevant benefits of your deal. They might want things like asset appreciation, residual income, tax benefits, or a combination.

- **Question:** How long do you typically need to review a deal?
  Ensure their timeline fits your runway and current needs to avoid cash flow issues.

- **Question:** Are you married? If so, is your spouse involved in investment decisions?
  Couples often make financial decisions together. Knowing this helps ensure all decision-makers are included in the process.

- **Question:** What do you do for a living?
  This gives insight into their likely income level, education, and potential networking opportunities.

- **Question:** Do you have any children?
  People with families often think long-term and may be more interested in investments that can grow generational wealth.

- **Question:** What are your hobbies? What would you do more of if you had the time or money?
  Hobbies can indicate income level, financial goals, and provide opportunities to strengthen personal relationships with potential investors.

# KNOWING WHEN TO SAY NO: SELECTING THE RIGHT INVESTORS

Money has a personality. What does that mean? It's not the best idea to just raise money blindly without considering your investors' personalities. Sure, funding is essential, but the investor you're working with is a big consideration too. When it comes to selecting investors, you'll quickly realize that not all capital is created equal.

Their personality matters because your investor doesn't just write a check and then disappear; they become your long-term partner in navigating your mutual investment journey, for better or for worse. When managing an SPV the allure of quick capital can be tempting, but beware—choosing the wrong investors can lead to trouble. Dealing with difficult people in business can be exhausting. Consider that you're interviewing investors just as much as they're interviewing you. You might even turn them down, even if they want to say yes to you.

Each investment decision should be made with care, considering both the immediate benefits and the long-term implications. Imagine being stuck on a long road trip with a backseat driver. Annoying, right? Now imagine that road trip lasting years. That's what partnering with the wrong investor can feel like.

The key is to find ways to say no without damaging the relationship. When turning down an investor, it's best to use a gentle approach known as a "soft no." This is especially important for investors who want to maintain good relationships. Instead of a blunt rejection, a soft no might sound like "Thank you for your interest. We'll keep you in mind for future opportunities." If it makes sense, it can be a good idea to suggest an introduction to another dealmaker that has an opportunity that might interest them. By offering helpful gestures, you can create goodwill that may prove beneficial to you later on.

So, what would make you say no to an investor? Every situation is different, but there are certain types of investors you should steer clear of. It's important to be aware of certain red flags during investor selection. This can save you not only a lot of time in fruitless matchmaking, but also a great deal of grief in avoiding a bad long-term relationship. Let's take a look at some of the different classifications of investors you might want to avoid for your deal.

## Short-Term-Focused Investors

It may be wise to avoid involving investors who lack patience and prioritize quick returns if you have a long-term investment strategy. You may face pressure from such investors to make decisions that jeopardize the long-term success of your venture. Quick cash might seem tempting, but remember, success takes time.

## Signs to Watch Out For

- **Pressure for Early Exits:** These investors might push for a quick sale of your technology or business before it reaches its full potential, sacrificing significant long-term profits for a short-term payout.

- **Focus on Flashy Metrics:** They prioritize impressive but unsustainable growth metrics over building a solid foundation for future success. This can lead to shortcuts in product development or aggressive marketing tactics that damage brand reputation in the long run.

- **Impatience with Development Timelines:** Investors who constantly pressure for quick results may lack understanding of the necessary timeframes for research, development, and market penetration.

## Potential Risks

- **Employee Demoralization:** A constant focus on short-term gains can lead to a culture of cutting corners and prioritizing quantity over quality. This can demotivate talented employees who thrive in environments that value long-term innovation and excellence.

- **Missed Opportunities:** The pressure to deliver quick results can lead to neglecting potentially game-changing long-term investments in research and development or strategic partnerships.

- **Undermining Long-Term Vision:** Short-term focused investors can create a pressure cooker environment, jeopardizing your long-term vision and strategic goals.

## How to Avoid

- **Clear Communication:** Be upfront about your investment timelines and the timeframes required for achieving your goals. Look for investors who understand and support your long-term approach.

- **Track Record Matters:** Investigate an investor's past behavior. Do they have a history of supporting ventures that require a long runway for success?

- **Shared Values:** Seek investors who value innovation, sustainable growth, and building something of lasting value, not just a quick financial win.

- **Patience as a Strategic Advantage:** Partner with investors who understand the timeframes required for your specific industry and are willing to play the long game.

## Dishonest or Unethical Investors

You probably won't want to deal with investors with a history dishonest or unethical behavior. These problematic investors can cause serious trouble for you. They might try to deceive you or others involved in your deal, potentially breaking laws or engaging in fraud. Even worse, they could push you to make choices that go against your values or ethics, putting your reputation and integrity at risk. By associating with such investors, you might find yourself caught up in scandals or legal issues that could harm your business and personal standing. It's always better to work with trustworthy partners who share your commitment to ethical business practices.

## Signs to Watch Out For

- **Fraudulent Activity:** Look for signs of manipulated financial records, inflated valuations, or other deceitful practices. During due diligence, uncover any past legal issues, regulatory violations, or negative press coverage related to an investor's previous ventures.

- **Pressure for Unethical Decisions:** Be wary of investors who push you to cut corners on product quality, mislead customers, or engage in unfair business practices. These tactics may yield short-term gains but can cause long-term reputational damage.

- **Red Flags During Reference Checks:** Talk to former business associates, portfolio companies, or even competitors. Insights from these conversations can be invaluable in uncovering potential dishonesty.

- **Gut Feeling:** Trust your intuition. If something about an investor feels off, don't ignore that feeling. A nagging suspicion could be a warning sign of dishonesty lurking beneath the surface.

## Potential Risks

- **Legal Consequences:** Partnering with dishonest investors can land your SPV in legal trouble, resulting in hefty fines or even criminal charges. This can destroy your reputation and disrupt your business operations.

- **Reputational Damage:** Unethical practices by an investor can tarnish your SPV's reputation, jeopardizing future fundraising efforts and partnerships. A damaged reputation can be hard to rebuild and can deter potential customers and partners.

- **Constant Friction:** Misaligned ethical standards can lead to constant disagreements, hindering the overall growth and success of your venture.

- **Employee Morale:** A team working for a company associated with unethical behavior can become disillusioned and disengaged, impacting productivity and innovation.

## How to Avoid

- **Investigate Track Record:** Dig deep into an investor's history. Look for past legal issues, regulatory violations, or negative press coverage related to their business dealings.

- **Conduct Thorough Reference Checks:** Speak with former business associates, portfolio companies, or even competitors to gain insights into the investor's integrity and behavior.

- **Trust Your Intuition:** If something feels off about an investor, don't ignore that feeling. Intuition can be a valuable tool in assessing honesty and ethical behavior.

- **Prioritize Ethical Compatibility:** Ensure potential investors share your core values and vision for the business. Misalignment in terms of values, ethics, or goals can lead to conflicts down the line.

- **Seek Long-Term Alignment:** Don't be afraid to say no to seemingly "perfect" investors solely based on a mismatch in values. Financial resources are replaceable, but shared vision and ethical alignment are crucial for a thriving SPV.

## Fading Star Investors

The term "Fading Star Investors" captures the essence of their situation – once seen as successful investors, their financial woes have caused their "star" to fade. These investors might mislead you based on their past reputation rather than their current financial reality. We see these investors emerge whenever the stock market, real estate market, or general economy experiences a significant slowdown or correction. People who once had a reputation as high-flyers, referred to you as potential investors, suddenly face serious liquidity problems. They might still be at the country club every day, but now they're running up a tab.

The problem is, they won't act or behave any differently. If you contact them, they may even agree to meet with you. They can't let word get out that they are no longer running with the big dogs. If news of their difficulties spread, they would lose important status in the community and be excluded from the A-list parties. Unfortunately, your potential investor now has very limited liquid capital. Someone who once looked like a great opportunity is now a major gamble. These aren't bad folks, and sometimes they can be back on the rise, but be cautious and take your time to vet them if you decide to include them in your deal.

## Signs to Watch For

- **Sudden Liquidity Issues:** Economic downturns can expose vulnerabilities. The flashy lifestyle Mr. Bigshot maintains might be fueled by dwindling reserves, not ongoing success.

- **Focus on Maintaining Appearances:** Despite financial struggles, they often prioritize projecting an air of success. They might still frequent exclusive clubs, but now it's on credit, not cash.

- **Name-Dropping and Status Anxiety:** They might bombard you with connections to wealthy individuals, hoping to impress and deflect scrutiny. Remember, past associations don't guarantee present resources.

## Potential Risks

- **Limited Capital:** Their promises of hefty investments might be hollow, leaving your SPV underfunded and hindering your growth plans.

- **Negative Press:** If word gets out about Mr. Bigshot's struggles and your association, it could damage your reputation and deter other potential investors.

- **Wasted Time and Resources:** Pursuing these types of investors can divert your attention from securing reliable partners, delaying your investment timeline.

## How to Avoid Fading Star Investors

- **Prioritize Due Diligence:** Don't rely on past reputation. Investigate an investor's current financial standing, focusing on verifiable assets and recent investment activity.

- **Seek Transparency:** Ask direct questions about their current financial situation and commitment capacity. A genuine investor will be upfront and honest.

- **Look Beyond the Name-Dropping:** Don't get swayed by impressive connections. Focus on concrete evidence of current financial strength.

## Inexperienced and Uninformed Investors

Investors who lack experience or knowledge in your industry can be risky partners. Just because someone has money doesn't mean they understand the complexities of your business. These inexperienced investors might not realize how challenging your industry can be or appreciate the risks involved. They may have unrealistic expectations about how investments typically perform. When setbacks happen, these investors might panic or react poorly because they don't have the background to put issues in context. This can lead to additional stress and complications for you as a business owner.

## Signs to Watch Out For

- **Limited Industry Understanding:** Inexperienced investors may not understand the specific risks and challenges inherent to your sector. For example, an investor unfamiliar with real estate development might underestimate permitting hurdles or construction delays that could impact your project timeline.

- **Misguided Advice:** Without a solid understanding of industry dynamics, their suggestions, while well-intentioned, might be off-base or detrimental, leading to wasted time, resources, and missed opportunities.

- **Unrealistic Expectations:** They might not grasp the inherent volatility of early-stage ventures and expect immediate, consistent growth. This lack of understanding can lead to frustration and hostility when faced with inevitable setbacks.

- **Emotional Volatility:** Inexperienced investors can be susceptible to panic during challenging periods, creating unnecessary tension and hindering your ability to navigate difficulties effectively.

## Potential Risks

- **Hindered Progress:** Inexperienced investors might push for decisions that prioritize immediate gains over long-term success, potentially jeopardizing your growth strategy.

- **Limited Strategic Guidance:** While their wealth might be impressive, their lack of experience likely translates to limited strategic guidance and support. Building a successful venture requires more than just financial resources.

- **Micromanagement Tendencies:** These investors may attempt to dictate every move, stifling your ability to leverage your expertise as the GP and creating a stifling work environment.

- **Lack of Trust:** Their constant need for control might stem from a lack of trust in your capabilities, breeding resentment and hindering your ability to build a strong, collaborative partnership.

## How to Avoid

- **Investigate Track Record:** Look for investors with experience in your industry or a related field. Don't settle for just financial muscle; seek out partners who bring strategic expertise to the table.

- **Conduct Thorough Reference Checks:** Speak with founders and CEOs of their portfolio companies. Did they find the investor to be a source of valuable guidance or unnecessary pressure?

- **Understand Their Investment History:** Research their past investments. Do they have a track record of supporting ventures through challenges, or a history of abandoning ship at the first sign of trouble?

- **Assess Their Questions:** Pay close attention to the questions they ask during meetings. Are they digging into the nuances of your business model and market dynamics, or focus on superficial topics?

## Sweat Equity Seekers

Remember, not everything that glitters is gold and you may encounter a sweat equity seeker. This is a character every entrepreneur should recognize and approach with caution. Initially, this type of investor seems like a dream come true. They're enthusiastic, charming, and eager to dive into your venture. They'll offer advice, introduce you to their network, and become a fixture in your office. It's easy to get caught up in their excitement and feel like you've struck gold. Here's the thing, when the capital call gets issued, they might not have enough to cover it. They might expect you to cover the difference because of the work they've done, even though there was no agreement beforehand.

## Signs to Watch Out For

- **Initial Enthusiasm:** These investors are often overly enthusiastic and charismatic, making them seem like the perfect partner. They offer advice and connections, and quickly integrate into your business.

- **Frequent Presence:** They become a regular presence in your office, showing a keen interest in your operations and making themselves indispensable.

- **Promises of Future Contributions:** They make vague promises about future efforts and contributions that are hard to quantify or verify.

## Potential Risks

- **Reduced Financial Commitment:** When it comes time to discuss the actual financial investment, the promised amount often shrinks dramatically. They push for a significant equity stake based on their past involvement and future promises rather than a concrete financial contribution.

- **Pressure Cooker Situation:** By the time their true intentions are clear, they might have already told others about their involvement. Backing out can damage your reputation and harm relationships you've worked hard to build.

- **Equity for Effort:** They argue that their "sweat equity" – the time and effort they've already put in and claim they'll continue to provide – is just as valuable as actual cash, putting you in a tough spot.

## How to Avoid Sweat Equity Seekers

- **Set Clear Expectations:** Establish clear expectations about financial contributions early in your discussions with potential investors. Ensure everyone understands the importance of real capital for your business.

- **Get Agreements in Writing:** Before allowing anyone to become deeply involved in your business, get agreements in writing. This protects you from future disputes over what was promised versus what was delivered.

- **Conduct Thorough Due Diligence:** Investigate potential investors' track records thoroughly. Look beyond their charm and enthusiasm to understand their financial stability and past behavior.

- **Maintain a Diverse Network:** Avoid becoming dependent on any single individual by maintaining a diverse network of potential backers. This ensures you have multiple options and aren't pressured into accepting unfavorable terms.

## Financially Unstable Investors

It's crucial to check a potential investor's financial health. Even if they seem to be doing well, their finances could actually be in a fragile state. This is why it's so important to dig deeper and really understand an investor's financial situation before partnering with them. If an investor doesn't actually have enough money or has a history of financial problems, they might not be able to keep their commitments. This can leave you in a tough spot. To avoid these issues, focus on finding investors who are truly financially stable. Take the time to thoroughly investigate potential investors' backgrounds and finances. This extra care in choosing your investors can make a big difference in the success of your business deals.

## Signs to Watch Out For

- **Inability to Meet Commitments:** Financially unstable investors might pledge a certain amount but struggle to deliver, leaving your SPV underfunded and hindering your growth plans.

- **Pressure for Short-Term Gains:** Faced with their own financial pressures, these investors might push for a quick exit strategy, sacrificing long-term value creation for a short-term payout.

- **Inconsistent Financial Background:** During due diligence, look for red flags such as overextension in other ventures, a history of financial difficulties, or a lack of liquidity.

## Potential Risks

- **Underfunded Ventures:** If an investor fails to meet their financial commitments, your SPV could be left underfunded, jeopardizing your ability to meet existing obligations and maintain momentum.

- **Derailment of Long-Term Strategy:** Financial pressures on the investor might lead them to push for premature exits, undermining your long-term vision for the SPV.

- **Operational Stress:** Constantly worrying about an investor's ability to fulfill their commitments can distract you from focusing on core business strategies, increasing operational stress.

## How to Avoid

- **Scrutinize Financial Records:** Request audited financial statements and delve into their details. Look for consistent profitability, a healthy debt-to-equity ratio, and a strong track record of managing finances.

- **Investigate Investment History:** Research their past investments. Did they meet their funding commitments in previous ventures? What was the overall success rate of those investments?

- **Assess Liquidity:** Understand the liquidity of their assets. Can they readily access the capital they've pledged to your SPV?

- **Conduct Thorough Due Diligence:** Go beyond impressive presentations and past successes. Focus on the current financial health of potential investors to ensure they have a stable financial foundation.

## Overbearing or Micromanaging Know-It-Alls

Be wary of those who try to exert excessive control or push their own agendas. Emotional intelligence is crucial in business relationships, so consider how potential partners handle challenges. Successful partnerships are built on mutual respect, so treat potential investors with respect and expect the same in return.

Remember that accepting investment is about more than just funds; it's about building a supportive partnership. Look for investors who value collaboration, respect your leadership, and support your vision. Avoid those who dominate discussions, belittle your ideas, or act condescendingly due to their perceived superiority. These overbearing investors can manifest their controlling tendencies in ways that stifle your ability to leverage your expertise as the GP.

### Signs to Watch Out For

- **Micromanagement:** Overbearing investors might bombard you with detailed instructions on how to run the business, creating a stifling work environment.

- **Disruptive Decision-Making:** They insist on being involved in every decision, regardless of their understanding of your specific industry, causing delays and hindering swift action on critical opportunities.

- **Erosion of Trust:** Their constant need for control signals a lack of trust in your capabilities, breeding resentment and making it difficult to build a strong, collaborative partnership.

- **Relentless Negativity:** They focus on potential pitfalls and worst-case scenarios, draining your team's morale and hindering their ability to take calculated risks.

- **Disruptive Influence:** Their arrogance might alienate other investors, potential partners, and even talented employees, fracturing the foundation of a successful SPV.

## Potential Risks

- **Stifling Creativity:** Constant micromanagement can second-guess every decision you make, hindering your ability to execute your vision and creating a tense, unproductive work environment.

- **Lowered Morale:** Relentless negativity can sap your team's optimism and drive, making it hard to maintain the energy crucial for success.

- **Alienation:** Disruptive influence can alienate other investors, partners, and employees, weakening the collaborative spirit necessary for a thriving SPV.

## How to Avoid

- **Clear Communication:** From the outset, establish clear expectations regarding communication and decision-making processes. Ensure the investor understands your role as GP and the level of autonomy you require.

- **Focus on Shared Goals:** Emphasize the alignment between your vision for the SPV and the investor's financial objectives. A shared sense of purpose fosters trust and collaborative decision-making.

- **Track Record Matters:** Investigate an investor's past behavior. Do they have a reputation for being collaborative or overly controlling with portfolio companies?

- **Assess Communication Style:** Pay close attention to how they interact with you and others during meetings. Do they listen actively or dominate the conversation? Do they value diverse perspectives or only see things their way?

- **Conduct Reference Checks:** Talk to founders and CEOs of their portfolio companies. Did they find the investor to be a supportive advisor or a controlling presence?

- **Observe Their Online Presence:** Social media posts and interviews can reveal a lot about an investor's personality. Do they focus on their own achievements or celebrate the successes of their portfolio companies?

## Time Wasters and Tire Kickers

It's important to be cautious about potential investors who may waste your time. While dealmakers can sometimes get overly excited about even slight interest from investors, not all interested parties are genuine. Some investors might string you along for various reasons, without any real intention of writing a check. For instance, they might use the due diligence process to explore a new industry or technology, with no plans to invest. Others might drag out the process to avoid saying no, thinking they're being kind, but actually just prolonging false hope. And some people simply enjoy the attention and feeling of importance that comes with being courted for an opportunity. It's crucial to recognize these "tire kickers" and time wasters to avoid investing too much energy in unproductive pursuits.

## Signs to Watch Out For

- **Never-Ending Due Diligence:** Procrastinating investors might drag out the due diligence process indefinitely, requesting mountains of information without ever reaching a decision.

- **False Hope and Empty Promises:** They might dangle the possibility of an investment but offer little to no concrete timeline or clear criteria for moving forward.

- **Information Vampires:** They might engage in lengthy "diligence" processes as a way to glean valuable industry insights or market intelligence, with no real intention of investing.

## Potential Risks

- **Delayed Funding:** Procrastinating investors can delay your ability to secure funding from other sources, hindering your overall momentum and delaying critical business operations.

- **Emotional Rollercoaster:** The constant back-and-forth can be demoralizing, causing stress and frustration as you wait for a decision that may never come.

- **Lost Opportunities:** Time-sensitive opportunities may slip away while you are stuck waiting for a non-committal investor, ultimately impacting your SPV's growth and success.

## How to Avoid

- **Set Clear Deadlines:** From the outset, establish clear timelines for the decision-making process. This keeps everyone accountable and prevents your pitch from languishing in an endless "maybe" pile.

- **Track Communication:** Pay attention to an investor's communication style. Do they respond to emails and inquiries promptly? Do they stick to scheduled meetings, or are they prone to last-minute cancellations and rescheduling?

- **Conduct Reference Checks:** Talk to other entrepreneurs who have pitched to this investor. Did they experience similar delays and a lack of clear communication?

## Disguised Brokers

Be cautious of brokers who pretend to be investors. These individuals or firms claim they're ready to invest in your deal, but their real goal is to collect fees, not provide capital. They typically don't actually intend to invest at all. Instead, they'll eventually ask you to sign an agreement to pay them for introducing you to real investors. When questioned about their funding sources, they tend to give vague answers and can't provide specific details. Entrepreneurs, often tired from their search for capital, might feel tempted to sign these agreements out of desperation. While it's not inherently wrong to hire someone to help find investors, it's crucial that they're honest about their role from the start. Remember, a business relationship that begins with deception is unlikely to improve over time. It's always better to work with those who are upfront about their intentions and capabilities.

## Signs to Watch Out For

- **Smoke and Mirrors Marketing:** Brokers might boast impressive-looking brochures and cultivate an aura of wealth and investment prowess. Don't be fooled by glossy presentations – dig deeper to understand their true track record.

- **Vague Investment Promises:** They might dangle the possibility of funding but offer little concrete information about their investment capacity or decision-making process. These empty promises can waste your valuable time and emotional energy.

- **The "Close Associates" Gambit:** When questioned about their investment capital, they might deflect with ambiguous terms like "close associates." This lack of transparency is a red flag that they lack the resources they claim to possess.

## Potential Risks

- **Wasted Time and Resources:** Engaging with brokers posing as investors can waste valuable time and resources, diverting your focus from securing genuine investment.

- **Emotional Frustration:** The constant back-and-forth with brokers can be emotionally draining, causing frustration and disillusionment.

- **Financial Loss:** Signing fee agreements with brokers can lead to financial loss, especially if no real investment materializes from their introductions.

## How to Avoid

- **Investigate Their Background:** Research their firm and track record. Do they have a history of successful investments or simply a history of collecting fees for introductions?

- **Conduct Reference Checks:** Talk to other entrepreneurs who have interacted with them. Did they experience similar tactics or a lack of transparency?

- **Clear Communication:** Ask direct questions about their investment capacity and decision-making process. A genuine investor will be happy to address your concerns head-on.

Choosing the right investors is a decision that will shape your deal's future. Throughout this process, trust your instincts – if something feels off, take a step back and reassess. Remember that each investor you bring on board should complement your vision. By choosing wisely, you're not just securing funding, but building a team that will help shape your success and legacy.

Keep in mind, properly profiling investors helps narrow your focus and can improve your chances of success. Having a clear picture of your ideal investor helps you raise capital better, attracting investors who truly get and appreciate your offering. This targeted strategy is your ticket to standing out in the competitive world of private investments, resulting in more efficient and successful capital raising. To help you effectively develop your ideal investor avatar for capital raising purposes, we have created this worksheet:

| DEMOGRAPHICS | |
| --- | --- |
| Name | [Investor's Name] |
| Age | [Age Range] |
| Occupation | [e.g., Venture Capitalist, Angel Investor] |
| Annual Income | [Income Range] |
| Net Worth | [Estimated Net Worth] |
| Education | [Highest Degree, Field of Study] |
| Industry Experience | [Years, Sectors] |
| Location | [City, Country] |
| Firm Size (if applicable) | [Number of employees, AUM] |

| AVATAR DESCRIPTION | |
| --- | --- |
| Avatar Description | [A brief narrative description of the ideal investor, including their background, expertise, and general approach to investing] |

| PSYCHOGRAPHICS | |
| --- | --- |
| Personal Characteristics | [e.g., Risk-tolerant, analytical, visionary] |
| Investment Philosophy | [e.g., Value investing, growth-oriented] |
| Decision-making Style | [e.g., Data-driven, intuitive] |
| Risk Tolerance | [e.g., High, moderate, low] |
| Investment Horizon | [e.g., Short-term, long-term] |
| Preferred Level of Involvement | [e.g., Hands-on, passive] |
| Interests | [e.g., Emerging technologies, sustainable businesses] |
| Professional Goals | [e.g., Portfolio diversification, industry disruption] |
| Personal Aspirations | [e.g., Leaving a legacy, societal impact] |
| Pains | [e.g., Deal flow quality, market volatility] |
| Main Challenges | [e.g., Finding promising startups, regulatory compliance] |
| Needs | [e.g., Reliable due diligence, strong founder relationships] |
| Communication Preferences | [e.g., Direct, frequent updates] |

| INVESTMENT PROFILE | |
| --- | --- |
| Typical Investment Size | [Range] |
| Stage Preference | [e.g., Seed, Series A, Growth] |
| Industry Focus | [Specific sectors] |
| Geographic Focus | [Regions of interest] |
| Track Record | [Past successful exits, notable investments] |
| Network and Connections | [Key industry relationships] |
| Value-add Beyond Capital | [e.g., Mentorship, strategic partnerships] |
| Exit Strategy Preferences | [e.g., IPO, acquisition] |
| Co-investment Requirements | [Yes/No, preferences] |
| Due Diligence Process | [Typical timeline, key focus areas] |
| Board Seat Expectations | [Yes/No, under what conditions] |
| Reporting Requirements | [Frequency, depth of information] |
| Follow-on Investment Capacity | [Yes/No, typical amounts] |
| Reputation in the Industry | [e.g., Respected, controversial] |

# WEALTH IN NUMBERS

*"The perfect pitch has three ingredients: it shows why something must exist, why you must build it, and why now is the time."*
— *Peter Thiel, Co-founder of PayPal, Palantir and Founders Fund*

# BUILDING A WINNING PITCH

To succeed with your Special Purpose Vehicle, you need one crucial element: capital. We thought this book wouldn't be complete without some tips on how to pitch your deal to investors. This section will show you how to pitch your deal like a pro to potential investors. We'll show you how to refine your pitch, so you can confidently attract investors and build a solid foundation for long-term success. Start by getting your head in the game. You need to identify why you're offering this opportunity to investors.

Ultimately, you get to decide what inspires you, but for your business, think about a purpose that's larger than yourself. It'll lead to greater meaning and better results in the long run. Start off with the right mindset and genuinely serve your investors - that's what leads to success.

## PREPARING BEFORE YOUR PITCH

Great supporting documents and thorough preparation are necessary for a successful capital raising effort. The key to attracting potential investors lies in a carefully constructed investment package. It is vital to keep in mind that the success of raising capital depends on several factors. There are various elements that contribute to the successful and consistent raising of capital.

Raising capital for a Special Purpose Vehicle takes careful planning and hard work. To succeed, you need two key things: detailed supporting documents and thorough preparation. These are the building blocks for making a strong case to potential investors. With these, you'll have a better chance of getting people to fund your idea.

You need an amazing investment package to get people interested in funding your venture. Make sure this package has a plan, financial projections, market analysis, and a clear explanation of how the invested money will drive growth and generate returns. Prove you're serious about this opportunity by having all your documents in order.

You need to realize that multiple factors play a role in the success of any capital raising initiative. The current economic climate, your industry, your team, and what sets your deal apart are all important things to consider. Also, how well you communicate your vision and strategy is a big factor in getting investors on board.

Consistency is a big deal when it comes to successful fundraising. This means not only maintaining a steady approach in your outreach and presentations but also showing a track record of reliable performance and meeting milestones. Investors are more likely to commit funds when they see a history of consistent progress and achievement.

Just keep tweaking your strategy and focusing on these different things, and you'll have a better chance of getting the funding you need for your SPV.

### Analyzing Your Competition

As you're getting things in order, checking out the competition is super important when raising capital for an SPV, because investors don't just look at your opportunity alone. They have plenty of other investment options and will compare your deal to others they're considering, deciding where to put their money. The investment market is saturated with opportunities, so investors have to be picky about where they invest their time, energy, and capital.

Your analysis of the competition is key to understanding this situation. It helps you see what others in your industry are offering, how they position themselves, their investment structures, sponsor terms, fees, transparency, and overall terms. Plus, you can check out how competitors handle investor relationships, their image, brand, and who they're trying to reach.

Knowing this inside out helps you stand out. The point is not to show you have no competition, but to prove you have a path to success. Find gaps in the market or areas that investors want to improve, and focus on what sets you apart.

Some examples could be being more responsive, having a unique niche, being flexible, or having competitive fees. In the end, a solid analysis of the competition shows why a busy investor should pick your SPV over all the other options out there, giving you an enormous advantage in a crowded market.

## Executive Summary / One Pager

You'll need a basic document called a "one-pager" or "tear sheet" to show potential investors. This summary highlights the most important and interesting parts of your proposal. This is a big part of your SPV presentation and gives a quick summary of what's being offered.

This short document is your sales pitch, it gives a 30,000 foot explanation of how the investment will work and showcases the standout features of your deal. In the executive summary, you typically break down each key factor in a paragraph or two, so investors can grasp your proposal quickly. Make sure you get your attorney to look over the marketing materials before you give them out.

## Pitch Deck

Your pitch deck is basically a condensed version of your business plan, made with PowerPoint or similar software. It's all about presenting your idea directly to investors, either in a group or one-on-one. Investors often ask for pitch decks before meetings so they can quickly understand your idea. So, get your deck in order before you approach potential investors. You'll usually have around ten slides to make a killer first impression.

Investors will check out your tear sheet and pitch deck to decide if they want to dig deeper into meeting with you to learn more. Your goal should be to to create a concise, visually appealing presentation that conveys the most important information to potential investors in a format they can easily digest. As with the executive summary, it is wise to have legal counsel review your pitch deck ahead of time.

## Set Your Desired Result

Before you even think about what to say to an investor, figure out what you want to achieve with your pitch. The first thing to consider is what you want to to achieve with your prospect by the end of the meeting. We know you want capital, but there could be more to do after the first meeting.

Choose one thing to focus on and make that your goal. For example, you might want this investor to agree to viewing see your data room and look at more specifics or if you're running a property deal, maybe you want the investor to go with you to check out a physical location in person.

Your desired outcome should be something that you're confident will move you closer to sealing the deal. It should also be a task that you want your prospective investor to complete, rather than a step you'll need to take. Decide the outcome you want to achieve, write it down, and remember this going in to your next meeting. Just take it slow and set small goals, and you'll naturally move things forward while you complete each step.

You need to know your material inside and out. It's a good idea to prep answers to potential questions before your pitch. We've noticed that most investors will ask a lot of the same questions and sometimes they'll have their own checklist so they can see if the deal works for them. Your responses to their questions really count. Depending on your response, it could either result in securing a new investor or having that prospect decide to pass on your deal. Give your full attention to the questions they ask, and don't hesitate to admit if you don't know the answer. Don't make something up on the fly. Tell them you want to verify the information and you'll get them an answer back soon. Another quick tip, if you don't know a lot of the terminology around finance and investments, dedicate some time to expanding your vocabulary and the concepts that they define - the jargon, the trends, and what makes it all happen. When you understand the context of someone's question, it's easier to give suitable answers.

# INVESTOR QUESTIONS
# TO PREPARE FOR

When pitching to investors, expect them to have questions about your deal. Anticipating what questions your potential investor may have is an important part of your preparation so you will be able to respond confidently and thoroughly. Here are some common questions investors may ask, along with some ideas how to address them effectively.

- **Question:** What are the risks?

  Don't pull any punches or soften things up on this one. Tell them that there are risks associated with investing. You want to tell them clearly what the most likely downsides are and how probable they may be. Most important, tell them what you are doing to mitigate and avoid those risks.

- **Question:** How and when am I going to get my money back?

  If you don't answer this one the right way, you're finished. You need to have a clear path to exiting the deal for them to feel comfortable working with you. Be prepared to go into that in detail and tell them exactly when you plan to get them out.

- **Question:** How much of your own money are you putting in? Are you bringing your own money into the deal?

  This question gets asked quite a bit, so be prepared for it. If you are putting your own cash in, bring this up early, and it will cut through many of their other concerns. Investors love to see that you are willing to put your money where your mouth is and see your coinvestment as a sign of your belief in the deal. If you are not investing alongside them, that's OK too. Please don't respond to it with "Well, I don't have any money, so I'm not putting in anything!" Even if you aren't investing in the deal, you need to frame this properly for your investors to accept that. Show them the amount of work you are going to do to keep the deal moving. It's called sweat equity, and it's of value. If they see the value of your involvement in the deal, they can look past how much cash you have in it.

- **Question:** How will this affect my taxes?

  If they haven't invested before, you will need to explain that the money they make with you is taxable. You need a good CPA on your team before you jump into these deals. A good CPA will make this process easy for your investors and may even be willing to help you prepare something to explain the process for them.

- **Question:** What are the logistics?

  This question is never worded the same, but in general, your investors will want to know the details on how they get the money to you, how it's protected, and the legal documents that set things up.

- **Question:** What's the minimum investment?

  Investors will want to know the financial commitment required upfront. Clearly state the minimum investment amount, and explain why this threshold is set. It might be due to the overall size of the deal, the need to cover certain costs, or to ensure that the investor base is manageable. Be transparent about how the minimum investment helps in achieving the project's goals and maintaining operational efficiency.

- **Question:** What's the plan if the economy changes and you can't sell? This question addresses risk management and contingency planning. Explain your strategy for navigating economic downturns or changes in the market. Discuss any measures in place to protect the investment, such as holding periods, diversification, or alternative exit strategies. Assure investors that you have considered various scenarios and have plans to mitigate risks, emphasizing your proactive approach to managing uncertainties.

- **Question:** What is the deadline for getting my funds in?

  Clearly communicate the timeline for funding, including any specific deadlines. Explain why these deadlines are important, such as for securing the deal, coordinating with other investors, or meeting project milestones. Providing a clear timeline helps investors plan accordingly and ensures a smooth funding process.

- **Question:** What do you like about the deal?

  When answering this question, focus on the strengths and unique selling points of the deal. Highlight factors such as market potential, the strength of the management team, projected returns, or any competitive advantages. Your enthusiasm and thorough understanding of the deal will help build investor confidence.

- **Question:** What DON'T you like about the deal?

  This question requires a balanced and honest assessment. Acknowledge any potential risks or downsides, but also explain how you plan to address or mitigate these issues. Being transparent about challenges shows that you have thoroughly evaluated the deal and are prepared to manage any potential problems, which can actually increase trust with investors.

- **Question:** Who else likes this deal?

  This question seeks third-party validation. Share any endorsements, due diligence reports, or expert opinions that support the viability of the deal. Mention any reputable partners, co-investors, or industry experts who have reviewed or are participating in the investment. This external validation can reassure investors about the credibility and potential success of the deal.

- **Question:** What if I have an emergency and need out?

  Investors want to know about liquidity and exit options. Explain any terms regarding early withdrawal or selling their stake in the investment. Be upfront about any restrictions, penalties, or processes involved in accessing funds in case of an emergency. Providing clear information helps manage expectations and prepare investors for all scenarios.

- **Question:** What fees will I be paying, and when?

  Be upfront about any management fees, performance fees, or other expenses associated with the SPV. Explain what each fee covers—such as operational costs or performance-based incentives—and when they will be charged. Investors appreciate knowing the fee structure in detail, as it impacts their overall return. Clarity around fees also shows transparency, which builds trust.

- **Question:** How often will I get updates?

  Describe your approach to regular updates, financial reporting, and major project announcements. Explain the frequency and format of communication, whether through quarterly reports, investor meetings, or direct messages. Emphasizing transparency in communication assures investors they'll stay informed about their investment's progress.

- **Question:** What happens if there are delays?

  Explain your contingency plans for handling potential delays, whether due to regulatory approvals, supply chain issues, or market fluctuations. Describe how you would mitigate delays, including any adjustments to timelines, budget buffers, or alternative strategies. Being upfront about delay management assures investors that you have practical solutions for keeping the project on track.

- **Question:** What's the competition, and how does this deal stand out?

  Discuss any competing investments or similar projects in the market and explain why this particular deal is attractive. Describe any advantages the SPV might have, such as unique positioning, access to exclusive assets, or competitive pricing. This answer demonstrates that you've thoroughly evaluated the market landscape and considered how to make this investment compelling amid potential competition.

# WEALTH IN NUMBERS

*"A great pitch is a mix of business logic and theater."*
*— Guy Kawasaki, Legendary Marketer and Venture Capitalist*

# INVESTOR OUTREACH

You can't expect for all of your potential investors to just stop by your home and tell you they're looking for a great deal to invest in. The next thing you need to be doing is actually reaching out and setting up meetings with people. When you're doing outreach, keep phone calls short and have something handy to jot down notes. Keep in mind that everyone is busy and it can be difficult to manage the demands of work, family, and other obligations. Your potential investors are no exception. They're swamped and won't give you their full attention unless they think it's worth their time.

Prior to reaching out, think about what might grab the attention of your investor. Highlighting mutual connections or interests can create a sense of familiarity and help build trust from the start. Having a persuasive "elevator pitch" is essential - a powerful synopsis of your idea that can be presented within a short elevator ride. Whether it's a spontaneous encounter or a planned introduction, this pitch can adapt to any situation. The aim is to generate enough curiosity for a future meeting. Remember, people's attention spans are limited, so organize your information in a digestible way. While crafting a short, consistent pitch may seem simple, it actually requires significant thought and effort to distill your message effectively.

You'll be using your elevator pitch in many situations — in intro emails, presentations, and even during random elevator encounters. Keep refining it while you highlight the things that make your deal stand out. Skip the buzzwords and remember that a solid explanation of why your offer is great will be more convincing than hype. When you're finishing up your pitch, ask an open-ended question that gets them talking. And don't forget, give them some space to share their thoughts. This could be as straightforward as asking something like, "Does this resonate with you?" or "Have you ever invested in anything like that?" These kind of questions not only grab the listener's attention but also can reveal some good info on what they're really interested in.

How the investor responds to your initial pitch is extremely important. It supplies valuable insights into their interest level and steers your next decisions. If they express enthusiasm, you can proceed with your presentation confidently. However, if their response is lukewarm, it's worth exploring further. Their lack of interest might stem from an unconvincing pitch or unfamiliarity with alternative investments. When an investor expresses satisfaction with their portfolio, you can request more details about their investment strategy. By using this approach, you can gain a deeper understanding of their preferences and create an opportunity for them to share. Often, people who could benefit from increased returns are hesitant to admit it, especially when meeting someone for the first time. Your initial pitch isn't intended to close the deal immediately; rather, it's an opportunity to establish rapport and highlight the potential value of your offer. If the investor responds positively, suggest scheduling a follow-up meeting to discuss the opportunity in more detail. This demonstrates your commitment and keeps the conversation moving forward.

When preparing to pitch to investors, start with a big-picture approach rather than diving into a lengthy presentation. Focus on introducing yourself, your business, and its importance concisely. Don't overload them with details and leave them wanting more.  If people hear your story and get curious, then you've hit the mark. Remember that investors need to trust you before they'll seriously consider any deal. Building trust takes time and usually involves a few interactions. Basically, your first pitch should start a conversation, not seal the deal. The goal is to spark interest, build credibility, and leave the door open for future discussions.

As you're preparing for your investor outreach, aim to reach out to a specific number of investors every day. Once you start setting up meetings, you will need to figure out how many of those you can realistically handle as well. The key is to push yourself but also set realistic goals. Finding that balance will make your efforts much more effective.

You might have an old-school image of raising capital from the movies wih roadshows, fancy cars, and over-the-top expenses. The game has totally changed from the good ol' days of raising capital. Video calls are the new normal. Let's face it, we've all embraced this modern way of doing things. Yeah, the travel was cool, but constantly trying to impress people in different cities every day was tiring, expensive, and took up a lot of time.

Think about it: the jet lag, the endless meals, the forced small talk – it's enough to wear anyone down. The settings were posh, but it could become a blur. With video conferencing, raising capital is much easier now. The virtual format has its own set of challenges, for sure. It's a bit trickier to maintain charisma on a screen, and building a real connection is more challenging. But there's no denying the trade-offs.

Imagine the amount of time and resources preserved by not having to travel across the country. No more packing and unpacking, navigating unfamiliar airports, or giving up sleep. Instead, you can have your meetings from your cozy home office, with your team right there to back you up. This flexibility isn't just for you, it helps the investors too. You can both easily fit in a quick Zoom call during a busy day, making the process more efficient for everyone. Also, you might want to consider hosting group calls to deliver your initial pitch to investors. This method will allow you to get more people through the door at a high level and and set up individual follow-up meetings for those who need more information or want to move forward.

Even though virtual fundraising is a a fantastic way to scale your efforts, don't forget that meeting in person still matter. Building strong relationships with potential investors requires a personal touch that video calls can sometimes struggle to replicate. Studies have shown success and close rates being anywhere from 15 to 30% higher with people who have met in person. When you take your initial calls virtually, you get to be more selective with your travel to finalize things and close a big deal. That means you can gauge interest ahead of time and ensure each trip is for a significant prospect that you're willing to travel for. That's why using a mix of methods is our recommended strategy for your SPV capital raising efforts. It's all about finding the right balance between the traditional roadshow charm and the convenience of the online world.

You have everything you need to start reaching out and scheduling meetings. Reaching out to your contacts about your deal might feel intimidating, especially if you haven't caught up in a while, but it's a surefire way to get the ball rolling. Be friendly and stick to the point when you chat so you can hit your targets while explaining your deal and requesting a meeting. When you start reaching out to investors, expect a mix of reactions. While some may be immediately interested, others may require some convincing. No need to stress, rejection is a completely normal experience. Don't worry if someone isn't feeling it - just move on to the next potential investor on your list.

## Investor Outreach Call Script

We love scripts, whether it's for calls, sales, or whatever. They set you up with a solid foundation. So, here's the deal: don't start calling people and reading word-for-word like a robot. But you can use them as a guide to stay focused on the main goal of the call. We put together a sample call script to help you chat with investors and start setting up some meetings. The goal is to introduce yourself, explain your opportunity, and ask for a meeting. Personalize it and tweak it to fit your unique style and situation.

[Ring, ring]

**Prospect:** Hello?

**You:** Hey [Prospect's Name], it's [Your Name]. How've you been? [Pause for response]

Hey it's great to hear that. Listen, I won't take much of your time. I'm calling because I'm working on something really cool and I immediately thought of you.

I've got a deal I'm working on that's honestly keeping me up at night – and I mean that in a good way. It's a [whatever type of deal it is] and I really don't want to miss out on it but I can't take the whole thing on myself right now.

So, I was thinking – and stop me if I'm being too forward here – but would you be open to grabbing a coffee this week? I'd love to walk you through the details in person. I promise it'll be worth your time.

[If they hesitate]

Look, I completely understand if you're skeptical. In fact, I'd be worried if you weren't. I'm not asking you to make any decisions right now. All I'm proposing is a quick meeting – 30 minutes tops. If nothing else, it'll be a chance for us to catch up, and I'll pick up the tab.

So, would [suggest a specific day and time] work for you?

[If they agree]

Fantastic! I'll send you a calendar invite with all the details. I'm looking forward to it.

[If they still hesitate]

No problem at all, I completely understand. How about this – why don't I send you a quick overview of the deal via email? That way, you can look it over at your convenience. If it piques your interest, we can always set up a meeting later. Sound fair?

[Wrap-up]

Alright, [Prospect's Name], I don't want to keep you, [either "I'll see you on [day]" or "keep an eye out for my email"]. Take care!

[End call]

## Email Outreach

Many successful people read their own emails and messages, always on the lookout for new opportunities. However, they often skip over messages that don't immediately grab their attention or seem unnecessary, given their limited time. Your challenge is to make your message stand out. Most cold emails fail because they're overly salesy, miss the mark with their audience, or are too long-winded.

When pitching an SPV opportunity via email, you need to strike a balance between providing information, being persuasive, and keeping it brief. The main goal is to start a conversation, not to secure immediate investment. To increase your chances of getting a reply, focus on making your email easily digestible. Given that professional investors receive hundreds of emails daily, yours should take no more than 30-60 seconds to read. Aim for 4-5 brief sentences, and test it by reading it aloud before sending. Be ready to provide more details, answer thorough questions, and build relationships with potential investors as you move forward. A few considerations to keep in mind when you're putting this message together:

- **Compliance and Legal Review:** Ensure your email adheres to all relevant securities laws and regulations. Consider having your attorney review your email template.

- **Attachments and Links:** Include a pitch deck or executive summary as an attachment. Use a secure data room solution for more sensitive documents.

- **Follow-up Strategy:** Plan a follow-up sequence, typically sending a reminder email 3-5 days after the initial outreach if no response is received.

The subject line is your first and sometimes only chance to grab attention. For SPV pitches, consider finding a way to highlight exclusivity with something like "Exclusive SPV Opportunity: [Brief Description]." For your opening paragraph, begin with a personalized greeting and a concise intro of yourself and the SPV opportunity you're presenting. We'll share an example email for you to work off of to build your message:

[Investor's Name],

We're running an SPV to invest in [brief description of investment opportunity], and given your background, I believe it could be in alignment with your investment strategy."

**i) SPV Overview:** Provide a succinct explanation of the SPV's purpose and structure.

**Example:** "We've created this SPV to allow a select group of investors to participate in [Company/Asset]'s [funding round/acquisition]. The SPV will hold a direct stake in [Company/Asset], providing investors with exposure to [key value proposition]."

**ii) Investment Highlights:** Present 3-5 bullet points highlighting the most compelling aspects of the investment opportunity.

**Example:** "[Company] has demonstrated 300% year-over-year growth for the past two years. Led by former executives from [Notable Companies]. Proprietary technology with 12 approved patents. Strategic partnerships with [Major Industry Players]. TAM estimated at $50B by 2025"

**iv) Urgency and Exclusivity:** Create a sense of urgency or exclusivity to prompt action.

**Example:** "Due to high demand, we're limiting this opportunity to 20 investors. The SPV is already 60% subscribed, and we expect to close within the next 30 days."

**d) Closing and Call-to-Action:** End with a clear next step and express openness to further discussion.

**Example:** "I've attached our detailed pitch deck for your review. Would you be available for a 20-minute call next Tuesday or Wednesday to discuss this opportunity in more depth?

Thank you for your time and consideration. I look forward to potentially collaborating on this exciting venture.

Best regards, [Your Name] [Your Contact Information]"

# BALANCING CONFIDENTIALITY

Managing exclusive investments is a high-stakes process that frequently involves sensitive information, and understanding the nuances of confidentiality can be tough for novice dealmakers. While you may be tempted to request Non-Disclosure Agreements (NDAs) before any discussion, experienced investors often hesitate to sign these for initial talks.

This is because reviewing many opportunities in related fields can make signing numerous NDAs impractical and legally cumbersome. The key is finding a balance that respects confidentiality needs while acknowledging how investment discussions work. When dealing with exclusive investments requiring confidentiality, it's crucial to be strategic in your communication. You need to spark investor interest without compromising sensitive information. Investors prefer individuals who show sharp and strategic thinking skills. Remember, ideas are common, but execution is rare and more valuable. To win over investors, demonstrate your ability to handle the details effectively.

A good approach is to start by sharing the non-confidential or publicly available information with potential investors. This gives them a general idea without revealing sensitive details. If they want to learn more, ask them to complete a brief online form, showing their serious interest. Once their genuine curiosity is established, you can request they sign a confidentiality agreement. They'll be more open to the idea because they're already intrigued by your offer. After signing, you can share more specific investment details and discuss potential involvement. While this might take more time, it's safer and more effective. It protects sensitive information by sharing it only with truly interested parties.

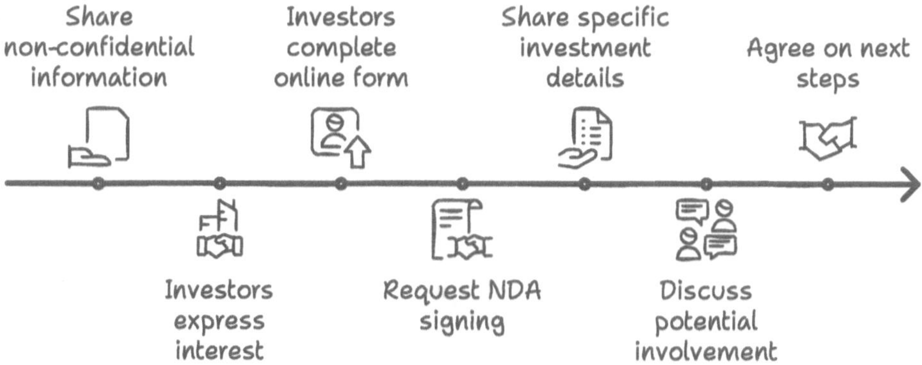

# WEALTH IN NUMBERS

*"The best advice I've ever gotten? Simple: Listen to those who've done it before. Every mistake you can make has been made before, and usually many times."*

*— Stephen Schwarzman. Co-founder, Chairman and CEO of The Blackstone Group*

# ERRORS TO AVOID IN CAPITAL RAISING

When raising capital, understanding investors' expectations is key. They look for big ideas, quick execution, and presentations that address their main concerns. To help your investor interactions, we put together a list of common mistakes to avoid. These aren't meant to be condescending but are based on actual experiences. Making mistakes is a common thing for successful entrepreneurs, and it's all part of the journey. The goal here isn't perfection, but always finding ways to improve. Practice makes dealing with investors feel more natural, but you still have to be prepared and have some self-awareness. You gotta be honest, attentive, and direct to make those investor relationships work. If you steer clear of these mistakes, you'll be in a better position to pitch your idea, gain trust, and get the funds. Take advantage of this list as a tool for advancing your professional development and maximizing your opportunities for success in the fiercely competitive world of investment.

- **Don't fall in love with your deal:** Creating stubbornness, inflexibility, and defensiveness is a deal killer. Be passionate about a good deal, but be open to criticism and changes. If your deal becomes not viable, don't be afraid to stop.

- **Don't fail to understand the investor's needs:** Tailor your presentation to the investor's style of learning and real needs. Remember that most investors are very busy and hate to have their time wasted.

- **Don't overload your presentation:** Keep it simple and get to the point. Provide a clear, concise deal presentation with all necessary information. Size matters and shorter is better.

- **Don't misjudge timing:** Timing is everything. Don't raise money at the last minute or misjudge the time it will take to close a deal. The best time to raise money is when you can afford to be patient.

- **Don't be overly secretive:** Being so afraid of sharing your idea that you don't tell anyone about it is counterproductive. You can't sell if you don't tell.

- **Don't neglect professionalism:** Show up on time, dress appropriately, have business cards aimed at investors, and be prepared with your equipment and materials.

- **Don't forget to practice:** Rehearse your presentation thoroughly before speaking to investors with real money.

- **Don't shy away from the ask:** Never forget to explicitly ask the investor for money.

- **Don't set unrealistic expectations:** Under-promise and over-deliver. Be realistic about your business prospects and avoid overly optimistic projections that can damage your credibility. Maintain integrity by only committing to what you're certain you can achieve. Your reputation is at stake.

- **Don't ignore investor feedback:** Listen attentively to investor insights and be open to their suggestions for improvement. Follow up to get feedback about your pitch.

- **Don't present without clear value proposition:** Clearly articulate what's extraordinary about your company's solution and its compelling benefits to a large number of consumers.

- **Don't assume knowledge:** Provide clear context and background. Remember that investors aren't as immersed in your business as you are.

- **Don't ignore presentation style:** While substance is more important, a polished presentation style can enhance your message and demonstrate professionalism.

- **Don't fixate on terms:** Avoid becoming overly focused on deal terms before establishing value and interest.

- **Don't hide significant problems:** Be transparent about challenges your business faces.

- **Don't expect immediate decisions:** Understand that investors often need time to evaluate opportunities thoroughly.

- **Don't dodge questions:** Know what you can and cannot disclose before you start talking, so that you do not stumble over awkward questions.

- **Don't switch off:** Be an active listener as you will always learn something.

- **Don't embellish facts or projections:** Present accurate and honest information about your business and its potential.

- **Don't forget about the team:** Highlight the strengths and experiences of your team members.

- **Don't use peripherals rather than focusing on content:** Ensure that any visual aids or props enhance rather than distract from your core message.

- **Don't start with a lengthy historical overview:** Avoid beginning with a long company history, mission statement, or current capitalization tables. Get to the point quickly to maintain investor interest.

- **Don't distribute lengthy handouts:** Avoid handing out long documents that might distract from your verbal presentation.

- **Don't be off your guard or too "salesy":** Maintain a professional demeanor. Be prepared and strategic in your approach, avoiding overly aggressive sales tactics.

# WEALTH IN NUMBERS

WEALTH IN NUMBERS

*"The art of communication is the language of leadership."*
*— James Humes, Presidential Speechwriter, Author, and*
*Former White House Advisor*

# CRAFTING YOUR INVESTOR PITCH

While you're fine-tuning your investor outreach and perfecting your elevator pitch, keep in mind that successful fundraising goes beyond just setting up meetings. Once an investor is interested and you've landed that prized in-person (or virtual) meeting, you need to step up your game even more.

It's important to run through your pitch and so you can keep it on target and cover all the important information in way that's easy to understand. In the near future, you are going to have a meeting with someone that might invest with you. You need to understand that successful pitching is an art form requiring finesse, preparation, and adaptability. Let's discuss how to convert your initial connections into impactful presentations that attract investors and result in successful fundraising.

You should recognize that investors' time is precious, and as we discussed, their attention spans are often limited. Make sure to get your point across quickly and effectively in your presentations. Share the right details at the right moments to keep investors interested and engaged.

Wondering how to make your potential deal more intriguing? Trust us, you can come up with an interesting mission statement for anything if you put your mind to it. One thing that dealmakers often get wrong is presenting their big plan and then throwing in a request for funding as an afterthought. Don't do that! Instead, make the investor feel like a crucial part of the story from the start. Let's say you're doing a roll-up of tire shops. Pretty dull, huh? So, what do you think about presenting something like this?

"We're revolutionizing car care by infusing tire shops with efficiency and cutting-edge technology. Our vision is to deliver unparalleled value to customers, foster rewarding careers for our team, generate solid returns for investors, and positively affect our communities. We invite you to join us in building this future." This approach transforms a potentially mundane investment opportunity into an exciting venture that investors want to be a part of.

As part of the process, showcase your expertise to prove you're the perfect person to lead this investment deal. For instance, if you're seeking investment for a software company, it would be appropriate to mention your experience as a consultant in the tech industry. That said, if your current job has nothing to do with your proposed business, it's best not to mention it. Others might question if you're really qualified. Just imagine, if you start off by saying you're a professional dog groomer when pitching an energy sector investment, people might raise an eyebrow.

Just a reminder, investors care about more than just the numbers. Don't forget that your body language and attitude play a role. If you stay professional and authentic, you'll have a better shot at getting investors interested and supporting you. While maintaining your authenticity, it's you need to be adaptable in your approach. The most effective dealmakers recognize that a one-size-fits-all approach falls short. Instead, make some tweaks as needed and adapt your presentations to different situations and who your potential investors are, just don't lose sight of your core message.

To do this, read the room and adapt your communication style to their unique personalities. Prepare both a summary and a detailed presentation to accommodate various investor styles and time constraints. Quickly assess the investor's preferences at the start and adjust your approach accordingly. One thing to consider is thinking about where this person falls on the extrovert-introvert scale. If you're outgoing and meeting with someone reserved, dial back your enthusiasm a bit and be more direct. If you're more on the shy side and you're meeting someone who's outgoing, be prepared for some small talk before getting into business.

You should approach initial investor meetings with a focus on relationship-building rather than immediate commitments. By arriving early, setting clear expectations, and actively listening to understand the investor's background and preferences, you'll lay the groundwork for long-term partnerships.

Don't forget to clearly ask for the deal. State you request for capital before leaving the meeting. Way too many people assume that investors will just offer money without being directly asked. I can't begin to tell you how many times that has resulted in a missed opportunity. You want to be upfront about what you need for funding, explain how the investment is structured, and ask when the time is right.

Feeling a bit nervous about asking for money is completely normal, but in the wise words of Young Jeezy and Lil' Wayne, "Scared money don't make no money." It's helpful to reframe your thinking about what you're actually doing here, too. Instead of seeing it as asking for a handout, consider that you're actually offering a valuable investment opportunity. You're a professional investor who is presenting other investors with chances to potentially earn returns on their money. This relationship is mutually beneficial - investors gain from your expertise and the opportunities you provide, while you benefit from their capital. It's important to recognize that you're helping investors achieve their financial goals. Overcoming your fear of fundraising is crucial for your success. Keep pushing through these fears and remember the value you bring to investors. By adopting this mindset, you'll build confidence in raising private money. This will enable you to clearly communicate your funding needs and confidently ask for investment when the time comes.

While confidence is key, it's equally important to be prepared with clear and thorough information about your investment opportunity. Here's one thing to note—many people, even experienced investors, are hesitant to invest in a business they don't fully understand and might not know much about SPV investments. Make sure to clearly explain how things work, the market potential of your deal, and your plan to generate returns.

This need for clarity extends beyond just the basics of the investment itself. Transparency should be paramount in your approach. You need to provide detailed information about your investment structure, communication frequency, and level of transparency. Be upfront about your fee structure, including management fees, carried interest, and profit distribution, enabling investors to make informed decisions.

When it's time to get into the details of the finances, impressing investors is all about being creative and presenting solid facts. At the end of the day, investors are laser-focused on one thing: a positive return on their investment—and if you can provide them with an exceptional one, even better. Here's how to knock their socks off:

- **Show Your Due Diligence:** Flex those research muscles! Demonstrate that you've dissected the market and sized up the competition like a pro. This isn't just guesswork—it's a masterclass in market analysis that'll have investors nodding in approval. Enhance your presentation with visual aids like charts and graphs when appropriate.

- **Keep It Real:** While it's tempting to paint a picture of unicorn-level success, seasoned investors can spot inflated numbers from a mile away. Present realistic estimates that showcase your potential without crossing into fantasy land. Credibility is your best friend here.

- **Present Your Timeline:** Some investors are adrenaline junkies chasing quick returns, while others are marathon runners in it for the long haul. Make sure to clearly communicate the timeline for returns so that they can accurately evaluate the deal.

- **Make it Digestible:** Don't drown them in data. Distill your financials into key metrics that tell a compelling story. Think of it as creating a highlight reel to get their interest and show the most important metrics.

- **Invite Them To The Deal Room:** Once you've discussed your strategy, you can encourage the potential investor to explore the more detailed financials in your SPV's deal room.

- **Know Your Material:** Be prepared to explain your assumptions and back up your figures with evidence to show that you've done your homework and have a solid grasp of your deal's potential.

By following this approach, you're not just asking for an investment—you're inviting investors to be part of an exciting journey. You're showing them that you've got the vision, the know-how, and the numbers to back it all up. The next level of conversation is just around the corner, and with this strategy, you're well-equipped to get there.

We've found that concluding your pitch with a compelling call to action is essential. After presenting your deal, it's imperative to move towards closing and securing commitments. This stage can be daunting, but asking closing questions prevents promising deals from slipping away. Create a sense of urgency or exclusivity when appropriate, tapping into the fear of missing out on a great opportunity. The close should be strategic, directly inquiring if potential investors are ready to proceed or what additional information they need.

Begin with a statement that encourages further exploration, such as "The more you examine this opportunity, the more compelling you'll find it." Then, transition to a direct question about their investment intentions: "Based on what you've seen, do you envision investing in this opportunity within the next [specific timeframe]?" If you receive a positive response, be prepared to discuss next steps for paperwork and due diligence. Follow up with a statement like "Would you prefer I walk you through our process, or should I send you a detailed overview?" This approach demonstrates preparedness, maintains momentum, and gives the investor control over how to proceed.

While most investors won't commit immediately and will want to review your data room, some might be ready to move forward right away. In such cases, promptly solidify their commitment and grant access to your data room. Even if you don't get an immediate "yes," progressing to the due diligence phase is still a positive step. When faced with a "maybe," acknowledge their feedback and encourage them to be open and honest with what they're thinking.

Invite them to review your deal room to help build some further interest and gives them time to think things over. You want to ensure your deal room is comprehensive and contains everything you're presenting. Make sure to respond promptly to any requests for further info. Remember that investor relationships develop at different paces; don't discount slow-burning relationships. Seasoned investors may be thorough in their review and take longer to commit initially. Once you're able to get them involved though, you'll often be able to count them as loyal, repeat investors once they're comfortable with your process.

So what if you deliver flawlessly, only to be met with a crushing "We're going to pass." This scenario is all too familiar in the world of raising capital. Successful fundraising requires realistic expectations; meeting with an investor doesn't guarantee funding, and many entrepreneurs face multiple rejections before finding the right investor. Even for visionaries like Steve Jobs, Sara Blakely, and Elon Musk. Remember, PayPal was once voted one of the worst business concepts of 1999. The key isn't avoiding rejection, but mastering how you respond to it.

As you encounter rejections, you'll build resilience. The fear that once held you back will diminish, allowing you to view these setbacks as a bump in the road on your journey to success. See rejection as an opportunity to learn and improve, rather than letting it bring you down. Regardless of the reason, continuing to refine strategy will guide you toward the right investment partners and ultimately lead to your success.

Bear in mind that investors can decline proposals for a variety of reasons so don't let the personal choices of others discourage you. A rejected deal doesn't reflect on you personally. Investors may have their own blind spots and biases that can be beyond your control. It's important to acknowledge and respect their different investment preferences. Don't let their limitations become yours.

It's common for investors, including us, to pass on good deals. We're not ashamed to say that we've missed out on numerous opportunities that turned out to be very successful. Even though things weren't ideal for us to get involved at the time, the deal got done and the investors who got on board were rewarded. Should your proposal be turned down, responding with gratitude and professionalism is the most effective approach. Showing appreciation for the investor's time is essential after a meeting. A brief email expressing thanks for their consideration of your proposal and acknowledging the value of your discussion can leave a lasting positive impression.

Remember that today's rejection doesn't close the door on future opportunities for working with this investor. A gracious response can lead to brilliant advice or valuable introductions in the highly interconnected investment community. By showing resilience and courtesy, you not only strengthen relationships but also establish yourself as a professional and capable dealmaker. Keep in touch with investors who say no, and maintain visibility. Persistence is key—they may be interested in a future opportunity that you put together.

It is crucial to maintain a mindset of continuous improvement as you deliver your pitch, always looking for ways to refine and enhance it. This process of rehearsal and refinement can make the difference between an interesting presentation that attracts investors and one that falls flat.

Back in 2008, Brian Chesky and Joe Gebbia, the co-founders of Airbnb, were struggling to get their startup off the ground. They came up with this cool idea: a platform where you can rent out your home or spare rooms to travelers looking for affordable and unique places to stay. But when they presented their concept to investors, they got a ton of rejections. Lots of investors didn't believe in the idea of random people crashing at someone's place and didn't think it would take off.

Brian and Joe saw that their pitch wasn't resonating, so they're gonna go back to the drawing board. They started by practicing their pitch a lot with their friends, mentors, and each other. They realized that their presentation was too technical and didn't highlight the story or the problem their idea solved.

With this insight, they got to work on an even more compelling story to show to potential investors. They zeroed in on four big things to make their idea more appealing. First off, they were talking about how Airbnb can give travelers a way more authentic and personal experience compared to regular hotels. This made people imagine how awesome it would be to use Airbnb. Secondly, they didn't shy away from addressing potential issues. They explained their plan to keep people safe, build trust, and create a comfortable community. Third, they used numbers to show that lots of people wanted affordable places to stay, and that many homeowners were interested in renting out their spaces. This revealed a great opportunity for their business. Lastly, they told stories about folks who had tried Airbnb and absolutely loved it. These real-life examples showed investors how Airbnb could actually work. These changes really boosted the appeal of their pitch and made their idea way more convincing and exciting for potential investors.

Airbnb's success story is proof that honing your pitch can really pay off. Brian and Joe, kept improving their pitch until they got it right. When they finally presented to Y Combinator, they were ready. They clearly explained their business idea and showed how passionate they were about making it work. Y Combinator loved it and invested in Airbnb. This gave them the support they needed to get things off the ground and made other key players take them seriously.

Get a friend to help you practice your pitch. This initial run-through can reveal surprising insights about how your carefully crafted words translate when spoken aloud. What sounds eloquent in your mind might come across differently when verbalized, so this step is invaluable for identifying and correcting any unintended messages or tones.

These mock presentations should include any supporting materials you plan to use. Pay close attention to your audience's reactions: Which parts capture their interest? Where do they seem to disengage? Encourage honest feedback about both the content and delivery of your pitch. This constructive criticism is gold for honing your presentation.

Make it your mission to memorize the pitch so you can crush it no matter where you are – whether you're stuck in an elevator or run into an investor at the grocery store. Being able to clearly and compellingly explain your SPV opportunity can make a huge difference.

To be really good, analyze your presentation piece by piece. This approach helps you spot any unnecessary parts of your pitch that distract from your message. Just a reminder, a short and powerful pitch is way better than a long and scattered one. Your story should be super well-crafted and concise so it sticks with your audience.

Keep in mind, you'll be telling this story countless times as you fine-tune your pitch. The sharper and more refined it gets, the stronger it will be. Your pitch should feel as effortless as an alarm going off – ready to use whenever the chance comes up.

The journey of honing your pitch is super important, just like the idea itself. Follow in the footsteps of Brian and Joe and never stop improving. Keep practicing your pitch, be open to constructive criticism and don't let initial setbacks discourage you. Remember, each rejection or stumble is an opportunity to learn and strengthen your presentation. By spending time on this refinement process, you'll end up with a pitch that's not only well-rehearsed but sincerely compelling. Preparing like this can really up your chances of connecting with the right investors and bringing your vision to life. Ultimately, it's not just the best ideas that win, but the entrepreneurs who never give up and keep going.

## Checklist for a Great Pitch

☐ **Understand Your Audience:**

- Research the potential investors' backgrounds, interests, and investment history.
- Tailor your pitch to align with their values and investment goals.

☐ **Craft a Compelling Opening:**

- Start with a strong hook or an intriguing question.
- Introduce yourself and your venture succinctly to grab attention immediately.

☐ **Clearly Define the Problem:**

- Articulate the specific problem or need your venture addresses.

☐ **Present Your Unique Solution:**

- Explain how your deal uniquely solves the problem and highlight what differentiates your solution alternatives.

☐ **Demonstrate Market Opportunity:**

- Provide evidence of market demand and size.
- Discuss industry trends and growth potential.

☐ **Explain Your Business Model:**

- Outline how your venture will make money.
- Discuss revenue streams, pricing strategies, and scalability.

☐ **Showcase Traction and Milestones:**

- Share any progress, such as user adoption, sales figures, or partnerships.
- Highlight key milestones achieved and outline future goals.

☐ **Detail Your Go-to-Market Strategy:**

- Explain how you plan to reach and acquire customers.
- Discuss marketing channels, sales strategies, and customer retention plans.

☐ **Conduct a Competitive Analysis:**

- Identify your main competitors in the market.
- Explain your competitive advantage and how you plan to maintain it.

☐ **Introduce Your Team:**

- Present the key team members and their relevant experience.
- Highlight any advisors or mentors associated with your venture.

☐ **Provide Financial Projections:**

- Offer realistic and data-driven financial forecasts.
- Include projected revenues, expenses, and break-even analyses.

☐ **State Your Funding Needs Clearly:**

- Specify the amount of funding you are seeking.
- Explain how the funds will be used and the anticipated return on investment.

☐ **Prepare a Strong Closing:**

- Summarize the key points of your pitch. End with a clear call to action, inviting further discussion or questions.

☐ **Develop Professional Supporting Materials:**

- Create a visually appealing and informative pitch deck.
- Include charts, graphs, and images that reinforce your message.

☐ **Practice Your Delivery:**

- Rehearse the pitch multiple times to build confidence.
- Pay attention to pacing, tone, and clarity.

☐ **Anticipate Questions and Objections:**

- Prepare thoughtful answers to potential investor questions.
- Be ready to address concerns about risks and challenges.

☐ **Ensure Clarity and Simplicity:**

- Avoid jargon and overly technical language.
- Keep explanations straightforward and easy to understand.

☐ **Test All Technical Aspects:**

- Ensure all of your AV equipment and software function properly.
- Have backups ready in case of technical difficulties.

☐ **Manage Time Effectively:**

- Keep your pitch within the allotted time frame.
- Allocate appropriate time to each section without rushing.

☐ **Dress Appropriately:**

- Choose attire that is professional and suits the context of the meeting. Aim to make a positive first impression.

☐ **Prepare for Different Scenarios:**

- Be ready to deliver your pitch in various settings, from formal meetings to impromptu encounters.
- Adapt your presentation style as needed.

☐ **Stay Informed About Legal and Compliance Issues:**

- Ensure all statements and claims are accurate and verifiable.
- Be aware of any regulatory requirements related to your venture.

☐ **Develop a Follow-Up Plan:**

- Have supplementary materials ready to share after the pitch.
- Plan how you will maintain communication and move forward with interested investors.

☐ **Review and Refine Your Content:**

- Double-check all facts, figures, and calculations for accuracy.
- Edit your materials for clarity, coherence, and impact.

By meticulously preparing each aspect outlined in this checklist, you'll be well-equipped to deliver a pitch that is not only flawless but also persuasive and memorable. Remember, the key to a successful pitch lies in thorough preparation, genuine passion, and the ability to connect with your audience on both a logical and emotional level.

# WEALTH IN NUMBERS

*"Trust is built in drops and lost in buckets."*

*— Kevin Plank, Founder, Under Armour*

# UNDERSTANDING TRUST CURVES

Don't underestimate the power of trust in determining the success of an investment, no matter how good the numbers appear. Building trust takes time, and we call it the Trust Curve. Knowing this concept can help explain why some deals work out while others don't, even if they seem promising.

What's your definition of trust in relationships? Merriam-Webster defines trust as "assured reliance on the character, ability, strength, or truth of someone or something." Trust involves believing that someone will do the right thing, and it requires accepting some risk in doing so.

In business, it's a major factor in decision-making and is established through time, expertise, and being dependable. People typically want to work with people they know, like, and trust, so it's really important for converting prospects into long-term partners.

Investors need to trust your ability to manage their capital and run a deal successfully. The Trust Curve framework helps us wrap our heads around how trust is developed in business relationships.

Understanding these curves can provide valuable insights into why some deals succeed while others falter, even when everything looks promising on paper. This invisible currency of business often explains why you might feel uneasy about a deal or be drawn to a company despite knowing little about their product.

# THE THREE TRUST CURVES

## Team Trust:

This curve represents the investor's confidence in the leadership and management team behind the venture or investment opportunity. Having trust is built by your potential investor getting to know you as the General Partner and others who are involved that will be managing the money or operations of the deal they might invest in. Trust in the individuals involved often matters more than the opportunity itself. This is why many start by seeking investment from friends and family—these individuals are already high up the Trust Curve with you and your team. They trust your abilities and are willing to overlook their lack of knowledge in other areas because of this trust. We're naturally drawn to people we connect with, trust, and believe in.

## Industry Trust:

This curve indicates how well the investor understands and feels comfortable with the industry or sector in which the investment opportunity lies. Imagine you're offered a chance to invest in a cutting-edge AI startup. It sounds exciting, right? But if you can't tell machine learning from a washing machine, you might hesitate, no matter how impressive the pitch. When we lack industry knowledge, our brain throws up red flags, and you know that if you do move forward, you'll likely have your thoughts filled with doubt and second-guessing. The lack of industry knowledge could stall the investment process.

### Opportunity Trust:

This curve reflects the investor's familiarity with and confidence in the specific deal or investment opportunity, often tied to its locality or unique characteristics. Does the deal itself make sense Are the terms fair? Does it align with the investor's goals? Even if trust in you and your team is strong, and the industry knowledge is solid, the specifics of the opportunity itself must make sense. Investors need to ensure that the deal is sound, aligns with their goals, and is fair. Due diligence is essential at this stage—trust but verify. A bad deal will still be a bad deal, even if the other elements of trust are in place.

How an investor feels about you in relation to these Trust Curves will really impact whether they want to get in on a deal. Imagine a situation where a seasoned investor is offered a chance to invest in a really promising apartment complex. They have a good relationship with your team (high team trust) and the property has strong financials and excellent collateral (high opportunity trust). The investor is hesitant because they don't know much about the multifamily real estate market. This knowledge gap could deter them from an otherwise attractive investment. If one thing area lacking, it can cause an investor to pause.

To improve your capital raising process and increase your success in closing deals, it's crucial to master these Trust Curves. Think about what you want to achieve before meeting with the investor. Are you trying to show how good your team is, educate the investor about your industry, or convince them to do something specific? If you see any trust gaps, handle them proactively so your potential investor feels confident in every aspect.

Think about where you stand on the Trust Curve when working on your proposal. Are you making progress on all three tracks, or is something holding you back? Figure out which part of the Trust Curve needs the most attention, so you can customize your presentation for the biggest impact. You want to move potential partners up the Trust Curves to increase your success in raising capital. Every interaction you have with your potential investor is a chance to get closer to sealing the deal.

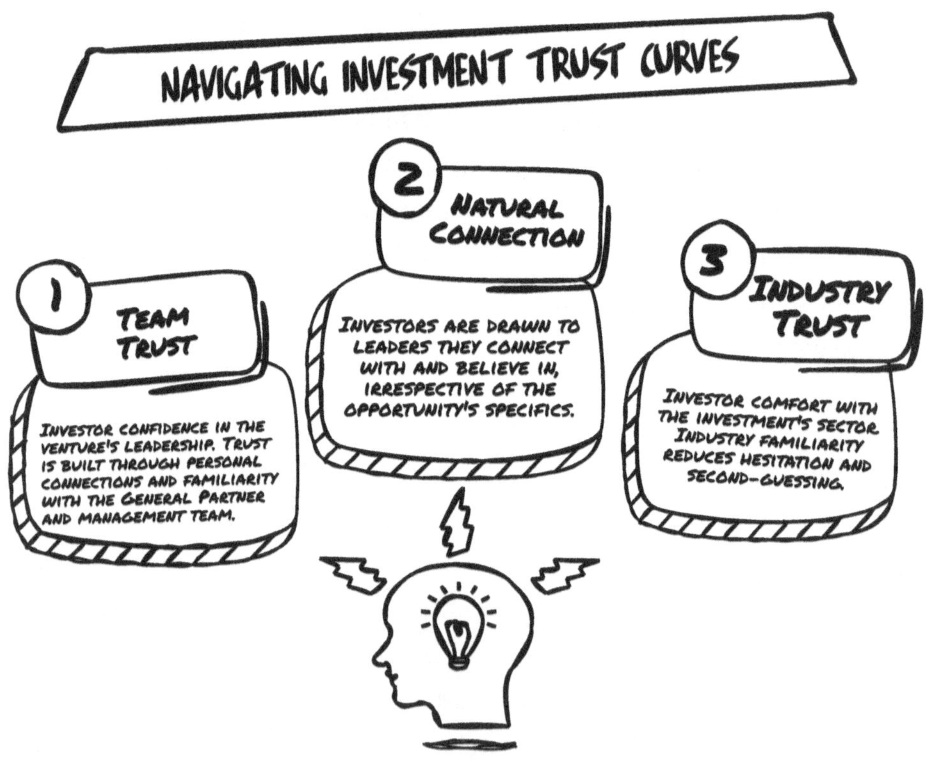

# WEALTH IN NUMBERS

*"I believe in analysis and not forecasting."*

— *Benjamin Graham, Father of Value Investing and*
*Author of The Intelligent Investor*

# DUE DILIGENCE

If you're entering the due diligence process, congrats! We're entering a pivotal moment in the investment process. Getting here took a ton of hard work, but now it's time to enter an intense stage to get even closer to the finish line. Validating the deal's integrity and potential is an essential function of due diligence. Both dealmakers and investors can check if the opportunity matches their criteria. This process lets everyone fully evaluate the deal before making a commitment. This is a great chance to identify risks, confirm the potential and take care of any issues.

For investors, due diligence signifies serious interest. As dealmakers, we must use this chance to demonstrate our competence, dedication, and alignment with the investor's goals. Make sure to reply promptly to any questions and maintain good communication with investors. If you take too long to respond to an investor's request, it might cause them some concern. To ensure success in the due diligence process, it's important to be thorough and transparent. This begins with compiling all relevant deal information, from corporate filings and government records to financial statements and insurance documents.

To provide access to these items, you need to have a well-organized data room where investors can easily access important documents. A data room is a secure digital repository for storing and sharing sensitive information during the due diligence process.

In the past, these were physical rooms with paper documents, but now virtual data rooms (VDRs) provide secure online access from anywhere, streamlining the investment process. By being proactive and maintaining a clear, organized presentation of your opportunity, you make it easier for investors to review and make informed decisions quickly.

If you're prepared, it'll make a big difference with investors. Keep your documents updated to stay accurate and maintain credibility. Every interaction counts. Because the info is sensitive, your data room needs good security like encryption, access control, and secure backups. Keeping your data room up-to-date and secure not only protects your information but also increases the likelihood of investors wanting to move forward with your opportunity.

Organize the required items for a data room by grouping them logically and providing clear labels for navigation. Set access rules for users, add security measures like encryption and two-factor authentication, and launch the data room after testing it out. Make sure only authorized users are invited and keep track of how they handle the data. Your data room will most likely include some of these:

- **Investor Presentation:** The investor presentation serves as a deck or summary overview sheet for the deal being presented. It should clearly convey the key points and value proposition to potential investors, ensuring they quickly grasp the essentials of the deal.

- **Financial Documents:** In your data room, include income statements, balance sheets, cash flow statements, tax filings, auditor reports, and detailed financial projections and budgets. These documents provide a clear picture of the financial health and future prospects of the deal. Your LPs will conduct a thorough evaluation of the financial health of the SPV, examining the expected return on investment for investors based on projected profits and the duration of the investment.

- **Personnel Documents:** Personnel files, payroll records, and benefits information should also be included. This ensures that investors have a comprehensive understanding of the company's human resources and compensation structures.

- **Corporate Legal Documents:** Ensure you have articles of incorporation, shareholder agreements, bylaws, minutes of board meetings, and details of any past or ongoing legal issues. These documents are crucial for understanding the legal framework and governance of the company. Review Legal Structure and Agreements: Examine the legal framework of the SPV, including its formation documents, contractual agreements, permits, licenses, and any legal issues that may affect the project's viability. Ensuring compliance with local, state, and federal regulations is crucial.

- **Business and Operational Documents:** Business plans, detailed descriptions of products or services, organizational charts, staff details, and information about key suppliers and customers should be part of your data room. These documents help investors understand the operational aspects and strategic direction of the business.

- **Intellectual Property Documentation:** Include patents, trademarks, copyrights, and associated legal paperwork. Protecting intellectual property is vital, and these documents assure investors of the company's proprietary assets. This includes information about trade secrets and any other proprietary business information. These documents highlight the unique value propositions and competitive advantages of the company.

- **Marketing Materials:** Presentations, brochures, flyers, ads, and other marketing collateral should be available to showcase the company's market presence and promotional strategies.

- **Technical Information:** Include product specifications, engineering drawings, and technical reports. These documents provide insight into the technical aspects and innovation within the company.

- **Environmental and Safety Information:** Environmental impact studies and health and safety reports are essential if relevant to your industry. They demonstrate the company's commitment to compliance and safety.

- **Due Diligence of the Parties Involved:** Your Limited Partners may want to investigate the reputation, experience, and financial capacity of all parties involved in the project. The vetting helps ensure participants are trustworthy and capable of fulfilling their responsibilities.

- **Additional Information:** Your data room should also contain a disclaimer, information security policy, privacy policy, and compliance documentation for the Bank Secrecy Act (BSA), Anti-Money Laundering (AML), and Know Your Client (KYC) screening processes. These documents emphasize your commitment to regulatory compliance and data protection.

# WEALTH IN NUMBERS

*"When dealing with people, remember you are not dealing with creatures of logic, but with creatures of emotion."*

— *Dale Carnegie, Author of* How to Win Friends and Influence People

# MOVING INVESTORS TO SAY YES

After you prepare your materials and do your due diligence, you're almost ready to complete the investment deal. At this point, investors have access to all the information about your business through your data room. But, turning their interest into a commitment needs your effort and a distinct set of skills.

In this phase, transition from information sharing to active engagement for investment. As a General Partner, offer strategic guidance patiently. Investors evaluate your opportunity against their criteria. Maintain timely, thoughtful communication—be persistent without overreaching. Mastering this balance significantly improves your funding success. Remember, investors operate on their own timelines, often juggling multiple options. Understand that some investors can have a lengthy due diligence process. This is one reason we suggested you start your capital raise early. It would allow time for their decision without added stress.

That being said, If you're raising capital for the first time, keep your expectations in check. While experienced dealmakers might close deals in 30 to 60 days, your process may take longer.

One thing you should do after each investor meeting is discuss a specific date for your next follow-up. This sets an expection and keeps communication open without being pushy.

During this period, be available and responsive. Let your potential investor know you're ready to answer questions or concerns, but don't bug them. You shouldn't be trying to pressure investors into writing a check. That is a quick way turn a "maybe" into a "no." Just keep your eyes open to nudge them when the time is right.

When that time comes, asking the right closing questions can help you figure out if they're into it and ready to commit. Just ask, "How do you see this opportunity fitting into your portfolio?" or "What's your timeline for deciding about this investment?" These open-ended questions can give us some great insights into their thought process. Another approach is to suggest a next step. For example, "How about a follow-up call to address questions before we draft paperwork?" This builds momentum without applying too much pressure. Remember, the goal is to make it easy for interested investors to say yes. By presenting a clear path, you can smoothly shift from exploration to getting a commitment.

Recognizing the psychological factors that influence investors is extremely important. As you get initial commitments, you build your funding base. You also create social proof that can speed up your fundraising.

This is where momentum plays a role. It taps into a powerful motivator in investing: the Fear of Missing Out, or FOMO. This psychological factor can greatly influence investors. It can also help your fundraising efforts. If you play your cards right with the commitments you've got, more investors will come flocking to your opportunity.

Many investors that initially respond with a "maybe," often disguised as statements like "it's too early for us" or "check back when you have more traction." These responses can be genuine. But, they often let investors keep their options open. This is when your ability to leverage FOMO becomes critical.

Time and time again, it's been shown that FOMO can really boost your ability to attract investors. When faced with new opportunities, people often seek their peers for a signal to decide. You can use this psychology to your advantage. You might tell a potential investor, "We've secured commitments from several top industry investors." Highlight commitments from respected investors (with their approval). Or, emphasize the amount of capital you've raised. This creates urgency and appeal for your SPV. Think of it like a snowball rolling down a hill. As it gathers more snow, it continues to grow larger and move faster.

Keep in mind that investors are not just evaluating your opportunity - they're also looking at who else is interested. Sharing info about other commitments can provide social proof. It may help convince hesitant investors to join in. Setting a target close date can push investors to commit sooner by creating a sense of scarcity. Successfully using FOMO involves crafting a narrative that emphasizes how desirable and exclusive your opportunity is. In essence, each "yes" you get can help you get more "yeses" down the line.

Even as you start to close deals with some investors, it's important to keep reaching out to others. Don't stop exploring options for Limited Partners to join your deal. This approach has several benefits. First, it helps you maintain your momentum and enthusiasm. Second, it gives you a backup plan in case some deals fall through. Finally, it can motivate investors to decide faster. They might fear missing out if they wait too long.

Remember, investing isn't quick. It takes time. You want to follow up effectively with potential investors. When you follow up, use it as a chance to keep investors interested in your opportunity. Share updates about your deal. New info can show your opportunity's value. This keeps your opportunity fresh in their minds and can help them decide to give you the green light.

Once you have an investor that likes the deal wants to move forward, it's a good time to formalize their interest. It's common to have preliminary agreements in place for private investment deals. These include Letters of Intent (LOIs) and Pledge Agreements for Capital Transactions (PACTs). While not legally binding, these serve as a bridge between your initial discussions and formal commitments. LOIs are the traditional choice, while PACTs, introduced by the Founder Institute in 2018, were designed to address oversubscription issues.

Both LOIs and PACTs outline key investment aspects. These include the amount, structure, rights, obligations, and timeline. They usually ask investors for a bit of info. They also want to know who's involved in the investment. Investors may choose to invest individually or through their own LLC. Save time by giving investors a pre-drafted LOI to fill out and sign. Having these in place is a huge step in the process because they show the investor is serious about moving forward.

These agreements also classify investors. They are "Hard Circled" (committed) or "Soft Circled" (casually exploring). They don't transfer funds right away. But, they clarify pledged amounts and prove the agreement. This allows a clear calculation of the "Hard Circled" total. It reduces uncertainty when closing multi-party investment rounds. When you use these tools to clarify investor interest, you can confidently move towards finalizing your investment deal.

Closing deals is an art. It blends strategy, psychology, and perseverance. Every interaction is a chance to build trust and show your value. Use it to get closer to your funding goals. The tricks and tips we've learned - like leveraging FOMO and making use of LOIs - are what you need to win in this game.

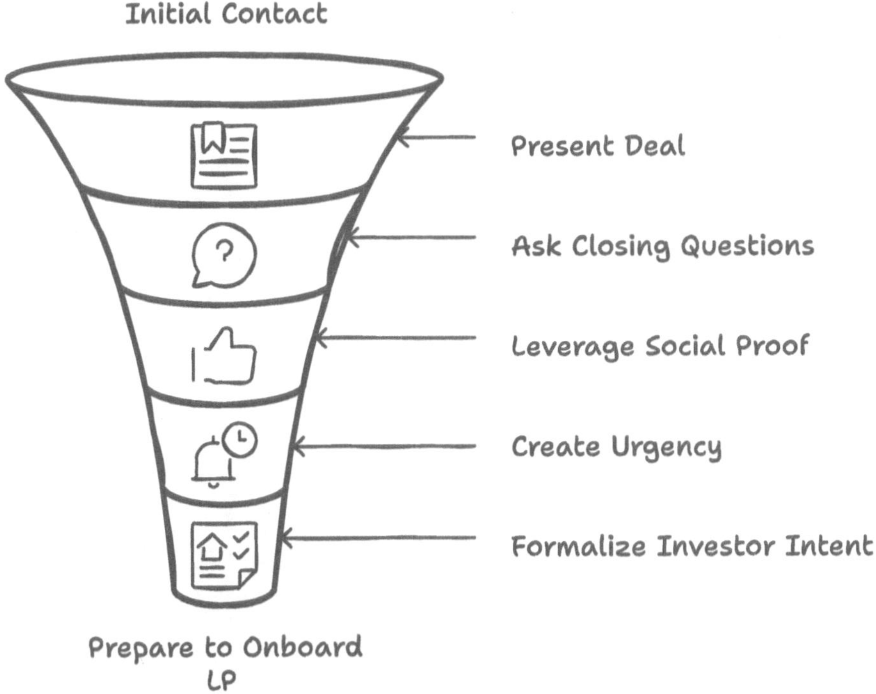


Beyond all these tactics, lies a truth: successful capital raising is about building relationships. It's about knowing your investors' needs and motivations. You must align your opportunity with their vision. As you start raising money, remember to be patient, observant, and resilient. Using the strategies we've discussed, you aren't just closing a deal. You're opening the door to huge opportunities that will define your path to success

# FINALIZING YOUR SPV INVESTMENT DEAL

You've reached a critical point in your investment journey. Your potential new Limited Partner has signaled their commitment, perhaps via a Letter of Intent (LOI) or a PACT agreement. You're close to finalizing the deal. However, closing an SPV investment has many pitfalls that could derail your efforts at the eleventh hour. Avoiding them demands your attention.

As you near the finish line, you may want to relax. But, now is the time to stay alert and manage every detail. From document reviews to fund verification, each step is vital. It helps you ink the deal and build a prosperous partnership. Let's explore the key elements and best practices. They will ensure a smooth, compliant, and efficient closing for your SPV investment.

It's wise to add buffer time for unexpected setbacks. Even if you manage your schedule well, others may not share your urgency. Starting each step too early gives flexibility. It helps ensure the smooth execution of your plan. It's also important to remain open to potential changes until the very end. Just when you think you have it all figured out, an investor you were counting on might withdraw unexpectedly. To reduce this risk, avoid rejecting other investors too soon, even if you have a preference. Keep the

SPV open for investment until you reach your desired subscription level and the funds are in its bank account.

Now that you have a serious investor that is ready to proceed, take concrete steps to finalize the deal. This usually means getting all necessary documents signed. It also means formally documenting the established capital commitment. Be prepared with the required paperwork and a clear understanding of the next steps in the process. Your closing approach should be direct, yet tactful. It should show your professionalism and readiness to move forward with the partnership.

When closing an SPV deal, perform a thorough check of all the necessary paperwork. This is one of the most important parts of the process. You can't consider an investor fully on board until you've completed a few key steps. First, take a close look at all the subscription documents to make sure they're complete. Check that no important information is missing. This careful review is vital. Even one forgotten signature could prevent the deal from closing. Attention to small details can mean success or failure in your investment deal.

Maintaining meticulous records of all onboarding activities is crucial. This documentation serves several purposes:

- It ensures compliance with laws and regulations.

- It provides a clear audit trail.

- It can help resolve future disputes or misunderstandings.

Next, conduct a final Know Your Customer (KYC) and Anti-Money Laundering (AML) check. This is to meet regulatory requirements and mitigate risk. These checks are not mere formalities. They are vital safeguards. They protect your SPV and your investors. Check that all required signatures are in place. This will confirm each investor's commitment and understanding of the terms.

As you progress through the finalization process, it's essential to prepare for capital calls. Ensure everything is set to call capital when ready. This will help a smooth transition from onboarding to active investment. An investor completes all these steps before becoming onboarded and ready to invest.

To simplify things, leverage digital platforms to sign documents and transfer funds. These tools can significantly expedite the process and reduce the likelihood of errors or delays. At each step, give investors clear, concise instructions. Be responsive to their questions and concerns throughout. This communication helps close deals faster. It also builds a positive relationship with your investors.

Remember, the onboarding process serves many important purposes in SPVs and investing. It ensures compliance with laws and regulations. It also provides investors with key info about the investment opportunity. This allows them to make informed decisions. The process protects the SPV and investors. It defines terms and expectations. This reduces the chance of misunderstandings or disputes down the line. Always remember that the deal isn't done until every 't' is crossed, every 'i' is dotted, and every dollar is in the bank. Stay vigilant and prepare for last-minute challenges.

After all this, you may be feeling overwhelmed by all the details and risks. To help you through this phase, we've made a checklist. It outlines the key steps and best practices. On the next page, you'll find a checklist. It will be your roadmap to a successful deal and will ensure that no key element is overlooked.

# INVESTOR ONBOARDING CHECKLIST

- Gather Essential Information

  - ☐ **Personal information:** Name, address, contact details
  - ☐ Government-issued ID
  - ☐ **Tax-related information:** Your Tax ID numbers and entity type (Individual or Company)
  - ☐ Completed Investor Questionnaire

- Compliance Checks

  - ☐ Conduct Know Your Customer (KYC) checks
  - ☐ Perform Anti-Money Laundering (AML) screening
  - ☐ Accreditation Verification (if required)
  - ☐ Complete any other associated regulatory compliance checks as required by law

- Document Preparation and Execution

  - ☐ Signed Private Placement Memorandum (PPM)
  - ☐ Signed Subscription Agreement
  - ☐ Completed W-9 or W-8 Form
  - ☐ Signed ACH Authorization Form (Optional)
    - Required if the Limited Partner elects for automatic fund transfers
    - If declined, the LP must specify their preferred alternative method for submitting funds during capital calls

# UNDERSTANDING KYC & AML

Now that you're running private investment deals, you need to understand how important it is to know your investors and prevent money laundering. Your job isn't just about getting raising capital, you also need to make sure every investor in your group is legitimate. This protects your investment group from unnecessary risks and keeps you out of trouble with the authorities.

No matter what business you're in, if you help people move money, criminals might try to use your service for illegal purposes. That's why it's crucial to have good practices in place.

KYC and AML are often mistaken for the same thing, but in reality, they are two segments. They work for a company's efforts to follow laws against money laundering and terrorist financing. Countries worldwide have enacted laws to require this. KYC, also known as Customer Due Diligence (CDD), is just one part of all-encompassing AML programs. AML is about how companies use people, processes, and technology to find and stop money laundering. KYC is about knowing and checking your customers to understand the risks they bring to your business. Basically, this all means doing your homework on potential investors. It's your first line of defense against risks. Because investments like yours are complex and involve a lot of money, it's even more important to take the right precautions.

One of the common obstacles criminals come across is finding ways to use their unlawfully obtained money. AML refers to the steps that firms must take to stop criminals from using illicit funds. This applies to financial institutions and other firms. This is where your role as a gatekeeper becomes critical. AML regulations aim to stop terrorist financing and crime, like human trafficking.

AML policies require businesses to report when a customer deposits a lot of cash. In simple terms, money laundering is about making dirty money look clean. Criminals do this by processing transactions through various activities. Their goal is to reintroduce their illegal funds into the financial system. This is a strategy to make the funds "clean" and appear legitimate. Since restrictions exist through AML policies, criminals are constantly seeking new ways to get their illegal money into the financial system without raising suspicion.

The money laundering process has three stages: Placement, Layering, and Integration.

- **Placement:** This stage involves introducing the "dirty money" into the legitimate financial system while concealing its origin.

- **Layering (or "structuring"):** This step obscures the money's source through a series of transactions and accounting maneuvers. By breaking the funds into smaller transactions, it becomes harder to trace and detect the laundering activities.

- **Integration:** In the final stage, the laundered money is withdrawn from the legitimate account and records, making it available for the criminals to use for their intended purposes.

Anti-Money Laundering (AML) activities aim to fight financial crimes. They do this by setting up rules and processes to monitor business relationships. These efforts aim to prevent things like market manipulation, illegal trading, tax evasion, and bribery. Your company may follow the rules, but your partners might not. So, it's important that you are taking the right steps to properly vet all entities that are participating in your investment deal.

A good Anti-Money Laundering program has three parts. First, it must have careful record-keeping that can withstand audits. Second, it must train employees on regulations. Lastly, it must monitor transactions for any suspicious activity. If you spot suspicious activities, you must report them to the proper authorities. The goal of these reports help law enforcement detect and catch financial criminals.

Many countries have implemented AML regulations. This is due to international standards set by groups like the Financial Action Task Force (FATF). As a General Partner of an SPV, you need to stay updated on these regulations and adjust your compliance program as needed. As the secondary component of this, here's what a comprehensive KYC process for your SPV should entail:

- **Identity Verification:** This is the foundation of KYC. You need to confirm that each LP is who they claim to be. This typically involves collecting government-issued identification documents and cross-referencing them with official databases. This process includes matching tax identification number (SSN or EIN) with IRS database.

- **Accredited Investor Verification:** For most SPVs, especially those using 506(b) or 506(c) exemptions, you'll need to verify that your LPs are Accredited Investors, per the SEC's definition. This involves reviewing financial statements, tax returns, or obtaining third-party verifications.

- **Source of Funds Verification:** Understanding where your LPs' investment capital originates is crucial. This step helps prevent the SPV from aiding money laundering or other crimes.

- **Beneficial Ownership Identification:** For LPs that are entities, you must identify and verify their ultimate beneficial owners. These are the people who truly control or benefit from the entity.

- **Risk Profiling and Prohibited Persons:** Investors have different levels of risk. Because of this, it's important to monitor them in different ways. By considering each investor's risk level, you can adjust your compliance work to fit the issues they might raise. This approach is especially important when checking for sanctions and high-profile people and its vital to check that none of your investors are on international sanctions lists. Dealing with banned individuals or companies could cause legal issues and damage your reputation. It's also important to identify politically exposed persons among your investors. These are people with important public jobs who need extra checking to avoid risks of corruption or money laundering. A good KYC & AML provider can help you assess risk. This will help you follow the rules. It will also protect your investment from compliance issues. Risk checks include:

- **Politically Exposed Person (PEP) List:**
    - Identifies individuals entrusted with prominent public functions
    - Higher risk for potential involvement in bribery and corruption

- **Sanction Lists:**
    - Prohibit business interactions with certain entities or individuals
    - **Sources:** OFAC, EU, UN, BOE, FBI, BIS, and others

- **Watch Lists:**
    - Indicate caution when interacting with listed individuals and entities
    - Over 20 embargo and caution lists checked (e.g., FBI, World Bank, Interpol)

- **Enforcement Lists:**
    - Information on potential and historical criminal activity
    - Includes data on terrorist financing

- **Adverse Media Checks :**
    - Search traditional news outlets, broadcasting media, internet media, and unstructured news sources
    - Report news associated with money laundering, fraud, drug trafficking, and other criminal activities

This process isn't a one-time task, but an ongoing responsibility. Your investors' risk levels can change due to personal events, money matters, or new rules. The risk from your current investors can change over time as various ban lists are updated. It's important to have a good process to check your investors and their info regularly. This helps you stay ahead of these changes. Knowing your investors protects your investment group. It creates a better ecosystem for everyone involved.

To make this process easier, we highly recommend that you make use of technology to your advantage. There are a ton of online services that can help with knowing your investors. Some software can gather, check, and monitor information. These tools will help you follow the rules and reduce your paperwork.

# ACCREDITATION VERIFICATION

Accreditation verification is a key part of due diligence for investors. It acts as a safeguard. It ensures that only qualified people can access private investments that have specific regulations. For those managing Regulation D offerings, the choice between Rule 506(b) and Rule 506(c) determines how to verify investors.

Rule 506(b) allows some self-certification. Rule 506(c) permits general solicitation but requires stricter verification. Under 506(b), investors can self-verify their status. This is easier for issuers but requires careful documentation. In contrast, 506(c) requires issuers to take "reasonable steps" to verify each investor's accredited status. This makes it a more thorough process. This may involve reviewing financial documents, like tax returns, bank statements, and brokerage accounts. The stricter approach of 506(c) helps ensure SEC compliance and protects against fraud.

Some people hesitate to choose the 506(c) election. It requires verifying investors' accreditation status. This concern was especially strong when the election was first introduced and still exists today, albeit to a lesser degree. People that are new to running deals tend to worry about how to verify an investor's status, what counts as acceptable verification, and how investors might react when they ask them to provide proof. They also are afraid that the investors they approach might get scared off and not want to participate. Still yet, there are concerns that the process could become too burdensome. Despite these concerns, we hope to put your mind at ease when we tell you that our experience has been largely positive.

Most investors will accept that verification is a legal requirement. It shows your commitment to compliance and quality fund management. Some investors may find the process frustrating. This is especially true if they struggle to provide necessary information or have complex asset combinations. However, we see this as a chance to showcase your professionalism and dedication. Overall, the verification process has been a positive experience for us, contrary to initial fears.

As we mentioned, the SEC can require issuers to take "reasonable" steps to verify investors' accredited status. But, it doesn't define "reasonable" in detail. Instead, it offers a "safe harbor" provision with three options. It agrees these will provide "reasonable" verification. This approach lets issuers choose their verification methods. It also ensures compliance with regulations.

For small securities offerings, manual verification might be manageable. However, for larger Rule 506(c) offerings with lots of investors, the process can become overwhelming. Running dozens of Accredited Investor verifications will quickly become a challenging and time-consuming task.

Fortunately, the SEC lets issuers use third-party verifiers to streamline this process. These services not only conduct the necessary research but also provide a "safe harbor" letter stating each investor's accredited status. A verification document from a qualified SEC-recognized professional confirms the investor's accredited status. It shifts the responsibility for accuracy to the third party if they incorrectly assess an investor's status. These services will save you a lot of time. They'll reduce repetitive work and let you focus on other parts of your deal.

You can receive verification with a written confirmation from one of these service providers. The letter you receive will confirm that they verified the investor's accredited status within the last ninety days. Recognized parties that can provide Accredited Investor verification include:

- **Certified Public Accountants (CPAs):** Professionals who are licensed to provide financial auditing and attestation services.

- **Attorneys:** Licensed legal professionals who can provide opinions on an investor's financial status.

- **Registered Investment Advisors (RIAs):** Professionals registered with the SEC or a state regulatory authority to provide investment advice with Series 7, Series 65, or Series 82 licenses or authorized signatories of SEC-Registered Investment Advisers.

- **Broker-Dealers:** Individuals or firms registered with the SEC and members of a self-regulatory organization like FINRA, authorized to buy and sell securities on behalf of their clients Series 7, Series 65, or Series 82 licenses.

- **Specialized Accredited Investor Verification Services:** There are many service providers that meet SEC criteria and specialize in verifying Accredited Investors. Often, providers that handle KYC and AML checks also offer this service, making your onboarding process more efficient.

When you use a third-party verification service, the letter you receive should list which accreditation criteria the investor meets. The validator should sign and date the letter to confirm they reviewed it on your behalf.

Using this type of service adds costs to your deal. However, the saved time, effort, and reduced liability justify the cost. You can't put a price on having peace of mind, knowing that the validation is thorough and trustworthy.

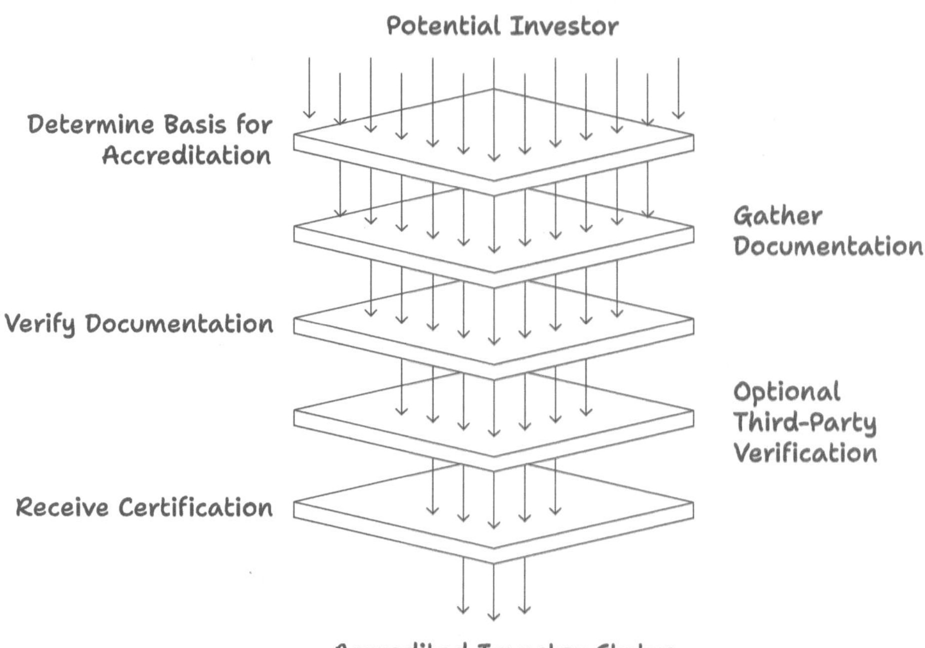



Take note that Regulation D defines "Accredited Investor" for only US citizens and residents. For international investors, there's no direct equivalent. However, issuers can use an equivalency determination process. It involves checking if an investor's finances meet US accredited standards.

For international investors, acceptable documentss may include audited financial statements, translated into English as well as legal opinions from attorneys in jurisdictions with similar Accredited Investor definitions. In some cases, it is possible to receive third-party verifications from certain institutions that assist with international investors.

As a general outline, an Accredited Investor letter will need to include a the date the letter is issued, the full legal name of the investor seeking accreditation, a statement verifying that the investor meets the criteria outlined in Rule 501 of Regulation D under the Securities Act of 1933, and the signature along with the printed name of the qualified professional who assessed the investor's financial standing and verified their Accredited Investor status. However, the document you'll have drafted is typically more thorough.

After exploring Accredited Investor verification, you may wonder what a proper verification document looks like. To help you, we've included an example of a comprehensive Accredited Investor verification letter on the next page. This sample document will give you a clear idea of the format, content, and level of detail expected in a professional verification letter and help you spot valid verification documents. Having this understanding will help ensure compliance in your investor onboarding processes.

# WEALTH IN NUMBERS

**ACCREDITED INVESTOR VERIFICATION LETTER**

_____________________________ ("Investor") has requested that the undersigned provide [General Partner Entity Name] (the "Manager"), with this Accredited Investor Verification Letter (the "Letter") to assist the Manager in its verification of Investor's status as an "Accredited Investor" within the meaning of Rule 501(a) of the Securities Act of 1933, as amended (the "Securities Act"), in connection with Investor's potential subscription for a partnership interest (the "Interest") in [SPV Entity Name] (the "Partnership").

I/We hereby certify that I am / we are (please check the appropriate box):

◻ a registered broker-dealer, as defined in the Securities Exchange Act of 1934, as amended (the "Securities Exchange Act");

◻ an investment adviser registered with the U.S. Securities and Exchange Commission (the "SEC");

◻ a licensed attorney in good standing under the laws of the jurisdiction in which I am admitted to practice law; or

◻ a certified public accountant in good standing under the laws of the place of my residence or principal office.

Based on my/our review of the Investor Materials (as defined below), the undersigned hereby advises you that Investor satisfied one or more of the following criteria (check all boxes that apply):

◻ a natural person whose individual "net worth," or joint net worth with his or her spouse or spousal equivalent,* excluding the estimated fair market value of his or her primary residence, exceeds $1,000,000;†

◻ a natural person who had an individual annual income‡ in excess of $200,000 in each of the two most recent years, or a joint annual income with his or her spouse or spousal equivalent in excess of $300,000 in each of those years, and has a reasonable expectation of reaching the same income level in the current year;

◻ a natural person holding in good standing one or more professional certifications or designations or credentials from an accredited educational institution that the SEC has designated as qualifying an individual for Accredited Investor status;§

◻ a "family client," as defined in rule 202(a)(11)(G)-1 under the Advisers Act of 1940, as amended (the "Advisers Act"), of a "family office," as defined in rule 202(a)(11)(G)-1 under the Advisers Act, whose prospective investment in the Partnership is directed by such family office, and such family office is one (i) with assets under management in excess of $5,000,000, (ii) that was not formed for the specific purpose of investing in the Partnership and (iii) whose prospective investment in the Partnership is directed by a person who has such knowledge and experience in financial and business matters that such family office is capable of evaluating the merits and risks of such prospective investment;

◻ a "family office" as defined in Rule 202(a)(11)(G)-1 under the Advisers Act which was not formed for the purpose of investing in the Partnership, has assets under management in excess of $5,000,000 and whose prospective investment in the Partnership is directed by a person who has such knowledge and experience in financial and business matters that such family office is capable of evaluating the merits and risks of such prospective investment;

◻ a "knowledgeable employee" as defined in Rule 3c-5 of the Investment Company Act, who is:

  i.   an Executive Officer**, director, trustee, general partner, advisory board member, or person serving in a similar capacity, of the Partnership or an Affiliated Management Person†† of the Partnership; or

  ii.  an employee of the Partnership or an Affiliated Management Person of the Partnership (other than an employee performing solely clerical, secretarial, or administrative functions with regard to such company or its investments) who, in connection with his or her regular functions or duties, participates in the investment activities of the Partnership, other Covered Companies‡‡, or investment companies the investment activities of which are managed by an Affiliated Management Person of the Partnership; provided that such employee has been performing such functions and duties for or on behalf of the Partnership or such Affiliated Management Person, or substantially similar functions or duties for or on behalf of another company for at least twelve months.

◻ Any organization described in Section 501(c)(3) of the Internal Revenue Code of 1986, as amended, corporation, Massachusetts or similar business trust, limited liability company or partnership, not formed for the specific purpose of acquiring the Interests, with total assets in excess of $5,000,000;

◻ Any personal (non-business) trust, other than an employee benefit plan trust, with total assets in excess of $5,000,000, not formed for the specific purpose of acquiring the Interests, whose purchase is directed by a sophisticated person as described in Rule 506(b)(2)(ii) under the Securities Act;

◻ An entity registered with the SEC as a broker or dealer or an investment company or that has elected to be treated or qualifies as a private business development company as defined in Section 202(a)(22) of the Advisers Act, or is registered as an investment adviser pursuant to Section 203 of the Advisers Act or registered pursuant to the laws of any U.S. state, or is an investment adviser relying on the exemption from registering with the SEC under Section 203(l) or (m) of the Advisers Act, or is a Small Business Investment Company licensed by the United States Small Business Administration under Section 301(c) or (d) of the Small Business Investment Act of 1958, or is a Rural Business Investment Company as defined in Section 384A of the Consolidated Farm and Rural Development Act;

☐ Any bank as defined in Section 3(a)(2) of the Securities Act, or any savings and loan association or other institution as defined in Section 3(a)(5)(A) of the Securities Act, whether acting in its individual or fiduciary capacity;

☐ Any insurance company as defined in Section 2(13) of the Securities Act;

☐ Any plan established and maintained by a state, its political subdivisions, or any agency or instrumentality of a state or its political subdivisions, for the benefit of its employees, if such plan has total assets in excess of $5,000,000;

☐ Any employee benefit plan within the meaning of the U.S. Employee Retirement Income Security Act of 1974, as amended ("ERISA"), if the investment decision is made by a plan fiduciary, as defined in Section 3(21) of ERISA, which is either a bank, savings and loan association, insurance company, or registered investment adviser, or if the employee benefit plan has total assets in excess of $5,000,000 or, if a self-directed plan, with investment decisions made solely by natural persons that would themselves qualify as eligible investors;

☐ Any entity in which all of the equity owners are Accredited Investors (if checked, this Letter must be individually completed and submitted for each equity owner of the entity);

☐ Any trust in which all of the grantors are Accredited Investors (if checked, this Letter must be individually completed and submitted for each grantor of the trust); or

☐ Any entity of a type not listed above which was not formed for the purpose of investing in the Partnership and that owns not less than $5,000,000 in "investments."

In connection with this Letter, the undersigned has reviewed the original or photocopies of the following documents as provided by Investor (the "Investor Materials") (please check the appropriate box or boxes):

☐ Form 1040 filed with the Internal Revenue Service by Investor for the two most recent years;
☐ Form 1099 filed with the Internal Revenue Service by Investor for the two most recent years;
☐ Schedule K of Form 1065 filed with the Internal Revenue Service by Investor for the two most recent years;
☐ Schedule(s) K-1 of Form 1065 issued to Investor by an independent third party for the two most recent years;
☐ Form W-2 issued to Investor by an independent third party for the two most recent years;
☐ Other official documents issued by or filed with the Internal Revenue Service (please specify): ________________________________________________________________;

☐ Bank statements, brokerage statements and other statements of securities holdings, certificates of deposit, tax assessments, or appraisal reports, in each case, issued by independent third parties to Investor, dated within two months of the date of this Letter ("Asset Statements");
☐ Balance sheet listing current assets and liabilities dated within two months of the date of this Letter, along with supporting documentation issued or audited by independent third parties to verify such amounts;
☐ A consumer report (also known as a credit report) from at least one of the nationwide U.S. consumer reporting agencies (a "U.S. Consumer Report");
☐ Other documents (please specify): ________________________________________________________.

In delivering this Letter, I/we have relied upon and assumed the accuracy of the Investor Certifications below. I/We do not have any basis which causes me/us to believe the Investor Materials are not accurate or complete or that Investor is not an "Accredited Investor" within the meaning of Rule 501(a) of the Securities Act; however, I/we have not conducted any independent investigation of the accuracy or completeness of the Investor Materials or the underlying information reflected therein, provided that to the extent I/we have relied on Investor Materials that are not (i) forms issued by or filed with the Internal Revenue Service, (ii) Asset Statements or U.S. Consumer Reports, in each case, issued by independent third parties, or (iii) the Investor Certifications, I/we have taken such other reasonable steps I/we deemed necessary for me/us to reasonably believe the Investor is an "Accredited Investor" within the meaning of Rule 501(a) of the Securities Act. I/We make no representation or warranty that Investor Materials were accurately prepared, agree with source documents, or were properly filed. This Letter is limited to the matters expressly set forth herein. Nothing may be inferred or implied beyond the matters expressly contained herein. This Letter may be relied upon by the Partnership in connection with the offering of Interests.

Dated: _________________
Name: _________________
Signature: _______________
By: _________________ (if applicable)
Title: _________________ (if applicable)

# WEALTH IN NUMBERS

*"A commitment made must become a commitment honored."*
— *Tony Robbins, Entrepreneur, and Best-selling Author*

# ISSUING CAPITAL CALLS

As you know, the main goal of the capital-raising process is to get the funds needed for investment. Understanding the intricacies of capital calls is crucial for your fund's success. Capital calls are formal requests to your Limited Partners. They are to contribute their agreed-upon capital. This is essential for funding your SPV's activities and maintaining its investment capabilities. When using a software platform like Syndicately, General Partners gain access to a streamlined capital call process. The platform adds this ability to your GP dashboard. It lets you efficiently and securely initiate fund transfers with Limited Partners.

Some capital can come early. In some deal structures, when an LP signs on to your SPV, they submit a portion of their investment upfront, known as "paid-in capital." They have agreed to invest a total amount called "committed capital." The difference between these two figures is "uncalled capital." For example, if an LP commits $100,000 but only transfers $25,000 initially, their uncalled capital would be $75,000.

However, you'll find that many GPs prefer not to draw capital until the deal is fully subscribed. This boosts investor confidence and lets them keep their capital until needed. It also lets you adapt your strategy to the market. You can avoid the pressure to deploy the money now and risk creating partially funded deals. Issues could arise if you've drawn capital and the deal goes bad before closing. Keep your LPs updated. Most often, you'll want to use email or secure portals for capital call notices.

To initiate the capital call, you'll have a notice to send to your Limited Partners. Include specific instructions, like wire transfer details or ACH info. The request usually includes the subscription amount and any fees in your deal structure. It should look something like this:

Dear [Investor Name],

In accordance with Section [X] of the [SPV Name] Operating Agreement dated [Date], this letter serves as formal notice of a capital call. We are requesting a capital contribution of $[Amount] from each investor, representing [X]% of your total capital commitment. This capital will be used to fund our investment in [Brief description of investment opportunity]. Please remit your contribution no later than [Due Date] to the following account:

[Bank Name] Account Name: [SPV Name] Account Number: XXXXXXXX Routing Number: XXXXXXXXX Reference: [Investor Name] - Capital Call [Date]

If you have any questions or concerns, please don't hesitate to contact us. We appreciate your prompt attention to this matter and your continued support of [SPV Name].

Sincerely,

[Your Name]

[Your Title]

[SPV Name]

Take a moment to review your outline of any penalties for defaulting on a capital call, as specified in your initial agreement with the LPs.

Penalties might include fees and compensation for legal expenses from any resulting damages. By setting clear expectations from the start, you can reduce defaults and ensure smooth SPV operations.

It is pretty standard to give LPs 10 days to transfer funds to the SPV's omnibus bank account. After that window has passed, as part of your process, you need to ensure that you have received all funds. Don't ever assume the deal is closed. Take time to verify that the SPV's bank account has received all the committed funds. If you haven't received all the called capital, you may have a problem when it's time to deploy capital.

If the funds don't arrive on time (which you should never assume they will), don't wait for the investor to notice and fix the issue. Be proactive; unusual situations can come up, and you should account for Murphy's Law that "Anything that can go wrong will go wrong." Always remember, it's not finalized until the money is in the bank. By actively managing this process, your investors will see that you're a competent GP and committed to making things happen.

# WEALTH IN NUMBERS

*"Numbers tell the truth when words don't."*

*— Ray Dalio, Founder of Bridgewater Associates*

# BUILD AND MANAGE CAPITALIZATION TABLES

A capitalization table[i], called a "cap table" for short, is a vital document for your SPV. It is an overview of ownership. It shows who owns what percentage of the SPV and their type of ownership. They're important for anyone in private investments. This includes deal managers and investors. Having a clear, organized, and up-to-date cap table is essential. A messy cap table can make your deal look unprofessional. Even worse, it may scare away a potential investor.

The importance of well-managed cap tables has become even more apparent in recent years. From 2019 to 2023, the number of SPVs formed rose 300%. That's a massive spike to show their popularity among investors in private deals. However, this rapid growth came with some problems. A study in 2023 found that more than two-thirds of startups (68% to be exact) had mistakes in their cap tables. These weren't small errors either - on average, companies had to spend $50,000 on legal fees to fix these mistakes. That's not a cost you want to have to make up for,

---

i     *A notable early instance of a cap table can be linked to the Fairchild Semiconductor company, founded in 1957. Fairchild Semiconductor is considered one of the pioneering companies of Silicon Valley, and it received venture capital from Sherman Fairchild and the Fairchild Camera and Instrument Corporation. The structuring of ownership shares among the eight co-founders (later known as the "Traitorous Eight") and the venture capital firm would have required a clear breakdown of shares, which mirrors the modern concept of a cap table.*

especially when it can be easily avoided. With that note, we hope you'll understand how important it is to keep your cap table accurate and well-managed.

As you're getting things going, it's really in your best interest to start building out your cap table before you deploy capital for your investment. This will help you in the process of determining the pre-money valuation of the asset or company and will come in handy as you make updates in the future. Also, the cap table is vital for your SPV's liquidity event. It shows how to distribute profits among all stakeholders. It lets investors know their stake in the SPV and its assets. You may need to revise the cap table after the asset transfer if the final terms differ from initial plans.

Also, remember that there are strict rules on the number and type of investors allowed under different exemptions. You can create a en entry column on your cap table to note your LPs' accreditation status. When you list your Limited Partner accreditation status, you'll have a quick point of reference to maintain compliance within the required investor counts for a 506(b) offering.

The first step in creating a cap table for an SPV investment is to clearly define the SPV's structure. This includes specifying the total number of units or shares issued, any different classes of shares, and the initial price per unit. The next step is to create a comprehensive list of all investors in the SPV. This list should include each investor's name, contact information, and the number of units or shares they own. To find each investor's ownership percentage, divide their investment by the total fund size.

At an absolute minimum, your cap table needs to include the investor or entity name, capital contribution amount, SPV units, ownership percentage, and committed capital. Don't forget to include a line item for any management fees or carried interest associated with the SPV. A cap table is a living document that tells the story of your SPV's ownership. Every time something happens that affects who owns what in your SPV, you will record it in the table.

Don't get lazy with your updates, take a moment to promptly update the cap table after each transaction takes place to ensure it remains accurate. Everyone gets busy and if you put this off, it can get out of hand fast. Each new transaction (like an additional investment round) is added as a new row. After each transaction, an "Updated Total" row is added to show the new total number of shares and overall valuation. Transactions are usually in chronological order. This makes it easy to follow the history of events and see how your SPV's ownership has changed over time, just by reading down the table. If it applies to your deal, add lock-up period details to the cap table. and specify the dates and conditions for each investor. This helps prevent misunderstandings and ensures all parties know where they stand.

## Capitalization Table

**Capital Contribution**
Represents the amount of money invested by each investor.

**SPV Units**
Denotes the specific units allocated within a Special Purpose Vehicle.

**Investor Name**
Identifies the individuals or entities providing capital.

**Ownership Percentage**
Indicates the proportion of the company owned by each investor.

It's also a good idea to establish a regular schedule to review your cap table. You'll want to revise the SPV's documents over its lifetime to show any valuation changes. This may include quarterly or annual audits to ensure all info is accurate and up to date. Set a reminder on your calendar and have someone like your CPA or attorney review your cap table from time to time as well. This ensures everything is correct and builds trust with your Limited Partners. To make things easier, we recommend using cap table management software to manage your cap table instead of a basic spreadsheet.

Good management software can automate tasks and make your life as a General Partner a lot easier. Things like calculating ownership percentages and generating reports can be done effortlessly. When we were building the Syndicately platform, we drew from our own experience on how much friction there was in cap table management. We had tons of Limited Partners across multiple deals to manage while juggling all of our other daily tasks. As a result, our platform automates cap table management and makes a complex, time-consuming task simple. This automation not only saves time but also reduces the likelihood of errors.

Outside of our own solution, there are lots of other cap table management solutions out there you can check out as well. While choosing to make use of a software solution might cost you some money, it's absolutely worth it to save yourself a lot of time and lower the risk of legal issues down the line. You might even work to include the software costs as part of your deal management fees.

Now that you're familiar with creating and managing cap tables, let's  move on to the next topic of putting your raised capital to work. Before we do, though, we prepared an example of a (very) basic cap table that assumes the SPV is investing in a single company and has multiple investors that you can check out to get an idea for a starting point.

## Capitalization Table

SPV Name: NewCo Startup SPV I LLC
Target Investment: NewCo Startup Inc.

| Investor Name | Capital Contribution | SPV Units | Ownership % | Committed Capital | Remaining Commitment |
|---|---|---|---|---|---|
| Lead Investor | $500,000 | 500 | 25.00% | $750,000 | $250,000 |
| Limited Partner 1 | $300,000 | 300 | 15.00% | $400,000 | $100,000 |
| Limited Partner 2 | $250,000 | 250 | 12.50% | $250,000 | $0 |
| Limited Partner 3 | $200,000 | 200 | 10.00% | $300,000 | $100,000 |
| Limited Partner 4 | $150,000 | 150 | 7.50% | $200,000 | $50,000 |
| Limited Partner 5 | $100,000 | 100 | 5.00% | $150,000 | $50,000 |
| Limited Partner 6 | $100,000 | 100 | 5.00% | $100,000 | $0 |
| Limited Partner 7 | $75,000 | 75 | 3.75% | $100,000 | $25,000 |
| Limited Partner 8 | $75,000 | 75 | 3.75% | $75,000 | $0 |
| Limited Partner 9 | $50,000 | 50 | 2.50% | $75,000 | $25,000 |
| SPV Manager | $200,000 | 200 | 10.00% | $200,000 | $0 |
| Total | $2,000,000 | 2000 | 100.00% | $2,600,000 | $600,000 |

### SPV Details
- Total Fund Size: $2,600,000
- Total Invested: $2,000,000
- Remaining Capital: $600,000
- Price per Unit: $1000
- Management Fee: 2% on raised capital
- Carry: 20% over 8% hurdle

### Target Company Details
- Company Valuation: $20,000,000
- SPV Ownership in Target: 10.00%

# WEALTH IN NUMBERS

*"The three most important things in investing are: First, the quality of what you're buying. Second, the price you're paying. Third, the timing of deployment. Most people only think about the first two."*

*— Howard Marks, Co-founder & Co-Chairman of Oaktree Capital Management*

# DEPLOYING CAPITAL

Once all investors have fulfilled their commitments and signed the docs, it's time for you to deploy the capital for the investment. This marks the final stage in your capital-raising lifecycle. Deploying capital involves actively putting the funds raised from your Limited Partners to work in the chosen investment. This stage means moving from fundraising to executing your investment strategy, allocating the capital towards the assets or opportunities that you've outlined for your SPV.

When getting ready to deploy capital, it's a good idea to prepare a purchase agreement, which is a legally binding contract between you and the other party in the transaction. It helps build your documentation and defines the deal terms, while also providing a path for legal recourse in the event of a dispute or failure to fulfill obligations. A well-drafted purchase agreement will typically:

- clearly identify the assets or projects the SPV will manage or invest in.

- detail the total investment amount and payment structure.

- specify ownership percentages and associated rights.

- stipulate the closing date.

- outline conditions to meet before finalizing the investment.

- include representations and warranties from both the SPV and the investors.

A purchase agreement is not always legally required. But, it is highly recommended, especially in larger transactions, as it helps define responsibilities for a smooth transfer. After signing the purchase agreement, you must transfer the funds from the SPV's bank account. To avoid delays in asset acquisition, transfer the funds promptly. In return, the seller will start the process of transferring the equity or assets in its name to the SPV.

Now that you've completed this process, it's a good time to reach out to your Limited Partners and congratulate them on a successful closing. Make this an upbeat message and thank them for their efforts and involvement. While we call this stage the "closing," remember that it's still very early in this journey with your Limited Partners and there's a long road ahead until you exit your deal.

We have included an example purchase agreement here to illustrate what you might expect to see for typical structure. Understand that this template is a starting point. Examine this sample closely, but work with your attorney to create one unique to your specific investment. A thorough agreement needs to address the aspects of the deal.

**EXAMPLE PURCHASE AGREEMENT**

This Purchase Agreement (the "Agreement") is made and entered into on [DATE], by and between: SELLER: [SELLER NAME] ("Seller") Address: [SELLER ADDRESS] and BUYER: [GENERAL PARTNER NAME], acting on behalf of [SPV NAME] ("Buyer") Address: [BUYER ADDRESS]

WHEREAS, Seller owns certain property as described herein and desires to sell said property; WHEREAS, Buyer desires to purchase said property;

NOW, THEREFORE, in consideration of the mutual covenants and promises contained herein, the parties agree as follows:

1. PROPERTY DESCRIPTION

Seller agrees to sell and Buyer agrees to purchase the following described property (the "Property"): [DETAILED DESCRIPTION OF PROPERTY, INCLUDING ADDRESS AND LEGAL DESCRIPTION IF APPLICABLE]

2. PURCHASE PRICE AND PAYMENT

The total purchase price for the Property shall be $[AMOUNT] (the "Purchase Price"). Buyer shall pay the Purchase Price as follows: a) An initial deposit of $[AMOUNT] upon execution of this Agreement. b) The remaining balance of $[AMOUNT] to be paid at closing.

3. OWNERSHIP STRUCTURE

Upon completion of the purchase, the ownership structure of the Property shall be as follows: a) [SPV NAME] shall own [PERCENTAGE]% of the Property. b) [LIST ANY OTHER OWNERS AND THEIR PERCENTAGES]

4. OWNERSHIP RIGHTS

The following rights are associated with ownership of the Property: a) Right to receive proportional share of income generated by the Property. b) Right to vote on major decisions regarding the Property, with voting power proportional to ownership percentage. c) [LIST ANY OTHER SPECIFIC RIGHTS]

5. DUE DILIGENCE PERIOD

Buyer shall have [NUMBER] days from the date of this Agreement to conduct due diligence on the Property ("Due Diligence Period"). During this period, Buyer may terminate this Agreement for any reason by providing written notice to Seller.

6. CLOSING

The closing shall take place on [DATE] or such other date as mutually agreed upon by the parties (the "Closing Date").

7. TITLE AND DEED

Seller shall convey marketable title to the Property by [TYPE OF DEED] free and clear of all liens and encumbrances, except as stated herein.

8. REPRESENTATIONS AND WARRANTIES

Seller represents and warrants that:

a) Seller has full authority to enter into this Agreement and sell the Property. b) The Property is free from all encumbrances except as disclosed in writing to Buyer. c) There are no pending or threatened legal actions or governmental proceedings against the Property.

Buyer represents and warrants that:

a) Buyer has full authority to enter into this Agreement and purchase the Property. b) Buyer has sufficient funds or has secured necessary financing to complete the purchase. c) Buyer is a duly formed and validly existing Special Purpose Vehicle under the laws of [JURISDICTION].

9. CONDITIONS PRECEDENT

This Agreement is contingent upon: a) Buyer's satisfactory completion of due diligence. b) Buyer's ability to secure necessary financing. c) A satisfactory title search and property survey.

10. CLOSING COSTS

[OUTLINE WHO PAYS FOR WHAT CLOSING COSTS]

11. RISK OF LOSS

Risk of loss to the Property shall remain with Seller until closing.

12. GOVERNING LAW

This Agreement shall be governed by and construed in accordance with the laws of [STATE/JURISDICTION].

13. ENTIRE AGREEMENT

This Agreement contains the entire agreement between the parties and supersedes all prior agreements, whether oral or written.

IN WITNESS WHEREOF, the parties hereto have executed this Agreement as of the date first above written.

SELLER: [SELLER NAME]

Signature

BUYER: [GENERAL PARTNER NAME], on behalf of [SPV NAME]

Signature

# WEALTH IN NUMBERS

WEALTH IN NUMBERS

*"Capital goes where it's welcome and stays where it's well treated."*
— *Walter Wriston, Former Chairman and CEO of Citicorp/Citibank*

# DEAL MANAGEMENT

Now that you've closed your deal and taken a moment to celebrate with your LPs, it's time to get back to business.

Effective deal management after deploying capital is essential to your SPV's success and your reputation as a General Partner. Securing initial investments may have felt like a finish line. But, it's just the start of a deeper journey. The true measure of an SPV's success goes beyond its initial fundraising success. While securing funds and closing deals are significant milestones, they merely set the stage for the work ahead.

Your relationship with your LPs will suffer if you disappear after raising capital. You want to respond to your investors promptly when they have questions. Provide consistent updates and set regular office hours for LP communication.

There are very few legitimate reasons to neglect communication with Limited Partners. They have trusted you with their hard earned capital and it's your responsibility to provide updates.

Investors are not just passive participants. They're stakeholders. Investors want to feel valued and informed. They want to know that they're more than just a name on a ledger. They expect—and deserve—

to be kept informed about their investments' progress and challenges. Regular, transparent communication isn't just polite. It's key to trust and credibility.

In addition to keeping your investors updated, it is also extremely important to listen to their feedback. In order to create a culture that cultivates great investor feedback, we must set up clear ways to receive and address it. Consider regular surveys and feedback sessions at investor meetings. These tools let investors share their insights and concerns. Acting on their feedback shows you respect their opinions and want to improve.

By seeking their feedback and advice on key decisions, you will improve your SPV management and communication. You will also deepen the trust and inspire collaboration, which are vital for long-term success. Too often, new dealmakers will treat investor relations like a routine task—a box to be ticked. But, with the right approach, investor relations can be a powerful tool. It's easy to get caught up in the hunt for new deals and fresh Limited Partners. The excitement of closing, funding, and structuring a deal can be intoxicating. However, true success comes from sustained effort. It's about managing the deal, meeting your vision, and—most importantly—exceeding expectations. Yes, delivering on promised financial returns is crucial. But, what sets successful General Partners apart is their effort. Great GPs work to provide a positive experience for their investors, even when challenges arise. If you can provide a genuine "WOW" factor, you'll quickly set yourself apart in a crowded field.

Throughout this book, we've emphasized the importance of your story—who you are and what you stand for. Your ongoing relations with investors should reinforce their decision to work with you. Keep in mind that your interactions with investors can have a lasting impact. They may open doors to future opportunities or close them permanently. Investors who have a positive experience are far more likely to reinvest with you. And let us tell you, these repeat investors are worth their weight in gold. They save you the time and effort of finding new LPs. Plus, they come with built-in trust. Each deal has its own intricacies. That said, knowing the basics of fund administration will help you navigate complex deals and avoid problems. Effective deal management has three, interconnected pillars:

- Accurate accounting

- Timely reporting

- Clear investor communication

These elements serve as the foundation for building and maintaining successful SPV deals. By mastering these segments you can build a strong deal management system. Being successful in this business is about building lasting relationships with those who have placed trust in you. Your goal should be to create a culture where your LPs are eager to hear from you for the next opportunity. Regular communication, transparency, and mutual respect are not just nice-to-haves. They are essential components of a successful investor relations strategy.

Done right, this approach secures repeat investments. It creates a virtuous cycle of growth and investor confidence It also turns your investors into advocates. They will drive your SPV—and your reputation—to new heights. Your journey to greatness is a quest for excellence. Every interaction with your LPs should galvanize their confidence in you as the General Partner.

# CAPITAL ACCOUNT STATEMENTS

Now that you're entering the next phase of your SPV journey, there's a key test waiting for you. It's what sets apart the good from the great in fund management. Your ability to maintain detailed records plays a vital role in establishing transparency and trust with your investors. Central to this practice is the Partner Capital Account (PCAP) statement.

PCAP statements provide transparency and keep your Limited Partners informed. These statements are an information bridge for GPs and LPs. They show each investor's financial stake in the SPV or fund. In addition, they provide a more detailed view of the SPV than your cap table.

The PCAP statement tracks each investor's financial position in the SPV by recording contributions, distributions, and current value. It's typically updated quarterly or annually for investor reporting and fund management. In contrast, a cap table is a snapshot of a company's ownership. It details shareholders, shares owned, and ownership percentages. Both tools are essential in their contexts. They provide vital info for investors, fund managers, and stakeholders. You can think of it as detailed ledger. This level-of-detail meets regulatory requirements and builds investor trust by providing visibility. After you deploy the capital and acquire the asset(s) for your SPV, the time for preparing your PCAP begins. You'll also prepare initial individual statements for each SPV investor.

Some GPs find it hard to provide accurate, timely PCAP statements. It is understandable to feel overwhelmed with tight deadlines and the need for perfect accuracy. Gathering, analyzing, and presenting data can be a lot of work. It's especially tough with many investors. So, once again, we recommend using specialized software to help generate these statements more easily. Syndicately allows you to generate individual PCAP statements and reports in minutes. This was a must-have feature we decided on when we began building our platform.

The information your PCAP contains will vary slightly depending on the SPV's specific financial structure, reporting needs, and partnership agreements. Generally, a standard PCAP for an SPV will include:

- **Commitment Summary:** Details like total commitment, amount called, remaining commitment, recallable distributions, and partnership percentage. This section shows each partner's financial commitment and capital obligations within the SPV.

- **Partner's Capital Statement:** Often presented in sections like "Quarter to Date," "Year to Date," and "Inception to Date," this part includes:

  - **Beginning Balance:** The partner's starting balance at the reporting period's start.

  - **Contributions:** Additional capital injected by the partner.

  - **Distributions:** Capital returned to the partner, often from investment exits or profits.

  - **Management Fees:** Any fees paid to the SPV managers for their services.

  - **Investment Gains/Losses:** Net gains or losses resulting from investment activities.

  - **Appreciation/Depreciation:** Realized and unrealized appreciation (increases in value) or depreciation.

  - **Ending Balance:** The partner's balance at the reporting period's end. This structure aligns with standard practices in SPV reporting, ensuring transparency and clarity for investors. However, details can vary. Some SPVs may include additional categories like preferred return allocations, carry distributions, or even footnotes explaining specific line items.

Once you have collected the required information, the typical steps for preparing a Capital Account Statement for an SPV are as follows:

- **Gather Necessary Information:** To prepare a Capital Account Statement, collect all the required financial details. This includes each member's initial capital, any extra contributions, and any distributions or withdrawals made by the members.

- **Create a Template:** Utilize appropriate software or design a template for generating the Capital Account Statement. The template needs to have columns for member name, initial capital, additional capital, capital distributions, and ending capital balance.

- **Enter Necessary Data:** Fill in the template or accounting software with the collected financial information. Verify the accuracy and consistency of data you're putting in.

- **Calculate the Capital Account Balance:** The final calculation of each LP's capital account balance should incorporate all relevant details.

- **Review and Revise:** Check the Capital Account Statement. It must be accurate and complete. Do a final review and revise as needed.

- **Distribution:** The last step is to submit the Capital Account Statement to the right parties. These may include the SPV's members or shareholders. It may also be part of the parent company's consolidated financial statements.

Nailing this part of the process will help with some of the next steps in deal management. We've prepared an example PCAP Statement for you to review:

Dear [Investor Name],

Please find on the following page your Partners Capital Statement for [SPV Name].

Should you have any questions regarding this correspondence, please don't hesitate to contact us.

Yours sincerely

[your name], General Partner, [SPV Name]

**Sample SPV FUND I**

**Unaudited Capital Account Statement**

**For the Period Ended December 31, [YEAR]**

**(Amounts in USD)**

**Commitment Summary**

| Item | Amount |
|---|---|
| Commitment: | $50,000,000 |
| Commitment Called to Date: | ($18,500,000) |
| Recallable Distributions: | $750,000 |
| Unfunded Commitment: | $31,500,000 |
| Percentage of Partnership | 4.00% |

**Statement of Partner's Capital**

| Period | Quarter to Date | Year to Date | Inception to Date |
|---|---|---|---|
| Beginning Balance | $1,800,000 | $1,650,000 | - |
| Contributions | $125,000 | $350,000 | $18,500,000 |
| Distributions | - | ($25,000) | ($6,750,000) |
| Net Management Fees | ($30,000) | ($120,000) | ($1,200,000) |
| Net Investment Gain / (Loss) | $5,000 | $15,000 | ($150,000) |
| Realized Appreciation / (Depreciation) | $10,000 | $45,000 | $850,000 |
| Unrealized Appreciation / (Depreciation) | $90,000 | $85,000 | $2,500,000 |
| Ending Balance | $2,000,000 | $2,000,000 | $2,000,000 |

# INVESTOR UPDATES

Investor updates are essential for strong ties with your limited partners. These reports give a complete view of your progress, challenges, and future plans. Updates are shared every month or every quarter, depending on the type of investment. They are a vital communication tool. They keep stakeholders informed about their investments and the business's health.

As we touched on earlier, a major issue that exists in SPV management is poor communication. Unfortunately, it's more prevalent than many realize. We know of many cases where LPs struggled to reach their GPs, even for simple requests. LPs expect (and deserve!) regular updates on their investments. As a General Partner, you must be available to provide them. This commitment to transparency will strengthen your investor relationships. It will also enhance your reputation as a trustworthy General Partner.

A well-crafted investor update typically includes several key elements. It starts with an overview of your key performance indicators (KPIs). They should be specific to the industry and business model, and will vary depending on the deal type. Financial metrics, such as revenue growth, burn rate, and runway, provide a clear picture fiscal health. The update should highlight items such as achievements, product developments, and new hires. It should also address any challenges faced during the reporting period.

By sharing both the wins and setbacks, you'll show a commitment to open communication and good management. This practice keeps investors engaged. It can also help in future fundraising. Also, these updates are a powerful marketing tool for your brand. They show your business acumen and leadership. This gives investors good talking points to promote you to their colleagues. Well-informed investors are more likely to join later opportunities or to introduce you to new potential LPs.

By prioritizing clear and consistent updates, you can build strong relationships with your investors and build a supportive ecosystem that will contribute to your long-term success. Consider the following best practices when preparing your documentation:

- **Detailed Explanations and Footnotes:** Investors will likely seek to understand the nuances behind the numbers. Be prepared to offer detailed explanations for significant transactions or changes in financial position. Use footnotes and supplementary materials to provide additional context and clarity.

- **Regulatory Compliance:** Ensure that your statements comply with all relevant laws and regulations. Include all necessary disclosures, such as risk factors, related-party transactions, and other pertinent information that investors should be aware of.

- **Professional Presentation:** Present your update in a professional format with consistent styling, clear headings, and a logical layout. This attention to detail reflects the quality of your management and enhances readability.

On the next page, you'll find a sample investor update template to inspire your own. Feel free to modify this format to suit your specific deal structure, adding or removing sections as needed to tailor it to your SPV.

# WEALTH IN NUMBERS

## Subject: [SPV Name] - Quarterly Investor Update - [Quarter/Year]

---

**Dear [SPV Name] Investors,**

We hope this update finds you well. Below is a summary of [SPV Name]'s performance for the quarter ending [Date].

## TL;DR

- **Wins:**
  [List 2-3 key accomplishments from the quarter]
- **Challenges:**
  [List 1-2 key challenges encountered]
- **Priorities:**
  [List 1-2 top priorities for the upcoming quarter]

## Portfolio Overview

- **Recent Performance Summary:**
  [Provide a brief summary of the portfolio's performance]
- **Significant Milestones or Achievements:**
  [Highlight any notable milestones or achievements from the quarter]

## Investment Highlights

- **[Investment 1]:**
  [Provide a brief description of the investment and performance during the quarter, including any developments or milestones]

## Performance

- **Overall Valuation:**
  [Briefly discuss the overall valuation of the SPV compared to the previous quarter]
- **Market Conditions:**
  [Discuss any relevant market conditions that impacted the SPV during the quarter]

## Looking Forward

- **Investment Pipeline:**
  [Discuss the current investment pipeline and any upcoming investment opportunities]
- **Strategic Initiatives:**
  [Outline any key strategic initiatives planned for the upcoming quarter]

## Market Trends and Industry Insights

- **Market Trends:**
  [Mention any relevant market trends affecting the SPV]
- **Industry Developments:**
  [Discuss industry developments that could impact future performance]

## Liquidity Outlook

- **Potential Exit Strategies:**
  [Provide information on any potential exit strategies]
- **Estimated Timeline for Liquidity Events:**
  [Include an estimated timeline, if applicable]

## Investor Relations

- **Upcoming Events or Meetings:**
  [List any upcoming investor events or meetings]
- **Ways Investors Can Support:**
  [Mention any ways in which investors can provide support]

## Asks

- **[Specific Ask]:**
  [Clearly outline any specific requests for your investors, such as introductions to potential investors or requests for domain expertise]

## Closing Thoughts

Thank you for your continued support. We are excited about the progress of the SPV and look forward to keeping you updated.

# SCHEDULED ACTIONS

A key part of your communication strategy is to create a calendar. It should outline the timing of your updates and interactions with investors. This calendar should include updates on distributions and capital accounts, as well as performance reports. You will typically schedule these actions quarterly. However, for some projects, more frequent updates may be appropriate. Consider monthly status briefings to keep all parties aligned and informed.

Transparency and regularity are key components of your communication strategy. Provide detailed reports on the SPV's performance at consistent intervals, usually quarterly. These reports should cover financial performance, operational updates, and strategic decisions. Don't wait for investors to ask questions. Engage them with updates, particularly after significant changes or unexpected issues. This approach strengthens relationships and allows you to address concerns before they escalate.

For a wider reach, send a monthly newsletter. It should inform your investors about ongoing projects and new deals.

Put in place a follow-up strategy that includes regular check-ins with investors every two to four weeks. Treat your emails like a "drip campaign." Send small updates to keep relationships warm. This approach keeps you fresh in their minds, even outside of active fundraising periods.

Personal touches can have a substantial effect on your investor relationships. Consider a program to call investors on their birthdays. Or, set aside time for periodic check-in calls with individual LPs. These gestures show your commitment to the relationship beyond the financial aspects.

By following these strategies, you create a communication framework that keeps investors informed, engaged, and confident in your management. This approach satisfies current investors. It also positions you well for future investments.

Moreover, consider the long-term benefits of this proactive communication strategy. GPs who meet or exceed these communication benchmarks often find their LPs becoming valuable partners. They introduce new investment opportunities, share industry insights, and invest in future funds. This can give a strategic advantage in the crowded SPV market. Remember, when it comes to deal management, silence is not golden. Your voice, shared with your investors, is your most valuable asset. It is key to building and maintaining successful long-term partnerships.

How to Implement this System Well:

- **Use Technology Tools:** Leverage investor communication platforms and CRMs to automate emails, manage call schedules, and track investor interactions. Tools like MailChimp, HubSpot, or other CRM systems can help implement drip campaigns and track personal milestones like birthdays.

- **Be Consistent:** Make consistency the core of your communication strategy. Missing an update can erode trust, while predictable communication fosters confidence in your management.

- **Tailor Communication:** Segment investors based on their preferences. Some may prefer detailed financial reports, while others may appreciate high-level updates. Tailor content to keep all parties engaged.

- **Monitor Feedback:** Collect feedback from investors to fine-tune the communication process. Adjust the frequency, tone, or content based on what resonates with your investor base.

By integrating these steps into your fund administration system, you ensure consistent, transparent, and personalized communication with investors.

These steps will make your fund admin system better. They will ensure consistent, transparent, and personalized communication with investors. This serves to maintain current relationships. It could also help attract new opportunities and investment partnerships in the future.

To get started with your scheduled actions, the specific tasks may differ depending on the deal. However, here are a few key items to consider including in your plan:

- **Capital Account Statements:** Provide detailed capital account statements on a regular basis to keep investors informed about their individual investments, contributions, distributions, and the overall value of their holdings.

- **Quarterly Performance Reports:** Provide detailed reports that include financial performance, operational updates, and strategic decisions. Be proactive in sharing information to prevent investors from needing to ask for updates.

- **Written Performance Updates:** Send periodic written performance updates that include both financial metrics and operational highlights, ensuring investors have a clear understanding of how their investments are performing.

- **Conference Call Updates:** Host scheduled conference calls with investors to provide updates on performance, answer questions, and discuss upcoming plans. These calls help maintain direct communication and transparency.

- **Monthly Project Status Updates:** For short-term deals or unstabilized long-term rental projects, send monthly updates that include: current project status, photos and/or video updates, and updated timelines.

- **Monthly Newsletters:** Send a monthly newsletter to keep the entire investor base informed about current and potential deals.

- **Regular Updates on Expenses:** Include expense ratios and updates in regular reports.

- **Financial Audits:** Conduct audits by reputable third-party firms. Share audit summaries or findings with investors to enhance transparency.

- **Operational Reviews:** Periodically review and report on operational efficiencies and risk management practices.

- **Tax Information:** Provide timely and accurate tax documents (e.g., K-1 forms) to investors. Update investors on any tax law changes that may affect their investment.

- **Legal Compliance:** Keep investors informed about any legal proceedings or changes in laws/regulations impacting the SPV.

- **Investor Surveys:** Conduct periodic surveys to gauge investor satisfaction and gather feedback. Use insights to improve communication and fund management practices.

- **Birthday Calls and Check-ins:** Show personal attention to investors by implementing a program to call them on their birthdays or scheduling periodic check-in calls. These personal touches help solidify relationships beyond just financial interactions.

# MANAGING INVESTOR RELATIONSHIPS DURING DIFFICULT TIMES

In private investments, dealmakers can face unexpected challenges that can test their resilience. A sudden loss or collapse of a deal is daunting. These situations can be deeply frustrating and potentially damaging to investor relationships. You need to develop a strategy for managing investor relations in tough times. In doing so, you need to have a plan to take swift action, provide clear communication, and practice adaptive problem-solving. These skills will help you handle crises and improve your reputation and relationships.

These situations can feel like a gut punch after putting in a lot of hard work and time to put a deal together. Just picture yourself nailing down an allocation, doing all the due diligence, and getting everything ready for your LPs. You can feel the excitement building as you approach the end. Suddenly, you're told that your allocation has vanished without any warning. You can feel the disappointment, and the frustration is undeniable.

There are multiple explanations for why this could happen. One particularly painful scenario occurred recently to a colleague in the industry. Everything was in place - the bank account and paperwork was ready to go. Then, at the eleventh hour, the deal fell apart. Such rare experiences show the need for flexibility and resilience in facing setbacks.

When faced with a lost allocation, it's crucial for GPs to act swiftly and transparently. Be clear with your LPs about the situation. Provide context, but don't breach any confidentiality agreements. Be ready to discuss alternative investments or how to return capital to investors.

When active deals go bad, things can get even more stressful. If your results in an investment are less than favorable, approach the investor sooner rather than later. New dealmakers often fear reporting bad news or mediocre results to their investors. However, as we frequently emphasize, the most important thing is to communicate with investors as soon as you identify a problem.

A well-thought-out communication strategy can make a significant difference. This should involve honest, and direct communication about the situation, its impact on the SPV, and the steps being taken to address it.

Start by assessing the seriousness of the problem. For example, short-term issues like negative cash flow for a few months or a vacant property are not as alarming in the grand scheme. Although these situations are unfortunate and uncomfortable, they are not critical and most likely won't sink your deal. Assess how to improve the situation. If the business plan is sound, reassure your investors. Tell them what you're doing to fix the issues.

For more serious problems, such as sustained losses or a significant drop in the value of an asset, you need to investigate thoroughly. Identify the root cause. If the issue stems from something you or your team overlooked, take corrective action. Present your action plan, outlining the options and what is required. This collaborative approach ensures you are both on the same team and working towards a solution. Additionally, update your internal processes to prevent similar problems in the future.

If the problem is external, like a market downturn, revisit the plan to see if it remains viable. Determine if the numbers will still work in the long term and if there are immediate actions that can be taken to expedite recovery. Some can be mitigated with solid processes and systems, while others are beyond control. When risks become reality, focus on navigating through the challenges together with your investor.

If there is a complete failure or a catastrophic event, it is imperative to address it quickly. If this happens while managing LPs' capital, you must act in their best interest. You need to maintain open and honest communication with your investors. It may feel overwhelming, but it's not the end of the world.

Inform your investors about any chance to recover value. Update them on the winding down of the investment and your efforts to reduce their losses. Open communication is essential during these times. Failure in business is painful, especially when it affects your investors who trusted you. However, facing your investors and explaining what went wrong shows integrity. It is professional, even when you can't deliver the expected results. This honesty helps maintain their trust in you. Besides your action plan, take the opportunity to learn from the experience.

Handling these situations well can help your reputation in the investment community. Use it as a chance to position yourself for success in future deals. But enough doom and gloom, let's talk about what you can do to celebrate your wins when things go right.

# MAKING THE PROCESS ENJOYABLE

While SPV management can be demanding, it's important to enjoy the journey. This business can be incredibly rewarding, not just financially but also in the impact you have on others. Embrace the process and take pride in the fact that your investments have the potential to positively influence many lives. Remember, this isn't just about numbers; it's about making a difference in the lives of others.

Empowering your investors with knowledge is a key aspect of successful SPV management. For less experienced investors, educational content related to the SPV's market sector, investment strategy, and structure can be invaluable. This info helps investors understand the SPV's goals and strategies. It builds their confidence in their investment decisions. This not only strengthens their connection to the SPV but also positions you as a knowledgeable leader.

As we keep trying to reinforce, taking great care of your clients and turning them into advocates for your SPV is essential for long-term success. By maintaining strong, healthy relationships, you create a network of satisfied investors who are more likely to support future ventures and recommend your SPV to others.

Understanding the mindset of your Limited Partners is essential for building a strong investor base. While financial returns are undoubtedly important, many investors are driven by deeper motivations that go beyond profit. Recognizing and addressing these underlying factors can lead to more meaningful relationships.

Some want the thrill of new ventures. Others seek the prestige of exclusive investments. Some wish to make a positive impact on the world. Skilled dealmakers can engage their investors by tapping into their desires. You should consider a range of engaging experiences for your Limited Partners. For instance, you could host exclusive events for your LPs to meet and interact with thought leaders in various fields. Another approach could be to let investors collaborate directly with portfolio companies. This would let them share their expertise and feel more involved. Also, you could stress the good social or environmental impact of their investments. Some other ideas could be to organize volunteer days where investors can participate in community service events alongside your team. This would appeal to those wanting to make a difference. These can all create a more rewarding experience by catering to investors' deeper motivations.

In addition to this, creating a sense of community among Limited Partners (LPs) can be a powerful strategy for General Partners. This approach adds value to your business and benefits the LPs. It creates a symbiotic relationship that can lead to successful deals and long-term partnerships.

Some GPs have kept their investors in separate bubbles, not interacting with each other. Building relationships among LPs can lead to a lot of perks.

When you build a diverse network of LPs, they can get more deal flow as partners with varied backgrounds and expertise contribute valuable insights and opportunities, potentially leading to new and lucrative deals. This connected investor community also facilitates knowledge sharing, allowing for the exchange of market intelligence, industry trends, and investment strategies.

Fostering a sense of community can create a feeling of belonging and loyalty among LPs, increasing the likelihood of their participation in future deals - a phenomenon often referred to as tribal loyalty. Finally, when faced with challenges, a united group of LPs can offer diverse perspectives and solutions, leading to more effective collaborative problem-solving. By breaking down the traditional barriers between Limited Partners, you can create a more dynamic, informed, and committed investor base, ultimately leading to stronger performance and more successful investments.

To cultivate a sense of community among Limited Partners, consider implementing a range of strategic approaches. Organizing LP gatherings is a key initiative, where events can be hosted to explore potential new markets, and collectively brainstorm ideas. These gatherings can be tailored to suit geographical constraints and preferences, taking place either in-person or virtually.

Additionally, creating digital platforms can significantly enhance community building by establishing secure online forums or communication channels where your investors can interact, share ideas, and discuss investment opportunities.

Take steps to actively facilitate networking by introducing investors with complementary skills or interests to one another, thereby encouraging organic relationship-building within the community.

Celebrating successes with your investors is crucial. When you share milestones, achievements, and positive outcomes, you not only boost confidence in your abilities as a dealmaker, but also strengthen the sense of community among your investors. This approach goes a long way in fostering loyalty and enthusiasm.

Organizing investor appreciation dinners can be a great strategy. Consider holding these in different cities where your investors are concentrated. These exclusive gatherings are first offered to our current investors, with some that haven't yet committed but are in our pipleine attending as our guests. These lucky attendees often enjoy special perks, such as meeting guest speakers in person.

For a more modern touch, you might launch an investor podcast series. This platform allows you to interview successful investors from your community, sharing their stories and insights with your wider investor base.

These initiatives aim to create a more engaging experience for your investors. By going beyond traditional communication methods, you can foster a strong sense of belonging and excitement about their investments. Remember, the money you spend on people who have already invested with you typically yields a much higher return than general marketing efforts.

Establish a virtual book club focused on investment, business, and personal growth literature, encouraging intellectual discussion and knowledge sharing. Additionally, host informal virtual coffee chats in small groups, providing a casual setting for investors to connect with you and each other. These initiatives can help create a more cohesive and engaged investor community, enhancing relationships and potentially leading to more fruitful collaborations.

By creating a fun and immersive investment experience, you distinguish yourself from other capital-raising entities in the market. This approach not only helps retain your current investors but also attracts new ones, setting a strong foundation for future growth.

Remember, building a community takes time and effort, but the long-term benefits can be substantial. As your LP community grows and strengthens, you may find that it becomes one of your most valuable assets, providing a competitive edge for your future as a dealmaker.

Work to align your communication and engagement strategies with these psychological drivers. As a result, you can foster a sense of partnership and shared purpose. This deeper connection boosts investor satisfaction. It also strengthens your relationships, helping them withstand challenging situations.

# WEALTH IN NUMBERS

*"Good governance begins with great compliance."*
— *Mary Shapiro, Former SEC Chair and Former CEO of FINRA*

# REGULATORY COMPLIANCE

Compliance is not just a legal obligation—it's a fundamental pillar of success. As a General Partner or SPV manager, you must know and follow the complex regulations. This serves to protect your investors while also enhancing your reputation.

The legal and regulatory landscape governing SPVs is intricate and ever-evolving. Compliance encompasses both domestic and international regulatory frameworks. This demands attention to detail and a commitment to staying informed of regulatory updates.

Securities compliance forms a critical component of SPV management. This requires a thorough understanding of securities laws. These include registration requirements, disclosure obligations, and anti-fraud provisions.

Equally important is tax compliance. SPVs must adhere to relevant tax laws to ensure proper reporting and payment of taxes. This includes understanding the tax implications of the SPV's activities, such as the treatment of income, expenses, and capital gains. Given the complexity of tax regulations, seeking expert advice from qualified tax professionals is often necessary. By doing so, you can optimize tax efficiency while remaining within legal boundaries.

Beyond securities and tax compliance, SPV managers must also navigate other regulatory areas. This includes having a robust due diligence processes and following anti-money laundering (AML) standards. You must remember that compliance isn't a one-time task but an ongoing commitment that requires regular review and adaptation.

Failure to comply with securities laws can have severe repercussions for those involved in SPV management. Understanding these potential consequences is crucial for maintaining a compliant and successful operation. Here's an overview of the possible outcomes:

- **Financial Penalties:** Regulatory bodies like the Securities and Exchange Commission (SEC) and state securities regulators have the authority to impose substantial fines. These can apply to both the SPV entity and its individual officers and directors, potentially causing significant financial strain.

- **Operational Restrictions:** Regulators may issue orders that limit or prohibit certain activities. This could include orders to stop selling securities, correct false statements, or sell certain assets. It would hurt the SPV's ability to function as intended.

- **Profit Forfeiture:** In cases where securities law violations have led to financial gains, regulators may demand disgorgement. This requires returning any ill-gotten profits, including earned interest or dividends. It could wipe out any gains from non-compliance.

- **Legal Injunctions:** Regulatory bodies can seek court orders to prevent ongoing or future violations. These injunctions might restrict securities sales, protect records, or appoint external management for the SPV's assets.

- **Professional Consequences:** Individuals found in violation of securities laws may face bans or suspensions from the securities industry. This can include prohibitions on serving as officers or directors of public companies, severely limiting future career prospects.

- **Criminal Prosecution:** Serious violations like securities fraud or insider trading can lead to criminal charges. These may result in substantial fines and even imprisonment, underscoring the gravity of securities law compliance.

- **Reputational Damage:** Non-compliance can harm the SPV and its managers. It can damage their reputations, beyond the legal and financial consequences. This loss of trust can have long-lasting effects, making it difficult to attract future investors or business partners.

The severity of these consequences often correlates with the nature and extent of the non-compliance. Regulatory authorities consider factors such as the scale of the violation, its impact on investors, and the degree of intent when determining appropriate actions. SPV managers must prioritize compliance. It's a legal duty and a key to responsible, sustainable business.

Compliance is also about creating a culture of responsibility and trust. Compliance protects your investments and investors. It also positions your SPV for long-term success. By demonstrating a commitment to transparency and adherence to regulations, you create a foundation of credibility. Having this reputation can set you apart in a competitive market.

# SECONDARY SALES

In private placements, lock-up periods are typically established through agreements between buyers and sellers, rather than by SEC regulations. However, other rules, such as Rule 144, can also impact holding periods. Private placement offering documents often include transfer restrictions or lock-up provisions. SPVs must manage secondary sales to avoid registering under the Investment Company Act.

When investing in a Special Purpose Vehicle (SPV), several common provisions often apply to secondary sales of interests. These provisions are designed to maintain control, ensure investor quality, and align with the SPV's long-term strategy. They usually include a Right of First Refusal (ROFR). This gives existing investors or the SPV priority to buy interests before they are offered to outsiders. Many SPVs also require manager approval for any transfer of interests, ensuring oversight of ownership changes. To comply with legal requirements, transfers may be limited to "qualified purchasers" as defined by the Investment Company Act. Lastly, to maintain stability and discourage short-term trading, firms often implement lockup periods of 1 to 3 years. These provisions collectively help protect the interests of all parties involved in the SPV.

While SPV investments often come with restrictions, there are ways for investors to sell their interests before the SPV concludes. These early exit options should be addressed during initial discussions and documented in the legal agreements signed at the outset. Despite careful planning, investors might still need to exit early due to unexpected personal expenses or changes in financial circumstances. In such cases, the SPV structure may present challenges, but various mechanisms exist to provide some flexibility and liquidity options. It's important for both SPV managers and investors to understand these potential scenarios and have clear protocols in place for handling early exit requests.

Specific procedures must be followed if an investor wishes to exit an SPV early. An effective method involves GP-led secondaries, where the general partner actively facilitates a structured sale process. This method allows existing limited partners to sell their interests to new investors or even to other partners already involved in the SPV. It's a controlled way to introduce new capital while providing an exit opportunity for those who wish to sell. First, the investor notifies the General Partner in writing. The

GP then informs other investors anonymously about the sale opportunity. This is done by you reaching out to the other investors to inform them of a member's desire to sell due to a personal matter. Remember, it's important to respect your LPs privacy and maintain anonymity. Existing investors can make offers, which the seller can accept, reject, or negotiate. In the absence of a deal, the GP has the ability to offer to make an offer directly. In the event of another seller rejection, the seller can search for a third party interested in purchasing their equity, possibly through someone they know. If an acceptable offer is received by the investor, they will disclose this price to you and the other investors, giving you the opportunity to match the offer and obtain the shares.

To meet the rising demand for liquidity in private investments, new secondary platforms have emerged. They offer an option for sellers. These platforms must comply with broker-dealer rules. This often means restricting access to Accredited Investors. Accredited Investors can trade private securities, including SPV interests, on these platforms' marketplaces.

Another way secondary sales occur is through tender offers, where the SPV or a third party may offer to buy interests from current limited partners. Investors looking for liquidity may find this option attractive, as it offers a clear way to exit. Investors need to evaluate the suggested valuation and any accompanying conditions since the terms of these offers can vary significantly.

These explanations should remind you to educate investors about limited liquidity in private investments. It can hinder quick cash-outs. Let's stress again how important it is to screen investors carefully and remind them not to invest money they might need soon. If you feel like investors are putting all their money in without thinking about unexpected personal expenses, it's your job to address it.

There are unique considerations and potential complexities for each mechanism.

Investors planning to sell their SPV interests must:

- Review the SPV's governing documents.

- Consult with legal and financial advisors.

- Understand any tax and regulatory issues related to the sale.

Despite this, there are SEC rules that become relevant when an investor plans to resell securities obtained through a private placement, specifically Rule 144. This regulation is applicable to "restricted securities." These generally consist of securities obtained through private placements.

Regulation D Rule 506(b) and 506(c) offerings result in investors receiving "restricted securities." These securities cannot be immediately resold in public markets. Instead, investors must comply with Rule 144, which provides conditions for safely reselling restricted securities. Regardless of the offering type, issuers bear the responsibility of clearly informing investors about resale restrictions. Issuers are also expected to explain the specific conditions under which resale might become possible, with particular emphasis on the requirements set forth in Rule 144.

Rule 144 typically doesn't apply to trades within an SPV. Internal transfers among existing members are usually governed by the SPV's Operating Agreement, not SEC rules. These private transactions don't involve public market resales, which is what Rule 144 regulates. However, securities laws may still apply if transfers significantly change the investment's nature or investors' rights. Rule 144 becomes relevant only when an investor sells to an outsider, potentially creating a public resale. Be cautious if the SPV makes major changes or adds new investors through internal trades. This could create new securities offerings that must comply with regulations.

Under Rule 144, investors in public companies must hold the securities for at least six months before reselling. For non-public companies, the required holding period extends to one year. This system aims to prevent indirect public offerings that would bypass normal registration requirements.

Once more, we must emphasize the significance of these disclosures, as they directly affect an investor's investment liquidity. Potential investors need to understand that they may be required to hold the securities for an extended period before being able to sell them. This transparency allows investors to make well-informed decisions, fully aware of the potential constraints on their ability to liquidate their investment.

To illustrate this, let's consider a publicly traded company listed on NASDAQ. This publicly traded company creates a Special Purpose Vehicle (SPV) to raise capital for a new research and development project through a Rule 506(c) offering.

> Investors who purchase securities through this SPV are subject to a six-month holding period before they can resell their securities. After six months, if all other Rule 144 conditions are met, these investors can begin to sell their securities in a marketplace. The shorter lockup period reflects the greater transparency and existing public market for the public company's securities.

Now, let's look at an example of a startup that raises capital through a Rule 506(b) offering:

> Investors are subject to a one-year holding period before they can consider reselling their securities. Even after one year, resale options may be limited since the company is not a public company and doesn't have a ready market for its securities. Investors might need to rely on private transactions or wait for a liquidity event (such as an IPO or acquisition) to sell their shares.

In both cases, it's important to note several key points regarding the resale of securities under Rule 144. The holding periods, which differ for public and non-public companies, begin from the date of purchase of the securities. For public companies, a critical requirement is the availability of current public information for resales to occur under Rule 144. Also, investors deemed "affiliates" of a public or non-public company face stricter rules, including limits on the volume of securities they can trade.

This measure helps prevent market manipulation by those with insider knowledge. Lastly, to comply with Rule 144, transactions must be conducted through unsolicited broker's transactions or with market makers. This requirement aims to ensure that sales are made in the market's ordinary operations, not through pre-arranged deals that could disadvantage other investors. These provisions collectively work to balance the needs of investors seeking liquidity with the broader goal of maintaining fair and efficient markets.

A thorough understanding of the legal framework, a detailed analysis of contractual terms, and a meticulous evaluation of practical issues are essential. Successfully navigating these challenges is crucial for completing secondary sales of SPV interests.

# BOI REPORTING

The BOI Reporting Rule, in the Corporate Transparency Act, requires some U.S. and foreign businesses to report their owners to FinCEN, a branch of the U.S. Treasury. This rule applies to companies formed or registered in the U.S., unless they're exempt. These companies must report their beneficial owners. These are individuals who control or own 25% or more of the company. For entities formed after January 1, 2024, they must also report their company applicants. These are the people responsible for registering the company. The reports must include specific information about the company. This includes its legal name and location. They must also include personal details of beneficial owners and applicants, such as their names, addresses, and IDs. Some entities are exempt from reporting. This includes subsidiaries of certain exempt entities, like registered investment advisers and large operating companies. However, subsidiaries of pooled investment vehicles may still need to report. It depends on their individual circumstances.

# DOCUMENT RETENTION

So picture this: years from now, you're sitting in your office when suddenly there's a knock at the door. There's someone asking questions about a deal you closed ages ago. Your heart races for a moment, but then you smile. Why? Because you've got a meticulously organized archive that would make your high school librarian swoon.

Now, we know what you're thinking. "Do I really need to keep all this stuff?" The answer is a resounding yes. Every closing document, every investor record, every offering piece - they're all parts of a puzzle. They tell the story of your SPV's journey. And let us tell you, it's a story you want to be able to tell with confidence.

Even though SPV activities are usually simple, it's essential to keep complete records of all business activities. As part of this, it's a good idea to keep a separate set of books and records for each SPV.

Don't be tempted to improvise. A plan for your document management will help you use your time well. Having a written process helps ensure that everything is properly retained.

Here's why having a plan for document retention can help you succeed:

- **Transparency and Accountability:** A comprehensive record-keeping system fosters transparency for investors and regulators. Furthermore, a well-structured, accessible archive is a powerful tool. You'll be able to easily go back to review parts of your previous deals when necessary. Easy access to documentation allows quick responses to inquiries. It also shows compliance with regulations. This transparency builds a reputation for reliability among investors. Having quick access to any document not only demonstrates compliance, but it also shows your competence as a General Partner. In the investment world, competence is a key element of your overall reputation. This system also supports good governance practices, which are crucial for both legal and ethical reasons.

- **Dispute Resolution:** In the event of challenges or disputes, organized records are invaluable. They provide a clear audit trail, vital for evidence in legal disputes. Additionally, they help defend your actions in management of the investment.

- **Compliance:** Regulatory bodies often impose specific record-keeping requirements on SPVs. Strong retention policies ensure compliance with regulations and avoid penalties. Also, investors and regulators prefer SPVs with clear, accessible records.

- **Risk Management:** Proper document retention is key to effective risk management. You'll have the ability to identify and reduce potential risks. You can also analyze past experiences by reviewing historical documents. When you review your past deals, you can identify patterns and use this to make better decisions in the future. This proactive risk management approach protects the SPV's interests. It also helps ensure your long-term success.

Some of the primary documents you need to retain include:

- **Formation Documents:** This includes the SPV's Articles of Incorporation, Operating Agreement, and all amendments. These foundational documents establish the legal framework of the SPV.

- **Closing Documents:** Keep all legal documents for the SPV's creation. This includes subscription, purchase, and financing agreements. These documents are critical for verifying the terms and conditions under which the SPV was formed and funded.

- **Investor Records:** Keep detailed records of all investors. Include their contact info, investment details, KYC records. Accurate, up-to-date investor records are indispensable. They help manage relationships and ensure compliance with regulations.

- **Correspondence:** In addition to investor records, keep all communications. This includes both electronic and physical messages with investors, regulators, and others. This provides a thorough audit trail of interactions.

- **Offering Materials:** Keep all marketing materials used to attract investors. This includes prospectuses, private placement memoranda, and subscription documents. These records provide a clear history of the information shown to potential investors.

- **Financial Records:** Keep financial statements, audit reports, tax returns, and any other documents related to the SPV's financial performance. They assess the SPV's health, guide management decisions, and meet reporting requirements.

- **Meeting Minutes:** Record detailed minutes of all meetings, capturing discussions and decisions made. These minutes serve as an official record of the governance and operational decisions of the SPV.

Digital record-keeping has changed how we handle, store, and access information. It is a big improvement over paper-based systems. This digital transformation brings unmatched security, access, and efficiency to document management.

Modern digital document management relies on several key pillars. Enhanced Security is one pillar. Modern digital platforms use top security, including strong encryption and fine access controls. These features are great for protecting sensitive data from unauthorized access. This is critical in the high-stakes world of investment deals.

Accessibility is another significant advantage. Instead of digging through a filing cabinet, digital systems let authorized parties access documents from anywhere. This facilitates seamless collaboration and instant information retrieval, vastly improving operational efficiency.

Choosing the right digital tools is essential for optimizing efficiency and ensuring security. A key advantage of cloud solutions is disaster-proof storage. They offer built-in redundancy and automated backups.. This approach greatly reduces the risk of data loss from disasters or hardware failures. As a result, you can ensure that records are maintained.

The game-changing feature of digital document management is its ability to conduct powerful searches. By using advanced search, users can find specific documents in seconds. The search includes keywords, metadata, and custom fields. This streamlines information retrieval and increases productivity. This not only streamlines operations but also provides a competitive edge.

# DATA PROTECTION AND CONFIDENTIALITY

Let's discuss why keeping information safe and private is so important for your SPV to succeed. SPVs often deal with sensitive data, including financial details, business secrets, and personal information of investors and partners. Because of this, protecting data is a big deal for any SPV. We need to talk about how you can use the best methods to handle this information carefully. Doing this right is crucial because it helps your SPV run smoothly and builds trust with the people involved.

Strong data protection is mainly about keeping your investors' interests safe. When people commit capital to your SPV, they're not just betting on a business idea - they're putting their trust in you. By using solid security measures, you show that you take this trust seriously. This builds confidence in your SPV, which is key to long-term success in investing. Essentially, good data protection isn't just about following rules - it's about proving to investors that their faith in you is well-placed.

Protecting data isn't just about keeping investors happy - it's also about avoiding serious problems. In the U.S., there's no single law that covers all types of private information, but there are laws for specific kinds of data, like the Privacy Act of 1974. It's important to also think about laws in other countries. For example, the European Union has strict rules called GDPR that even affect U.S. businesses. GDPR isn't the only set of rules to worry about, though. Many places have similar laws, and you need to know which ones apply to your SPV. If you break these laws, you could face fines, legal issues, and harm to your reputation. So, it's crucial to figure out which laws matter for your SPV and follow them carefully.

Let's talk about how to handle data protection and privacy the right way. Start by figuring out what information needs extra protection. This could be things like your investors' personal and money details, secret investment plans, or private business information from companies you might invest in. Once you know what needs protecting, set up safety measures to guard against outside attacks and inside mistakes. Improve your online security by using a VPN, antivirus software, and secure data systems. Remember, even the best security can fail if someone isn't careful. So, make sure to control who can see sensitive information by only giving access to people who really need it. Think of it like having a strong lock on your door, but also being careful about who you give the key to.

## Data Governance and Risk Management

To safeguard your SPV's data, it is wise to plan ahead and establish governance measures. Think of data governance as a set of rules for handling information from start to finish. It covers how you collect, store, use, and get rid of data. By having clear guidelines, everyone in your company knows how to handle information safely.

One important part is deciding how long to keep different types of data. This helps you follow the law and avoid problems with old information. When you need to share data with others, only share what's absolutely necessary. Use safe ways to transfer it and make clear agreements about how it can be used. Don't forget about getting rid of data properly when you don't need it anymore. This could mean deleting files securely or making sure they can't be traced back to people. It's also a good idea to regularly check your data practices, like a health check-up, to spot and fix any weak points. Go a step further by training your team about data security to create a culture where everyone understands information protection.

## Data Breach Management and Notification

Despite your best efforts, it's important to prepare for the worst. Data breaches in SPVs are inevitable risks that require thorough preparation. Should a data breach occur, you need to have a comprehensive incident response plan that outlines exactly what steps to take in case of a data breach or security incident. Your incident response plan should outline steps for detection, investigation, containment, and communication. This plan should address both technical and communication aspects, including strategies for notifying affected parties and stakeholders.

You should also familiarize yourself with the legal requirements for breach notification. Depending on jurisdiction and breach severity, notification protocols may differ and include direct communication with individuals, regulatory bodies, or public announcements. Timely notification is often mandated, with specific deadlines. Having an incident response plan in place demonstrates dedication to data protection and crisis management, which can build trust with all involved parties.

### Third Party Data Protection Officer Services

Don't be afraid to ask for help when it comes to protecting your SPV's data. As regulations evolve and the threat of cybercrime increases, it's smart to talk to experts. Some dealmakers are hiring special data protection officers or advisors. These experts can help you follow the rules and spot potential problems before they happen.

If you're running multiple deals or have a complex SPV, you might want to hire a part-time Data Protection Officer (DPO). These experts can oversee your data protection efforts without the cost of a full-time employee. They're called Fractional Data Protection Officers (FDPOs), and they can tailor their help to fit your specific needs.

FDPOs make sure you're collecting and using data properly and following all the rules. They'll check your current practices, suggest changes if needed, and keep an eye on new laws that might affect your business. They can also review any new services or apps you want to use to make sure they're suitable and compliant.

Whether you hire a DPO or not, remember that protecting data is an ongoing job. It's not something you can do once and forget about. You need to regularly review and update how you handle data to keep up with new threats and changing rules. It's a good idea to check your data protection setup from time to time to make sure everything is working as it should. Data protection for SPVs goes beyond compliance—it's a an essential step for building trust, mitigating risk and achieving success as a General Partner.

# WEALTH IN NUMBERS

## Data Protection Policy
**Last Updated**: [Insert Date]

### Definitions
- **General Partner**: [Insert GP entity name]
- **Responsible Person**: [Insert name of the individual responsible for data protection].
- **Register of Systems**: A record of all systems or contexts where the General Partner processes personal data.

### 1. Data Protection Principles
The General Partner is committed to handling data according to its obligations under relevant law and ensuring that personal data is:
- Handled legally, fairly, and transparently.
- Collected for specific, explicit, and valid purposes, without further processing that contradicts those purposes.
- Relevant, adequate, and limited to what's necessary.
- Accurate and updated when required.
- Stored only for as long as necessary for its purpose.
- Processed securely to protect against unauthorized access, loss, or damage.

### 2. General Provisions
- This policy applies to all personal data processed by the General Partner.
- The Responsible Person will ensure adherence to this policy.
- This policy will be reviewed annually.

### 3. Lawful, Fair, and Transparent Processing
- To ensure data processing is lawful, fair, and transparent, the General Partner will maintain a Register of Systems.
- The Register of Systems will be reviewed annually.
- Individuals have the right to access their personal data, and requests will be addressed promptly.

### 4. Lawful Purposes
- All data must be processed under one of the following lawful bases: consent, contract, legal obligation, vital interests, public task, or legitimate interests
- The General Partner will document the lawful basis in the Register of Systems.
- If consent is used as the lawful basis for processing, evidence of opt-in consent will be retained.
- Communications based on consent will provide an option to revoke consent, and systems will ensure revocation is accurately reflected in the General Partner's records.

### 5. Data Minimization
- Personal data will be relevant, sufficient, and limited to what's required.
- [Include specific considerations relevant to the General Partner's systems]

### 6. Accuracy
- The General Partner will take reasonable measures to ensure personal data remains accurate.
- Where required, measures will be in place to keep data current.
- [Include specific considerations relevant to the General Partner's systems]

### 7. Archiving / Removal
- To keep personal data only as long as necessary, the General Partner will implement an archiving policy and review it yearly.
- The policy will define what data should be retained, for how long, and why.

### 8. Security
- The General Partner will store data securely using modern, up-to-date software.
- Access will be limited to necessary personnel, and suitable security measures will prevent unauthorized sharing.
- Backup and disaster recovery solutions will be maintained.
- Data deletion will ensure it is destroyed and unrecoverable

### 9. Breach
- If a security breach leads to accidental or illegal destruction, loss, alteration, or unauthorized disclosure of personal data, the General Partner will assess the risks to individuals and report if necessary.

# MONITOR AND
# REVIEW COMPLIANCE

As we mentioned, you need to ensure ongoing compliance with your SPV. Regularly monitoring and reviewing compliance is essential for investment management. Why is this so important? Compliance monitoring will keep you on the right side of things with regulations. It keeps everything on track, ensuring all policies and procedures are followed and well-documented. You need to do it to keep everything running smoothly.

But compliance monitoring isn't just about avoiding trouble; it also improves performance. It finds gaps and sets up a strong compliance program by completing regular checks. You'll want to stay updated and informed on any regulatory changes that might affect the SPV. Your system needs to have processes in place to monitor compliance with securities laws, Anti-Money Laundering regulations, investor checks and reporting requirements.

It's always wise to work with your legal and compliance experts while following your strategy. Internal audits, third-party assessments, and legal reviews can help. They can find areas for improvement, reduce risks, and strengthen governance. Another good way that you can  stay up-to-date on industry best practices and regulatory developments is by joining professional organizations in your industry. In the end, preventing risk is only possible if you have procedures to assess it. Proper compliance monitoring will certainly reduce risk while building a reputable, successful operation.

# NAVIGATING REG D & FORM D

Maintaining compliance for your SPV requires attention to legal and regulatory guidelines. As we covered earlier, a major piece of this process relies on Regulation D. It provides what is called a safe harbor exemption[i] which allows you to raise capital and sell securities for your SPV without SEC registration. It's important for you to know the nuances of Regulation D so you can remain compliant.

The completion and filing of Form D creates a valid offering under Regulation D. It gives regulators a clear view of your offering and helps ensure compliance with securities laws. The SEC requires Form D to be submitted when unregistered securities are sold under the 1933 Securities Act. This applies to offerings that claim exemption from registration under these specific rules:

- Rule 504 of Regulation D

- Rule 506 of Regulation D

- Section 4(a)(5) of the Securities Act

If you sell securities without SEC registration, and you're using one of these exemptions, you must file Form D. To stay compliant, you need to submit it to the SEC in a timely manner. Form D provides the SEC with key details about your offering. It includes the names of the principals, the capital being raised, the industry, and other relevant information. You will want to avoid any discrepancies that might raise concerns by ensuring alignment between the information on your Form D and your PPM.

You really can't overstate the importance of filing Form D properly. Even large companies have gotten into some serious trouble for not doing it properly. As an example, Facebook (now known as Meta) faced charges

---

i        *A safe harbor exemption is a legal provision that can reduce or eliminate legal or regulatory liability in certain situations. This means that you're protected from a penalty as long as certain conditions are met.*

from the SEC in 2019 for misleading disclosures[ii] about the risk of user data misuse. In addition to these charges, the SEC's complaint included charges against Facebook for not filing a Form D when they sold securities to Instagram's shareholders during the acquisition. Facebook agreed to a $100 million penalty to settle the SEC's charges. This was due to alleged securities law violations, including a failure to file Form D.

When it comes to filing under Regulation D, you can choose to file before or after the closing of your offering. You can pre-file before the fund closes without disclosing how much you've raised. For post-close filings, the notice to be filed within 15 days after the first sale of securities in the offering. When the first investor becomes contractually committed to invest, that is considered the "date of first sale" for your deal. If the deadline lands on a Saturday, Sunday, or holiday, it is pushed to the next available business day. The SEC does not charge any filing fee for a Form D notice or amendment.

To file your Form D, you'll need to prepare specific information about your Special Purpose Vehicle. This includes details about who's running the SPV, its financial health, and the specifics of the investment you're offering. Take your time while gathering all this information to check it for accuracy. It's important to double-check every detail you put on the form. The SEC has strict requirements about what needs to be included, so make sure you've covered everything they ask for. Getting this right from the start can save you from potential problems with the SEC down the line. Remember, the goal is to provide a clear and honest picture of your offering to the regulators.

If your offering is open longer than a year, you'll need to provide an annual update for your Form D. You should file this update before the anniversary of your first filing. If you're done raising money and not taking new investors, you likely won't need to submit an update. The

---

ii          *https://www.sec.gov/newsroom/press-releases/2019-140*

exemption from annual amendments for some private funds that have finished fundraising applies to both 506(b) and 506(c) offerings.

As a note, even if you aren't required to perform an annual update, you should update your Form D if important information changes. This could include things like a new address, changes in who's running the company, or a significant change in the number of investors. It's also a good idea to keep copies of everything you submit. If the SEC decides to take a closer look at your offering, they'll probably want to see your Form D filings and your Private Placement Memorandum (PPM). Having good records will make this process go much smoother.

Now that you have a handle on this important part of the process, it's time to shift our focus from theoretical to the practical aspects of this process. Knowing the rules is essential, but your SPV's success depends on you (accurately) completing and submitting Form D. So, let's go through how to get this done. We'll break down Form D, giving you the info you need to fill it out correctly and stay compliant.

## Steps to Complete Form D

### Issuer's Identity

This section is all about who is responsible for filing the security with the SEC, not the sponsor details. It includes:

- Issuer's name
- Jurisdiction of incorporation (e.g., Delaware LLC)
- Previous names (if applicable)
- Entity type (usually LLC)
- Year of incorporation
- Year it was formed

### Principal Place of Business and Contact Information

Usually, this part has the sponsor's address and contact info for notifications.

### Related Persons

This section identifies the executive officer, often the manager of an LLC or the manager's manager. Only one person needs to be identified. Their details should include:

i. Last name, first name, middle name
ii. Street address
iii. Contact information

In some situations, "executive officer" refers to directors or promoters.

### Industry Group

This info is used by the SEC to classify industries under Reg D. You have a few common choices, like:

- Real estate (residential, commercial, etc.)
- Technology
- Business services
- Private equity
- Venture capital

### Issuer's Size

You can either share the revenue range or total asset value. You can say no to disclosing but consider how providing this info may be beneficial for your offering.

### Exemptions

Specify the exemption under Rule 504, 504(b), or 504(c)

### Type of Filing

Most often, clients use the "new notice" type of filing. "Amendment" is used if there are changes or mistakes in a previous filing.

### Date of First Sale in This Offering

This date marks when funds from investors were received and deposited, making them non-refundable.

### Duration of the Offer

Regulation D offerings are usually valid for one year. If the duration is longer, select "no" and ensure you renew the offering as needed.

### Types of Securities Offered

Select "Equity" for ownership interests or "Debt" for contractual obligations. Other options, such as options or warrants, are less common.

### Security to Be Acquired Upon Exercise of the Option

This is typically left blank but may apply in specific cases.

### Business Combination Transaction

Indicate "no" unless this offering is connected to a merger, acquisition, or exchange offer.

### Minimum Investment Amount

Specify the minimum amount that is required from investors, as stated in your private placement memorandum.

### Sales Compensation

Leave this blank unless you are paying sales commissions to a licensed broker-dealer.

### Offerings and Sales Amount

Provide the total offering amount and the total amount already sold as of the filing date. The remaining amount is the difference between these two figures.

### Investor Section

Report the number of non-accredited investors, if applicable, and the total number of investors, regardless of their accreditation status.

### Sales Commissions and Finder Fees

Avoid paying finders' fees, as it can lead to regulatory issues.

### Use of Proceeds

Specify the portion of funds allocated for payments to persons marketing the security, such as acquisition or marketing fees.

### Signing the Form D

Fill in the issuer's name, the signer's name, signature, and title. If you are the executive officer, indicate this in the title.

### Additional Pages

Pages 5 through 11 contain instructions and continuation pages for multiple issuers, related persons, or those paying sales compensation. Complete these pages only if applicable.

# FILING FORM D ON EDGAR

After preparing your Form D, it's time to submit it to the SEC. This is where the Electronic Data Gathering, Analysis, and Retrieval system comes back into the picture. Like we talked about before, EDGAR is the SEC's online platform for filing and accessing regulatory documents. Filing your Form D through EDGAR ensures that your SPV's offering information is officially recorded and made available to the SEC and potential investors.

Now, let's walk through the process of sending in your completed Form D using the EDGAR system. This part of the process is just as important as filling out the form correctly, so pay close attention to each step to ensure a smooth filing experience.

To file Form D on the EDGAR system, follow these steps:

- **Log in to EDGAR:** Start by logging into your EDGAR account. You'll need the Central Index Key (CIK) number, CCC number, which is your CIK Confirmation Code and password you obtained when you first registered with EDGAR. Once logged in, you'll follow the prompts to submit the form and any other required documents.

- **Review Form D:** Make sure you've completed all necessary sections of Form D, including issuer information, the offering details, and any exemptions you're claiming. The form must be prepared and saved in a format compatible with EDGAR, The formats that are accepted include ASCII, HTML, XML, XBRL and PDF.

- **Submit the Form on EDGAR:**

  - Go to the "Submit Filings" section.

  - Follow the on-screen prompts to upload your prepared Form D and any other required documents. You will be asked to verify the information before submission.

- After confirming the details, complete the filing by submitting the form through the EDGAR system.

- **Receive Confirmation:** After successfully submitting, you'll receive a confirmation from EDGAR. This confirmation will include a submission ID and other details verifying the form was filed.

Make sure to check for any required updates to the Form D filing if there are significant changes to your offering.

# SEC EDGAR FILING CODES

The CIK and CCC codes are used to make submissions to the SEC on behalf a filer. We will require these codes before we can file documents on your behalf.

## CIK (Central Index Key)

The CIK is a unique, public number that is assigned to each entity that submits filings to the SEC. Use of the CIK allows the SEC to differentiate between filing entities with similar names.

## CCC (CIK Confirmation Code)

The CCC is a code used in combination with the CIK to submit a filing via EDGAR. The CCC is eight characters having at least one number (0-9) and at least one special character (@, #, $, *). The CCC is also case-sensitive and must be entered exactly as created, in lower case.

While Regulation D and Form D filings are major aspects of federal securities regulation, it's important to remember that they're not the only compliance consideration. We must also take into account state-level requirements, commonly known as "Blue Sky" laws. For a long time, the United States didn't have robust laws governing the sale of securities and financial investments.

In the early 20th Century, the US Economy went through major change, and in 1909, Joseph Norman Dolley emerged as a champion for Kansas investors. Dolley's appointment as state bank commissioner exposed him to the rampant fraud that targeted unsuspecting citizens. This made him become increasingly frustrated with the lack of regulation. Swindlers sold worthless investments in fake mines and imaginary plantations. They pitched outlandish schemes that promised huge returns. These investments, Dolley remarked, that the ventures were backed with "no more basis than so many feet of blue sky." Which is where the term "blue sky laws" originates.

He witnessed how these scams were devastating people's lives, some of them having their savings wiped out overnight. Dolley was determined to shut down these scams and got to work on ways he could protect investors from these predators. He achieved a monumental win in 1911 through relentless lobbying. Kansas made history as the first state to enforce a comprehensive securities law, which included the registration of investments and the licensing of salespeople. Dolley's work on this pioneering legislation led to the establishment of similar regulations nationwide.

The absence of regulatory oversight allowed for widespread fraud. Companies capitalized on this by issuing stocks and marketing investments. Their exaggerated promises attracted many inexperienced investors. Despite attempts to create safeguards, these investment schemes were widespread. Ultimately, these practices contributed towards the infamous 1929 stock market crash.

While there were a few "blue sky laws" in place, they were inadequately enforced and easily evaded by unethical operators who shifted their businesses to other states. The 1929 crash showed the need for federal regulation. It led to the Securities Acts of the 1930s and to the SEC in

1934. The Uniform Securities Act of 1956 served as a blueprint for state securities laws, establishing the basis for current blue sky laws.

The National Securities Markets Improvement Act (NSMIA) of 1996 aimed to standardize the regulation of national securities offerings. This introduced the concept of "covered securities" exempt from state registration. Covered securities consist of stocks on major exchanges such as Nasdaq and NYSE, mutual fund shares, and specific government and municipal securities. While NSMIA lessened certain obligations, states still possessed the power to uncover and take legal action against fraudulent practices.

All Blue Sky laws focus on key provisions. They require registration and work to prevent fraud by disallowing misrepresentation. An example of the latter can be found in the Uniform Securities Act of 1956, a model statute that forms the basis for Blue Sky laws in most states:

It is unlawful for any person, in connection with the offer, sale, or purchase of any security, to directly or indirectly:

- (1) employ any device, scheme, or artifice to defraud;

- (2) make an untrue statement of a material fact or omit a material fact that makes the statements misleading, given the circumstances;

- (3) engage in any act or practice that would operate as a fraud or deceit upon any person.

While these laws vary between states, they share a common intent of safeguarding the interests of investors. Federal law preempts state registration and qualification under Rule 506. However, states can require notice filings and collect fees. In most states, issuers of Rule 506(b) or 506(c) offerings must notify state regulators within 15 days of the first sale to an in-state investor. Some states require a pre-offering notice filing. You should should check requirements for all states where you intend to offer securities, as regulations can change.

Typical filing requirements include a notice of sale, qualification of the offering, state-specific forms or disclosures, and payment of filing fees, which vary by state. The submission process differs among jurisdictions. Some states accept electronic submissions through the North American Securities Administrators Association's ( https://www.nasaa.org ) Electronic Filing Depository System. Others may still require paper filings. Deadlines and renewal requirements also lack uniformity across states.

For general partners and fund managers, understanding blue sky laws is essential. The cost of Blue Sky notice filings depends on the geographic distribution of limited partners, as filings must be submitted to each state where LPs reside. The North American Securities Administrators Association has info on state filing fees. They can vary significantly. Some jurisdictions require annual updates, while others do not mandate such amendments.

Issuers should track filing deadlines and renewal requirements in multiple states. It's also advisable to budget for varying filing fees and compliance costs ahead of any capital raise. Also, fund managers and issuers should know that some states may require extra filings or registrations before offering securities to their residents. You must comply with these requirements. It will help avoid penalties or legal issues. Failure to meet compliance could jeopardize the offering and damage investor trust.

The general process for filing Blue Sky fees typically involves the following steps:

- Research state requirements
- Prepare the necessary documents
- Submit the documents to the state securities regulator
- File Blue Sky fees within 15 days of collecting capital, with fees varying by state.
- Pay the filing fees

- Wait for approval

- Keep records

Failing to comply with state notice filing requirements can lead to penalties, legal issues, and even the cancellation of the offering. Additionally, non-compliance can harm investor trust and make it harder to raise capital in the future. Therefore, it is crucial for any issuer offering securities in multiple states to thoroughly research and carefully follow each state's regulations.

You can easily find third-party services to handle your blue sky filings for a fee. These services are often worth the investment. They ensure proper filing, reduce your workload, and keep you compliant across all jurisdictions.

Your SPV's annual maintenance obligations are heavily dependent on the state in which it operates. Just like filing requirements and annual fees, these can vary depending on the jurisdiction. Let's check out the typical compliance needs:

- **Annual Reports:** Filing these reports keeps your SPV in good standing with the state.

- **Documentation:** Maintaining accurate and up-to-date documents is crucial for smooth operations and potential audits.

- **Legal and Regulatory Compliance:** Staying on top of changing laws and regulations helps ensure your SPV operates within legal boundaries.

- **Taxes and Fees:** Be prepared for state franchise taxes and registered agent fees, which are standard expenses.

As we have covered time and time again throughout this book, running an SPV isn't a set-it-and-forget-it task. It needs ongoing attention, and ignoring this can lead to big problems like fines, legal issues, and damage to your reputation. As the General Partner, you're responsible for various fees and annual filings. You also need to stay up-to-date with legal changes and keep accurate records.

The cost of maintaining an SPV can vary depending on where it's set up. Many managers find it helpful to work with legal and accounting experts to handle these tasks smoothly and avoid mistakes. In fact, many prefer to hand these jobs over to professionals entirely. This way, they can avoid the complexity and potential pitfalls of SPV maintenance.

By letting a trusted third party handle your SPV maintenance, you free yourself up to focus on what's really important: finding deals and growing your business. Working with a specialized service provider, like Syndicately or similar companies, can give you peace of mind. This sets you up for long-term success as an SPV manager.

Imagine being able to pour all your energy into running deals, meeting investors, and finding new opportunities, while your SPV runs smoothly in the background. Whether you use Syndicately or another service, having a third party manage these tasks is highly recommended. It allows you to build momentum and focus on what you do best.

# TAX IMPLICATIONS AND STRATEGIES

To maximize success with SPVs, dealmakers need to go beyond just following the rules and develop smart tax planning strategies. SPVs have a unique structure. When you implement effective tax strategies, it becomes possible increase investor returns. As a result, you will improve the overall value proposition for investors.

Tax planning is complex and what is involved can vary depending on where you are located. It's crucial to get professional tax advice. Some important things to think about are how the SPV's income is taxed, how capital gains are treated, and special investment structures that can save on taxes. You also need to consider state tax laws. There are various factors to consider. Strategies for tax-efficient profit sharing, loss offsetting, and using tax treaties can all enhance the SPV's performance.

Let's take a moment to review the key tax details you'll need to know as the General Partner of your SPV, and how to handle them effectively.

Understanding the Tax Environment: A thorough understanding of the tax environment is the first step in optimizing tax benefits for an SPV. This includes federal, state, and local taxes in the SPV's home jurisdiction, as well as any relevant international tax treaties if the SPV operates across borders.

Strategic Use of Jurisdiction: The choice of jurisdiction for an SPV can have significant tax implications. Jurisdictions like Delaware, the Cayman Islands, and Luxembourg are popular for their favorable tax laws and beneficial treaties. Selecting the right jurisdiction should align with the SPV's investment goals while optimizing tax efficiency.

Leveraging Tax Incentives: Many jurisdictions offer tax incentives for investments in specific industries, technologies, or projects, such as renewable energy or real estate development. Identifying and utilizing these incentives can substantially reduce the tax burden on an SPV.

The primary tax form for Special Purpose Vehicles is Form 1065, also known as the U.S. Return of Partnership Income. This form gives a full overview of the SPV's financial activities for the tax year. It includes total income, deductions, credits, and other tax items. It is the cornerstone of tax reporting for partnerships and LLCs taxed as partnerships, which are structured as SPVs.

It is critical to understand Form 1065 due to the pass-through tax nature of SPVs. Unlike corporations, SPVs typically don't pay entity-level taxes. Instead, individual investors bear the tax liability. This form serves as the main way to report the SPV's financial performance to both the IRS and investors. The information on Form 1065 is used to generate Schedule K-1 forms, which specify each investor's share of income, deductions, and credits. Errors on Form 1065 can lead to incorrect K-1s, which may cause tax problems for both the SPV and its investors.

Form 1065 has several schedules and attachments. They detail specific aspects of the SPV's operations. Schedule B is for partnership info. Schedule L has balance sheets. Schedule M-1 is for income reconciliation. These components contribute to a transparent picture of the SPV's financial status.

As the General Partner, it's your responsibility to prepare and file Form 1065 on time with the tax authorities. This includes generating and distributing K-1 forms to each investor. K-1 forms report gains, losses, interest, dividends, earnings, and other distributions from the investment for the past tax year. Although individual investors don't submit the K-1 form themselves, the information it provides is fundamental for filing their personal tax returns.

Timely and accurate preparation of these forms is vital for maintaining compliance. The K-1 forms are due by March 15 or the 15th day of the third month following the end of the entity's tax year. It is generally expected that partners receive their K-1 forms by this deadline.

Given the complexity and importance of this process, it is advisable to engage a tax professional to prepare and distribute K-1s. The associated fees can be included in the SPV's costs and shared among all investors. Proper planning and management of K-1 forms help ensure compliance and timely tax filings for all parties involved.

When we started developing Syndicately, we designed a workflow to anticipate and fix common K-1 distribution issues. We aimed to make documentation and reporting easy to access. This would allow partners to file their taxes on time and comply with regulations.

Tax planning and accurate reporting are key to maximizing the performance of Special Purpose Vehicles. SPV taxation is complex and daunting. But, tools like Syndicately are designed streamline these processes. However, due to complex tax laws, they may affect investor returns. So, it's best to get professional tax advice. Your tax plan should be tailored to your SPV structure and investment goals. In short, SPVs can enhance their value to stakeholders by combining expert guidance with efficient management.

While complex, the Form 1065, Schedule K-1 offers valuable insights into the financial health of an investment. Investors should review this form carefully. It will help them assess their investment's performance and report their taxes. Again, this form's complexity often requires expert help. Misinterpreting it can cause compliance issues in the future. To grasp the structure of a K-1, let's analyze the information it contains:

# UNDERSTANDING YOUR SCHEDULE K-1

### Final K-1

At the top of the form, there's a box labeled "Final K-1". As a GP, you should check this box if it's the last K-1 for a particular partner. This could be because the partner sold their share, ownership was transferred to someone else, or the partnership was dissolved. Checking this box notifies the IRS and the partner that they should not anticipate receiving future K-1s from this partnership.

### Schedule K-1 Part I

Part I of the Schedule K-1 form is a critical section that establishes the identity of the partnership or fund issuing the document. It includes the partnership's name, address, EIN, and the IRS center where it filed its return. For Special Purpose Vehicles, use the specific SPV name and tax ID for the investment. This section gives the legal entity's ID. It ensures all info is accurate and matches the partnership's tax return. This section may seem simple. But, it is foundational for tax reporting of the partner's income, deductions, and credits. It ensures accurate records and links to the right investment entity.

| **Part I** | **Information About the Partnership** |
|---|---|
| **A** | Partnership's employer identification number |
| **B** | Partnership's name, address, city, state, and ZIP code |
| **C** | IRS Center where partnership filed return |
| **D** | ☐ Check if this is a publicly traded partnership (PTP) |

## Schedule K-1 Part II

Part II of the Schedule K-1 form is critical. It details the partner's relationship with the partnership or fund. This section links the entity info in Part I and the financial details in Part III. It shows a clear picture of the partner's stake and role in the entity. Part II includes:

- **Partner Identification:** This includes the partner's name, address, and Taxpayer Identification Number (TIN). For individual partners, this is typically their Social Security Number, while for entity partners, it's their Employer Identification Number (EIN).

- **Partner Classification:** It specifies whether the partner is a general or limited partner, which is crucial for determining tax treatment and liability.

- **Foreign Partner Status:** This indicates whether the partner is domestic or foreign, which can affect tax withholding requirements and reporting obligations.

- **Capital Account Information:**
  - Beginning and ending capital account balances
  - Capital contributions made during the tax year
  - Current year increase (decrease) in capital account
  - Withdrawals and distributions

- **Profit, Loss, and Capital Sharing Percentages:** These percentages (found in Boxes J, K, and L) show the partner's share in the partnership's profits, losses, and capital. They are critical for calculating the partner's tax liability and understanding their economic interest in the partnership.

- **Partner's Share of Liabilities:** This includes the partner's share of nonrecourse, qualified nonrecourse, and recourse liabilities at the year's end.

- **Tax Basis Capital Account Information:** This provides insights into the partner's tax basis in their partnership interest, which is crucial for determining gain or loss upon sale of the interest or partnership liquidation.

- **Section 704(c) Information:** This relates to built-in gains or losses on property contributed to the partnership.

Your Limited Partners need to take time to review this section and ensure it is accurate. They must also understand their place in the partnership structure. The capital account information is particularly important for reference here, as it shows changes in the partner's investment over the year. This includes contributions, distributions, and their share of the partnership's income or loss.

## Section J

Section J of the Schedule K-1 form details a partner's capital account in a partnership or fund. It provides key insights into their ownership percentage. Box J includes two important figures: Beginning Capital and Ending Capital. For new investors, the Beginning Capital is typically 0%, reflecting their initial entry into the investment. The Ending Capital percentage represents the investor's share of the total investment. It is calculated by dividing their contribution by the total amount raised. For example, an investor who contributes $100,000 to a $1 million fund would have an Ending Capital of 10%. Investments may start before January 1 but fund after. This can cause discrepancies between the Beginning and Ending Capital figures. This indicates a shift in the investor's stake over the year. Additionally, if an investment is closed and repaid within the tax year, the Ending Capital will be recorded as 0%. Investors must accurately analyze these figures. They need to track their ownership percentage and their investment's performance.

## Section L

Section L of the Schedule K-1 form, titled the Capital Account Analysis, offers a detailed overview of the changes in a partner's capital account over the tax year. This section begins with the prior year's capital balance and tracks all financial activities to determine the year-end balance. The key components of Section L include the beginning capital amount, capital contributions made during the year, any increases or decreases in the current year (calculated by subtracting interest expenses from interest income), and withdrawals or distributions. The ending capital account, which results from these calculations, is a critical indicator of potential taxable gain or loss if the partnership interest were to be sold. A negative ending balance generally suggests a capital gain upon sale, while a positive balance indicates a potential loss. It's important to note that the timing of transactions can cause discrepancies between the figures reported in the K-1 and an investor's personal records, so investors should refer to the "Effective Date" of transactions in their portfolio for accurate reconciliation. The ending capital account also serves as the beginning balance for the following year's K-1, ensuring continuity in tracking an investor's ownership in the partnership over time.

| Part II | Information About the Partner |
| --- | --- |

**E** Partner's identifying number

**F** Partner's name, address, city, state, and ZIP code

**G** ☐ General partner or LLC member-manager  ☐ Limited partner or other LLC member

**H** ☐ Domestic partner  ☐ Foreign partner

**I1** What type of entity is this partner? _______________

**I2** If this partner is a retirement plan (IRA/SEP/Keogh/etc.), check here . . . . . . . . . . . . . . . . . . ☐

**J** Partner's share of profit, loss, and capital (see instructions):

| | Beginning | Ending |
| --- | --- | --- |
| Profit | % | % |
| Loss | % | % |
| Capital | % | % |

**K** Partner's share of liabilities at year end:

| | |
| --- | --- |
| Nonrecourse . . . . . . | $ __________ |
| Qualified nonrecourse financing . | $ __________ |
| Recourse . . . . . . . | $ __________ |

**L** Partner's capital account analysis:

| | |
| --- | --- |
| Beginning capital account . . . | $ __________ |
| Capital contributed during the year | $ __________ |
| Current year increase (decrease) . | $ __________ |
| Withdrawals & distributions . . | $ ( __________ ) |
| Ending capital account . . . . | $ __________ |

☐ Tax basis  ☐ GAAP  ☐ Section 704(b) book
☐ Other (explain)

**M** Did the partner contribute property with a built-in gain or loss?
☐ **Yes**  ☐ **No**
If "Yes," attach statement (see instructions)

## Schedule K-1 Part III

Part III of the Schedule K-1 form outlines a partner's share of the entity's financial activities. It is essential for accurate tax reporting. This section breaks down income sources like interest, dividends, and both short- and long-term capital gains. It also covers various deductions and credits. Investment entities must report interest income earned during the tax year. This can be derived from transaction records. Also, some may report "Other deductions." This might include investment interest deductions from pre-funded opportunities. Part III also covers ordinary business income or loss, rental income, royalties, and any applicable tax credits. This info affects the partner's tax return. It shows their share of the partnership's profits, losses, and tax liabilities. Partners must use this data to accurately report their share of the entity's financial activities. The items in Part III vary based on the partnership's nature and activities. So, your Limited Partners must review each entry. This ensures tax compliance and effective financial planning. As the General Partner, you must allocate these items to each partner based on their ownership percentage or the partnership agreement. To accurately report on the Schedule K-1 form for Limited Partners in an SPV, pay close attention to these specific important items:

- **Box 1 - Ordinary Business Income (Loss):** This box reflects the partner's share of the SPV's ordinary business income or loss for the tax year. As the General Partner, you must ensure that this amount accurately reflects the SPV's performance. It must also be allocated based on each partner's share or the partnership agreement. Any errors in this section can significantly impact the partner's individual tax liability.

- **Box 5 - Interest Income:** Box 5 reports the partner's share of interest income earned by the SPV during the tax year. This income typically comes from interest-bearing accounts or investments made by the SPV. As the GP, make sure to carefully track all interest income and allocate it correctly to each partner according to their share in the

SPV. Accurate reporting of this income is essential for the partner's tax return, as it will be subject to taxation.

- **Boxes 8 and 9:** Short-Term and Long-Term Capital Gains (Losses) These boxes report the partner's share of capital gains or losses realized by the SPV during the tax year. Box 8 reflects short-term capital gains or losses. These apply to assets held for one year or less. Box 9 covers long-term gains or losses for assets held longer than one year. It is essential to distinguish between these two types of gains or losses, as they are taxed differently. Accurate allocation of these amounts is critical. It ensures each partner's tax return reflects their share of the SPV's investment performance.

- **Box 19 - Distributions:** Box 19 shows the total amount of distributions made to the partner during the tax year. This includes any cash or property distributions from the SPV. As the GP, you must ensure that the amount reported in this box matches your records of all distributions made to each partner. Discrepancies in this section can lead to confusion and potential tax issues for the partner, so thorough record-keeping and accurate reporting are vital.

Paying close attention to these items on the Schedule K-1 form will help ensure your Limited Partners receive accurate tax documents. This will aid in proper tax compliance and financial reporting. K-1s contain various line items depending on the SPV's activities. Here's a table outlining some common ones:

| Line Item | Description | Relevance for Investors |
| --- | --- | --- |
| Ordinary Income | The SPV's regular taxable income from operations | Affects investors' taxable income |
| Capital Gains/Losses | Gains or losses from selling capital assets (e.g., investments) | May impact investors' capital gains tax treatment |
| Foreign Income | Income derived from foreign sources | May be subject to additional tax reporting requirements |
| Guaranteed Payments | Fixed payments made to certain partners, irrespective of profits | Reported separately as income for the receiving partner |
| Credits | Applicable tax credits the SPV can claim | Investors can benefit by reducing their tax liability |

| **Part III** | **Partner's Share of Current Year Income, Deductions, Credits, and Other Items** | | |
|---|---|---|---|
| **1** | Ordinary business income (loss) | **15** | Credits |
| **2** | Net rental real estate income (loss) | | |
| **3** | Other net rental income (loss) | **16** | Foreign transactions |
| **4** | Guaranteed payments | | |
| **5** | Interest income | | |
| **6a** | Ordinary dividends | | |
| **6b** | Qualified dividends | | |
| **7** | Royalties | | |
| **8** | Net short-term capital gain (loss) | | |
| **9a** | Net long-term capital gain (loss) | **17** | Alternative minimum tax (AMT) items |
| **9b** | Collectibles (28%) gain (loss) | | |
| **9c** | Unrecaptured section 1250 gain | | |
| **10** | Net section 1231 gain (loss) | **18** | Tax-exempt income and nondeductible expenses |
| **11** | Other income (loss) | | |
| | | **19** | Distributions |
| **12** | Section 179 deduction | | |
| **13** | Other deductions | | |
| | | **20** | Other information |

*Remember: The specific line items on a K-1 will vary based on the SPV's tax situation. As a GP managing an SPV, you must complete Schedule K-1 forms accurately. It's required for compliance and for providing partners with info for their tax returns. While this guide provides a comprehensive overview, tax laws and regulations can be complex and subject to change. Always consult a qualified tax professional to ensure compliance with current tax laws.*

# STATE AND LOCAL TAX CONSIDERATIONS FOR SPVS

As you know, federal tax obligations are uniform across the United States. But SPVs may face complex state and local tax rules. These vary by their location, structure, and activities. Tax matters demand your utmost attention. Careful consideration of these implications safeguards both personal and partnership interests.

## State Income Tax

You must be prepared to navigate each state's income tax rules. This can be tough due to varying nexus definitions, like physical presence or economic thresholds. State income tax treatment of SPVs often differs from federal treatment and varies by jurisdiction.

- **Pass-Through Taxation:** Many states mirror the federal approach, treating SPVs as pass-through entities. In these cases, the SPV's income "passes through" to its owners, who report their share on their individual state tax returns.

- **Entity-Level Taxation:** Some states impose entity-level taxes on SPVs, requiring them to file separate state tax returns and pay taxes directly.

- **Composite Returns:** Certain states allow or require SPVs to file composite returns on behalf of their non-resident owners, simplifying compliance for multi-state operations.

## State and Local Sales & Use Tax

SPVs may encounter sales and use tax obligations depending on their activities and operating locations. If an SPV sells taxable goods or services, it might need to register as a sales tax vendor, collect sales tax, and remit it to the appropriate authorities. When purchasing taxable items for use, your SPV may owe use tax if sales tax wasn't collected at the time of purchase. Some states offer exemptions for specific types of SPVs or transactions, which can lead to significant tax savings. Take steps to analyze your activities in each jurisdiction. This is to find their sales and use tax obligations and possible exemptions.

## Property Tax

SPVs that own real or personal property may be subject to state and local property taxes. Real property, such as land and buildings, is typically taxed based on assessed value. In some jurisdictions, business personal property, including equipment, furniture, and inventory, is also taxed. Additionally, an SPV that is leasing a property may face property tax on their leasehold interests. SPV managers should budget for property taxes. They should also check for tax exemptions or abatements for their owned or leased properties.

## Other State and Local Taxes

Your SPV may also be subject to other state and local taxes based on their nature and activities. Franchise taxes, imposed by some states on the privilege of doing business, are often based on an entity's capital structure or net worth. Certain jurisdictions levy gross receipts taxes on businesses regardless of profitability. Additionally, SPVs in specific industries, such as energy or telecommunications, may face industry-specific taxes or fees.

Managing state and local taxes requires careful planning and ongoing compliance. Set aside time to carefully review tax obligations in all relevant jurisdictions, and consult experts once again. By proactively addressing state and local tax issues, you'll once again be taking steps to avoid penalties and optimize tax strategies.

# INTERNATIONAL TAX CONSIDERATIONS FOR SPVS

The tax treatment of SPVs differs significantly depending on their structure and the country in which they operate. When SPVs involve cross-border investments, international tax complexity increases greatly. The Foreign Account Tax Compliance Act (FATCA) plays a vital role in this regard, establishing a comprehensive framework for reporting and compliance. Under FATCA, foreign financial institutions must report information about accounts held by U.S. taxpayers or foreign entities in which U.S. taxpayers have significant ownership interests. Failure to comply with these requirements can result in severe penalties, including a 30% withholding tax on certain U.S.-source payments.

Here's a practical example: An SPV in the Cayman Islands gets dividend income from U.S. investments, and it may face a 30% withholding tax on those dividends. But if the SPV's investors are from countries with tax treaties with the United States, they may be eligible for lower withholding rates - as low as 5-15% depending on the treaty terms. The complexity also applies to reporting requirements.

U.S. persons owning interests in foreign SPVs may need to file extra forms with their tax returns, like Form 8938 (Statement of Specified Foreign Financial Assets) or FinCEN Form 114 (Report of Foreign Bank and Financial Accounts).

Even in an instance where the SPV doesn't generate any taxable income in a given year, these reporting obligations definitely still apply. The tax implications of an SPV can also vary depending on its investment strategy. For example, an SPV that invests in real estate may be treated differently for tax purposes than one that invests in securities or intellectual property.

The type of income (ordinary income or capital gains) and when it's recognized can greatly affect the overall tax efficiency of the structure. Given the complexities and potential financial consequences, it's essential that both SPV managers and investors consult qualified tax experts. These professionals can help set up the SPV in the best possible way from the start and ensure it continues to meet all tax laws and reporting requirements in every relevant area.

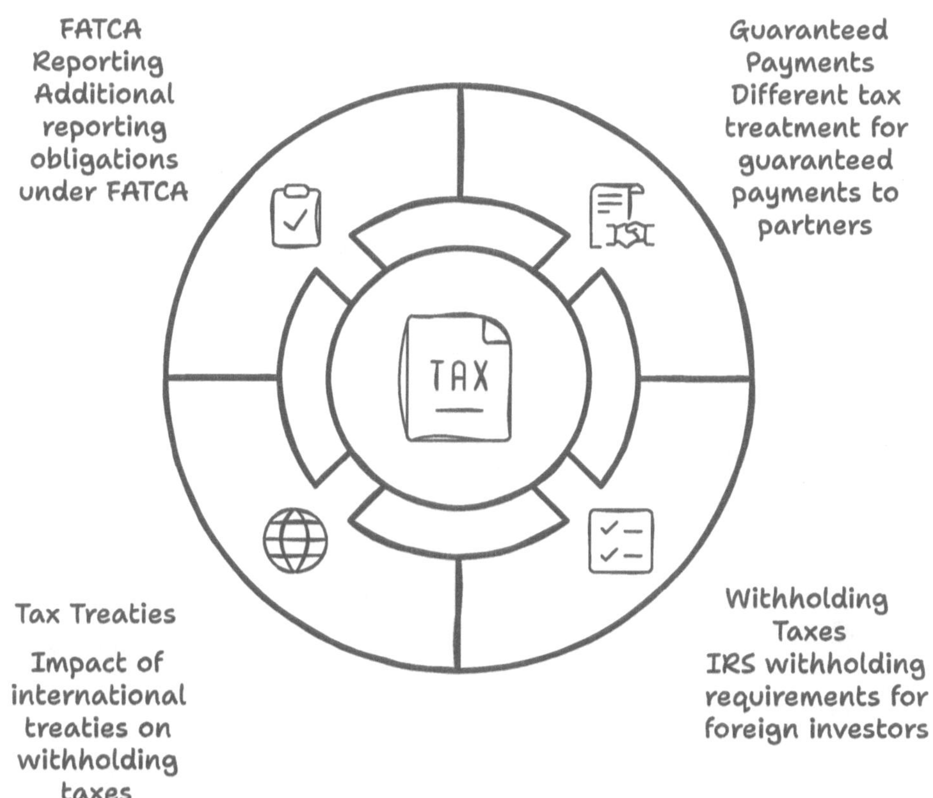

# WEALTH IN NUMBERS

*"The goal isn't just to sell high - it's to ensure that when you distribute returns, you've built lasting relationships that will fuel future opportunities."*
— *Henry Kravis, Co-founder, Co-Chairman, and Co-CEO of KKR*

# EXITING THE DEAL

The exit process and distribution of proceeds represent the pinnacle of an SPV's lifecycle. This critical phase transforms the SPV's investment strategy into tangible results, marking the fulfillment of its core purpose. It doesn't just mark the end of your efforts, but the moment when months or years of work, strategic decisions, and risk management culminate in measurable returns for investors. To achieve success and keep your Limited Partners satisfied, they need to to understand this process.

Timing is key when selling the assets from your SPV. You need to keep an eye on several things at the same time: the state of the overall economy, what's happening in their industry, and the SPV's overall performance.

It's important to pay attention to big economic trends and how easy it is to raise money, as these can affect who might want to buy the SPV's assets and at what price. Changes in the industry, like new technologies or laws, can also create good selling opportunities. Because things are so complex and interconnected, you need to stay alert and be ready to take action at the right moment.

Exiting an SPV investment is often a delicate balancing act between maximizing returns and mitigating risk. While waiting for the perfect conditions might be tempting, you must recognize that market timing is inherently difficult. Be ready to make a decision with the best information that you have available. Perfect timing is rarely achievable.

Consider partial exits or phased selling strategies if appropriate. This approach can reduce timing risks. It lets you capitalize on good conditions while keeping exposure to potential future gains.

When they think it's the right time to sell, winding down the SPV and distributing the profits signals the end of the investment. This task needs careful planning and expert guidance to ensure everyone gets their fair share.

# CALCULATING AND DISTRIBUTING PROCEEDS

When calculating your distributions, your first step is to review the SPV's Operating Agreements to ensure your distribution aligns with the agreed-upon terms. Next you'll calculate what needs to be distributed to your Limited Partners. Take into account all expenses and debts from the SPV's operations. Once complete, you'll be ready to follow the distribution plan laid out in the agreement. This plan usually involves several steps and can vary depending on your deal structure. Be precise and transparent. This will ensure everyone gets their fair share per the agreement.

The importance of precision in these calculations cannot be overstated. When allocating funds, even a small mistake can cause errors. Investors may receive incorrect amounts, either too much or too little. Take time to double-check everything carefully to make sure each investor will get exactly what they should. Errors might damage your reputation and make LPs wonder if you're trustworthy.

The cap table is central to this process and is key to ensuring accurate distribution. You must ensure that all changes in ownership and allocations are correctly updated in the cap table. This is one reason that it's so important to keep detailed records throughout the SPV's lifecycle.

# EXECUTING THE DISTRIBUTION

After finishing all the calculations, it is time to actually send the money or assets to the investors. If it's a cash payout, they simply transfer the calculated amounts to each investor's bank account. Most distributions come in the form of cash, but occasionally investors may receive other assets, such as stock shares, instead. For stock-based events, like when a company goes public, you'll need to arrange for shares to be sent to the investors' brokerage accounts instead. No matter what type of payout it is, it's very important that you give each investor a detailed statement. This statement must explain, clearly, how the returns were calculated. It must show each investor's individual results. Being open about this process helps build trust with the investors. Here's a checklist of the process:

- **Distribute Returns:**

    - ☐ **Calculate Carried Interest:** Subtract the GP's carried interest from the total proceeds.

    - ☐ **Direct Distribution:** Allocate the remaining proceeds directly to investors based on their percentage ownership in the SPV, after accounting for any fees or expenses.

- **Arrange for Distributions Based on the Nature of the Exit:**

    - ☐ **Cash Distributions:** For liquid exits, transfer the calculated cash amounts to each investor's designated account.

    - ☐ **In-kind Distributions:** In cases of stock-based liquidity events, arrange for the transfer of shares to investors' brokerage accounts.

- **Provide Documentation:**

    - ☐ Supply detailed distribution statements to all investors, clearly outlining the calculation methodology and their individual returns.

The exit and distribution process is a key point in an SPV's lifecycle. It turns paper gains into real returns for investors. It's the end of the SPV's investment strategy where theoretical value becomes realized profits. This process validates investors' faith in you as a dealmaker. When capital and returns flow back to stakeholders, it proves that your investment thesis was correct and shows that your deal successfully created value. If you nail the distribution process, it can open up more opportunities down the line. Satisfied investors are more likely to invest again or refer others to you.

When you handle payouts carefully, accurately, and openly, several important goals are achieved. You provide the best returns possible for investors, meet your legal obligations, and set yourself up for future success. Doing this well isn't just about finishing one good investment. It's about building a great reputation that will attract more investors and opportunities in the long run. In essence, the exit is not merely the conclusion of one investment cycle, but a pivotal moment that can define your career trajectory in the competitive landscape of alternative investments.

# POST CLOSE ACTIVITIES

The wind-down process for a Special Purpose Vehicle (SPV) begins after the final distribution to shareholders. This crucial phase requires careful attention to legal, tax, and administrative details. First, verify all original investors and SPV members to ensure accurate record-keeping. Next, liquidate any remaining assets efficiently to maximize returns.

File final tax returns and settle any outstanding fees or obligations. This step is complex, so it's advisable to enlist tax professionals and legal experts specializing in SPV dissolutions. Engaging professional assistance for the wind-up procedures is crucial to ensure compliance and minimize risk. They can help you complete and submit the paperwork to notify regulators of the SPV's closure. Proper documention helps prevent future legal complications and records the SPV's orderly dissolution. Experienced advisors can navigate the complex process of:

- Notifying relevant authorities about the SPV's dissolution.

- Completing jurisdiction-specific forms.

- Managing IRS requirements.

For administrative closure of your SPV, you'll need to take several important steps. Start by filling out all necessary forms and paying any required fees to the relevant government agencies. If you registered your SPV in any state, make sure to file a dissolution form there and settle any associated costs. Next, you'll need to create and send out final K-1 tax forms to all your investors, as this is crucial tax documentation. Lastly, file the appropriate dissolution forms with the Internal Revenue Service (IRS). The specific forms you'll need depend on your SPV's legal structure. By completing these tasks, you'll ensure that your SPV is properly and legally closed.

# FORMS AND DOCUMENTS REQUIRED FOR SPV DISSOLUTION

- **State-Specific Dissolution Form:**

  - Varies by state (e.g., Form LLC-4/7 in California, Form DOS 1563 in New York.) These forms officially dissolve the SPV in the state where it was registered.

- **IRS Form 966 - Corporate Dissolution or Liquidation:**

  - Notifies the IRS of a corporate dissolution or liquidation.

- **Final Tax Return:**

  - Depends on SPV structure (e.g., Form 1065 for partnerships, Form 1120 for corporations). This form reports final income/losses and indicates that this is the final return for the entity.

- **Final Schedule K-1:**

  - This provides each investor with their final share of the SPV's income, losses, and other tax items.

- **Form 8594 - Asset Acquisition Statement:**

  - This form reports the sale or distribution of business assets (if applicable).

- **Form 4797 - Sales of Business Property:**

  - This form reports the sale or exchange of business property (if applicable).

- **State Tax Clearance Certificate:**

  - This form certifies the payment of all state taxes, which varies by state.

- **Forms 940 and 941 (if the SPV had employees) - Final Employment Tax Forms:**

  - This form reports final wage and tax information.

- **Local Business License Cancellation Form:**

  - Local business licenses or permits are cancelled by these forms, the specifics of which vary by locality.

> **NOTE: The exact forms you need may vary depending on your SPV's structure, location, and specific situation. Again, consulting with a tax professional or attorney is a wise step to ensure proper completion of all necessary forms.**

With all forms submitted, fees paid, and debts settled, the SPV's closure marks the end of its lifecycle. This final step not only fulfills legal obligations but also safeguards the interests of all stakeholders involved. While it signifies the end of one investment vehicle, the process imparts invaluable experience and insights for future ventures. By carefully following these procedures and seeking expert guidance when needed, you ensure a proper and professional conclusion to the SPV. As this chapter closes, the knowledge gained paves the way for more refined and efficient management of future Special Purpose Vehicles.

# PERFORMANCE EVALUATION METRICS FOR SPV INVESTMENTS

When evaluating your SPV's performance, consider a range of metrics. These metrics show the investment's financial health and success. They also reveal the overall success of your SPV. Regular, thorough performance evaluation is key to maximizing an SPV investment's financial returns. With these metrics, stakeholders can make informed decisions by analyzing the financial results, asset performance, and risk profile.

## Financial Performance:

A thorough analysis of the SPV's financial performance begins with revenue generation. Check the income sources, like rents, sales, and dividends. Compare them to past figures, industry benchmarks, and forecasts. This comparison helps assess the SPV's financial health and the sustainability of its income streams.

Equally important is the evaluation of expenses, including operating costs, management fees, and interest payments. Scrutinize these expenditures for efficiency and identify potential areas for optimization.

Any deviations from budgeted amounts should be carefully analyzed to ensure proper cost control.

Profitability metrics offer valuable insights into the SPV's ability to generate revenue and profit. These are items such as net profit margin, return on assets (ROA), and return on equity (ROE). These ratios should be evaluated both at the overall SPV level and for individual assets or business lines within the structure.

Cash flow analysis is another critical component of financial performance evaluation. Examine the SPV's cash flows from operations, investing, and financing. Also consider working capital, capital investments, and debt obligations. Positive cash flow means good liquidity and financial health. Negative cash flows may signal financial strain or a need for additional capital injections.

### Asset Performance:

For SPVs with tangible assets, it's essential to evaluate their performance. This includes assessing value appreciation. It involves analyzing historical and projected price movements of the assets. It also considers market trends and economic indicators. Thorough market research can help identify potential drivers or risks that may impact asset values in the future.

If the SPV is a property that generates rental income, analyze the stability and growth of this income stream. Consider factors such as rental rates, occupancy levels, lease agreements, and tenant quality. Assess the potential for rental income growth and lease renewals. This will gauge the SPV's assets' long-term income potential.

Asset quality is another important consideration. Regular inspections and valuations ensure that assets are well-maintained. Consider future market demand, tech changes, and regulations. They may affect the asset's value and relevance.

You want to know these numbers because they provide valuable insight into your performance and investment strategy. Being able to review what went right, what you can do better next time, and what you learned is ideal for your growth as an investor and General Partner. By examining the numbers, you can objectively assess the success of your deals. This includes analyzing returns and comparing them to your projections. Also, you'll better understand the factors that helped or hurt your success.

The lessons learned from each deal allow you to fine-tune your investment strategy. You might identify patterns in successful investments or recognize potential red flags to avoid in future deals. This will help manage risk in future investments. You can identify which risk factors had the most significant impact and develop strategies to mitigate them.

Each deal provides a wealth of data that can inform your future decision-making process. You'll develop a keener sense of which opportunities align with your strengths and investment thesis.

By doing this review process, you'll build a strong, impressive track record. This track record is more than just numbers on a page; it's a testament to your expertise, learning capacity, and ability to generate returns. As you demonstrate consistent performance and a thoughtful approach to investing, you'll find that more investors are attracted to your deals. They'll see not just the potential for returns, but also the value of partnering with someone who is constantly striving to improve and adapt.

Also, this track record can lead to bigger, more lucrative opportunities. As your reputation grows, you may be able to raise larger amounts, attract new investors, and access more exclusive deal flow. In essence, the numbers you track and the lessons you learn today are laying the foundation for your future success in the investment world.

# WEALTH IN NUMBERS

# BENEFITS OF USING AN ONLINE PLATFORM

So, if you've gotten this far in the book, all this might seem pretty complex because, well, it is complex and can be a bit overwhelming. New dealmakers face many barriers. One is unpacking legal and tax complexities. They must also manage branding, operations, and investor relations. Administrative tasks often hinder GPs. The traditional way of managing SPVs causes extensive paperwork, time-consuming data entry, and leaves room for error.

So what if you had a powerful on-ramp for your Special Purpose Vehicle? A way to launch SPVs, track funding in real-time, and boost liquidity? As we've discussed, successful dealmakers need superior tools and processes to gain an edge in private investments. That's what motivated us to develop Syndicately—to streamline the entire deal process for General Partners.

We believe we have built a brilliant solution. It helps anyone, regardless of their experience, to get started in private investments. We respect your choice to manage deals manually or try other software. But, we believe our platform is the best for value and ease of use.

We created Syndicately because we saw how much friction there was when we did our own investment deals. We had this idea where software could help stakeholders communicate and make operating a SPV easier. The private investment world is a real maze, as you'll find out in this book. It's got a bunch of complicated terms and different professionals you'll work with, like lawyers, accountants, and tax advisors. Between the fees, complexities and multiple parties involved, it can be tough to get started. At the end of the day, being pulled in all directions can definitely slow down your deals. Consider the impact that a digital SPV management platform could have on your operations:

- How much time could you save by automating routine tasks?

- How might improved data accuracy and insights affect your investment decisions?

- What value could enhanced investor communications bring to your relationships?

- How would streamlined compliance processes reduce your stress and risk?

SPV management is going digital, and by embracing these advanced tools, you'll be ahead of the curve, ready to make the most of new opportunities. The difference between achieving success and stagnation often comes down to the tools you have. As we've seen in this book, deal-making can be complex and overwhelming, but it's not impossible to master. When you use a solution like Syndicately, you're not just streamlining operations, you're unlocking your full potential as an investor and dealmaker.

If you've enjoyed this book and would like to work with us, we'd be thrilled to support your investment journey as a valued client. Our goal isn't simply to sell you on our service, but to empower you with the tools and resources you need to succeed in the world of private investments. The primary aim of our technology is to let you focus on managing deals without distractions. Syndicately saves you time and keeps you focused. It cuts down on the administrative burdens that go along with raising capital and running an SPV. With Syndicately, you can focus on what's important and scale your operations. We take care of creating the entities and bank accounts, and managing users is made easy with just an invite link. Your investors can enter their info, commit capital, and link their accounts. Syndicately also makes signing and paperwork easy with eSignatures and online notary services. Filing regulatory documents also becomes much easier.

Another major thing is having predictable expenses and keeping it simple to calculate the cost for the General Partner. The Syndicately platform helps users factor in administrative cost into their evaluation process for investment decisions. Check out Syndicately now by visiting www.syndicately.com or get a demo by scanning this QR Code:

In this high-stakes game, efficiency gives you a strategic advantage. It's not just about saving time. It's about seizing opportunities, building relationships, and making smart decisions. They will help you get ahead of the pack. As you close this book and look to the future, ask yourself: Are you ready to transform the way you manage investments? Are you prepared to elevate your deal-making to new heights? The tools are here, the knowledge is in your hands, and the opportunities are boundless. Your next great investment journey begins now—will you take the leap?

# WEALTH IN NUMBERS

*"Every Stock, Bond, Currency & Commodoty will be Digitized and run on a Blockchain."*

*— Mark Yusko, Founder, CEO & CIO of Morgan Creek Capital*

# TOKENIZATION OF SPVS

One more thing to mention is that we baked in some next-generation technology to the Syndicately platform. As financial technology advances, tokenizing Special Purpose Vehicles represents a major innovation. We believe that tokenization is on the verge of revolutionizing the fabric of private investments. This combines SPVs with blockchain technology, bringing a new era of efficiency, transparency, and access to complex financial instruments. For those new to this subject, we want to provide a brief overview of what this technology can do and its potential advantages. This is just a glimpse of how blockchain is revolutionizing industries. We strongly encourage you to explore its wide range of applications.

Since blockchain has lots of practical applications, let's start by discussing its fundamental concept. Distributed Ledger Technology (DLT) is a decentralized system. It records and syncs data across multiple locations or institutions at once. It lets a network's participants verify information. Blockchain is a subtype of DLT, which is a larger category of technologies. It stores data in linked "blocks." It usually uses a consensus mechanism to validate new entries. All blockchains are DLTs, but not all DLTs are blockchains.

Public blockchains and private permissioned blockchains are two types of distributed ledger technology. Each has its own strengths and use cases. Public blockchains, like Bitcoin, Ethereum and the XRP Ledger, are open, decentralized networks. Anyone can participate and view transactions. They are transparent and resistant to censorship; however, their public accessibility results in reduced privacy. In contrast, private permissioned blockchains, such as those designed for financial institutions, operate on a closed network where participants are pre-approved. These systems offer better control over data access and faster transactions. They also enhance privacy. These are vital for businesses that handle sensitive financial data.

Public blockchains excel at achieving trust-minimized, global consensus. But, private permissioned networks are better for enterprises. They need to balance the benefits of distributed ledgers with compliance and data protection. This makes private permissioned blockchains ideal for tokenizing Special Purpose Vehicles. There, it's vital to keep financial data confidential while meeting legal requirements.

A huge benefit of tokenized SPVs is the enhanced transparency. Every transaction is on an immutable digital ledger. All history is fully documented. Having a clear audit trail boosts investor confidence and streamlines oversight.

One of the most significant things that tokenization addresses for SPVs is the lack of liquidity. Tokenized SPVs allow fractional ownership and simpler secondary market trading. They give investors unmatched flexibility. This increased liquidity has far-reaching effects. It improves portfolio diversification. It also encourages investment in overlooked high-growth sectors. Perhaps one of the most transformative aspects of SPV tokenization is the democratization of access. Tokenization opens private market investments to more participants. It reduces entry barriers and provides opportunities to previously excluded investors.

Tokenization also paves the way for improved portfolio management and risk assessment. By standardizing ownership representation across diverse assets, investors can conduct more sophisticated analysis. As a result, investors will be able to optimize their portfolios more effectively.

Blockchain networks are global. They can boost cross-border investments and help create access in emerging markets and niche investments. However, the path to widespread adoption of tokenized SPVs is not without challenges. Regulatory frameworks are still evolving globally and compliance with financial regulations is critical. Technological hurdles, particularly around scalability and interoperability of some networks, also persist.

As tokenization continues to evolve, we will inevitably witness more synergy between public and private markets. This could lead to better price discovery and new hybrid corporate financing models. The financial landscape stands to evolve dramatically. Expect to see new specialized intermediaries and adapted traditional institutions.

For all these reasons, the tokenization of SPVs represents a transformative development in private market investments. Through this technology, we can solve long-standing issues in private investments. As innovation advances and regulations evolve, we can create a more inclusive, efficient, and dynamic private investment ecosystem. It is set to drive growth and innovation in the global economy.

# WEALTH IN NUMBERS

# THE END

You've now reached the end, which is really just the beginning. The world of running Special Purpose Vehicles is challenging, but achievable. This book has given you the scaffolding to build your empire, and like you've learned, opportunities don't arise – they are always there!

It's up to you to identify them and leverage the power of your newly acquired knowledge to raise the capital that fuels your vision. Conquer "first deal syndrome" and turn your newly acquired knowledge into action. We genuinely hope you are able to take these tools and build something amazing.

We are eager to hear about your SPV success stories, challenges, and questions as well! Together, we can create a community of SPV champions. If you found value in this book, please leave us a review on Amazon, Books-A-Million, Barnes & Noble, Goodreads, or LibraryThing. Thank you! Remember, the greatest opportunities are often just beyond your comfort zone. So, take a deep breath, and start building.

# WEALTH IN NUMBERS

# GLOSSARY OF TERMS

You're now entering the world of private investments. It has many specialized terms, jargon, and complex concepts. Investors expect you to speak their language. We built this glossary to help you master the complex language of private investments and SPVs. It will expand your vocabulary. You'll then understand important information and be able to "talk the talk" when explaining your next deal. Some of the items we have included are relevant to SPVs, while others apply to the larger investment and financial markets as a whole. When you know what financial terms and investor buzzwords mean, you'll be able to present your offer more effectively, answer investors' questions confidently, and keep the process on track.

As you go through this glossary, keep in mind that it's a starting point, not an endpoint. We encourage you to place a priority on your continued education in the field, beyond this book. We hope you will seek new information to better position yourself and your partners for success. Remember, knowledge truly is power. So dive in, expand your financial vocabulary, and empower yourself to excel with SPVs and private investments.

409A Valuation

A formal assessment of a private company's fair market value, typically conducted by an independent appraiser. This valuation is used to set the exercise price for employee stock options and ensure compliance with IRS regulations. The process involves analyzing the company's financials, comparable companies, and market conditions.

Accredited Investor

An individual or entity that meets specific financial criteria set by the Securities and Exchange Commission (SEC). This typically includes having an annual income exceeding $200,000 ($300,000 for joint income) for the last two years or a net worth over $1 million, excluding primary residence. Accredited Investors are permitted to participate in certain private investment opportunities not available to the general public.

Acquisition

The process by which one company purchases a controlling stake in another company. This can involve buying all or a majority of the target company's shares, assets, or business operations. Acquisitions are often pursued for strategic growth, market expansion, or to eliminate competition.

Add-On Services

Additional support or resources provided by investors beyond their financial contribution. These may include mentorship, networking opportunities, operational expertise, or access to industry contacts. Add-on services can significantly enhance a startup's growth potential and chances of success.

Allocation

The amount of investment opportunity assigned to a particular investor or fund in a financing round. It represents the portion of available shares or securities that an investor is permitted to purchase. Allocation decisions are typically made by the company or lead investors based on various factors, including investor interest and strategic value.

AML (Anti-Money Laundering)

A set of laws, regulations, and procedures designed to prevent criminals from disguising illegally obtained funds as legitimate income. AML measures require financial institutions and certain businesses to monitor transactions, report suspicious activities, and maintain detailed records to help detect and prevent money laundering.

ARPU (Average Revenue Per User)

A metric that measures the average amount of revenue generated by each customer or user of a product or service over a specific period, typically monthly or annually. ARPU is calculated by dividing total revenue by the number of users or customers. It's an important indicator of a company's ability to monetize its user base.

AUM (Assets Under Management)

The total market value of all financial assets managed by an investment firm or financial institution on behalf of its clients. AUM includes the capital from all investors and any returns generated from those investments. It's often used as a measure of an investment firm's size and success.

Automated Clearing House (ACH)

An electronic funds-transfer system that facilitates financial transactions in the United States. ACH processes large volumes of credit and debit transactions in batches, including direct deposits, payroll, and bill payments. It's a crucial part of the modern banking infrastructure, enabling fast and efficient money transfers between accounts at different financial institutions.

Bankruptcy Remoteness

A legal structure designed to protect a Special Purpose Vehicle (SPV) from the potential bankruptcy of its parent company or originator. This arrangement ensures that the SPV's assets remain separate and unaffected if the parent company faces financial distress, providing security for investors in the SPV.

Basis Point

A unit of measurement used in finance to describe percentage changes in interest rates or financial instruments. One basis point is equal to 0.01% or one one-hundredth of a percentage point. For example, if an interest rate increases from 5.00% to 5.25%, it has risen by 25 basis points.

Benchmarks

Specific performance indicators or targets used to measure a company's progress and success. These can include financial metrics (e.g., revenue growth, profitability), operational metrics (e.g., customer acquisition cost, user engagement), or industry-specific standards. Benchmarks help investors and management assess a company's performance relative to its goals and competitors.

Beneficial Owner

An individual or entity that ultimately owns or controls a significant portion of a company or investment vehicle, even if the ownership is indirect. In the context of anti-money laundering regulations, identifying beneficial owners is crucial for transparency and preventing financial crimes. The threshold for beneficial ownership typically ranges from 10% to 25%, depending on the jurisdiction.

Big Gifts

Substantial financial contributions made to non-profit organizations or institutions. These large donations often come from wealthy individuals, foundations, or corporations and can significantly impact the recipient organization's ability to achieve its mission or fund major initiatives.

Blocker Structures

Legal entities, typically corporations, used to prevent certain types of income from flowing directly to investors. Blocker structures are commonly employed to shield foreign or tax-exempt investors from incurring Effectively Connected Income (ECI) or Unrelated Business Taxable Income (UBTI). While they add a layer of complexity, blockers can provide tax advantages for certain classes of investors.

Blue Chip Company

A large, well-established, and financially sound corporation with a history of reliable performance and stable earnings. Blue chip companies are typically leaders in their industries and are known for their ability to weather economic downturns. Their stocks are often considered less risky investments and may pay regular dividends.

Blue Sky Fees

Regulatory fees charged by individual states for registering securities offerings. These fees are associated with complying with state-level securities laws, known as "Blue Sky Laws," which are designed to protect investors from fraudulent offerings. The costs can vary significantly from state to state and depend on the size and nature of the offering.

Board Deck

A presentation or set of documents prepared for a company's board of directors meeting. It typically includes key financial and operational metrics, updates on strategic initiatives, and important decisions requiring board approval. A well-prepared board deck provides directors with a comprehensive overview of the company's performance and challenges.

Board of Directors

A group of individuals elected by shareholders to oversee a corporation's management and make major decisions on its behalf. The board's responsibilities include setting company policies, approving major financial decisions, hiring and evaluating top executives, and ensuring the company acts in the best interests of its shareholders.

Bootstrapping

The practice of starting and growing a business using personal finances or the company's own revenue, without relying on external investors. Bootstrapping often involves strict budget management, creative resource allocation, and a focus on early profitability. While challenging, this approach allows founders to maintain full control over their company.

Bridge Round

A short-term funding round designed to provide a company with additional capital to reach its next major milestone or financing event. Bridge rounds are typically smaller than full funding rounds and may use convertible notes or other flexible financing instruments. They're often used to extend a company's runway or prepare for a larger upcoming round.

### Broker-Dealer

A person or firm licensed to buy and sell securities for its own account or on behalf of its customers. Broker-dealers play a crucial role in capital markets by facilitating transactions, providing liquidity, and often offering investment advice. They must register with the SEC and comply with various regulatory requirements.

### Bull Market

A period of sustained increase in the value of financial markets, typically characterized by investor optimism and confidence. In a bull market, stock prices generally rise, and there's an expectation of continued upward movement. This term is often contrasted with a "bear market," which represents a period of decline.

### Business Cycle

The natural fluctuation of economic activity over time, typically characterized by periods of expansion, peak, contraction, and trough. Understanding the business cycle is crucial for investors and businesses as it affects various economic indicators, including employment rates, consumer spending, and investment levels.

### Buy-and-Hold Strategy

An investment approach where securities are purchased with the intention of owning them for a long period, regardless of short-term market fluctuations. This strategy is based on the belief that long-term returns will outweigh short-term volatility. It's often associated with passive investing and can reduce transaction costs and taxes.

### Buyout

The purchase of a controlling interest in a company, often with the goal of taking it private or significantly changing its operations. Buyouts can be conducted by management (management buyout), outside investors, or private equity firms. They typically involve a significant amount of debt financing and aim to improve the company's performance or realize value through restructuring.

### CAC (Customer Acquisition Cost)

The total cost associated with acquiring a new customer, including marketing expenses, sales costs, and any other related expenditures. CAC is a crucial metric for assessing the efficiency of a company's growth strategy. A low CAC relative to customer lifetime value indicates a scalable and potentially profitable business model.

### CAGR (Compound Annual Growth Rate)

A measure of the average annual growth rate of an investment over a specified time period, assuming the growth compounds each year. CAGR provides a smoothed rate of return that accounts for the effects of volatility and is useful for comparing investments with different time horizons or growth patterns.

Cap Table (Capitalization Table)

A detailed breakdown of a company's ownership structure, typically in spreadsheet form. It lists all the company's securities (common shares, preferred shares, options, warrants, etc.), who owns them, and their respective ownership percentages. The cap table is crucial for understanding equity dilution, valuation, and potential payouts in liquidity events.

Capital Call / Drawdown

A request made by a fund manager to limited partners (investors) to provide a portion of their committed capital. Capital calls are typically made as needed to fund investments or cover expenses, rather than collecting all committed funds upfront. This approach allows for more efficient cash management for both the fund and its investors.

Capital Gains Tax

A tax levied on the profit realized from the sale of a capital asset, such as stocks, bonds, or real estate. The tax rate can vary depending on how long the asset was held (short-term vs. long-term capital gains) and the taxpayer's overall income level. Understanding capital gains tax is crucial for investment planning and tax strategy.

Carried Interest (Carry)

A share of the profits of an investment paid to the investment manager as a form of performance fee. In private equity and venture capital, carried interest is typically 20% of the fund's profit above a certain threshold (usually 8% annual return). It aligns the interests of fund managers with those of their investors.

Churn

The rate at which customers stop doing business with a company over a given period. It's typically expressed as a percentage of lost customers relative to the total customer base. High churn rates can indicate customer dissatisfaction, strong competition, or other business challenges. Reducing churn is often a key focus for subscription-based businesses.

Co-Investment Vehicle

A separate investment structure that allows investors to participate directly in a specific deal alongside a private equity or venture capital fund. Co-investment vehicles provide investors with more control over their portfolio allocation and potentially lower fees compared to traditional fund investments.

Co-Investors

Additional investors who participate in a financing round alongside the lead investor. Co-investors can bring additional capital, expertise, or strategic value to the deal. Their participation can validate the investment opportunity and potentially provide follow-on funding in future rounds.

Common Stock

A type of security that represents ownership in a corporation. Holders of common stock typically have voting rights in corporate decisions and may receive dividends if declared by the board of directors. However, common stockholders have the lowest priority claim on a company's assets in the event of liquidation.

Control Person

An individual or entity with significant influence over a company's management and policies. This typically includes directors, executive officers, or large shareholders. Control persons often have additional responsibilities and potential liabilities under securities laws and are subject to certain reporting requirements.

Convertible Debt

A type of bond that can be converted into a predetermined number of shares of the issuing company's common stock. Convertible debt offers investors the potential for equity upside while providing some downside protection. For companies, it can be an attractive way to raise capital without immediately diluting existing shareholders.

CPA (Cost Per Acquisition)

A marketing metric that measures the total cost of acquiring a customer who takes a desired action (e.g., making a purchase or signing up for a service). CPA is calculated by dividing total marketing spend by the number of acquisitions. It's used to evaluate the efficiency of marketing campaigns and channels.

Data Room

A secure physical or virtual space where confidential documents are stored and shared during due diligence processes. Data rooms are commonly used in mergers and acquisitions, fundraising, and other complex transactions to provide controlled access to sensitive information for potential investors or buyers.

Deal Memo

A concise document that outlines the key aspects of a potential investment opportunity. It typically includes an overview of the company, market analysis, financial projections, and investment thesis. Deal memos are used by investors to evaluate opportunities and present them to investment committees.

Debt Financing

The process of raising capital by borrowing money, typically through loans or bonds. Unlike equity financing, debt financing doesn't dilute ownership but requires repayment with interest. It can be an attractive option for companies with stable cash flows and assets to use as collateral.

### Dilution

The reduction in existing shareholders' ownership percentage of a company that occurs when new shares are issued. Dilution typically happens during fundraising rounds when new investors acquire equity. While dilution decreases the percentage ownership of existing shareholders, it may increase the overall value of their holdings if the company's valuation grows.

### Direct Stock Exchange Program

A service that allows investors to buy shares directly from a company without going through a broker. These programs, also known as direct stock purchase plans (DSPPs), can offer lower fees and the ability to make small, regular investments. They're typically offered by larger, established companies.

### Discount Broker

A brokerage firm that executes trades for clients at reduced commission rates compared to full-service brokers. Discount brokers typically don't provide investment advice or research, focusing instead on efficient trade execution. They've become increasingly popular with the rise of online trading platforms.

### Distribution Waterfall

A method for allocating investment returns among partners in a private equity or venture capital fund. The waterfall structure typically prioritizes the return of capital to limited partners, followed by a preferred return, before the general partners begin to receive their share of profits (carried interest).

### Dividend

A distribution of a portion of a company's earnings to its shareholders, usually paid in cash or additional shares. Dividends are typically declared by the board of directors and can be regular (paid at set intervals) or special (one-time payments). They're often seen as a sign of a company's financial health and shareholder-friendly policies.

### Down Round

A financing round in which a company raises capital at a lower valuation than in its previous round. Down rounds can be challenging for existing investors and employees as they lead to dilution and may indicate that the company is struggling to meet growth expectations.

### Drag-Along Right

A provision that allows a majority shareholder to force minority shareholders to join in the sale of a company. This right is designed to protect the interests of majority shareholders and make the company more attractive to potential buyers by ensuring they can acquire 100% of the shares.

Due Diligence

A comprehensive investigation or audit of a potential investment or business deal. Due diligence involves reviewing financial records, legal documents, operational processes, and other relevant information to assess risks and verify the claims made by the company. It's a crucial step in the investment process for venture capital, private equity, and M&A transactions.

ECI (Effectively Connected Income)

Income that is considered to be connected with the conduct of a trade or business within the United States. For foreign investors, ECI is subject to U.S. income tax and may require filing a U.S. tax return. Many foreign investors seek to avoid ECI through the use of blocker structures or other tax planning strategies.

Employee Stock Purchase Plan (ESPP)

A company-run program that allows employees to purchase company stock at a discounted price, typically through payroll deductions. ESPPs are designed to align employee interests with those of shareholders and provide an additional form of compensation. The plans often include a "lookback" feature that can increase the potential for employee gains.

Equity Financing

The process of raising capital by selling shares of ownership in a company. This form of financing doesn't require repayment like debt, but it does dilute the ownership of existing shareholders. Equity financing is common for startups and high-growth companies that may not have the cash flow or assets required for debt financing.

ESOP (Employee Stock Ownership Plan)

A qualified defined-contribution employee benefit plan that invests primarily in the stock of the employing company. ESOPs provide employees with an ownership interest in the company and can be used as a corporate finance strategy to align the interests of employees with those of shareholders.

Exercise Price / Strike Price

The price at which the holder of an option can buy (for a call option) or sell (for a put option) the underlying security. This price is set when the option is issued and remains fixed for the duration of the option contract. The relationship between the strike price and the current market price of the underlying asset determines the option's value.

Exit

The process by which an investor (or founder) sells their stake in a company to realize a return on their investment. Common exit strategies include initial public offerings (IPOs), acquisitions by larger companies, or secondary sales to other investors. The choice of exit strategy can significantly impact the returns for investors and the future of the company.

Exit Strategy

A planned approach to ending an investment, typically with the goal of maximizing returns. Exit strategies are crucial for investors and entrepreneurs to define how and when they plan to sell their stake in a company. Common exit strategies include going public through an IPO, selling to a strategic buyer, or conducting a management buyout.

Fair Market Value (FMV)

The price that an asset would sell for on the open market when both buyer and seller have reasonable knowledge of relevant facts and neither is under compulsion to buy or sell. FMV is an important concept in various financial and legal contexts, including taxation, financial reporting, and business valuations.

Family Office

A private wealth management advisory firm that serves ultra-high-net-worth individuals and families. Family offices provide a wide range of services, including investment management, tax planning, philanthropy coordination, and intergenerational wealth transfer. They can be single-family offices (serving one family) or multi-family offices (serving multiple families).

Feeder Fund

An investment vehicle that pools capital from multiple investors and then invests that capital into a master fund. Feeder funds are often used in hedge fund and private equity structures to accommodate investors with different tax or regulatory needs. They can simplify administration for the master fund while providing investors with indirect access to the fund's strategy.

Financial Engineering

The use of mathematical techniques to solve financial problems or create financial products. In the context of private equity and venture capital, it often refers to complex financial structures used to enhance returns or manage risk. While financial engineering can create value, critics argue that excessive focus on financial manipulation rather than operational improvements can be detrimental.

Follow-On Investment

An additional investment made by an existing investor in a company they've previously funded. Follow-on investments are common in venture capital, where investors often reserve capital to participate in later funding rounds of successful portfolio companies. These investments can help maintain ownership stakes and demonstrate continued confidence in the company.

Form 3921

An IRS form that companies must file to report the transfer of stock to an employee upon the exercise of an Incentive Stock Option (ISO). This form helps the IRS track potential taxable events related to stock options and ensures proper reporting of income by employees who exercise ISOs.

Form ADV

A required submission to the SEC by professional investment advisors. Form ADV consists of two parts: Part 1 contains information about the advisor's business, ownership, clients, employees, business practices, affiliations, and any disciplinary events; Part 2 is a narrative brochure that includes information on the types of advisory services offered, fee schedule, disciplinary information, conflicts of interest, and the educational and business background of management and key advisory personnel.

Founders Shares

Common stock issued to a company's founders at the time of the company's formation, typically at a very low price. Founders shares often come with special rights or preferences, such as enhanced voting power or protection against dilution. They're designed to reward founders for the risk and effort of starting the company.

Fund of Funds

An investment strategy in which a fund invests in other investment funds rather than directly in stocks, bonds, or other securities. In the context of venture capital and private equity, a fund of funds provides investors with broad exposure to multiple managers and strategies, potentially reducing risk through diversification. However, this approach can also result in higher fees due to the additional layer of management.

GAAP (Generally Accepted Accounting Principles)

A common set of accounting principles, standards, and procedures used by companies to compile their financial statements. GAAP is a combination of authoritative standards set by policy boards and the commonly accepted ways of recording and reporting accounting information. Adherence to GAAP helps ensure consistency and transparency in financial reporting.

General Partner (GP)

The manager of a limited partnership, typically in the context of a venture capital or private equity fund. The GP is responsible for making investment decisions, managing the fund's portfolio, and handling day-to-day operations. GPs usually contribute a small percentage of the fund's capital and receive management fees and carried interest as compensation.

General Solicitation

The broad advertisement or marketing of an investment opportunity to the general public. Historically, general solicitation was prohibited for most private securities offerings. However, recent changes in SEC regulations (specifically, Rule 506(c) of Regulation D) now allow general solicitation for certain offerings, provided all investors are accredited and the issuer takes reasonable steps to verify their accredited status.

### Golden Handcuffs

Financial incentives designed to encourage key employees to remain with a company for a specified period. These can include stock options with long vesting periods, deferred compensation plans, or bonuses contingent on continued employment. Golden handcuffs aim to align employee interests with long-term company success and reduce turnover of valuable personnel.

### GP Lead Commitment

The amount of personal capital that a general partner (GP) invests in their own fund. A significant GP commitment is often seen as a positive sign by limited partners (LPs) as it aligns the GP's interests with those of the LPs and demonstrates the GP's confidence in the fund's strategy.

### Hybrid Vesting

A vesting schedule that combines elements of time-based and performance-based vesting. Under a hybrid vesting scheme, employees or founders might earn portions of their equity based on both their tenure with the company and the achievement of specific milestones or performance targets. This approach aims to balance retention incentives with performance motivation.

### IAS (International Accounting Standards)

A set of international accounting standards stating how particular types of transactions and other events should be reported in financial statements. IAS were issued between 1973 and 2001 by the International Accounting Standards Committee (IASC). In 2001, the International Accounting Standards Board (IASB) replaced the IASC and began issuing International Financial Reporting Standards (IFRS), which have since superseded most IAS.

### IFRS (International Financial Reporting Standards)

A set of accounting standards developed by the International Accounting Standards Board (IASB) that is becoming the global standard for the preparation of public company financial statements. IFRS is used in many parts of the world, including the European Union, and is increasingly being adopted globally to provide a common accounting language for international business.

### Incentive Stock Options (ISOs)

A type of employee stock option that offers potential tax advantages to the employee. If certain holding requirements are met, the profit from exercising ISOs can be taxed at the lower long-term capital gains rate rather than as ordinary income. However, ISOs may trigger alternative minimum tax (AMT) liability in the year of exercise.

Information Rights

Contractual provisions that give investors the right to receive certain financial and operational information about a company. These rights typically include access to regular financial statements, budgets, and business plans. Information rights are important for investors to monitor their investments and make informed decisions about future funding rounds or exits.

Initial Public Offering (IPO)

The process of offering shares of a private corporation to the public in a new stock issuance. An IPO allows a company to raise capital from public investors and provides an opportunity for early investors and employees to liquidate some of their holdings. Going public brings increased regulatory scrutiny and reporting requirements but can also enhance a company's profile and access to capital markets.

Internal Rate of Return (IRR)

A metric used to estimate the profitability of potential investments. IRR is the discount rate that makes the net present value (NPV) of all cash flows from a particular investment equal to zero. In private equity and venture capital, IRR is commonly used to evaluate and compare fund performance. However, it should be considered alongside other metrics, as it can be manipulated and doesn't account for the absolute size of an investment.

Investment Instrument

Any type of financial security or contract that can be bought, sold, traded, or used for investment purposes. Common investment instruments include stocks, bonds, options, futures, and various derivatives. Each type of instrument has its own characteristics, risks, and potential returns.

Issuer

The legal entity that develops, registers, and sells securities to finance its operations. Issuers can be corporations, investment trusts, or domestic or foreign governments. When a company conducts an IPO or issues bonds, it is acting as an issuer in the financial markets.

K-1

An IRS tax form used to report income, losses, and dividends of a business's partners or an S corporation's shareholders. Each partner or shareholder receives a K-1 showing their allocation of the entity's income and expenses, which they then use to complete their individual tax returns. K-1s are often more complex than standard W-2 forms and may delay individual tax filings.

### KYC (Know Your Customer)

A standard due diligence process used by financial institutions and companies to verify the identity, suitability, and risks involved with maintaining a business relationship. KYC processes are a crucial part of anti-money laundering (AML) efforts and involve collecting and analyzing client information to ensure the client is who they claim to be and that their financial activities are legitimate.

### Letter of Intent (LOI)

A document outlining the preliminary understanding between parties who intend to enter into a contract or agreement. In the context of investments or acquisitions, an LOI typically precedes a binding contract and outlines key terms such as purchase price, timeline, and conditions. While often non-binding, LOIs can help parties align expectations and identify potential issues early in negotiations.

### Liquidation Preference

A provision in a company's charter that dictates the order and amount in which investors will be paid in the event of a liquidation event (such as a sale or dissolution of the company). Liquidation preferences are typically associated with preferred stock and can significantly impact the distribution of proceeds, especially in scenarios where the exit value is less than the total invested capital.

### Liquidity

The degree to which an asset or security can be quickly bought or sold in the market without affecting its price. Cash is the most liquid asset, while real estate and private company shares are typically considered illiquid. In the context of startups and venture capital, liquidity often refers to the ability of investors or employees to convert their equity into cash, which typically occurs through an IPO or acquisition.

### Liquidity Event

A transaction that allows a company's shareholders to cash out some or all of their ownership stakes. Common liquidity events include initial public offerings (IPOs), acquisitions, or secondary sales of private company shares. Liquidity events are crucial for venture capital and private equity investors to realize returns on their investments.

### Lock-up Period

A predetermined amount of time following an initial public offering (IPO) during which major shareholders, such as company executives and investors, are restricted from selling their shares. Lock-up periods typically last 90 to 180 days and are designed to prevent the market from being flooded with too many of a company's shares immediately after the IPO.

### Look-Through Rules

Regulations that require certain investment entities to be "looked through" to their underlying assets or investors for tax or regulatory purposes. In the context of venture capital funds, look-through rules may affect how the fund is classified for tax purposes or how it's treated under certain investor regulations.

LP (Limited Partner)

An investor in a limited partnership, typically a venture capital or private equity fund. Limited partners provide capital but do not participate in the day-to-day management of the fund. Their liability is limited to the amount of their investment, and they receive returns based on the fund's performance after the general partners have taken their share.

LTM (Last Twelve Months)

A time frame used in financial statements and analysis that refers to the most recent 12-month period. LTM figures are often used to provide a more current view of a company's performance than fiscal year data, especially when there have been recent significant changes in the business. This metric is particularly useful for evaluating companies with seasonal fluctuations in their business.

LTV (Lifetime Value)

The predicted total revenue a business expects to earn from a customer over the entire duration of their relationship. LTV is a crucial metric for assessing the long-term value of acquiring and retaining customers. It's often compared with customer acquisition cost (CAC) to evaluate the efficiency and profitability of a company's growth strategy.

Management Company

A separate entity created by fund managers to handle the operational aspects of running an investment fund. The management company typically employs the fund's staff, leases office space, and provides other administrative services. It receives the management fee from the fund to cover these expenses and compensate the fund managers.

Management Fee

A periodic payment made by investors to the managers of an investment fund for their expertise and services in managing the fund's investments. In venture capital and private equity, management fees typically range from 1.5% to 2.5% of committed capital or assets under management annually. These fees cover the fund's operating expenses and provide income for the fund managers.

Milestone-Based Vesting

A vesting schedule where equity or options are earned based on the achievement of specific company or individual performance targets rather than the passage of time. Milestones might include reaching certain revenue levels, product launches, or other significant business events. This approach aims to align equity compensation more closely with value creation for the company.

Most Favored Nation (MFN)

A clause in investment agreements that ensures an investor receives terms at least as favorable as those given to other investors in the same or future rounds. If a company later offers better terms to another investor, the MFN clause typically requires the company to extend those same terms to the earlier investor. This provision is often used in convertible note or SAFE financings.

MRR (Monthly Recurring Revenue)

The predictable total revenue generated by a company from all active subscriptions in a particular month. MRR is a crucial metric for subscription-based businesses as it provides insight into the company's predictable and stable revenue stream. It's often used to track growth, forecast future revenue, and value subscription-based companies.

MOIC (Multiple on Invested Capital)

A financial metric used to evaluate the performance of an investment, calculated by dividing the total value returned to investors by the amount of money invested. For example, an MOIC of 3x means that the investment returned three times the original amount invested. MOIC is often used alongside IRR to assess private equity and venture capital investments, as it provides a simple measure of total value creation regardless of time.

Net Worth

The difference between an individual's or entity's total assets and total liabilities. In the context of investment regulations, net worth is often used to determine an individual's status as an Accredited Investor. For these purposes, the value of one's primary residence is typically excluded from the net worth calculation.

Non-Qualified Stock Options (NSOs)

A type of employee stock option that doesn't qualify for special favorable tax treatment under the Internal Revenue Code. Unlike Incentive Stock Options (ISOs), NSOs are taxed as ordinary income at the time of exercise on the difference between the exercise price and the fair market value of the stock. NSOs can be granted to employees, directors, consultants, and advisors.

NTM (Next Twelve Months)

A forward-looking time frame used in financial projections and analysis, referring to the upcoming 12-month period. NTM figures are often used in valuation models and to set performance expectations. They're particularly useful when a company is expecting significant changes or growth in the near future.

Off Balance Sheet

Referring to assets, liabilities, or financial activities that are not recorded on a company's balance sheet. While off-balance-sheet items are not inherently improper, they can sometimes be used to hide liabilities or risks from investors and regulators. Common examples include operating leases or certain types of joint ventures.

### Option Grant

The issuance of stock options to an employee, giving them the right to purchase a specific number of company shares at a predetermined price (the strike price) within a certain timeframe. Option grants are a common form of equity compensation, particularly in startups, used to align employee interests with company success and provide a potential financial upside.

### Option Pool

A portion of a company's shares reserved for future issuance to employees, typically as part of their compensation packages. The size of the option pool is usually negotiated during funding rounds and can impact the company's valuation. A typical option pool might represent 10-20% of a company's fully diluted equity.

### Ordinary Income

For tax purposes, any income that is not classified as capital gains. This includes wages, salaries, commissions, bonuses, interest income, rent, and most other forms of income. Ordinary income is typically taxed at higher rates than long-term capital gains, making the distinction important for tax planning purposes.

### Parallel Vehicle

An investment vehicle created to invest alongside a main fund, typically to accommodate investors with specific legal, tax, or regulatory requirements. Parallel vehicles invest in the same assets and at the same time as the main fund, with investments allocated pro-rata based on committed capital.

### Performance Vesting

A type of equity vesting schedule where shares or options are earned based on achieving specific performance milestones rather than the passage of time. These milestones could be company-wide (like revenue targets or product launches) or individual (like sales quotas). Performance vesting aims to more closely align equity compensation with value creation for the company.

### PFIC (Passive Foreign Investment Company)

A foreign corporation that meets certain income or asset tests related to passive income. Specifically, a company is a PFIC if 75% or more of its gross income is from passive sources (like interest or dividends) or if 50% or more of its assets produce passive income. U.S. investors in PFICs face complex and potentially unfavorable tax treatment, making PFIC status an important consideration in international investments.

### Pitch Deck

A brief presentation, often created using PowerPoint, Keynote, or similar software, used to provide investors with a quick overview of a business plan. A typical pitch deck includes information about the problem the business is solving, the solution it offers, the market opportunity, the team, financial projections, and the amount of funding sought.

Post-Money Valuation

The value of a company immediately after it receives funding. It's calculated by adding the amount of new funding to the pre-money valuation. For example, if a company raises $5 million at a $20 million pre-money valuation, its post-money valuation would be $25 million.

Pre-Money Valuation

The value of a company prior to receiving new funding. This valuation is used to determine how much equity investors will receive for their investment. For example, if an investor puts $5 million into a company at a $20 million pre-money valuation, they would typically receive 20% of the company's equity.

Preferred Shares

A class of stock that has priority over common stock in terms of dividend payments and asset distribution in the event of liquidation. Preferred shares often come with specific rights and preferences, such as liquidation preferences, anti-dilution protection, or voting rights on certain matters. They are typically issued to investors in private financing rounds.

Pro-Rata Rights

The right of an existing investor to participate in future funding rounds in order to maintain their percentage ownership in the company. Pro-rata rights allow investors to avoid dilution as the company raises additional capital. These rights are often a point of negotiation in early-stage investments and can be valuable as the company grows and attracts new investors.

Profits Interest Units (PIU)

A form of equity compensation used by LLCs and partnerships that gives the recipient a share in future profits without requiring an upfront capital contribution. PIUs can offer tax advantages compared to other forms of equity compensation, as they may be eligible for capital gains treatment if certain conditions are met.

Qualified Client

An investor who meets certain financial thresholds set by the SEC, allowing investment advisers to charge performance-based fees. As of 2021, a qualified client is defined as an individual or entity that has at least $1.1 million under management with the adviser, or a net worth exceeding $2.2 million (excluding primary residence), or is a qualified purchaser, or is an executive officer, director, or employee of the adviser.

Qualified Purchaser

An individual or entity that meets specific high net worth or investment thresholds set by the SEC. This designation allows participation in certain private investment opportunities. As of 2021, the criteria include individuals or family-owned businesses owning at least $5 million in investments, and institutions owning and investing at least $25 million on a discretionary basis.

Qualified Small Business Stock (QSBS)

A special category of stock in certain small businesses that, if held for at least five years, may qualify for partial or full exclusion from federal capital gains tax when sold. To be eligible, the stock must be in a C corporation with gross assets of $50 million or less at the time the stock was issued, among other requirements.

Recycling

The practice of reinvesting profits from early exits or distributions back into the fund rather than distributing them to limited partners. This allows the fund to make additional investments and potentially increase overall returns. The ability to recycle capital is typically defined in the fund's Subscription Agreement.

Registered Agent

A person or entity designated to receive official legal and tax correspondence on behalf of a business entity. Every corporation or LLC must have a registered agent in each state where it does business. The registered agent must have a physical address in the state and be available during business hours.

Registered Investment Advisor (RIA)

A firm or individual registered with the SEC or state securities authorities to provide investment advice. RIAs have a fiduciary duty to act in the best interests of their clients and are required to disclose any conflicts of interest. They typically charge fees based on assets under management rather than commissions.

Regulation D

A SEC regulation that allows companies to raise capital through the sale of equity or debt securities without having to register the securities with the SEC. Regulation D includes several exemptions (most notably Rules 506(b) and 506(c)) that are commonly used for private placements and other exempt offerings.

Return on Investment (ROI)

A performance measure used to evaluate the efficiency or profitability of an investment. ROI is typically expressed as a percentage and is calculated by dividing the net profit (or loss) from an investment by its cost. While simple to calculate and understand, ROI doesn't account for the time value of money or risk.

Right of First Refusal (ROFR)

A contractual right that gives its holder the option to enter a business transaction with the owner of something, according to specified terms, before the owner is entitled to enter into that transaction with a third party. In the context of startups, ROFR often applies to the sale of shares by existing shareholders.

Risk

The possibility of losing some or all of an original investment. Risk is often quantified using statistical measures such as standard deviation or beta. Different types of investments carry different levels of risk, and higher risk is generally associated with the potential for higher returns.

Rule 701

An SEC rule that provides an exemption from the registration requirements of the Securities Act for securities issued by non-reporting companies pursuant to compensatory arrangements. This rule is commonly used by private companies to issue stock options and other equity compensation to employees without having to register the securities.

Runway

The amount of time a company can continue operating before it runs out of cash, assuming current income and expense levels remain constant. Runway is typically expressed in months and is calculated by dividing current cash reserves by monthly burn rate. Extending runway is often a key consideration in fundraising decisions.

SAFE (Simple Agreement for Future Equity)

A financial instrument used for early-stage startup investing, created by Y Combinator as an alternative to convertible notes. A SAFE gives an investor the right to obtain equity in a future equity round, subject to certain parameters. Unlike a convertible note, a SAFE is not a debt instrument and therefore does not accrue interest.

Secondary Transaction

A transaction in which existing shares of a private company are sold to new investors, rather than the company issuing new shares. Secondary transactions allow early investors or employees to gain liquidity before a company goes public or is acquired. These transactions can be complex and may require approval from the company or other shareholders.

Securitization

The process of pooling various types of contractual debt or other cash-flow producing assets and selling their related cash flows to third party investors as securities. This can be done with mortgages, auto loans, credit card debt, or other assets that generate predictable cash flows.

Seed Capital

The initial capital used to start a business, often coming from the founders' personal assets, friends and family, or Angel Investors. Seed capital is typically used to support initial operations until the company can generate cash flow or attract larger investments.

Series LLC

A form of limited liability company that allows for multiple "series" within a single LLC, each operating as its own protected entity. This structure can provide liability protection between different series and can be useful for managing multiple properties or business lines. Series LLCs are not recognized in all states and have complex legal and tax implications.

SIV (Structured Investment Vehicle)

A type of special purpose entity that borrows money by issuing short-term securities at low interest rates and then lends that money by buying long-term securities at higher interest rates, making a profit for investors from the difference. SIVs were popular before the 2008 financial crisis but have since become less common due to increased regulatory scrutiny.

Sovereign Wealth Fund (SWF)

A state-owned investment fund that invests in real and financial assets such as stocks, bonds, real estate, or other investment vehicles. SWFs are typically created when countries have budgetary surpluses and have little or no international debt. They serve various purposes, including stabilizing the country's economy, generating wealth for future generations, or funding social and economic development projects.

SPV (Special Purpose Vehicle)

A subsidiary company formed to undertake a specific business purpose or project. SPVs are often used in structured finance transactions, such as securitizations, or to isolate financial risk. In venture capital, SPVs are sometimes used to pool capital from multiple investors for a single investment opportunity.

Stock Option Pool

A portion of a company's equity reserved for future issuance to employees, typically in the form of stock options. The size of the option pool is often a point of negotiation during funding rounds, as it impacts the company's valuation and the potential dilution of existing shareholders.

Stock Options

A form of equity compensation that gives an employee the right to buy a specific number of company shares at a predetermined price (the strike price) within a certain time frame. Stock options are often used by startups to attract and retain talent, aligning employee interests with company success.

Stock Split

A corporate action in which a company divides its existing shares into multiple shares. While the number of shares outstanding increases, the total dollar value of the shares remains the same. Stock splits are often done to make shares more affordable for individual investors and to increase liquidity.

TAM (Total Addressable Market)

The total market demand for a product or service, usually expressed in dollar terms. TAM represents the maximum potential size of a market and is often used in business plans and investor presentations to illustrate the growth potential of a business. It's typically calculated by multiplying the total number of potential customers by the average annual revenue per customer.

Tax Shelters

Strategies or investments used to reduce taxable income. While some tax shelters are legal and encouraged by the government (like retirement accounts or certain business expenses), others may be considered abusive and can result in penalties if used improperly. It's important to distinguish between legitimate tax planning and potentially illegal tax evasion.

Tearsheet

A one-page summary of a company or investment opportunity, typically including key financial metrics, business description, and investment highlights. Tearsheets are commonly used in finance to provide a quick overview of an investment opportunity or to track the performance of existing investments.

Tender Offer

A public offer to purchase some or all of the shares in a corporation, usually at a premium over the current market price. In the context of private companies, tender offers are sometimes used to provide liquidity to early shareholders or employees before a company goes public.

Term Sheet

A non-binding agreement outlining the basic terms and conditions under which an investment will be made. Term sheets typically cover key points such as valuation, investment amount, investor rights, and governance issues. While not legally binding (with some exceptions), term sheets serve as a blueprint for developing more detailed, legally binding documents.

Total Customers

The number of individual or business entities that have purchased a company's products or services. This metric is crucial for understanding a company's market penetration, growth rate, and overall business health. It's often analyzed alongside other metrics like customer acquisition cost and customer lifetime value.

Total Value Paid In (TVPI)

A performance metric used in private equity and venture capital to measure the total value of an investment relative to its cost. TVPI is calculated by dividing the sum of all distributions and the current value of unrealized investments by the total amount of capital invested. A TVPI of 2.0x means that the investment has doubled in value.

Traction

Measurable evidence of market demand for a product or service. Traction can be demonstrated through various metrics such as revenue growth, user acquisition, engagement rates, or strategic partnerships. For startups, showing traction is often crucial for attracting investment and validating the business model.

Tranche

A portion of a larger financial structure, typically used in debt issuances or investment rounds. In venture capital, tranches are sometimes used to structure investments where capital is provided in stages as the company meets certain milestones. This approach can help mitigate investor risk and incentivize company performance.

Trigger

An event or condition that initiates a specific action in a financial contract or agreement. In the context of equity compensation, triggers often refer to events that cause vesting to accelerate, such as a change in control of the company or termination of employment under certain conditions.

UBTI (Unrelated Business Taxable Income)

Income generated by tax-exempt organizations from activities unrelated to their primary exempt purpose. UBTI is subject to taxation at corporate rates. This concept is particularly relevant for tax-exempt investors in private equity and venture capital funds, as certain investment structures can generate UBTI and create tax liabilities.

Ultimate Beneficial Owner (UBO)

The natural person(s) who ultimately owns or controls a legal entity or arrangement. Identifying UBOs is an important part of anti-money laundering (AML) and know your customer (KYC) procedures. The threshold for beneficial ownership typically ranges from 10% to 25%, depending on the jurisdiction.

Unrelated Business Taxable Income (UBTI)

Income regularly generated by a tax-exempt entity by means of taxable activities. This income is subject to taxation when it is generated by an activity that is not related to the purpose for which the entity received its tax-exempt status. UBTI is particularly relevant for tax-exempt investors in private equity and hedge funds.

Valuation

The process of determining the current worth of an asset or company. In the context of startups and venture capital, valuation often involves projecting future cash flows and applying a discount rate, as well as considering factors like market size, growth rate, team quality, and competitive landscape. Valuation is a crucial factor in investment negotiations and can significantly impact the terms of a deal.

### Venture Capital Adviser Exemption

An exemption from certain registration requirements with the SEC for advisers who solely advise venture capital funds. To qualify, funds must meet specific criteria regarding the types of investments they make and the amount of leverage they use. This exemption allows venture capital fund managers to avoid some of the more burdensome regulatory requirements that apply to other types of investment advisers.

### Venture Round

A type of funding round specifically for venture capital financing, typically occurring after seed funding and before later-stage rounds. Venture rounds are often labeled alphabetically (Series A, Series B, etc.) and tend to involve larger amounts of capital and more formal processes than earlier funding stages.

### Vesting

The process by which an employee or founder earns the right to stock options or restricted stock over time. Vesting schedules are designed to incentivize long-term commitment to the company. A typical vesting schedule might last four years with a one-year cliff, meaning no shares vest for the first year, and then 1/48th of the shares vest each month thereafter.

### Warrants

A type of security that gives the holder the right, but not the obligation, to buy a certain number of shares at a specified price before a certain date. Warrants are sometimes issued alongside other securities (like bonds) as an added incentive for investors. They can also be used as a form of compensation or as part of a financing agreement.

### Waterfall

A method of allocating returns among different classes of investors in a fund or investment vehicle. The waterfall structure determines the order and proportion in which cash flows are distributed to various stakeholders. A typical private equity waterfall might include steps for returning capital, paying a preferred return, and then splitting additional profits between general and limited partners.

### Working Capital

The difference between a company's current assets and current liabilities, representing the capital available for day-to-day operations. Adequate working capital is crucial for a company's financial health and operational efficiency. In the context of venture capital, companies often raise money to increase their working capital and fund growth.

### Yield

The income return on an investment, typically expressed as a percentage based on the investment's cost, current market value, or face value. In the context of stocks, yield usually refers to the dividend yield, which is the annual dividend payment divided by the stock's current price. For bonds, yield typically refers to the current yield or yield to maturity.